Praise for
When China Attacks

"Grant Newsham's family intervention with the United States of America, a nation locked in a cycle of self-destructive behavior in its relationship with Communist China. It's the brave effort of a man who has dedicated his life to American national security and studying the Chinese threat to wake us up before it is too late. Newsham is articulate and knowledgeable. He also has the moral courage to tell the truth, clearly, directly, and unambiguously. If you want to slumber on, secure in your belief that somebody somewhere is busy handling the existential threat from the Chinese Communist Party, you'd best skip this book and put the cartoons back on. If you want your grandchildren to live in a democracy free of the dictates of Chairman Mao, buy this book now and don't put it down until you have read every page—then, get up, raise Holy Hell, and demand our 'leaders' put this nation on the right track before it is too late."

   —**Sam Faddis**, retired CIA operations officer and senior editor of AND Magazine

"America's war planners think China's war planners think like America's war planners. Not so! In his gripping *When China Attacks*, Grant Newsham shows us the horrific consequences that can result from American misperceptions of Chinese intentions and capabilities."

   —**Gordon Chang**, author of *The Coming Collapse of China*

"*When China Attacks* will make you uncomfortable—but by design. China wars on a distracted U.S. without effective challenge. Taiwan is critically endangered, our era's Sudetenland. Will we wake up and act in time?"

   —**Wallace C. Gregson**, lieutenant general (retired), former commander U.S. Marine Forces Pacific, and former Assistant Secretary of Defense for Asian and Pacific Security Affairs

"With disturbing clarity, Newsham brings his diplomatic, military, and business experience to bear on the critical question for the security of Asia and the globe: When is America going to wake up? His comprehensive description of China's 'whole of society' approach to warfare is a must-read for anyone with a stake in America's influence around the world. His narrative is edgy, well researched, convincing, and yes, it will make you uncomfortable—as it should!"

—**Robert Thomas,** vice admiral (retired), U.S. Navy, former Seventh Fleet commander

"*When China Attacks* is a clarion call to Americans about the existential threat from the People's Republic of China. Newsham doesn't rely on the usual 'China Hands'—the so-called experts who have brought us to this brink of war—but instead plumbs a new well of PRC experts who have not sold their souls to the Chinese Communist Party. The book provides a matter-of-fact and comprehensive description of the CCP's grand strategy, its individual elements of national power employed against America and its allies, and a vivid description of the impact to every American—the possible future of subservience to a totalitarian ideology and the regime in Beijing. Newsham not only describes the threat, but also provides a plan of action across all facets of national power, ending with an inspiring and historic call to action to save this land of the free. A book that should be read by every American today. Time is not on our side."

—**Jim Fanell,** captain (retired), U.S. Navy, former Director of Intelligence and Information Operations U.S. Pacific Fleet, fellow at Geneva Centre for Security Policy

"Newsham is one of the most seasoned and astute observers of U.S. strategy in the Indo-Pacific writing today. A former Marine officer with decades of experience in Asia, Newsham speaks from experience and is not afraid to talk about the reality much of the U.S. foreign policy establishment would prefer to ignore: the Chinese Communist Party is increasingly threatening America's dominance in Asia and globally. While the People's Liberation Army Navy is now the largest in the world, the U.S. Navy is steadily shrinking. The Air Force is flying aircraft older than their crews. Meanwhile, much of official Washington is focused on political correctness instead of war fighting. Newsham is unsparing in his description of the China threat and illuminating in his proposed remedies. This is a must-read for anyone who cares about the future of U.S. power in the twenty-first century."

—**Alexander B. Gray,** former deputy assistant to the President of the United States and chief of staff of the White House National Security Council, 2019–21

"Gripping, lucid, and jam-packed with strategic intelligence—*When China Attacks* is a Marine Corps–style boot camp for your mind. Make it to the end and you will be harder, sharper, and ready to defend yourself against Beijing's propaganda and psychological warfare machine. Think you know the China threat? Read this book—and think again!"

—**Ian Easton,** author of *The Final Struggle: Inside China's Global Strategy*

"Colonel Newsham outlines a frightening truth you won't hear from our political leaders or the self-proclaimed media experts. We have been at war for years and are losing, badly, and it could get much, much worse very soon. Our way of life and the future of our children, the nation, and freedom itself are at stake. China's dictators see us as weak and distracted. They believe we lack the will to resist and fight. Newsham exposes how they have the tacit and, in many cases, active support of useful idiots—and even some well-rewarded collaborators and traitors within our political and business class. Thankfully, he also points out that it's still not too late to save our nation, but we—all of us, together—need to act now."

—**David Reynolds,** former U.S. government Senior Intelligence Officer and China-based diplomat and business executive

"An urgently needed and hard-hitting primer on the grand strategy of China to achieve global hegemony, and the lack of effective countermeasures by the United States. The author knows Asia and the Pacific, having spent decades on the ground in those legal, financial, diplomatic, and military fields of battle."

—**Anders Corr,** publisher of the *Journal of Political Risk*

"A powerful call for America to get its house in order, appreciate the threat of China's multi-dimensional subversion, and fight back hard. Newsham draws on his extensive military experience and his deep understanding of Chinese strategy and operations to detail how much damage Beijing is doing to America. From aggressive industry policies to intellectual property theft, cyber assaults, ideological penetration of schools, and fentanyl supply, he reveals the details and he names names. While military reform is desperately needed, he emphasizes that an effective counter-offensive will require all of American society to rally to the cause. Important reading for anyone concerned about America's future security."

—**Ross Babbage,** chief executive officer, Strategic Forum, Australia, non-resident Senior Fellow, Center for Strategic and Budgetary Assessments

"Colonel Newsham brilliantly describes the Chinese Communist Party's insidious plans to defeat America in battle across the Pacific Ocean, and how it is devastating American society through savage, unrelenting political warfare to fatally subvert our national will and ability to fight back. As important, he provides sound recommendations regarding what America's leaders must do *now* to confront and defeat this existential threat. His descriptions and analysis are irrefutable, and his recommendations hard-nosed, achievable, and much more likely to succeed than the confused U.S. policies currently being pursued. Should be mandatory reading by the president, his national security team, and every member of the Congress of the United States. Time is short!"

—**Professor Kerry K. Gershaneck,** author of *Political Warfare: Strategies for Combating China's Plan to "Win without Fighting"*

WHEN CHINA ATTACKS

When China Attacks

A Warning to America

Col. Grant Newsham

Regnery Publishing
WASHINGTON, D.C.

The near-future scenarios that appear in portions of this book are presented as informed speculation. All characters and events portrayed therein are fictional, and any resemblance to real people or incidents is purely coincidental.

Cataloging-in-Publication data on file with the Library of Congress

ISBN: 978-1-68451-365-9
eISBN: 978-1-68451-394-9

Published in the United States by
Regnery Publishing
A Division of Salem Media Group
www.Regnery.com

Manufactured in the United States of America

10 9 8 7 6 5 4 3 2 1

Books are available in quantity for promotional or premium use. For information on discounts and terms, please visit our website: www.Regnery.com.

To those who were right about the
Chinese Communist Party and tried to warn us

Contents

Contents

Section One

A Cautionary Tale

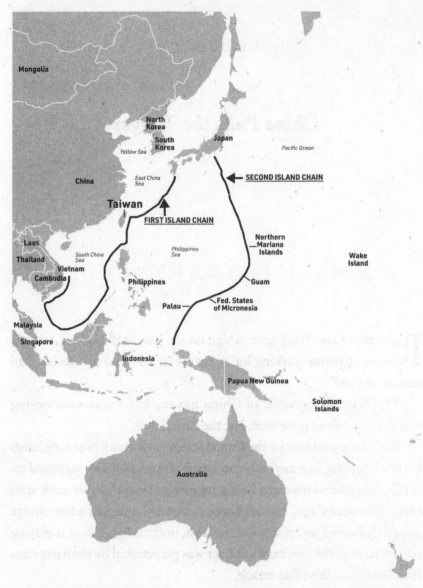

The First and Second Island Chains underpin the defense architecture of America and its allies. For this reason, Chinese strategists view free access through the chains as essential to the People's Liberation Army's ability to project power beyond the coast of China. If the PRC breaks or leapfrogs the chains, U.S. defenses in the Western Pacific will collapse. *Map courtesy of Pavak Patel.*

CHAPTER 1

China Pulls the Trigger

It's a year or two from now. A sign on the gate at the U.S.S. *Arizona* Memorial visitor parking lot at Pearl Harbor reads: "Closed until further notice."

The People's Republic of China has started a war—a shooting war—and it hasn't gone well. For the Americans.

Part of the problem for the United States is the way China is fighting. It's not behaving like anybody thought it would, like it is *supposed* to. A U.S. Navy submarine at a base a mile away from this gate sank at its berth two weeks ago, its hull blasted open by an underwater charge placed by parties unknown—or, at least, undeclared. China is playing coy. Its state media says maybe the act was perpetrated by the Americans themselves as a false flag attack.

Soon after, at the nearby Hickam Air Force Base, two U.S. Air Force aerial refuellers blew up—as did the F-22s parked nearby. A surge of hard-to-trace social media posts attribute it to BLM activists operating at the base.

Then a Navy replenishment oiler loaded with fuel and enroute to the Western Pacific was rammed and put out of commission by a fishing boat a couple miles outside the entrance to Pearl Harbor. The ship's escort shot up the fishing boat, but it was too late. The Mandarin-speaking crew said they lost control and are now calling the Americans murderers for killing "poor and unarmed fishermen." This is a charge echoed in the China-friendly press around the world.

Just today, mysterious drone swarms took out the communications and radar of several ships exiting San Diego naval base. TikTok influencers say the drones are *actual* aliens.

The news from farther west isn't much better.

The Chinese Foreign Ministry has announced: "Taiwan's reunification with the motherland is at hand." The People's Liberation Army is ashore on Taiwan in large numbers. Details are hard to come by—communications having been cut—and Elon Musk's Skylink network isn't working

The Americans think an all-out assault on Taiwan is impossible. But Xi Jinping thinks otherwise—and that's what matters. The PLA planners provide Xi with options. In this case, there are two:

Intimidate Taiwan into surrender by blockading Taiwan and seizing several of its tiny offshore islands, or...

Go for broke and launch a full-scale assault on Taiwan.

Chairman Xi likes option number two.

The timing isn't an accident. In January 2024, when China's favored candidate loses Taiwan's presidential election, it becomes clear that the Taiwanese are not going to come peaceably into the fold. Xi has staked his reputation on the long-sought goal of "reunifying Taiwan." It will be his path to making his mark as one of the legendary "great ones" of

Chinese history. He is as keen to take Taiwan as President Joseph Biden was to get out of Afghanistan in 2021.

But the timing of Xi's decision reflects the Chinese understanding of the American situation. Beijing sees the United States, its chief competition, as relatively weak and distracted. The U.S. economy is a mess, inflation is making life miserable (and eating away at defense budgets), and half the country considers the other half absolute demons—or semi-fascists. Riots are easy to stir up, and the media are fueling the fires.

The American president and administration are preoccupied—and nobody involved frightens the Chinese. A number of them are, in fact, longtime friends of the Chinese communists. The last thing the American administration wants is a war—or better said, another war.

The Chinese describe it bluntly: the Americans lack *will*.

So, the thinking in Beijing goes, why wait and take the chance things might stabilize? Or that another American administration might appear that will stop spending like a drunken sailor and will begin standing up to the People's Republic of China? For example, the Trump administration had shown backbone. Conditions could change. Under Trump, representatives in Congress from both sides were starting to wake up to the Chinese threat and to Taiwan's importance.

From Beijing, it seems that China has never been stronger, and America has never been weaker. Xi believes China has the military, political, and economic wherewithal to strike, and the United States—with its military, politics, and economy in disarray—either can't or won't stop it. And if the Americans won't, nobody else will, either.

So, with the timing right, the question becomes how to attack. Russia's invasion of Ukraine had shown half measures wouldn't work. Best to hit hard with everything, isolate Taiwan physically and electronically, then do whatever is necessary to keep the Americans and their friends from coming to the rescue.

Present them with a *fait accompli*, the thinking goes, and they'll soon enough shrug their shoulders, avert their eyes, and get back to business as usual.

So China hits. Hard.

The Chinese start by cutting Taiwan's internet so the world can't see what is about to happen. This buys the PLA time to attack the Taiwan military, and allows the CCP more time to seed the narrative of the inevitability of its success globally.

Washington is taken by surprise. U.S. Department of Defense assessments have recognized the impressive—if not alarming—advances in Chinese military power. Indeed, some American intelligence officers saw it coming. They sounded the alarm, but few people took them seriously. Those perceptive enough to recognize the peril were likely to get fired. In 2015, Pacific Fleet's intelligence chief, Captain James Fanell, was cashiered—supposedly at the request of the Obama White House—for publicly stating that China was gearing up for war.

If there were a danger, the dogma went, it would be a few years off.

The most common pushback on the possibility of an invasion, and a key component of the dogma on the military side, has been the idea that the People's Republic of China lacks enough "lift" (ships) to move an amphibious assault force across the Taiwan Strait. A condescending undertone has suggested the PLA simply isn't good enough to master amphibious operations—considered the most difficult military operation of them all.

The Americans figured they'd have plenty of notice as the Chinese collected their amphibious ships and barges and brought forces together. But in the Chinese amphibious assault plan, the large conventional amphibious force is just the reserve that rapidly transports reinforcements to the areas where they are required.

That time has come.

When the People's Liberation Army moves against Taiwan, it proves China has plenty of lift.

The main amphibious landings are provided by China's vast fishing fleets, the so-called maritime militia: cargo container vessels and dual-purpose civilian craft adapted for deployment of amphibious vehicles while underway.

This explains why the Chinese have built civilian ferries with rounded bottoms like World War II Landing Ship Tanks (LSTs). It certainly isn't for passenger comfort. Round-bottomed boats are the vomit express. But the design will come in handy during beaching operations.

The PLA moves from almost a standing start and is on the beaches before anyone can react. China dispatches forces from its long coast; they converge to arrive simultaneously with little advance warning, cloaked by civilian shipping turning east from highly-transited commercial shipping lanes.

They pick up follow-on forces from staging bases on artificial islands, cargo container ships, and cruise liners. In one case, waves of men use zip lines from the cruise liners down to a barge, and then step across to waiting Landing Craft Air Cushions (LCACs) pulled up alongside, before speeding towards Taiwan's beaches.

The element of surprise turns out to be a massive force multiplier—even though there have been plenty of photos over the years of amphibious tanks driving down the ramps of civilian roll-on/roll-off ships at sea or off cross-channel ferries. Too many experts didn't want to realize what they were seeing.

And the amphibious assault—with its own version of Iron Dome air-defenses—is just one part of the symphony of destruction the PRC is playing for Taiwan.

Rockets and missiles destroy the Presidential Palace in Taipei and hit every other government and military building and target of importance while peppering civilian areas for good shock and awe measure. Massive waves of attack drones neutralize hardened targets, and helicopter and airborne forces deploy in large numbers once anti-aircraft radar and missile sites are taken out.

Fifth-columnists and special forces (earlier infiltrated via smugglers' fast boats) are also at work, shooting up police stations, bus stops, and schools throughout Taiwan and leaving trouble, fear, and distraction in their wake.

The jewel in the crown for China's Ministry of State Security (MSS), the major port of Kaohsiung, opens its doors to the Chinese on day one, without a shot fired. The port authorities even have a welcome banner flying.

Kaohsiung is run by organized crime and has been for years. That means China's MSS, the Godfather of Chinese organized crime, effectively controls it. So now, the PLA invasion force has Taiwan's biggest port at its service. With its warehouses ready, stocked with supplies.

The Taiwanese are not the Ukrainians. The military fights, and most units stay at their posts until the end. But the million-man reserve proves to be a paper force, and the once-touted civil defense simply doesn't exist. The risks of fighting back are enormous. The occupier-to-population density ratio can be made much lower if, like the Chinese, an aggressor is willing to kill one hundred civilians for each PLA member that is killed. Hitler proved that in France.

Even citizens who want to defend their country have no idea how to do so. The Americans and the Taiwanese had never gotten together beforehand to train side-by-side—or even to plan for how they would defeat a Chinese assault. The Marines never even got onto Taiwan. They'd talked about it a lot, but the State Department had always refused. And they still did—even after the Chinese attacked. Too provocative and escalatory. Forty-plus years of American isolation of Taiwan's military—hoping this would make China happy—have come home to roost. The Chinese are indeed happy.

Where Is America?

The Chinese won't launch PLA rocket salvos against U.S. bases in Japan, Guam, or Hawaii. That might galvanize American and Japanese resolve. The Chinese are still dangling the possibility of off-ramps for an all-out war against the United States, just as the Americans have talked about doing to China.

The U.S. administration, losing critical time, waffles and whimpers like a helpless child. Once the president reluctantly gives the green light (or more likely, a cautious amber light) to assist, the PRC has the full measure of (the lack of) American resolve and goes to work against U.S. forces, whittling them down and making it clear that China won't allow

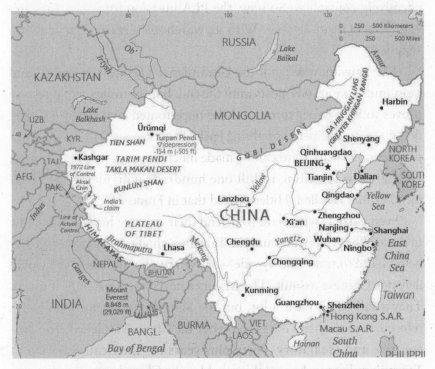

Map courtesy of The World Factbook 2021. *Washington, D.C.: Central Intelligence Agency, 2021.*

anyone, especially the United States, to interfere in its self-defined internal matter.

In the Philippines, U.S. Marines rush several of their new "littoral units" into position on Northern Luzon and the islands in the Bashi Channel between the Philippines and Taiwan. The New People's Army guerrillas and their Chinese advisors are waiting for the Americans, who never get the chance to deploy their anti-ship missiles against Chinese ships. There are pockets of bravery, but that is all.

Two U.S. Navy ships—a destroyer and a Littoral Combat Ship (LCS)—left Singapore's Sembawan Naval Base in a hurry, heading north through the South China Sea. PLA Navy guided-missile corvettes swarm and sink them from one hundred miles away. The American ships' anti-ship cruise missiles only have a range of seventy-five miles. The Chinese don't bother to look for survivors. Nor does anyone else. The zone is too hot.

The wide area of coverage and concentration of anti-ship and anti-aircraft weapons systems provide a formidable shield while China is silently prepping the battlefield. The Chinese irregular fishing vessels are providing both sentinels and subterfuge.

The U.S.S. *America*, an amphibious assault ship in name but an aircraft carrier in practice, with two dozen F-35 stealth fighters aboard, moves from Guam and heads toward Taiwan along with three escorts.

They are on alert. They saw several small ships on their radar, but those are identified as fishing boats. The Americans can't see any PLA Navy ships. By the time they detect the dozen anti-ship missiles headed their way at twelve hundred miles an hour, it is too late. U.S.S. *America* burns and eventually sinks. One of the escort frigates explodes and also goes down.

Several American aircraft dispatched from Kadena on Okinawa are shredded by the invisible teeth of the fishing fleet before analysts can figure out what's transpiring. The PLA doesn't have to attack Kadena, just the aircraft heading south from there.

The generals and admirals quickly realize there is too much clandestine firepower hidden among the fishing fleet, in the official PLA afloat, in the air, and on the mainland for the United States to penetrate and aid Taiwanese forces.

U.S. ships moving out of Japanese ports encounter smart mines, moored mines, and drift mines that magically appear in the wake of the fishing fleet, though nobody can quite prove who placed them.

All in all, it's like running a gauntlet—and it isn't just the U.S. forces in the far western Pacific.

U.S. Navy ships heading out of West Coast ports are taking fire from containerized anti-ship missiles launched from cargo ships and fishing boats. The PRC has been getting these so-called commercial vessels ready and has used them to track the U.S. Navy for years. Drones swarm other ships, destroying their radar and putting them out of action.

And then it gets worse. When the Americans don't back off, PLA Special Forces go to work in Hawaii, in Guam, and on the Japanese mainland.

On the main departure route from Iwakuni Marine Corps Station near Hiroshima, surface-to-air missiles (SAMs), firing from a solar farm built with Chinese and Yakuza money, shoot down U.S. Marine and U.S. Navy jets. The same thing happens at Yokota near Tokyo, Misawa, and elsewhere. The Japanese government was right to be worried about Chinese nationals buying property near U.S. and Japanese bases.

Even worse for the Americans, two U.S. nuclear submarines have disappeared. These were America's aces in the hole, but the Chinese were tracking them—once again with the PRC's massive fishing fleet—using sonobuoys to effectively run a zone defense in the Pacific.

What about America's Friends?

The Japanese? Beijing sends backchannel messages to Tokyo telling the Japanese to stand clear. They probably won't, but they also won't know what to do other than order the Japanese Maritime Self-Defense Force to assist the Americans.

The Japan Ground Self-Defense Force Amphibious Rapid Deployment Brigade moves to the southern islands but never fires a shot. The orders never come, and the Chinese stay far enough away not to trigger a response. The Japanese Navy sails out on its own initiative and does its best. And the Air Self-Defense Force is angrily buzzing around inside Japanese air space. But the central government hadn't done what's necessary. And when the Chinese attack Taiwan, the Japanese can't respond effectively. The government debates for several weeks if it is even legally allowed to attack. It never does figure out this legal point.

Beijing sends backchannel messages to Tokyo telling the Japanese to stand clear. They probably won't, Beijing realizes, but they also won't know what to do besides order the Japanese Maritime Self-Defense Force to assist the Americans.

Meanwhile, an Okinawa independence movement, long supported by covert Chinese funding, takes to the streets in Naha, along with an out-of-the-blue and well-funded peace movement in Tokyo.

PLA helicopters operating out of the northern Philippines use anti-ship missiles to make life difficult for U.S. and Taiwan Navy ships operating around southern Taiwan. The governor of Ilocos Norte Province is a Chinese proxy, as are the New People's Army guerrillas who have been operating in the region for decades.

The Australians try to help out, but they run into the Chinese fishing fleet—as did the Americans—and lose ships, aircraft, and people while heading north from the Southwest Pacific.

What about China's Friends?

Yes, it has some. Beijing is getting covering fire from several directions during its attack on Taiwan.

North Korea returns the favor for Beijing's decades of life support. A few missile salvoes into Seoul, the South Korean capital, are an adequate distraction. Taking too much initiative—say, engaging in a full-scale invasion that might get the Americans thinking about using nuclear weapons—is not what Beijing wants.

A few North Korean missiles—conventional ones—into Seoul are all that is needed. Maybe sending a few into Tokyo could be in order.

The Russians likewise return the favor to Beijing for its support during the Ukrainian invasion. The two powers had agreed to a no-limits partnership before Putin launched the attack. After the Russians attacked, Chinese officials ordered the media not to criticize Russia, because China expected Russia to do the same when the time would come for Taiwan. Now the Russians maneuver against the Japanese to threaten them, hold them in place, and further stress the Americans. Russia is also considering an opportunistic move in the Baltic.

China's new friend, Iran, has closed the Straits of Hormuz, shutting down a good chunk of global oil flows and launching missiles against Saudi Arabia and Israel. Just what the Americans don't need.

Closer to home, Russian and Chinese troops in Cuba and Venezuela set up long-range missiles aimed at the United States—one more distraction.

Don't expect India to help. They are busy now that the Chinese have made a move against their northern border.

Meanwhile, Argentina is eyeing up the Falklands.

China has friends inside the U.S. as well. The U.S.-China Business Council issues a statement denouncing the violence and loss of lives—and warning this could harm business ties between the two countries.The chairs of all six of Wall Street's leading firms sign a similar joint letter—urging restraint by all parties.

A team of Wall Street luminaries visits the White House and asks that it do something to restore the U.S.-China relationship—or the economy (and donations) will shrivel to nothing. That something? Accept Beijing's offer to hold talks and avoid further trouble over China's "domestic affairs." That is, abandon Taiwan, write it off as a loss, and look to the future.

The U.S. administration is overloaded.

During the Global War on Terror, a four-man U.S. Special Forces team was run down and killed by terrorists in Niger, West Africa. It was a national catastrophe, and Congress held hearings.

Over a thousand American sailors and Marines die in the attack on the U.S.S. *America* expeditionary strike group, and the numbers are adding up elsewhere. World War II's Greatest Generation knew all about such things—they remembered World War I but still gave it all they could (and more) just over twenty years later.

The 2020s version of Americans? Not so much. Modern Americans get upset at mean comments on Twitter. They are being fed a constant stream of TikTok videos about how an American intervention will just be more racist colonialism. To stand down isn't bad at all. It is a sign of virtue.

Meanwhile, article after article appear reminding readers of all the wargames in which America either got its ass handed to it or, in one outlier game, the fight was long and bloody, and the Americans only prevailed at huge cost.

Communist Party outlet *China Daily* runs a deluge of pieces saying that Beijing is in its rights to defend itself with nuclear weapons if Washington continues to interfere in Chinese domestic affairs.

That is the last straw for the U.S. administration—it figuratively goes into a fetal position under the Resolute Desk in the Oval Office.

Taiwan realizes no help is coming.

It sues for terms and gives up.

Immediately, the rest of Asia gets the message. The United States cannot keep twenty-three million free people free. U.S. military might can't do it. U.S. economic and financial power can't do it. And U.S. nuclear weapons don't matter, either.

But the United States will soon realize that Taiwan isn't the end point. Taiwan is the necessary launch point.

What Happens Next? China Will Not Stop at Taiwan.

Control of Taiwan is far more important than a sop to so-called national esteem. The CCP's show of wounded pride over Taiwan has always been, in part, a propagandistic sideshow. This will soon become obvious. To understand what will happen next, start with geography—and why Taiwan is the necessary starting point for achieving China's real ambitions. For China to reach its goal and drive the Americans out of the Pacific (for starters), it needs to be able to get its military beyond the First Island Chain—the chain of islands that run from Japan southwards through Taiwan and the Philippines and onwards to Indonesia and Malaysia.

From the Chinese perspective, the First Island Chain and its handful of narrow, easily defended straits block access to the Western Pacific Ocean.

If the United States and its allies wanted, their forces—armed with anti-ship missiles and anti-aircraft systems, and backed by air and naval forces and submarines—could keep the Chinese military hemmed inside the First Island Chain with relatively little effort.

Though the PRC may have carried out the biggest, fastest defense buildup in history—and might be a match for U.S. forces in certain instances—that doesn't matter if Chinese forces can't get through the First Island Chain.

The Chinese have been angling to break the chain for decades. Where are the weak links? Japan's Ryukyu Islands? Not likely, given what the Japanese and the Chinese think of each other. The Japanese might eventually fight.

The Philippines? Philippine geography and politics are too complicated. Many Filipinos are angry that China has already seized Philippine maritime territory—and regularly muscles in elsewhere, humiliating Filipinos in the process.

This leaves Taiwan. It is a juicy option for the People's Liberation Army and the Chinese Communist Party leaders.

Taiwan sits in the middle of the First Island Chain. Take it, and China will have a lodgment smack in the middle of the United States' (and its allies') first defense line that bottles up the People's Liberation Army. Imagine a castle wall collapsing.

With Taiwan captured, this is what will come next.

Taiwan's airfields and ports will allow the People's Liberation Army freedom of movement and extended range into the Western Pacific and beyond.

With Taiwan under Beijing's control, the PRC will have outflanked Japan's southern defenses. In this scenario, PLA submarines, ships, and aircraft will be able to operate regularly east of Japan's main islands, surrounding Japan. The PLA can then dominate the East China Sea and seize Japanese maritime and island territory. The Chinese, in fact, claim that the entire Ryukyu Chain belongs to China—just like they have claimed Taiwan.

This will seriously curtail the ability of the United States to operate from Okinawa and its other bases in Japan.

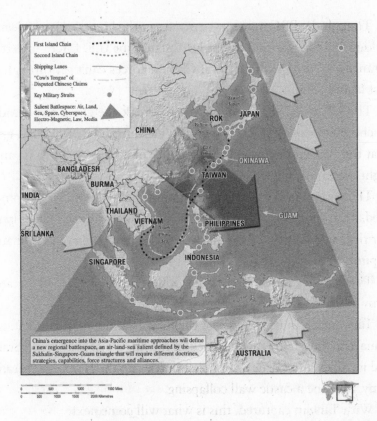

First Island Chain
Second Island Chain
Shipping Lanes
"Cow's Tongue" of
Disputed Chinese Claims
Key Military Straits
Salient Battlespace: Air, Land,
Sea, Space, Cyberspace,
Electro-Magnetic, Law, Media

China's emergence into the Asia-Pacific maritime approaches will define a new regional battlespace, an air-land-sea salient defined by the Sakhalin-Singapore-Guam triangle that will require different doctrines, strategies, capabilities, force structures and alliances.

As the People's Liberation Army looks to expand its operations into the Pacific, Taiwan is in the way. Conversely, if seized, Taiwan offers an excellent springboard for future operations. *Map courtesy of Paul Giarra.*

But PLA planners have much more in mind. They are always looking at the whole map.

From Taiwan, the PLA will drive a salient into the heart of the U.S. second layer defense in the Central Pacific, then push into the Southwest and South Pacific.

The PRC has bases in all but name across the area, including in the Solomon Islands. From these bases, the PRC can seriously constrain Australia. The Japanese understood this in 1941 but couldn't accomplish it. Beijing has laid the groundwork with thirty years of political warfare, economic and commercial inroads, and physical presence—greasing many palms in the process.

But PRC interests don't stop in the middle of the Pacific. The PLA is moving to operate east of Hawaii and off the West Coast of the continental United States. And it has been assiduously developing ties and so-called shipping routes to the west coast of Central and South America—where China-friendly leftist governments have come to power.

Taiwan is strategic geography if such ever existed. Taking Taiwan is the prerequisite for much greater things for the PLA and the PRC.

Once China takes Taiwan, every nation in Asia besides Japan—even Australia—will cut the best deal it can with Beijing.

Pacific Asia turns Red.

The rest of the world also gets it. This is just the start.

Destroying the Soul of America

The destruction and subjugation that follow a PRC takeover of Taiwan might seem horrific but far away. However, China has been fighting on another battlefield just as important, if not more so, and winning. If we lose there, it could destroy families, communities, and the very soul of America.

Just as the Chinese Communist Party (CCP) has spent unlimited amounts and devoted vast efforts to build up its military, it has likewise funded and worked on destroying our will to fight—or even defend ourselves.

The primary target? The American mind.

Your mind. And, even more frighteningly, the minds of those you love.

CHAPTER 2

The American Homefront

As the PRC swarms onto Taiwan and starts its takeover, here is what is happening at a kitchen table in a typical home in America. Imagine a family eating dinner. It's food that is bought readymade and microwaved at home. The parents regret it, but it will have to do. Mom and Dad work two service jobs each—homemade meals are holiday luxuries.

Their three teenagers, two boys and a girl, *should* be at the table, but only two of them *are* there. The middle child, their sixteen-year-old son, hasn't come home. It happens a lot. They long ago stopped trying to get him to stay. They don't know how to give him the hope he needs to work hard now for a better future.

This used to be a factory town, but the jobs left long ago for China. Their son, and they, know that even if he graduates high school, he will be lucky to get the same shelf-stacking, burger-serving jobs his parents had. The best the parents can do is hope he is with his good friends—the guys who don't do hard drugs—or at least that he has his Narcan with him.

The two other teens, a fourteen-year-old girl and a seventeen-year-old boy, are staring at their phones as they eat. So is Mom.

Dad scans his family, trying to catch someone's eye. He has spent the day—as with most days—doing brainless work, in a soulless building, for heartless bosses. He wants to talk to the people he does it all for, but he doesn't know what to say.

Conversation is usually a minefield. Last week, he asked his daughter what she was learning in economics and was promptly told that capitalism is evil, and the problem is "real communism has never been tried."

He didn't argue. He learned his lesson the year before when his daughter came home listing the unredeemable moral failings of the Founding Fathers—especially when compared to other national founders like Mao, who lifted so many out of poverty.

He mentioned that Mao had also killed tens of millions of his own people. She reported him to her teacher. The school banned him from school board meetings, something that went on his permanent social credit record for all future employers to see.

His only solace was that, by reporting him, his daughter got extra points on her own record, making her more likely to qualify for a government job once she graduated—assuming she kept her record pristine.

Suddenly, his son sits up straight and holds up his phone: "Dad, look at this."

Dad looks at the video on the small screen and knows immediately what he is seeing. He had served in the U.S. Marines—including deployments to the Pacific. He had been discharged with no benefits for refusing to denounce his faith as inherently discriminatory, but he still has friends in the Marine Corps. He follows news from the region. Everyone does, since the Chinese attacked Taiwan.

The men he sees on his son's phone are the missing Marines.

The video is clear. Two dozen male U.S. Marines standing in line facing the camera. Tired, sullen, unshaven, unarmed—and with hands on their heads. None of them look scared, just angry and defiant. There is no sound.

At the thirty second mark, they are gunned down. They flop to the ground. Two men who appear to be Asian step in front of the camera and systematically put a bullet into each of the Marines' heads. Some of the Marines, still alive, jerk and die. The video ends.

"What do you think, Dad? Deepfake?"

Dad doesn't answer. He's thinking, absorbing. He feels sick.

It hasn't been long since a forty-person U.S. Marine platoon on a small, empty island off the northern coast of Luzon, Philippines, went dark. It wasn't supposed to. The Marines from the Third Littoral Regiment based in Okinawa were part of the so-called stand-in force.

This was the previous commandant's plan that intended to deploy small teams of Marines throughout the First Island Chain. The Marines were to surveil Chinese ship movements and maybe take a shot with long-range anti-ship missiles should the People's Liberation Army Navy make its move.

This particular Marine unit was keeping an eye on the Bashi Channel—the hundred-mile-wide ocean gap between the northern Philippines and southernmost Taiwan. If the Chinese launched an assault on Taiwan, they would need to come through the Bashi Channel.

U.S. Marine headquarters on Okinawa tried repeatedly to contact the platoon and was worried, though not panicking. Sometimes comms go down. Nobody noticed that the Philippine New People's Army guerrillas had announced, without saying where it happened, that their Luzon front had eliminated an American spy team.

It wasn't surprising that nobody noticed.

Two days later, the Chinese People's Liberation Army attacked Taiwan.

In spite of Taiwan being cut off, details of the attack are starting to come out, and Dad had been learning what he could from old Marine friends. According to them, after the first twenty-four hours, the PLA had twenty thousand troops ashore, with armor, and had seized a foothold—or, in Beijing's words, a "liberated zone."

Getting rid of the Marines covering the Bashi Channel was necessary—and not particularly difficult, it seemed.

No, the video isn't a deepfake. The women Marines disappeared before reaching the beach, the men, unarmed, were executed, and the video was released as a message. The PLA likely used one of its proxies, the Philippine New People's Army guerrillas, so China's friends in the U.S. media could muddy the water on attribution. But Washington knows what it really means: "If we think you are in our way, we will kill you—quickly, if you are lucky."

Now, with the PLA ashore, Washington must decide what to do. Dad has been waiting for a statement from the president, but it isn't coming.

It still wasn't clear if the United States would defend Taiwan—despite plenty of earlier debate in Washington over the longstanding policy of strategic ambiguity towards Taiwan.

The debate on Capitol Hill and the talk shows have begun to erupt. Some people demand the United States immediately go all-out to save Taiwan. Others take a let's-get-more-details approach. And others insist that Taiwan is not worth risking nuclear war with China.

Dad tried to bring up the Taiwan invasion at the dinner table a few days ago. His daughter confidently said it was "only natural" for Taiwan to be reunited with "the rest of China." His son was mostly interested in the attack's dramatic visuals, trying to figure out how they were filmed and what had been enhanced. Mom wanted to change the topic—out of concern someone would say something that might end up on their record. Mom won the day, and the subject was changed to whether or not the family could afford a dog.

The same has been happening all over the country—and now this, a video of Marines being murdered.

Dad looks at his family. His daughter is uninterested. His son is moving through the video frame-by-frame, looking for odd shadows or lack of blinking that will allow him to declare it a deepfake that he can smugly ignore. Mom starts clearing the dishes.

This is it, Dad thinks. *If Washington doesn't act, we are done.*

Two Weeks Later

The American public—even on the coasts—is infuriated by the video and demands the government "do something"—though the message is muted, as reporting about PRC atrocities in Taiwan is repeatedly flagged by social media as fake news, with the so-called perpetrators losing their accounts.

Some columnists for major newspapers start arguing that the real villain isn't China but the Philippines, and that the United States needs Beijing's help with its Philippines problem.

The U.S. administration dithers, but eventually the Pentagon holds a grand press conference announcing that real action is being taken. But . . . it is action too secret to discuss publicly.

Meanwhile, Dad hears from friends still serving that the United States lost several ships to ramming by Marshall Islands–, Malta-, and Panama-flagged freighters while the ships were in port or just underway. Then the same thing happens with U.S. 7th Fleet ships moving out of Yokosuka Naval Base. It barely make the news, and Beijing remains silent.

Two Weeks Later

Dad now hears from friends that the American military is returning to base. The United States is ramping up for a vicious election. Rioting by leftists has begun in most major American cities, akin to the urban convulsions during the summer of 2020. His daughter spends most dinners explaining the virtue of the rioters' actions.

U.S. harvests are in trouble—some rumors say sterile seeds are to blame, though this problem doesn't seem to be affecting the crops grown by Chinese state-owned farms across the Midwest. Since those crops are immediately exported, and food prices are rocketing. Mom is thinking of trying for a third job, as a greeter at a big box store.

America finds itself not just unwilling to act to save Taiwan, but nearly unable to do so. To top it all off, according to many journalists, war with China isn't polling well.

A month after Dad watched the twenty-four young men shot in the head, he is at the dinner table again with Mom and his daughter. Neither son has come home tonight. The middle son has joined the Maoist protesters, to his sister's delight, and the oldest son has tagged along to film the action, hoping to strike it rich by catching a viral moment.

Dad's phone rings. A rarity. He doesn't have time or energy for friends. But it's one of his old Marine colleagues. Has he heard? The democratic government of Taiwan realized that help would not be coming. It has formally surrendered.

The rest of Pacific Asia—except for Japan and maybe Australia—was quietly reaching out to Beijing, and many had issued press releases stating they looked forward to a return to harmony in the region.

In 1990, the United States won the Cold War. Now it has lost a real war.

With the loss of Taiwan, America is finished in Asia.

An entirely new world is at hand.

Dad hangs up his phone, gets up from the table, and walks over to the window. He sees the pulsating red glow from the protest fires downtown.

He wonders if anyone will notice a difference. China had thoroughly destroyed America—destroyed his family—from the inside, long before it launched the first missile at Taiwan. This is just making it official. The Chinese Communist Party has beaten the United States of America.

From behind him, he hears his daughter calling her friend, excited and breathless: "It's me. Guess what? It's amazing! China just liberated Taiwan!"

This Doesn't Have to Happen

America still has plenty of military power and fight left in its soul. We can cause the Chinese all sorts of harm. It will be costly to save Taiwan directly, but we can, for example, spread the battlefield and make the fight global—including cutting all of China's trade along with its food and energy imports. Do this, and the Chinese Communist Party will be in big trouble.

What stopped the U.S. from fighting, *really* fighting, in this fictional future was the same thing that is stopping us from preparing and fighting now: a real go-order never came from the White House.

The world's most powerful military folded. The defeat was mental as much as military. How on earth did that happen? Gradually, and then all at once. It happened over thirty years, and few people noticed until it was too late.

To know what to do about it, you must know how it happened, where we are now, and where we are heading if we don't fight. Then you have to know what we are fighting and how to fight it. I'll tell you.

Let's start in Baltimore.

THE BATTLES CHINA IS ALREADY FIGHTING AND WE ARE ALREADY LOSING

CHAPTER 3

Witness to War: The Baltimore Battlefield

M y longtime friend from Baltimore describes what his city used to be, and what it is now.[1]

I remember Sparrows Point, and ARMCO Steel, and Maryland Drydock, and the GM Plant, and Locke Insulators.

When I was little, every man in my neighborhood worked either at the GM plant, the steel mill, or the shipyard at Sparrows Point. Yeah, Sparrows Point was like Disney World. Those guys worked hard, played in bowling leagues, raised kids, went to church, and retired with a modest pension.

As an 18-year-old, I tended bar from 0600 to 1300 in a little neighborhood joint in SE Baltimore. Sparrows Point, GM, and all the plants worked three shifts. The 2300-0700 overnight shift guys were awesome. They'd get off work, drink a few beers (25¢ cent drafts), eat a hot dog, shoot darts, and then home to bed. The bar was on a bus line that ran non-stop from the Point to the neighborhood. No one drove to work.

My wife did her internship and residency at South Baltimore General Hospital—now Harbor Hospital—down on the water. Our sons were born there. I was a patient there a couple of times. You could look out at the ships in the harbor. Sparrows Point was way in the distance.

I got two law degrees, a J.D. from the University of Maryland and an LLM from Georgetown. I started the J.D. in the fall of '69, a year after I "got back." Several times, I took the night train to New York City, and you could see them pouring steel at Sparrows Point. What a memory.

It's all gone now, without a trace. Sacrificed on the altar of so-called free trade.

My high school classmates who went to work at Bethlehem Steel in Sparrows Point, or the GM plant in Dundalk, were laid off by the 1980s. Many never again held a meaningful job.

Enormous Amazon "Fulfillment Centers" sit where those factories once stood, filled with goods from Chinese factories. The grandsons of those hard working men I served beer and hot dogs to now handle goods made in Beijing, not Baltimore, on the very spots where those two economic engines once stood. They make a couple bucks over minimum wage. Too many are either alcoholics or drug-addicted, or both. But the city is putting in a park for them. With artificial grass.

My old neighborhood is one step below a slum, with Section 8 housing. The tenants work those dead-end, low-pay jobs and happily let their rented property go to hell—having infiltrated a community that was almost 100 percent owner occupiers.

Old ladies like my 90-year-old mom—who, God bless her, still lives in the row house I grew up in—never leave their homes. Crime is rampant. Cops stay in their patrol cars.

My cousin is a Captain in the Baltimore City Fire Department. He used to spend most of his twenty-four-hour shift running the company, and fighting and preventing fires. These days, he is busier than ever, but fighting fires comes second. Most of his calls are to officially pronounce dead the zombies in Baltimore and Dundalk who have wasted their lives as addicts of fentanyl and/or heroin.

In 2020, in Baltimore, 954 people died opioid-related deaths[2]—more than two-and-a-half times the murder rate. Fentanyl is much deadlier than heroin, and almost all of it comes from China via Mexico and Mexican drug gangs. Over seventy thousand Americans died of fentanyl overdoses in 2021[3]—that's ten times the total number of American servicemen killed during the twenty years of war in Afghanistan and Iraq, and more than were killed during the twelve-year Vietnam War. You won't hear of it anywhere, and the TV news ignores it. My cousin sees it every day. Multiple times. My cousin is a war medic.

My old neighborhood is awash with the effects of this scourge. Hopeless men and women roam aimlessly, looking for their next dose. First responders spend most of their calls attending to overdoses. Police are unable to curb the gang violence connected to the drug problem. The drugs inside of George Floyd that led to his erratic behavior, and all that followed, likely came from China. He also had COVID at the time of his death.

My family has been pretty lucky. Just one cousin's son—a good, smart boy—died of a heart attack at sixteen. Or at least, everyone says it was a heart attack. For grandma's sake. Everyone knew it was fentanyl.

It used to be you could escape if you tried—especially if you were lucky enough to go to a Catholic school. The girls could go into nursing. The boys would join the military. But these days, the public schools are as demoralized and chaotic as the neighborhoods. What is a guidance counselor supposed to suggest they work towards? It's not easy to go into nursing or enlist when you can barely read, you use drugs, or you've been arrested—more than once—before you're seventeen. One U.S. Marine recruiter said the breaching party in Fallujah was easier duty than the recruiting station in Baltimore.

But the suburbs around D.C.—thirty miles away—are the richest in the nation. Members of congress, lobbyists, consultants, and Wall Street CEOs who bought their beach houses by ripping out and shipping out the heart of communities to China should be forced to take a stroll through Dundalk. Thank you, Nixon, Bush, Obama, and Biden for your poor and possibly traitorous foreign policy.

There should be a monument to those blue-collar workers who worked at Sparrows Point.

Useful Idiots, Collaborators, and Traitors

There are dozens of American cities and towns that, like Baltimore, have had their guts ripped out. These areas have been left with crumbling, warzone neighborhoods full of hopeless young men and women stuck with dead-end, menial jobs, or a one-way ticket to addiction, prison, or the grave.

Buffalo, New York; Erie, Pennsylvania; and Youngstown, Ohio are examples, as well as part of just about any city or town of any consequence in the United States. All took a hit. The specifics might vary, but not the basics.

The thing is, none of this was an accident. It wasn't the inevitable turn of events as businesses and industries flourished and then faded away as they always have. The core of America has been successfully attacked. And the assault continues, with help from the inside.

The United States is riddled with, at best, enablers, and at worst, collaborators—including some politicians, government officials, financiers, investment bankers, CEOs, journalists, academics, think-tankers, NGO leadership, military personnel, and others, many of whom benefit financially. Some are able to convince themselves what they are doing is decent, wise, unavoidable, or even statesmanlike. And some are just traitors.

Cutting a Wide Swath through the Political Class

The jobs that left Baltimore were some of the estimated 3.5 million manufacturing jobs that went to China[4] in the twenty years after the PRC was allowed to join the World Trade Organization (WTO) by being exempted from key membership requirements every other prospective member had to comply with.

Too much of the American business and industrial class eagerly shuttered U.S. facilities and moved the work to China. Some of the same companies that now tout their ESG scores exulted in cheaper labor costs, no environmental restrictions, and no troublesome labor unions. The Chinese would work long hours for next to nothing. Or else.

Every one of those jobs had supported a family, and its loss had a human cost and a ripple effect on future generations. It absolutely gutted neighborhoods and livelihoods—not just of the workers, but their families and the ecosystems of suppliers and retail establishments.

American politicians knew what would happen—and privately admitted it—but the donor class smelled Chinese money and was urging them to comply. By the time the WTO decision came around, Washington had been well trained for decades.

Richard Nixon started it all, begging the Chinese communists for a relationship when it should have been the other way around. His biggest mistake? Listening to a former Ivy League professor, Henry Kissinger, who knew little about China, and whom the Chinese played masterfully—and have played ever since.[5] Though perhaps he thinks he's played them, given he's made a bundle off his China business.

Jimmy Carter? He threw away Taiwan without ever explaining why.[6] Beijing presumably didn't ask. Even Ronald Reagan, who brought down the Soviet Union—and hated communism—listened to his too-clever-by-half advisors, handing over military technology to the PRC to "split" the Chinese from the Russians.[7]

George H. W. Bush was sure that he knew the CCP—having lived in Beijing for fifteen whole months—so he comforted the CCP after it massacred thousands of its citizens at Tiananmen Square. Around a month after the main massacre, Bush wrote to Deng Xiaoping in language that may very well be echoed in a future U.S. president's letter to a Chinese leader after the invasion of Taiwan:

> I write in the spirit of genuine friendship...from one who believes with a passion that good relations between the United States and China are in the fundamental interests of both countries. I have felt that way for many years. I feel more strongly that way today, in spite of the difficult circumstances.... I have tried very hard not to inject myself into China's internal affairs...[T]he actions I took as president could not be avoided [and] the clamor for stronger action remains intense.... I have resisted that clamor, making clear

that I do not want to see destroyed this relationship that you and I have worked so hard to build.... I explained to the American people that I did not want to unfairly burden the Chinese people with economic sanctions.[8]

His son, George W. Bush, was busy with Iraq and Afghanistan, and in any case lacked the stomach for challenging the PRC—as his treatment of Taiwan revealed.

The Clintons? Theirs is a saga of corruption. Read Peter Schweizer's books.[9] In fact, William C. Triplett II and Edward Timperlake laid out a prosecutor's brief on then president Clinton over twenty years ago in their book *Year of the Rat: How Bill Clinton and Al Gore Compromised U.S. Security for Chinese Cash*. Everyone knew what was going on, but nobody did anything.

President Obama was keen to "de-escalate" regardless of Chinese provocations or broken promises.[10]

Beijing made a clean sweep of U.S. administrations until Donald Trump came along.

And now? Then presidential candidate Joe Biden declared that China "was not competition for us."[11] Maybe the Chinese government's interest in his son's investment company[12] had more to do with manipulating the former vice president than with Hunter Biden's financial brilliance? Biden's rhetoric, at least, has gotten tougher, sort of, since taking office, but one wonders.

Of course, all leaders have their own reasons for engagement or appeasement. The go-to assertion: "We need China's help with climate change / North Korea / Ukraine / transnational crime / fill in the blank." Often, these are problems exacerbated, if not created, by Beijing in the first place.

To make things easier for China, top political leadership is often supported at the working level by officials keen to accommodate Beijing, generally in the name of statesmanship. Many are convinced they alone know China and how to handle the Chinese—especially if they speak some Mandarin. The communists gladly let them think so.

The Obama administration's Asia policy director, Evan Medeiros, was in Hong Kong not long after stepping down, advising American businessmen that to make money in China, they should align themselves with Chinese dictator Xi Jinping's interests.[13]

Another prominent former official, Susan Thornton, who nearly got the State Department's top Asia job in 2018, advised a Shanghai audience—that included Chinese officials—to wait out Mr. Trump until more accommodating people took over.[14] Ms. Thornton also said, "I haven't seen any evidence for the Chinese covertly interfering in domestic politics in the United States."[15]

The Biden administration has an inordinate number of people handling Asian and foreign affairs who, at some point in the recent past, have earned money from PRC-related business.[16]

It has likewise been easy pickings for the Chinese over on Capitol Hill.

Powerful Democratic senator Dianne Feinstein was curiously accommodating toward the PRC for decades, even musing, "I sometimes say that in my last life maybe I was Chinese."[17] Presumably, this had nothing to do with a Chinese agent being on her staff for many years.[18] Meanwhile, her husband made a fortune from Chinese business dealings.[19]

Up-and-coming Democratic congressman Eric Swalwell had a Chinese "friend"—who was also a Chinese agent.[20] That was not enough to cost him his seat on the House Intelligence Committee.

The Republicans can be equally subverted. Senator Mitch McConnell, the powerful House Minority Leader, has connections to Chinese money—a lot of it—via his wife, Elaine Chao, and her family's shipping company, the Foremost Group.[21]

You don't even need to be in power officially to be useful to Beijing. Former legislators are also juicy targets for the PRC.

Joseph Lieberman, once the conscience of the U.S. Senate, signed up to lobby on behalf of Chinese telecom firm ZTE in 2018 after it was hit with U.S. government sanctions.[22] Ex-senator Republican David Vitter became a shill for Hikvision USA—the American branch of the Chinese company whose equipment is a backbone of the PRC's surveillance state (including being complicit in the imprisonment of a million Uighurs).[23]

Former U.S. government officials advised Hong Kongers to take their medicine and accept enslavement. One of them, the respected former U.S. Consul General in Hong Kong Kurt Tong (who later joined the Asia Group), warned the Trump administration to "do no harm" when it came to Hong Kong.[24] In other words, the thinking was, and is, *don't do anything China won't like.*

The list goes on and on. Ex-secretary of defense, William Cohen, a former senator from Maine and a model of Down East sensibility, runs a consulting firm—the Cohen Group—pushing business with the PRC. He hired another ex-defense secretary a few years ago, retired Marine general James Mattis.[25] Say it ain't so, Mad Dog. What about those Chinese concentration camps, General? And the PLA greasing up to kill Americans?

China Today

There is footage of Shanghai during the COVID lockdowns of 2022. In one clip, residents go to their balconies to sing and protest lack of supplies and food. A drone appears and broadcasts: "Please comply [with] COVID restrictions. *Control your soul's desire for freedom.* Do not open the window or sing."[26]

Control. It's all about control. Look at what happened to Hong Kong. It had free press, elections, representative government, freedom of speech, and every other freedom we recognize as important. Universities were free, and you taught and said what you wanted. It had fiercely independent courts and judges that followed real laws based on British Common Law rather than PRC-dictated regulations. It had a currency that people wanted and accepted worldwide.

Two years later, after Beijing decided enough was enough, Hong Kong had none of those things. Reporters and editors were arrested—as were pro-democracy leaders and Cardinal Zen, the ninety-year-old head of the local Catholic Church. Brutal lockdowns and quarantines were enforced. Hong Kong was run by a Beijing-approved former policeman. The law became what the Chinese Communist Party said it was. It wasn't rule of law, it was rule *by* law.

Hong Kong went from being one of the freest places on the planet, as the economist Milton Friedman noted years ago, to being just another Chinese city. And that, by definition, means one of the least free places on earth.

That is China's goal for America: a country in which the people and state do nothing that matters without Beijing's permission. And it's not just America. When the British gave Hong Kong to China, it was supposed to be one country, two systems. It quickly ended up being one country, one system. Beijing's goal is 193 countries (or however many are listed at the United Nations), one system. Theirs.

Life in America will be different—though we are already being trained for it. In China, there is increasing use of a social credit system (actually a population control system) in which you accrue points for things like reading Xi Jinping's texts and lose points for searching for non-government-sanctioned churches. This dovetails with mass AI-powered surveillance technologies (including facial recognition) and use of a Chinese-government-created digital currency to provide levels of control at the micro level that would have made Stalin giddy.[27]

The government can cut off your money, deem you unemployable, block you from public transit, and watch as you pace back and forth in your tiny room at your wit's end until you comply.

Think you can escape by getting rid of your personal tracking and monitoring device (your cellphone)? You can also get punished for not keeping your phone topped up and charged. You pay for the privilege to be controlled. China doesn't need to build more prisons (even though it is). It is building a prison the size of a country.

Think that can't happen here? We are already doing it to ourselves—undoubtedly nudged along by information warfare operations by China and others. Take a look at the dynamics of so-called cancel culture, which was supercharged from 2020 onwards—creating immense turmoil, fear, and hatred inside America.

Canceling sure looks a lot like the Chinese Cultural Revolution, where people with wrong thoughts were berated by angry mobs, physically abused, forced to apologize, and sent away to the hinterland—or, in today's United States, banned from social media. And it is evolving to conflate with technologically enabled, U.S.-style informal and opaque social credit systems. Increasingly, taking positions that aren't illegal but that are considered wrong-think might mean you can't get banking services, certain jobs, or travel to certain places.

Pillow maker Mike Lindell, known for questioning the integrity of the 2020 election (which is controversial but not illegal), has not only been deplatformed from social media, but "debanked" by his financial institution over concerns of "reputational damage," and he had his cellphone taken by the FBI.[28]

Want to see what's coming? Just look north of the border. Some participants in the 2022 Canada trucker's convoy had their bank accounts frozen and trucks seized.[29] Canada's deputy prime minister

Chrystia Freeland said, "If your truck is being used in these protests, your corporate accounts will be frozen. The insurance on your vehicle will be suspended. The consequences are real, and they will bite."[30] Canada's justice minister said that "pro-Trump" major donors to the convoy "ought to be worried."[31] Major banks froze donations destined for the truckers.[32] Bear in mind, a judge found the Ottawa protests were "peaceful, lawful, and safe."[33]

Going forward, if you want to buy a plane ticket, access your bank account or an ATM, get a job, or get into a good school, your wrong-think better not have extended to being negative about the CCP anywhere in your digital past.

The control will only get easier. If you want to rent somewhere, buy something specific, or even travel across states, you may need a digital ID. That ID will be stored on the holy grail of social control, that self-carrying tracking and monitoring device, the cellphone. And the more control they have, the more control they want. Next up, government-backed digital currency.[34]

All this makes it even easier for China's agents and useful idiots to shape our economy and society. America will only have the industries China allows it to have, and that may not be many. The United States' main purpose will be to provide PRC manufacturers with natural resources and raw materials and Chinese citizens with food—likely grown on Chinese-owned land, and farmed by imported Chinese labor.

The Party will decide how many Americans there should be—and how many children Americans are allowed to have—just like it did in China. If the Chinese did it to their own, they will be even more brutal with others once they get the chance.

People will resist. We are Americans, after all. But they will be brought into line. If social coercion and control don't work, there will be beatings, possibly delivered by the regime's pet organized crime gangs, as we saw in Hong Kong.[35] Inconvenient cases will disappear into detention centers. Or maybe they will be called "reeducation centers."

Then there is the concept of generational punishment, in which your parents and children are punished for your transgression. If you think wrong, then your parents will have a hard time getting medical insurance, and your kids won't get into university or hold a government job.

There will be rewards for turning in your wrong-thinking family, friends, neighbors, and co-workers. You'll be suspected, and maybe punished, if one goes rogue and you didn't alert the authorities beforehand. The majority will fall into line, try to keep their heads down, and not catch the eye of the system.

There will also be plenty of Americans willing to help keep the new order for the common good, of course. There always are.

So lose this war and, at best, you're in a birdcage—constantly surrounded by cats. The mode of living will be akin to the one in the PRC (on a good day) or like Eastern Europe in the Communist era. Nobody knows what the rules are but, keep your mouth shut and don't do or say anything the regime and its "ears" can hear and won't like, and you're free enough. Until you aren't. You might even get an overseas trip now and then and the chance to buy some blue jeans. People who remember the good times know to keep their mouths shut. People who don't remember the good times, don't know any better. But it's a birdcage nonetheless. Do not open the window or sing.

In another clip from the 2022 Shanghai lockdown, a police officer roughing up a Shanghai citizen says, "You can't do what you want, like in America. This is China. So listen carefully (and) don't ask me why. There is no why!"[36]

For now, it's just China.

We are in a war that started a long time ago. We just chose not to recognize it, even though one could see it plain as day in Baltimore and any number of towns where communities were destroyed and societies were ripped apart under the incessant assault of the invisible soldiers of the PRC and its proxies.

The game isn't over yet, fortunately, and Americans are showing signs of finally waking up and gearing up to fight back. If we are going to have a chance, we need to understand what we are fighting so that we can put tactics and strategies in place that land serious blows. We must not become distracted into shadow boxing or, worse, allowing ourselves to be confused by Beijing into fighting each other.

If we do not respond intelligently, before we realize it, we will become the United States with Chinese characteristics.

CHAPTER 4

What's the Goal of the Chinese Communist Party?

L et's start with the end. We can see what the Chinese Communist Party is doing to the United States. How does that fit into its overall goals? What are the objectives of China's rulers? Do they really intend to take over the world? Isn't this exaggerated apprehension at best, and an idea bordering on conspiracy theory at worst?

Take them at their word. They do. The People's Republic of China may settle for dominance rather than occupation, but it does indeed aim to rule us all.

The U.S.-China Economic and Security Review Commission has been one of the few U.S. government entities to correctly assess China for many years. It stated in its annual reports to Congress:

- The CCP seeks to revise the international order to be more amenable to its own interests and authoritarian governance systems. It desires for other countries not only to acquiesce to its prerogatives but also to acknowledge what it perceives as China's rightful place at the top of the new hierarchical world order.[1]

- The CCP's triumphalism derives from a genuine belief in its own superiority and from the need to legitimize and sustain its one-party rule.[2]
- CCP leaders publicly express confidence that China will prevail in an ideological and civilizational clash with the United States and other democracies they refer to as "the West." Chinese leaders portray the United States as a waning superpower on a path towards inevitable decline and believe China will be able to continue expanding its power and influence globally.[3]

Don't underestimate the appeal of nationalism—crude as it may seem—in China. Humans haven't outgrown this, or the tribalism that's a part of most of us. Inside the PRC, appeals depicting China as "picked on," "contained," and "deprived of its rightful place in the world" do indeed resonate widely with the populace.

It's just as much as patriotism is part and parcel of the American psyche. But the Chinese Communist Party also has a large dose of resentment and vengeance, and that's different. And dangerous.

Indeed, the Chinese Communist Party nurses grudges. In 1999, during the Yugoslav Civil War, the U.S. Air Force shot a missile into the Chinese embassy in Belgrade. The PRC leaders simply could not believe it was an accident—perhaps, I would say, because someone in the embassy was doing something they shouldn't have been doing.

In an attempt to prove it was a mistake and to make up, a senior Chinese official was invited to meet CIA director George Tenet in his seventh-floor office. It did not go well.

The Chinese haven't forgotten. A Xinhua story on the twenty-third anniversary declared, "'The Chinese people will never forget

NATO's barbaric atrocities of bombing the Chinese embassy in Belgrade in 1999, and will never allow the historical tragedy to be repeated.'"[4]

And when countries don't act as Beijing thinks they should, it lets those countries know in no uncertain terms. One Chinese editor referred to Australia a couple years ago as being as inconsequential as "chewing gum stuck on the sole of China's shoes."[5]

But surely, Xi Jinping doesn't think he and the PRC can rule the world?

Actually, he does. There is even a word for it: *tianxia.*

Author Gordon Chang describes *tianxia* (literally, "all under heaven") as a Chinese concept of world order that puts China at the center of the world—and, in its modern form, Xi and the Chinese Communist Party are at the top.[6]

This may seem far-fetched to Americans, but not to Chinese Communist Party leadership. Combine *tianxia* with a Tony Soprano mindset—getting and keeping power, destroying rivals that one internalizes on the way to the top of a communist system—and you'll have a better sense of the CCP.

Observers debate whether the CCP is serious about *tianxia.* Some claim today's PRC leadership sees *tianxia* as just demanding mutual respect, not a Sino-centric vision of global dominance. But the research done in Chinese think tanks shows just how serious they are.

Comprehensive National Power

A foundational concept in Chinese foreign policy is Comprehensive National Power (CNP).[7] References to CNP are all over the Chinese literature, and it provides the key to unlocking the way the CCP looks at the world.

CNP is, as Michael Pillsbury notes, "something unique to China."[8] Pillsbury writes that CNP refers to the combined overall conditions and strengths of a country in numerous areas.... Chinese assessments of CNP are done both qualitatively, in general discussions of country strengths and weaknesses, as well as quantitatively, through the use of formulas to calculate numerical values of CNP. China's forecasts of CNP reject using gross national product (GNP) indexes or the measurement methods of national power used in the United States. Instead, Chinese analysts have developed their own extensive index systems and equations for assessing CNP.[9]

In other words, the CCP ranks each country on the planet according to a numerical CNP value. That value is calculated based on a range of factors. Some we would recognize as traditional elements of national power, such as the size of the military, but others are elements that give new meaning to the word "comprehensive," and might include things like control over human capital in someone else's country. So, those hundreds of American researchers—funded by the U.S. government and working in American labs doing cutting-edge research that is then suspected of ending up in China—count towards China's CNP, not the United States.[10]

China expert Captain Bernard Moreland (retired) explains:

One of the important things to understand about CNP is that it is an objective metric. Beijing constantly calculates and recalculates China's CNP relative to other nations the same way many of us watch our 401(k) grow. The [CCP is] obsessed with engineering and calculating everything and believe that all issues can be reduced to numbers and algorithms. This is what they mean when they euphemistically refer to scientific approaches.

For us in the West, concepts like national power are subjective vague concepts. We often talk of our own national power, but to us it's a byproduct of a strong economy from pursuing prosperity, or a strong military from pursuing defense. We don't build power for the sake of power. That idea is foreign to us. For the Chinese Communist Party, Comprehensive National Power as measured by a CNP score is a goal in itself and pursuit of CNP justifies just about anything.[11]

Entropic Warfare

Justifies anything? Yes, anything. Including biological attacks like the one launched in late 2019. We'll get to that soon.

There are two ways for a country to rise in the CNP rankings. The first is to improve—work harder, smarter, and govern better. The other is to knock competitors down and, in the process, end up *relatively* higher in the ranking. Remember, CNP is a relative ranking, not an absolute one. You don't need to reach a certain number to win, you just need to be higher than whoever is number two.

China uses these dual approaches to achieve its goal of being number one in the world in terms of CNP. It deepens its own comprehensive power base, at the same time undermining those of its competitors.

This means it actively seeks to destabilize and weaken other countries so that they are easier to dominate and control. The process has been described by Cleo Paskal as entropic warfare.[12]

The definition of entropy is "a process of degradation or running down or a trend to disorder." Paskal describes entropic warfare as a sustained attack that results in "paralyzing a target country's ability to respond or defend itself, and so allowing Beijing to win without fighting"[13] Want to know what entropic warfare looks like? It looks like Baltimore.

Baltimore didn't just happen—it was the result of wave after wave of assaults—China's entry into the WTO, its floods of fentanyl, the capture of the Washington elite, and more. And China has a name for that also.

Unrestricted Warfare

We are used to war being kinetic, meaning the overt use of physical force. The word "kinetic" came along at some point during the Global War on Terror and has burrowed itself into U.S. military and defense jargon since. In a military context, kinetic just means using force—shooting, bombing, blowing things up, and killing people. Presumably, the Mongols, Tamerlane, Attila, William Tecumseh Sherman, and others had their own terms.

But we are not (yet) in a war where the People's Liberation Army has gone on the attack and is killing Americans directly. That's the kind of war we're familiar with, and indeed, more comfortable with.

It is important to keep in mind that the Chinese Communist Party does not distinguish between peacetime and wartime like Americans do. To the communists, there is no distinction. Instead, it considers itself in a constant state of war with its enemies—with the United States being the main opponent. Non-kinetic warfare measures and an actual shooting war are on the same spectrum from the Chinese viewpoint.

And when the time is right—assuming non-kinetic efforts haven't worked well enough—the knives come out.

How do we know this? The Chinese told us.

James Lilley, the former U.S. ambassador to China and ex-CIA officer, often said the Chinese telegraph their punches.

In 1999, two People's Liberation Army colonels published their book *Unrestricted Warfare: China's Master Plan to Destroy America.* They call for economic warfare, attacks on key infrastructure, propaganda and influence efforts to weaken and tear apart an opponent's society and political system, and any number of lines of attack.

They write that, with unrestricted warfare, "all means will be in readiness,…information will be omnipresent, and the battlefield will be everywhere. [All] weapons and technology can be superimposed at will, [and] the boundaries lying between the two worlds of war and non-war, of military and non-military, will be totally destroyed."[14]

The two colonels describe at least twenty-four different warfares. Only a few are kinetic warfare in the Western sense (for example, "atomic warfare" and "bio-chemical warfare"). The rest fall under the political warfare umbrella category and include "media warfare," "ideological warfare," and "psychological warfare."

Military Category	Trans-military Category	Non-military Category
Atomic warfare	Diplomatic warfare	Financial warfare
Conventional warfare	Network warfare	Trade warfare
Bio-chemical warfare	Intelligence warfare	Resources warfare
Ecological warfare	Psychological warfare	Economic aid warfare
Space warfare	Tactical warfare	Regulatory (Legal) warfare
Electronic warfare	Smuggling warfare	Sanction warfare
Guerrilla Warfare	Drug warfare	Media warfare
Terrorist warfare	Virtual warfare (deterrence)	Ideological warfare

"Political warfare" is a popular expression these days, but it is a term of art. It's not exactly warfare in the traditional sense, but it is a struggle for power, dominance, and control—which is what warfare, and politics, are ultimately about. The weapons of political warfare seek to undermine, subvert, and demoralize an opponent without actually fighting. They are the tactics used to wage—and win—entropic warfare, and so increase Comprehensive National Power.

Political warfare makes use of various non-kinetic warfares such as economic and financial warfare, cyber, legal warfare, influence operations, and others. These are the actual devices with which the war is fought.

Say you are Beijing, and you want another nation to act a certain way—either voluntarily or involuntarily. It could be anything from supporting your desired candidate for a key post at the United Nations to ceding its territory to you.

All measures short of actual violence by your armed forces are employed as needed—bribery, social media manipulation, targeted blackmail, swarming by your fishing fleet to push back their ships, and so forth. There is one exception to the no-violence rule: you sometimes have so-called proxies commit violence on your behalf.

Done correctly, political warfare bends the target to your will, he changes his behavior, and you win without direct fighting. Or else the entropic warfare weakens him and sets you up for the successful use of actual force—kinetic warfare. Either way, you move up in the CNP rankings, and he moves down.

Using combinations of these unrestricted warfares, you coerce, threaten, persuade, entice, deceive, embarrass, distract, and upset your opponent. Economic and financial stratagems are particularly effective, and you play rough if needed: bribery, drug peddling, debasing currency are all in the political warfare tool kit. Fear of embarrassment and appealing to an opponent's sense of playing by the rules can handcuff an adversary. Your military can be used to intimidate and demoralize while stopping just short of actual violence. This all works best when your opponent's *own* citizens, agents of influence, do the work for you.

Some scholars argue that the colonels' book gets too much credence from Westerners and that unrestricted warfare is not official Chinese doctrine. That may be so on the doctrine issue, but it may not matter either.

Professor Kerry Gershaneck, author of the seminal book *Political Warfare: Strategies for Combating China's Plan to "Win without*

Fighting," notes that unrestricted warfare at least characterizes the underlying philosophy for Chinese warfare—kinetic and political.[15] Nothing is prohibited. The two colonels just drew a lot of things together and had their day—getting famous.

What are the limits to Chinese behavior? There really aren't many... beyond what Beijing can get away with and a preference for avoiding outright and direct force that might provoke an opponent (or its friends) to respond in kind. That's the reason, for example, China has not taken a shot at the Japanese Navy and Coast Guard ships around the Senkaku Islands. The Americans are nearby and have said they will protect the Japanese. Instead, Beijing sends in its fishing fleet and Coast Guard to test, harass, and wear down local responders, and change facts on the ground.[16]

Sometimes political warfare will be directed at other nations as a way of influencing, pressuring, or isolating (and thus, weakening) the main target.

Since political warfare is about shaping an opponent's behavior and ultimately influencing his thinking, it has a huge psychological component. Indeed, the most successful political warfare conditions the opponent to think he is acting out of his own free will, or at least taking the wisest and only sensible course of action.

Once you understand that unrestricted political warfare is a different sort of warfare, it is not hard to recognize.

But you can better understand unrestricted political warfare by looking at how it works in practice. One observer commented that unrestricted warfare's most important principle is "opportunity." In other words, take advantage of any opportunity that injures the enemy (or its friends), especially in the long-term. So, sometimes, the PRC will hold back, often for quite a while, even years, until it spots an opportunity and makes its move. Want to know what that looks like? Think back to 2019.

Unrestricted Warfare: Opportunistic Biological Warfare

Biological Warfare? Yes, Indeed

The COVID virus may or may not have been deliberately set loose on the world by the Chinese Communist Party. But once the virus appeared in Wuhan, China, in late 2019 (or earlier), and was unlikely to be contained, the CCP went into unrestricted warfare mode and took full advantage.

If China's Comprehensive National Power was going to be affected, Beijing was going to make sure that everyone else was hit even harder so that, in a relative sense, the Chinese would come out ahead.

It had been planning for an event like this since at least 2002 when it faced an outbreak of severe acute respiratory syndrome (SARS) that quickly spread worldwide, which prompted the World Health Organization (WHO) to declare a worldwide health threat.

For China, it was a major Comprehensive National Power loss. Premier Wen Jiabao said at the time, "China's national interest and international image are at stake."[17]

The outbreaks continued for around two years, and the WHO, still a largely independent body then, mostly did its job with professionalism. For example, in May 2004, following another outbreak, it put out a report that read: "The investigation has centered primarily on the National Institute of Virology in Beijing where experiments using live and inactivated SARS coronavirus have been carried out. Two researchers at the Institute developed SARS in late March and mid-April. The outbreak was reported on April 22 and the Institute was closed a day later."[18]

For China, it was a major threat to have an organization that it didn't control shaping the narrative around a crucial event. Beijing didn't want to be put in that position again. So not only did it study the health-related lessons learned from SARS, it also studied the unrestricted warfare lessons.

By the time COVID came around, Beijing had a much more compliant leadership in place at the WHO, making it easier for the Chinese government to conceal details of the disease, including human-to-human transmission. Sure, it affected the credibility of the WHO—but that was fine with Beijing. From a Comprehensive National Power perspective, whether the WHO is a weapon Beijing can deploy to advance its own interests, or is weakened to the point of ineffectiveness and so can't be used against China, it's a CNP win for Beijing either way.

With the WHO tamed, China could then lock down Wuhan—blocking travel to other parts of China while allowing Chinese travelers, including from Wuhan, to travel overseas, seeding the rest of the world.

Remember that, in 2019, the United States economy was humming along—and starting to bring manufacturing back from overseas. The Chinese economy was stumbling, and the Communist Party itself was on the back foot owing to the Trump administration's efforts.

The CCP allowing the international spread of a virus they knew to be deadly (biological warfare) probably cost President Trump another four years in office—to the CCP's considerable relief. Trump's was the first administration in the last fifty years that stood up to the Chinese Communist Party rather than accommodating and overlooking Chinese misbehavior in hope the Chinese would liberalize and become "responsible stakeholders."

The Trump team—including Secretary of State Mike Pompeo, his advisor Miles Yu, Assistant Secretary of State for East Asian and Pacific Affairs David Stilwell, Deputy National Security Advisor Matthew Pottinger, and Assistant to the President Peter Navarro—scared the Chinese. They fought effectively on the political warfare battlefield with tariffs, investigations, going after Chinese state media, shutting down the suspect Houston consulate, and much more. Beijing wanted them off the field. It got its wish.

By mid-2020, the United States cowered—economically, psychologically, and physically. The majority of Americans voluntarily gave up their freedoms, enduring lockdowns without much protest. Until COVID, "lockdown" was a word only used for prisoners. When American churches closed down but strip clubs and liquor stores remained open, one knew America had lost its collective mind, or been effectively and meticulously driven crazy, including through effective social media political warfare operations pushed by China.

The U.S. military also lost its nerve. A U.S. Navy aircraft carrier put itself out of commission and docked in Guam—despite the young, physically fit crew members being at little risk from COVID. Meanwhile, the United States realized it was dependent on China for pharmaceuticals and medical supplies.

All in all, quite a win for the Chinese communists, who sensibly sat back and watched their propaganda and proxies work with willing Americans to shut down the United States of America.

Once it was shut down, people moved online and became even easier to reach and manipulate (and a more captive market for online retailers selling Chinese goods). As fear and desperation were stoked, the stage was set for the Marxist-led mobs.

Marxist? Yes. Don't take my word for it, take theirs. The Black Lives Matter co-founder proudly proclaimed she was a "trained Marxist."[19] One of the goals of the organization was the Marxist aim to "disrupt the Western-prescribed nuclear family structure requirement."[20]

Riotors, taking inspiration from BLM and its agenda, started in a major way by protesting the killing of George Floyd. They began to destroy parts of U.S. cities—causing $2 billion in property damage[21] in already vulnerable areas, increasing the despair. They also went after the state, attacking police physically and ideologically, and burned down government buildings.

Chinese Accessories

The Chinese Communist Party was an accessory to all this (as was possibly Russia). Chinese media egged on the violence publicly and, covertly, CCP operations worked to manufacture dissent in part through online mass-customized manipulation. The Trump-era focus on China was lost as the United States looked inward and fought not the CCP, but itself.

So, there you have it. The methods (unrestricted warfare, including political warfare) create the desired outcome (an entropic warfare win). The result is that the U.S. Comprehensive National Power takes a hit and so, in a relative sense, China's increases.

This extremely effective entropic warfare has fragmented the United States, the only country that might have prevented Beijing from building an economy and a military able to challenge and conceivably defeat America.

Galactic Hegemony?

But Beijing's ambitions are even bigger than that. As detailed by researchers including Clive Hamilton and Anne-Marie Brady, they are global—even galactic, if one looks at their space program.[22] To achieve that, Beijing isn't just trying to create states of entropy within countries, but also between allies to weaken alliances and expand its own sphere of influence.

According to one analyst with many years of experience observing Chinese political warfare:

> Academics dismiss the Cold War-era domino theory (that warned of communist takeover in one country in a region leading to other countries falling to the communists) without giving credit to U.S. actions in Korea and Vietnam to slow

the spread of communism in the Pacific or the Cuban missile crisis directly confronting Russian ambitions in our hemisphere. The Chinese stealth approach to the game of Go is yielding better results. By my count, Brazil will soon be our last ally south of the Mexican border.[23]

Take a look at even the smallest countries. You'll see large CCP footprints, especially in the most remote locations. An American businessman with decades of experience in China explains why:

> The CCP strategy is to encircle the U.S. This comes from Mao's famous strategy parallel during the civil war to liken China to a great pond with some smaller islands in it (cities) and one big island (Beijing). If the fish swimming between the smaller islands and the one large island can control this open space, they can control the islands and eventually cut them off one-by-one, and inevitably the big island will fall, too. The fish will end up controlling the whole pond.... It is their pond.
>
> For all the time I have been in China, I have heard this story over and over again from party members and business entrepreneurs. No matter the product or service.
>
> I would ask, "So what is your marketing plan for, let's say, vocational training via satellite?"—vocational training companies are very competitive in China. The answer: "Mr. John, our marketing plan is built on the same principle as Mao's taking the pond civil war strategy...we will be the fish that take the countryside first, encircle the mass city markets, and take them one by one until we take all of China's major vocational education markets."
>
> There is a side-story to this: if you are starting up a small private company in China the odds are stacked

against you big time. One way to ingratiate yourself with the local party secretary whose support you need is to let him or her know you have a Mao-inspired marketing plan.

One more thing: in China, "Mao Marketing," as I came to call it, actually worked. Mao was right.

It is obvious China is using Mao Marketing as their strategic geopolitical policy as well. The world is a pond dominated by the Big Island United States. CCP fish go out and fill the open spaces between U.S. island and the smaller islands, taking the open parts of the pond. Then, one-by-one, start isolating and eventually taking over the smaller islands. Western Europe [is] one of these smaller islands, urban areas of Latin America and Africa are other small islands. Take the open spaces in Latin America and Africa first, surround their urban areas, eventually cut them off, and isolate them from America. Keep repeating the process around the world until America itself is isolated.[24]

And so, here we are. The Chinese Communist Party has pulled off a breathtakingly successful political warfare campaign against the United States over the last five decades. We are increasingly isolated, fragmented from within, and under attack from so many unrestricted warfares that we can't even tell the source, and don't know how, or whom, to fight. So we end up fighting each other, not realizing that that's China's goal. They are winning.

Counterattack?

But certainly, the United States has its own offensive political warfare campaign against the Chinese?

We used to, back in the Cold War, but it all disappeared after 1990. The U.S. government just doesn't do political warfare. U.S. Air Force brigadier general Rob Spalding, fluent in Mandarin and a former defense attaché in Beijing, understood how the Chinese communists operate. When assigned to the U.S. National Security Council in the early days of the Trump administration, General Spalding made it his mission to do something about Chinese political warfare. He was resisted and ultimately forced out.[25]

The Trump administration got its legs, however, and was the first in decades to challenge China. Did Trump start a "sea change" that will roll back Chinese political warfare successes?

Don't bet on it. People in the Trump administration understood political warfare and what the Chinese were doing and attempted to do something about it. However, they faced a constant internal fight inside their own administration from, among others, Wall Street's men—led by Steve Mnuchin, the treasury secretary, formerly of Goldman Sachs.[26]

You'll often hear the PRC only wants a "peaceful rise," "win-win solutions," and insistence that China does not meddle in other countries' internal affairs. Alex Joske, formerly with the Australian Security Policy Institute, concluded that the concept of China's "peaceful rise" originated from a Chinese Ministry of State Security influence operation.[27] It worked.

I once had a conversation with a young Marine officer who insisted China posed no threat as it was on a "peaceful rise."

"How do you know?" I asked. "They said so."

If we can't name the enemy, we can't even start to fight it. And sometimes it seems we will do anything not to see what's in front of us.

Kurt Campbell is currently the National Security Council's Indo-Pacific Coordinator. Ely Ratner is Assistant Secretary of Defense for Indo-Pacific Security Affairs. In 2018, they wrote "The China

Reckoning: How Beijing Defied American Expectations" for *Foreign Affairs* about how the PRC had baffled American hope that engagement with and accommodation of the Chinese communists would lead to the regime liberalizing and becoming a responsible, peaceful member of the international community.[28]

A retired diplomat friend who read the article noted, "All of us who had experienced Tiananmen and spent two or more tours in Beijing or even read authors like James Mann and many other experts had no positive expectations whatsoever. [Former U.S. ambassador to China and ex-CIA officer James] Lilley sure understood Beijing. But Campbell and Ratner sounded like they had discovered gravity."[29]

Absolutely nothing about Chinese behavior over the last forty years should have surprised anyone. It's what repressive communist regimes do (not that there's another kind of communist regime). And making things even easier, the Chinese always telegraph their punches, as James Lilley often said.

For example, in 1992, the PRC passed the Law on the Territorial Sea and the Contiguous Zone, which claimed the South China Sea—vital global sea-lanes and international waters, though parts were claimed by several neighboring states.[30] Nobody took Beijing seriously, and anyway, China couldn't enforce the law. Twenty years later, in 2012, China began building artificial islands in the South China Sea, and gradually turned them into military bases. In the process, it established de facto control of the South China Sea. In 2021, the PRC passed another law codifying its right to assert administrative control over ships passing through the SCS.[31] And China is very clear that U.S. Navy ships operating in the SCS only operate at China's sufferance—for now.

The Chinese were clear about their intentions early on; we just chose not to believe them. Campbell and Ratner in particular should have seen it coming. Campbell had been U.S. assistant secretary of state for East Asian and Pacific Affairs from 2009 to 2013, and Ratner had been deputy national security adviser to then U.S. vice president Joe Biden from 2015 to 2017. This covered the period during which China illegally took, and then militarized, islands in the South China Sea.

Despite China having no enemies, it is building up a massive military that can defeat the United States—and everyone else—pretending it must do so to defend itself. But name one country or person who has called for attacking China. Indeed, there has never been a country that was more welcomed and accommodated in hope—indeed, expectation—that it would liberalize and become a responsible nation.

In recent years, commercial imaging satellites have identified targets at Chinese missile ranges in the western China desert that are mock-ups of the U.S. naval base at Yokosuka, Japan, and a separate mock-up of the aircraft carrier U.S.S. *Ronald Reagan*.[32] The Chinese have also boasted about their DF-21 and DF-26 anti-ship ballistic missiles—the so-called carrier killers.[33]

It's never hard to figure out what Beijing has in mind. If you want to.

It's all laid out in detail in Ian Easton's excellent book *The Final Struggle: Inside China's Global Strategy*. In simple terms, the Chinese Communist Party seeks global domination and will fight its main enemy, the United States, to achieve it. Indeed, the destruction of capitalism and the triumph of Chinese-style socialism is seen as a historical inevitability.

As for the PRC liberalizing while under Chinese communist rule? Don't bet on it. *Central Committee Document No. 9*, issued in 2013 (when many Western China Hands insisted Xi Jinping was a closet reformer) and eventually leaked overseas, stated things clearly. Matt Pottinger and his co-authors size up *Document 9* as follows: "The party must eradicate Western 'false ideological trends' including constitutional democracy, the notion that Western values are universal, the concept of civil society, economic neoliberalism, journalistic independence, challenges to the party's version of history," and all the other things free people value.[34]

The Mongols are famous for their political warfare and psychological operations as they swept through Russia and into Eastern Europe in the thirteenth century. But they had to throw a few headless bodies over the town wall and give residents the choice: "Surrender now, or everyone dies tomorrow."

The Chinese communists have had it easier with the United States. Like all good political warfare campaigns, China understands its target and knows its vulnerabilities, capitalizing on American avarice, ignorance, naiveté, vanity, and hubris. Some combination of money, flattery, and a ten-course dinner is usually all that's needed with Americans. They'll do the rest themselves.

Sometimes you have to step back and gaze in awe at what the CCP has accomplished. The Chinese communists should have a victory parade through the streets of Baltimore—a conquering army marching through the town they devastated from tens of thousands of miles away, without firing a shot.

But it's not over. James Lilley used to say about the Chinese, "First they try to buy you. Then they try to scare you. After that, they're stumped."[35]

The key is clearly understanding how they are waging their various unrestricted warfares—who they are buying, how they are scaring us. That's what we'll look at in the next chapters.

Once we know that, we can craft a plan not only to defend ourselves, but to bolster our allies, fight back, and win.

We are, after all, America. For now.

CHAPTER 5

Psychological Warfare: How Communist China Does Your Thinking for You

O n November 28, 2020, Di Dongsheng, vice dean of the School of International Relations at Renmin University in Beijing, gave a videotaped lecture in which he said:

> Why did China and the U.S. used to be able to settle all kinds of issues between 1992 and 2016? It's just because we have people at the top. We have our old friends who are at the top of America's core inner circle of power and influence...for the past thirty years, forty years, we have been utilizing the core power of the United States.[1]

He went on to say he was miffed when Donald Trump took office. China's friends in Washington and on Wall Street couldn't get the U.S. administration to back off from its efforts to challenge China like they could with previous administrations. "During the U.S.-China trade war, [Wall Street] tried to help, and I know that my friends on the U.S. side told me that they tried to help, but they couldn't do much."[2]

Professor Di had higher hopes for the new Biden administration: "But now we're seeing Biden was elected, the traditional elite, the political elite, the establishment, they're very close to Wall Street."[3] Perhaps he had reason to be optimistic—given the number of new appointees (many of them Obama administration veterans) who came from "old friend" consulting firms that had serviced PRC clients.[4]

Peter Schweizer's books include detailed accounts of Chinese influence in Washington, D.C., highlighting the psychological dominance China has accumulated over many years. This has resulted in U.S. policies and actions (or inactions) in Beijing's favor.

The Most Important Warfare

Ultimately, psychological warfare is the most important of the political warfare techniques, so we will look at it first. Chinese psychological warfare seeks to change an opponent's thinking and behavior in a way that is favorable to PRC interests and objectives. Through non-kinetic means, it aims to weaken the opponent's will and ability to resist. Successful Chinese psychological warfare makes the other side more accommodating and less willing or able to resist. There is a point at which, even if you realize the danger and are willing to "go kinetic," you think there is no point—it's futile. It doesn't matter how big a stick you have if you aren't willing to use it.

When China talks about winning without fighting, it essentially means without us fighting *back*. And that comes down to getting into our heads and disabling us from the inside.

Most people have heard of psychological operations, or psyops.

Many of us think we are too smart, too well educated, and too discerning to be influenced by psychological warfare. But if you've ever said or thought any of the following, you've been influenced by Chinese psyops:

- COVID-19 couldn't possibly have come from a Chinese laboratory
- China wants to reunify with Taiwan
- The United States must have China's help on climate change, North Korea, and so forth
- We simply have to be invested in the China market
- China won't like it
- To make China an enemy, treat it like one
- How can I criticize China, given what the West has done?
- China is no longer communist. It is capitalist.
- Criticizing the CCP is racist
- China's rise is "peaceful" and "inevitable"
- Chinese culture isn't compatible with democracy
- China is militarizing/aggressive/expansionist because of the trauma of a century of humiliation
- Fentanyl is just payback for the opium wars
- China is not expansionist. It has never attacked its neighbors.
- China is just doing what all great powers do
- We welcome a strong China—the only thing worse is a weak China with nuclear weapons
- You can't say *that* about China! You will offend Chinese people

All of these downplay or excuse threats posed by the People's Republic of China and justify inaction, lethargy, or compliance in the face of outrageous, inhumane CCP behavior. It's all part of being conditioned to think the PRC is not a threat or cannot be resisted, as that will only make things worse.

Psychologcal Warfare and the Military

If you didn't pass the test, don't worry. Neither did America's premier warfighters, the U.S. Marine Corps.

At military exercise Dawn Blitz 2013, for the first time ever, the Japanese sent a small amphibious group to Southern California to train with the Marines and the U.S. Navy. Beijing was unhappy.

I was quoted in the press:

> Colonel Grant Newsham, who is the Marine liaison to the Japanese military, said improving [Japan's] military training was essential to strengthening the United States Asia-Pacific strategy.
>
> "If the twentieth century taught us anything, it is that when democracies are able and willing to defend themselves it preserves peace and stability. Most Asian countries welcome— even if quietly stated—a more capable (Japanese force) that is also closely allied to U.S. forces," Newsham explained to the Associated Press.[5]

Seemed pretty uncontroversial—just a basic reporting of facts. However, the Marine Corps ruling class and its public affairs *commissars* went berserk.

"You can't say that!"

"The Chinese will be mad!"

"They will think we're containing them."

If the United States Marines were too scared to say something that might upset the Chinese communists, you knew PRC psychological warfare was working well.

How well? Five years earlier, the Marine Corps had fallen for Beijing's assurances that it had peaceful intentions, and dispatched

U.S. Marine commandant, General James Conway, to visit the Chinese Marine Corps. He gave a speech encouraging the PLA Marines to master their profession. Unfortunately, they took his advice.

Too much of the American defense establishment has been conditioned over the years (with Chinese help) to believe that it faced no real threat from the PRC, and that engagement and understanding would solve any problems.

America's political class wasn't much different, but had even more of a preference for accommodation. The American business and financial classes were mostly in the bag for China—lulled by Chinese promises of access to the lucrative China market.

To its credit, the Marines (and the rest of the U.S. military) have mostly woken up to the Chinese threat in recent years. But it took them a while. In the meantime, the Chinese People's Liberation Army pulled off the biggest, fastest defense buildup since World War II—and probably in history. And they haven't stopped.

What led to Chinese psychological warfare's success, and too many American government and business elites missing the oncoming Chinese threat?

There's not one single reason, but the PRC understands its targets and, if it wants, has vast intelligence networks to draw on to create individual susceptibility profiles (something made even easier as we all moved online during the pandemic). It can, and does, use any combination of charm, blandishments, cash, flattery, threats (open and veiled), soothing language, in-person hospitality, promises of "opening up," and the allure of access and favors for special friends to entice and convince that with just more effort or time, everything will come right.

Chinese psychological warfare is sometimes so successful that its targets seem to have battered spouse syndrome—excusing away PRC actions that are in fact harmful, and even blaming themselves for having caused it.

Former assistant secretary of defense Professor Joseph Nye typified that approach in his 2013 *New York Times* article "Work With China, Don't Contain It": "When I worked on the Pentagon's East Asia strategy in 1994, during the Clinton administration, we rejected the idea of containment for two reasons. If we treated China as an enemy, we were guaranteeing a future enemy. If we treated China as a friend, we kept open the possibility of a more peaceful future."[6]

Internalize this idea, and it's easy to convince yourself that if China is acting like an enemy, it must be something America is doing wrong. This approach is still common currency among the so-called China Hands—that tight-knit and self-protecting coterie of China whisperers who try to ensure they are the only ones deemed worthy to explain China.

Exemplifying this phenomenon, Henry Kissinger—who has been the go-to guy regarding China for many people in both countries—was quoted in 2022 on the China-U.S. relationship: "We have to be conscious of the differences of ideology and of interpretation that exists. We should use this consciousness to apply it in our own analysis of the importance of issues as they arise, rather than make it the principal issue of confrontation, unless we are prepared to make regime change the principal goal of our policy."[7]

Maybe so, if it's Canada or France you are dealing with. But what if the other side sees differences in ideology as the main issue of confrontation and believes there will be a winner and a loser—and the winner will be the People's Republic of China, by force if necessary?

Dr. Kissinger seems to be suggesting America concede to the Chinese communists, or else *we* are the bad guys.

Sometimes this sort of analysis derives from one of the usual MICE (money, ideology, coercion, ego). Sometimes it's reputational or professional embarrassment at having completely misread the Chinese communists for decades.

Regardless, the PRC benefits from U.S. foreign policy elites being so invested in a largely non-threatening view of China, because debate was impossible for many years—and still isn't easy. Indeed, challenge the accepted wisdom in the mainstream media, academia, think tanks, or any of the other thought-shaping zones so thoroughly infiltrated and infected by the CCP, and you can expect to be roughly handled—at best marginalized, and at worst destroyed.

One American defense analyst suggested at a seminar a few years back that China intended to invade Taiwan. During the break, an irate former U.S. ambassador to Beijing berated him—to include a spittle fleck shower. Too often, this is considered reasoned debate in the China Hand world.

The Chinese communists could also often count on their friends in the United States to keep administrations from pushing back too far—and even to open doors for Beijing, as in the case of the Clinton administration vouching for China as a member of the World Trade Organization (WTO) in the early 2000s.[8] That one act, the result of hubris and greed-fueled blindness, did more to undercut America's strategic position against China than any other action in the last thirty years.

It opened the floodgates for the move of large swaths of American manufacturing to China, and the mostly unchecked transfer of technology and know-how with both commercial and military uses. Most Americans—at least in the elite—convinced themselves there was nothing wrong with this, and most people at the street level understood that the move was dangerous. Just ask a former factory foreman in Baltimore.

Chinese psychological warfare has also created a degree of fear on the U.S. side that has shaped policy and strategy.

U.S. policy towards Taiwan, for example, has for years been based on a fear of provoking China, thus leading to an attack on Taiwan or trouble in the U.S.-PRC relationship, all resulting in the interruption of supply chains or difficulties for U.S. companies in China. The fear and self-censorship are disguised, however, as "statesmanship" or "hard-headed realism."

So strong is the ingrained fear of challenging the Chinese that when a senior U.S. military officer at INDOPACOM in 2015 was asked why they were appeasing China, he answered: "What are we supposed to do? Go to war with them?"

Instead, the plan was that the U.S. forces would push back just enough to give the PRC "off-ramps" from their aggressive behavior. But that only works when the other guy is interested in the off-ramps—and when he doesn't think his behavior is yielding better results. This approach lost military planners valuable time and allowed the PLA to close the military capabilities gap even more.

Psychology Shapes Events, and Events Shape Psychology

This dangerously mistaken mindset isn't new. In 1991 and 1992, believing there was nothing to fear from the PRC, and feeling perhaps too proud of itself at having won the Cold War, the United States pulled out of its key military bases at Subic Bay and Clark Field in the Philippines. One Asia analyst I spoke with observed,

> America's departure from the Philippines and its stunning release of hard assets (Clark Air Base and Subic Bay) there did more than any other single event to embolden the CCP to embark on its current course at home and abroad. The Philippine exit exemplified for the Chinese communists the old Chinese saying, "Seek truth from facts," to confirm its

perception America had entered its irreversible, reactionary-state, decline.[9]

Nearly twenty years later, the Chinese applied some psychological pressure and got the United States to respond in a way that only suited Beijing. In 2012, Chinese Coast Guard ships occupied an islet called Scarborough Shoal, rich fishing grounds and well within the Philippines Exclusive Economic Zone (EEZ).

The Obama administration had no interest in a fight with China—whom it really didn't see (or want to see) as a threat. Remember, senior military officers were forbidden from even saying the Chinese communists might be a problem—and too many of them were keen to engage with the PLA anyway.

Beijing sensed weakness, and perhaps even fear. So it pushed to see how the Americans would respond to this assault on the Philippines sovereignty. The Philippines is a U.S. treaty ally that Washington is obligated to defend.

Instead of sending U.S. Navy ships to defend the overmatched Philippine Coast Guard, Obama's staff cut a deal requiring each side to withdraw. The Filipinos did. The Chinese did not. And the Americans did nothing.

Eventually, we produced a tortured explanation for why "some rocks" (that is, Scarborough Shoal) really did not come under the U.S.-Philippine Mutual Defense Treaty. It was a huge psychological win for Beijing. In the face of Chinese aggression and overt disregard for a recent agreement, Washington effectively said, "Nothing to see here," abandoned a treaty ally, and pretended everything was okay. Across the world, strategic communities took notice.

China took full advantage of the United States not just blinking, but closing its eyes. It went all-out on its island-building campaign in the South China Sea. Within five years, it established de facto control of legally international waters, through which vital trade routes transit. But what value is the law if no one can or, in this case, *will* enforce it?

The Philippines was distressed, and U.S. prestige took a massive blow throughout the region—akin to the damage done in 1975 when the Americans left South Vietnam (and their South Vietnamese allies behind) as North Vietnamese forces took over the country. And it happened again with the catastrophic withdrawal from Afghanistan in 2021.

This also helps Beijing's psychological warfare operations in other countries—to include telling those leaders that the United States can't be relied upon to help, so it had better cut a deal with China as soon as it can.

Psychological Warfare: Enlisting U.S. Media and U.S. Education

The Chinese communists figured out a long time ago that you can enhance control over what people think by controlling what they read, hear, and learn. They did this in China, but have been successful in the United States too.

Indeed, the PRC's psychological warfare against the United States has been much easier and effective, because American media—especially corporate houses with interests in China—largely averted their gaze or tried to give the Chinese Communist Party the benefit of the doubt.

American media gladly (and rightly) savage Russian aggression, but when it comes to China, it's too often the kid gloves treatment. When Donald Trump tried to protect the American economy from PRC predation, he was routinely disparaged by the mainstream media as a racist who just didn't like the Chinese.

While there have been, and still are, some good reporters and columnists covering the PRC—James Mann (*Los Angeles Times* in the

1990s), Joseph Kahn (*New York Times* in the 2000s), Austin Ramzy (formerly *New York Times*, now *Wall Street Journal*), and Kathrin Hille (*Financial Times*) —there's also the other kind. *New York Times* opinion columnist Tom Friedman sang Beijing's praises for years. In 2009, he wrote he'd like to be the Chinese government for a day so he could fix America, explaining, "One-party autocracy certainly has its drawbacks. But when it is led by a reasonably enlightened group of people, as China is today, it can also have great advantages."[10]

Indeed.

Newspapers print PRC government talking points and data, uncritically as often as not. Two years after the start of the pandemic, when the United States had reported over 825,000 COVID deaths, China was still reporting fewer than 5,000. And that number was being echoed in media across the United States,[11] often as the basis for justifying more Chinese-style lockdowns. Sometimes U.S. media outlets even accept overt Chinese-paid propaganda, as the *Washington Post* did with its *China Daily* insert. The *Wall Street Journal*, supposedly the best on PRC matters, did as well.[12]

The Chinese Ambassador to the United States recently got top billing in a *Washington Post* op-ed attacking the United States and its policies towards Taiwan.[13] Other Chinese officials have no difficulty finding outlets for their often-venomous propaganda.

Apart from promoting the PRC's line, there are frequent cases of suppressing stories that might "offend" Beijing. Bloomberg killed a well-researched story in 2013 on CCP leadership corruption, seemingly afraid of damaging its other money-making operations in the PRC.[14]

Then consider the fentanyl epidemic that is killing more Americans each year than died during the worst days of the Vietnam War. Major American media—including the *New York Times* and *Washington Post*—only occasionally mention that China is the ultimate source of most of the drugs and could turn the supply off in a minute.

Within China, Beijing benefits from U.S. administrations being too afraid to challenge Chinese restrictions and harassment of American reporters, and this while Chinese reporters and media companies operate freely in the United States. The Trump administration tried to do something about this, simply insisting on reciprocity for American reporters. But it no longer seems to be a priority for the Biden White House.

One longtime U.S. intelligence official describes even deeper problems with U.S. reporting in and on China:

> [Western reporters] tend to over-rely on the usual suspects—Chinese "think-tank" and academic sources—and utilize without skepticism "sources" steered to them by their local-hire "researchers" who, by the way, are recruited by the Ministry of State Security–controlled Foreign Enterprise Service Corp. to work in foreign news bureaus around China.
>
> Over the past decade, almost all major international news media actors have recruited large teams of PRC-Chinese, who have been trained in CPD (Central Propaganda Department) journalism or foreign language schools and have overseas Xinhua or China News Service tours under their belts (i.e., they have been trained as intelligence collectors).
>
> They are all instructed directly by the MSS on what intelligence to collect, and by the CPD in Beijing on what stories to cover, what angles to play-up, what statistics to use. Further, they are able to inject those biases into their unwitting non-PRC colleagues' PRC reporting and editorials.
>
> During COVID, for example, they…engaged in an intensive campaign to label U.S.G.-suspicions of COVID's Chinese origins as "racist" and to report all instances of "anti-Asian" violence as a direct result of the Trump administration's COVID worries.[15]

Academic Honesty Has Its Price

As for American universities, Beijing correctly calculated that the price of academia's principles equals the number of Chinese students paying full tuition. Until the COVID pandemic stopped the flow, over three hundred thousand Chinese students were studying at U.S. colleges and universities. Handsome donations to university "China centers" bring in money, as do visas, business class tickets, and seminar invitations for professors and administrators. No matter how dull they or their courses may be, those professors and administrators are ever so grateful for the chance to bask in their glory as they look out at a room filled with adulatory "students."

University faculty and administrators that allow conservative speakers to be hounded off campus and who go along with "Boycott, Divest, Sanction" movements against Israel don't say a word when Chinese agents—often students, and sometimes consular officials—intimidate Chinese students criticizing or protesting the communist regime.

As for Chinese communist human rights atrocities, try raising awareness on a U.S. college campus, and you should stand by for trouble. Even professors who say things about the PRC that Chinese students think are offensive can find themselves under investigation by campus administrators.

Once upon a time, American universities thought human rights mattered. Remember apartheid South Africa?

Confucius Institutes, funded by the Chinese Communist Party, sprung up from the 1990s on over a hundred U.S. college campuses. Nominally, they taught Chinese language and culture, but as much served as a useful platform for promoting the CCP party line and for monitoring activity on campus. The Trump administration sought to close them down by giving colleges a choice: do business with the U.S.

government or have a Confucius Institute. Most colleges did the cost/benefit analysis and shuttered the Confucius Institutes.

However, they appear to be reforming under different guises.[16]

While the Confucius Institutes get most of the attention, Confucius Classrooms have largely gone under the radar, even though their effects are even more pernicious. They teach Chinese language and culture like the Confucius Institutes, but they are targeted at American public schools, grades K–12, and there are over five hundred of them.[17]

That's a win-win from Beijing's perspective. A goodly number of young Americans grow up well disposed to the PRC, internalizing the idea that the People's Republic of China and the CCP are just lovable pandas. Can you imagine Beijing allowing the U.S. government to set up "George Washington Classrooms" in China? No, you can't. Maybe American universities should start teaching courses in reciprocity.

Psychological Warfare and U.S. Business

It's just as bad in other U.S. business sectors. The PRC's *China Daily* recently crowed that an American Chamber of Commerce paper in China stated that U.S. companies are saying, "If [you are] not in China, you can't be competitive globally."[18]

After fifty years, U.S. business is still keen to get into the People's Republic of China—and Beijing is keen to keep them interested. It isn't hard. There is the dangling bait of selling one of something to every person in China. And Chinese government perpetually promises to open up—this time, we mean it!

Americans routinely do the sort of business in China they would never do in Wisconsin, or in any of the other forty-nine states. Such is the effect of Chinese psychological warfare that they ignore the risks of an ersatz market controlled by a capricious dictatorship—a dictatorship in which a contract means nothing more than what the dictator says it means, and in which handing over key technology is the price of entry. The Americans studiously overlook the fundamental nature of the regime and its human rights atrocities, even when fellow investors and business owners are thrown in jail for, well...whatever reasons the dictator might have at the moment.

But the Chinese Communist Party understands the psychology involved and plays its hand well. The Chinese have an easy time. The smell of money will often make Westerners dance like sea lions performing tricks at Sea World for a mackerel snack.

I was corresponding with an American businessman who had years or experience in the China market. I wrote, "Like all good psyops campaigns, the communists knew their target's vulnerabilities. They capitalized on American avarice, ignorance, naiveté, vanity, and hubris."

He replied, "Yes, all of these characteristics led to giving away much of our technology to China. I witnessed it first-hand. I would add racism, too, not in all cases, but in many situations, latently and patently. I remember one colleague telling me, 'John, I'm going to let them have the tech manual (for free). They are Chinese. They will never figure it out.'"[19]

Another psychological warfare element to the way China does business is one that you've probably felt yourself and have certainly witnessed in others. The Chinese government subsidizes Chinese manufacturers so they can make the product for less than the Americans (and others) can. And the best part (for them) is that they create a dependency and get the Americans hooked on cheap products—to the point they (American importers of the cheap products) lobby the U.S. government to allow the Chinese to keep doing what they are doing for "the good of Americans."

The American businessman mentioned earlier describes it as follows:

China takes full advantage of our addiction to cheap. An American goes to a big box store to purchase four plastic lawn chairs. When he gets there, he discovers the chairs are really cheap (made in China by a PLA offshoot).

Instead of purchasing the four chairs he needs, he purchases six "because they are so cheap." The cost of the six chairs about equals the price of four higher quality chairs made in Youngstown, Ohio.

The sale, in USD, goes to China's State Administration for Foreign Exchange (SAFE). The PLA offshoot receives a yuandenominated payment from SAFE (maybe). The amount is usually not at the China-made exchange rate but a sum far lower. After all, the PLA offshoot is funded by the state.

China, and just about every other country around the world, knows Americans have this addiction, and they keep feeding it.

When I explained this to some Beltway types, their reaction was that China's cheap goods have provided lower socio-economic groups in America with a material lifestyle they would not otherwise be able to afford. They went on to say this was critical for maintaining the American belief in upward mobility.

I pointed out that paying a little bit more to purchase American goods was the price of freedom needed to keep us from becoming CCP party / state dependent. They dismissed the idea. They could not, or would not, accept or concede Made in China was eroding our own economy and strengthening, product-by-product, purchase-by-purchase, the CCP's party / state influence on the U.S.[20]

That is successful psychological warfare. It also reinforces Chinese economic warfare and makes chemical (fentanyl) warfare more effective by making sure manufacturing (and jobs) don't come back to America. At the same time, it is funding the PLA buildup for the day kinetic warfare begins.

The gravy for the PRC is that it is Americans making sure U.S. government policy doesn't change—even as their fellow citizens are harmed. The Chinese barely need to break a sweat. That's what Comprehensive National Power looks like.

Bottom line, Chinese psychological warfare has been very successful, and for decades.

No matter what the PRC does—threatens U.S. ships in international waters, harasses and sinks other nations' fishing boats, withholds life-saving medical care from a Nobel Prize winner and lets him die, locks up citizens *en masse* in concentration camps, or gets caught red-handed stealing American trade secrets and government secrets— there is an amen chorus of bureaucrats, Ph.D.s, business and financial types, government officials, politicians, and pundits who will tell you why there's nothing to worry about from communist China.

And, they add, anyone who says otherwise is racist, stupid, a hawk (or even a super hawk)—and anyway, it's all America's fault since we treated China like an enemy. And more than a few senior U.S. military officers and their courtiers (the colonels who hope to be generals) are willing to say the same thing.

One can argue why and where the blame should go, but one can't argue with the outcome. With only token opposition, the United States ceded its advantages and allowed—indeed, helped and encouraged—a self-avowed enemy to develop its economic and military might (and the psychological might that comes with it) to the point that the PRC can potentially defeat America, maybe even without fighting.

But there is some good news. Like a drunkard awakening from a stupor, the powers that be in U.S. military and the Department of Defense are starting to recognize the PRC as a threat. That's quite a change from the Obama era when you couldn't use the word "adversary" for China. Even Capitol Hill is more awake to the China risk than it has been since the Cold War—though the donor class that makes money from the PRC still carries plenty of weight.

Even some American businesses are starting to realize that being in the PRC market is riskier than they thought.

Others will require a punch in the nose to wake up, and even that probably won't be enough.

Wall Street and the financial class, unfortunately, remain fully committed to the PRC. It is somebody else's money, after all.

But we know what the People's Republic of China is about now—and it's getting harder for those who pretend it's something else.

We need to accept what reality tells us about the Chinese communists and not be lulled, confused, or cowed by what the CCP's psychological warfare operations try to make us think.

We have to keep our heads clear, because there are many more "warfares" ahead of us. We can only see them for what they are, and win, if we've liberated our mental battlefield.

CHAPTER 6

Lawfare: Rules for Thee but Not for Me

Another warfare the Chinese Communist Party has mastered is lawfare. To the CCP, the law's purpose is to help the CCP stay in power and advance Party interests. Justice, at least as understood in the West, has nothing to do with it.

The PRC pretends to obey the law sometimes, writes new laws to make the blatantly illegal seem justified, ignores laws when it feels like it, and often uses other countries' legal systems to target, slow down, or block rulings that could impede its activities. I'll give you some examples.

Using America's Legal System to Weaken American Security

In June 2020, the PLA ambushed and killed twenty Indian soldiers in the Himalayas. Two weeks later, Delhi retaliated by banning fifty-nine Chinese apps, including WeChat and TikTok. Indian security experts explained the apps could be used to gather sensitive information from cellphones, including locations, contacts, images, audio, and more, and then surreptitiously send it to servers outside India.[1] That opened users up to spying, influence operations, physiological manipulation, blackmail, industrial espionage, and more. Additionally, the harvested metadata could, given China's military-civil fusion doctrine, be used to refine AI weapon systems.[2]

The concerns were shared by American security professionals, and in August 2020, the Trump administration issued executive orders banning TikTok and WeChat. They were clear about the risks posed. The TikTok order read in part:

> TikTok automatically captures vast swaths of information from its users, including Internet and other network activity information such as location data and browsing and search histories. This data collection threatens to allow the Chinese Communist Party access to Americans personal and proprietary information—potentially allowing China to track the locations of Federal employees and contractors, build dossiers of personal information for blackmail, and conduct corporate espionage.
>
> TikTok also reportedly censors content that the Chinese Communist Party deems politically sensitive, such as content concerning protests in Hong Kong and China's treatment of Uyghurs and other Muslim minorities. This mobile application may also be used for disinformation campaigns that benefit the Chinese Communist Party, such as when TikTok videos spread debunked conspiracy theories about the origins of the 2019 Novel Coronavirus.[3]

The WeChat executive order specified that

the application captures the personal and proprietary information of Chinese nationals visiting the United States, thereby allowing the Chinese Communist Party a mechanism for keeping tabs on Chinese citizens who may be enjoying the benefits of a free society for the first time in their lives. For example, in March 2019, a researcher reportedly discovered a Chinese database containing billions of WeChat messages sent from users in not only China but also the United States, Taiwan, South Korea, and Australia.[4]

To put this in context, suppose the CIA or the National Security Agency could deploy a similar app used by hundreds of millions of people in the People's Republic of China. The CCP probably would not approve.

To give a sense of how creepy it all is, consider the experience of a BBC reporter based in China who was visiting Hong Kong to cover the thirtieth anniversary of the Tiananmen Square massacre.

He took some photos of the protests and sent them back to friends in China via WeChat.

He was quickly locked out of WeChat. When he tried to log back in, a message appeared: "This WeChat account has been suspected of spreading malicious rumors and has been temporarily blocked."[5]

When he was allowed to log in the next day, he was told, "Faceprint is required for security purposes," and was instructed to hold up his phone to "face front camera straight on" and "read numbers aloud in Mandarin Chinese."[6]

The reporter noted, "Capturing the face and voice image of everyone who was suspended for mentioning the Tiananmen crackdown anniversary…would be considered very useful for those who want to monitor anyone who might potentially cause problems."[7]

Which is exactly what Beijing wants to do, and they are taking no chances. Again, Hong Kong gives a glimpse of what the CCP has in mind for anyone who challenges the Party.

In 2015, the CCP rounded up and imprisoned over three hundred lawyers, legal assistants, and human rights defenders who were taking Chinese statutes about human rights a little too seriously and trying to use the Chinese courts to protect rights nominally guaranteed on paper. Many of the arrestees were charged with inciting subversion of state power, though "provoking quarrels" is another good one. As of 2022, many are still in jail.[8]

Now Back to Hong Kong

The Party also used a new National Security Law as cover to snuff out Hong Kong's freedoms a couple years ago—and along with them, potential opposition to the CCP. In the process, reporters, editors, former lawmakers, and pro-democracy activists were arrested and imprisoned.[9] A new communist-style electoral system was introduced that ensures Beijing's man or woman always wins.

Local officials crow that the National Security Law has brought order to Hong Kong, a condition that will now allow the city to flourish. Quite a change from the old British system where you had to commit a real offense and be proven guilty. Now, anger the Party and you'll find yourself in the dock, with a Yao Ming–sized guard on either side, and a 100 percent chance of conviction.

As evidence of how well PRC economic warfare works in support of lawfare, a prominent U.S. lawyer in Hong Kong praised the law in a video taken at a government ceremony in 2021 celebrating the first anniversary of the law's introduction: "I believe the National Security Law is a very important, positive piece of legal and regulatory framework in maintaining Hong Kong's leading role as a financial business

and investment center.... Why is it important? At the heart of everything, Hong Kong government's success is the rule of law."[10]

And in November 2022, in an implicit vote of confidence for the communist crackdown in Hong Kong, leading Wall Street and Western financial luminaries attended a Global Financial Leaders' Investment Summit in Hong Kong.[11] The keynote speaker, John Lee, is Hong Kong's current chief executive. Lee, a former police officer, was one of Beijing's front men when it snuffed out freedom in Hong Kong.[12]

Just give a Westerner a whiff of cash, and more often than not, they'll deliver for the Party.

This is directly relevant for America. The Chinese Ministry of State Security is active—along with its gangs—in the United States. It intimidates the Chinese American diaspora community to stay silent and not criticize or oppose the Chinese Communist Party, and to follow its orders.

In 2020, FBI director Christopher Wray announced the arrest of eight people for their "roles in a campaign to harass, stalk, and coerce certain residents of the United States to return to the People's Republic of China as part of a global, concerted, and extralegal repatriation effort known as Operation Fox Hunt."[13] He explained:

> Fox Hunt is a sweeping bid by General Secretary Xi and the Chinese Communist Party to target Chinese nationals here in the United States and across the world who are viewed as threats to the regime.
>
> In another case like this one, when it couldn't locate a Fox Hunt target, the Chinese government sent an emissary to visit the victim's family here in the United States. And the message they said to pass on?
>
> The target had two options: Return to China promptly or commit suicide. And what happens when Fox Hunt targets do refuse to return to China?

Their family members, both here in the United States and in China, have been threatened and coerced; and those back in China have even been arrested for leverage. These are not the actions we would expect from a responsible nation state. Instead, it's more like something we'd expect from an organized criminal syndicate.[14]

One observer I know describes the experience of his Chinese American in-laws in New York City: "[They] are former dissidents with over twenty years in the PRC re-education camps behind them. They tell me pro-PRC gangs are active in NYC. [Many] Asian residents in NYC believe pro-PRC gangs act with near impunity and may be inspiring attacks on Asians in hopes of isolating the community."[15]

Another expert on China I spoke with, who has testified as an expert witness, vouched for this: "Your in-laws are right about the gangs in NYC. I testified in one case. [The PRC] has a vicious junkyard dog of a lawyer, from a white-shoe firm. I was one of those who slugged it out with him. We won...but the PRC is well lawyered up.... It's a very unequal fight. [U.S.] State Department no help."[16]

Another aspect of this is that the PRC uses its own laws to give Chinese organizations (such as WeChat and TikTok) and citizens an obligation to cooperate. The PRC's 2017 National Intelligence Law states: "Any organization or citizen shall support, assist and cooperate with the state intelligence work.... The State commends and rewards individuals and organizations that have made significant contributions to national intelligence work."[17]

Given all this, banning the apps, as the Indians did, seemed a pretty clear case of protecting American citizens from illegal and predatory behavior by a malign power, right? Well, not according to the lawsuit launched by a WeChat users group that claimed the ban was unconstitutional. They were supported by the American Civil Liberties Union

(ACLU), which said it was a First Amendment violation. ACLU's explanation included the following:

> For many of WeChat's users, the app is their primary or only source of communication with friends and family in China, where the government blocks popular messaging platforms like Facebook, WhatsApp, and Instagram.
>
> In August 2020, the Trump administration issued an executive order declaring WeChat a threat to national security. As we explained at the time, WeChat, like many U.S.-owned social media and messaging apps, including Facebook and Instagram, does collect broad categories of user data. Concern about how this data is used and protected is warranted. In the case of WeChat, there is also some legitimate concern about whether user data is accessible by the Chinese government.[18]

Even though it's the Chinese government that is restricting freedom of speech and spying on users, the ACLU put the blame at the feet of the U.S. government:

> Here, the government has banned an undeniably unique and valuable platform for users to express themselves. As the district court found, WeChat is irreplaceable for its users in the U.S., particularly in the Chinese-speaking and Chinese-American community. Because the government's actions against WeChat suppress more speech than necessary, they violate the First Amendment.[19]

So, apparently, the CCP allows only one monitored, controlled, and easy-to-manipulate app to communicate with a captive Chinese population. That app can also be used to monitor, control, and manipulate users who have it on their phone in the United States, but trying to protect Americans from becoming victims, if not active participants, of China's intelligence state is against the First Amendment?

How about banning the app that tries to control and spy on you instead, and then seeing if China cares enough about staying connected to the United States to allow alternate modes of communication? This is China's problem, not America's.

What happened to the case? The Biden administration rescinded the TikTok and WeChat executive orders and paid $900,000 in legal fees to the WeChat users' group.[20]

And that, ladies and gentlemen, is how you do lawfare.

Xiaomi and Forty-Three Others

This sort of thing happens all the time. Shortly before leaving office, President Trump issued another executive order prohibiting investment in a number of Chinese companies with connections to the Chinese military. The first thing those companies did was ring up the American lawyers and get the lawsuits in motion. Ever heard of a U.S. company suing in a Chinese court under similar circumstances? Didn't think so.

The telecom companies Huawei and ZTE were also sanctioned by the Trump administration earlier in his term for being extensions of the Chinese Communist Party's surveillance state, not to mention for their unfair trade practices.

Neither company had any trouble finding former U.S. politicians to lobby for them, or American law firms—including the most prominent ones—to handle their cases. That is our system, of course. But one notes that those whose interests that happen to dovetail with the Chinese Communist Party have an easier time hiring legal counsel than many of the January 6 protestors.

It's an open question whether the PRC government funds these legal maneuvers. In some cases, yes; in some cases, no. But there are others who simply see the genocidal Chinese Communist Party as just another client—such is the effect of extended political warfare in shaping perceptions and thinking.

And it's not only Donald Trump who found himself on the wrong end of PRC lawfare. Even President Joe Biden complained about Chinese efforts to use lobbyists (many of whom are lawyers) and work the American system—particularly the D.C. swamp—to interfere with passage of the so-called Competition Act that was intended to strengthen the U.S. semiconductor industry.

President Biden stated publicly: "Fundamentally, this is a national security issue. This is one of the reasons why the Chinese Communist Party is lobbying folks to oppose this bill. And it's an issue that unites Democrats and Republicans. So, let's get it done."[21]

You can hear the lawyers salivating.

Meanwhile, in 2020, the PRC passed an anti-sanctions law that prohibits Chinese companies—and any others—from complying with foreign (that is, U.S.) sanctions. You see the problem, say, for Apple or Ford that do business in China? Somehow, I don't think they'll find lawyers to take their cases against the CCP.

And that's in the context of PRC spokesman Zhao Lijian saying, "China is opposed to imposing unilateral sanctions on other countries without the authorization of international law and the United Nations."[22]

This, of course, isn't true. Just look at what Beijing did to Taiwanese pineapples or Australian wine. It's why China is trying to get ever more control over international law and the United Nations—so that it can get its proxies to back up its version of the law.

International Agreements

China is perfectly happy to go through endless rounds of negotiations on international agreements—for example the Paris Accord. They help Beijing get a read on other countries and, ideally, put in place rules, norms, and legislation that block others and benefit the PRC.

But just blocking others is a win in the Comprehensive National Power sweepstakes, especially as China has no intention to follow through on any commitments that might impede it anyway.

For example, on climate, it ostentatiously agrees to formal commitments to reduce greenhouse gasses, pretending they are legal obligations to be followed, while calling out countries like Australia for their seeming intransigence.

However, on closer inspection, Beijing's commitments are far out in the future and don't involve any real verification. It doesn't intend to live up to those promises that would hurt the CCP, and it is glad to have other nations go first in the shift towards so-called green and renewable energy—and take the economic hits that come with such a move. Meanwhile, China doubles down on coal, builds new coal plants, and belches out more emissions than just about everyone else combined. Legally. Not that it matters.

As another example of the PRC creating the illusion it is following international rules, it recently signed the Hague Agreement Concerning the International Registration of Industrial Designs, which covers ninety-four countries.

Ma Yide, an intellectual property professor at the University of Chinese Academy of Sciences, said,

> Working with the international community, China is addressing intellectual property protection and governance challenges....
> In addition, under the Hague Agreement, protection of IPR

should be further intensified and the protection of industrial designs will be extended, which will benefit IPR owners and will help China's IPR protection further align with international standards.[23]

Sounds good, right? And China claims to have strengthened IPR protection in the last few years—having revised its trademark law, patent law, and copyright law, and having established a punitive damages system with the highest international standards.

That ought to keep the foreign investment flowing into China (think economic and financial warfare).

However, read the United States Trade Representative's annual report on Chinese intellectual property practices, or talk to a foreign businessman whose IPR disappeared in China (or to China), and you can judge for yourself how precious little such laws mean to the CCP.

China is even trying to use international lawfare to gain *galactic* control. Really. When the PLA warns of "militarizing space," it is engaging in a pseudo law-based psychological operation against the West. It is aided in this by idealists who insist any militarization or military uses of outer space are bad. The United States, sensitive to being accused of lawbreaking or looking bad, slows efforts to protect itself on outer space's high ground (which also protects our remote-sensing eyes and ears). Meanwhile, China goes full speed ahead with militarization.

This brings up the issue of individuals and organizations who advocate, sometimes through the courts, for positions that might seem valid but just happen to dovetail with CCP aims. For example, according to some analysts and local observers, from the 2000s onward, the PRC-funded environmental groups that opposed and filed lawsuits against the U.S. military's efforts to build an amphibious and combined arms training area on an island in the Northern Marianas Chain.[24] It was to have been the only such facility west of California—and crucially important for training. Eventually, the Americans gave up.

The equivalent would be a Greenpeace-like organization filing suit in Hainan to close down People's Liberation Army training areas on Hainan Island. The United States and China have two very different systems and approaches to law. The CCP takes full advantage of this.

China will say, sign, or agree to whatever greases its way. But that doesn't mean anything, because China just isn't concerned about being caught. We can trust and verify all we like, but if we don't also enforce, what's the point? China has shown the world we don't enforce. Not anymore.

Court Ruling? What Court Ruling? And by the Way, What Court?

Another lawfare technique used by China is to simply ignore a ruling, employing the ancient legal argument, "So whaddyagonnadoabout it?"

The classic case involves the 2016 Permanent Court of Arbitration ruling that was a byproduct of the infamous Scarborough Shoal takeover. I mentioned it before in the psychological warfare section, but it's also worth looking at from a lawfare perspective.

As a reminder, the situation developed in 2012, when Chinese fishing boats backed up by the China Coast Guard occupied the rich fishing grounds at Scarborough Shoal—Philippine maritime territory in the South China Sea (SCS) about 120 miles from the Philippine coast, and 700 miles from the nearest Chinese land. Outmatched, the Philippine Coast Guard withdrew after a U.S.-brokered deal for both sides to pull back. The Filipinos kept their word, but the Chinese did not. (Nor did the Americans, for that matter.)

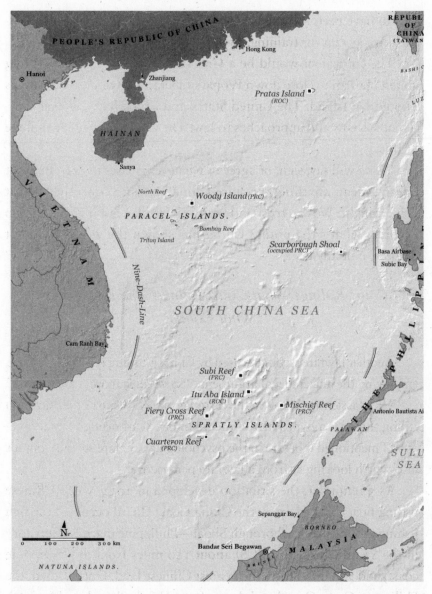

China claims sovereignty over nearly the entire South China Sea despite objections of neighboring states and a Permanent Court of Arbitration ruling against Beijing's claim. *Map courtesy of Louis Martin-Vézian and CIGeography.*

This was the latest in a long-running sequence of Chinese harassment and muscling in on Philippine waters—and Chinese claims to nearly the entire South China Sea under a legal fiction invented by

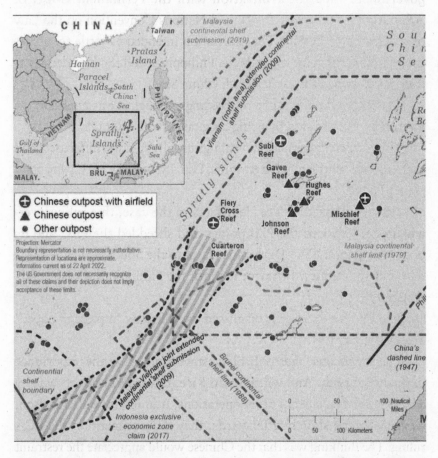

China's manmade island bases are in the middle of the South China Sea, far from Chinese territory. This allows the PLA to dominate key maritime terrain through which a huge amount of trade flows and facilitates military operations throughout the region. *Map courtesy of U.S. Department of Defense*, Military and Security Developments Involving the People's Republic of China, *2022, online version: https://media.defense. gov/2022/Nov/29/2003122279/-1/-1/1/2022-MILITARY-AND-SECURITY-DE VELOPMENTS-INVOLVING-THE-PEOPLES-REPUBLIC-OF-CHINA.PDF.*

Beijing, the so-called Nine-Dash Line. As far back as 1992, it passed a law declaring its ownership of the SCS.[25]

So, in 2013, with the United States' encouragement, the Philippine government filed for arbitration with the Permanent Court of Arbitration (PCA) under the United Nations Convention on the Law of the Sea (UNCLOS).[26] The arbitration intended to settle the issues over Chinese behavior towards the Philippines and the broader assertion that it owned the entire South China Sea.

The PRC did not join the proceedings, though it was bound to the arbitral panel's decision by being a signatory to UNCLOS.

These sorts of international rulings usually split the difference, and each side gets a little of what it wants. Usually, nobody goes away completely happy.

However, based on the clear facts in the case, this ruling overwhelmingly favored the Philippines and shredded the PRC and its position. China's Nine-Dash Line claim to the South China Sea was rejected, and Chinese behavior towards the Philippines was similarly rebuked.[27]

The PRC's response? It dismissed the ruling as "a piece of paper" and ignored it.[28]

The Americans made only bland statements about the importance of following rules. And when Susan Rice, Obama's national security advisor, and then chief of naval operations, Admiral John Richardson, went to Beijing shortly afterwards, they did not mention the PCA ruling. The thinking was that the Chinese would appreciate the restraint and somehow reciprocate.

They didn't. They pocketed the concession, smelling either weakness or stupidity (or maybe both), and went full speed ahead with their efforts to lock up the South China Sea.

The U.S. government had encouraged the Filipinos to bring the suit. So the American response to the tribunal's decision seemed like a betrayal.

A *second* one, given the initial failure to act after the Chinese broke the 2012 agreement to withdraw. Once could be a mistake; twice was seen as a pattern.

The Obama administration thus turned Beijing's stinging lawfare defeat in court into a victory for the PRC in reality.

Manila was demoralized, and everyone else in the region noticed. America's reputation as a reliable ally was badly damaged. Beijing carried on with its island-building campaign, further militarized its man-made island bases, and became increasingly aggressive against foreign militaries operating in the South China Sea.

It also went on a lawfare offensive, aware that if you want to freeze Westerners in their tracks, just accuse them of breaking the law, no matter how outrageous the charge.

Beijing passed new laws asserting Chinese administrative control over certain types of ships transiting the area, as well as a law giving the China Coast Guard legal authority to shoot at trespassers in waters the PRC claimed as its own.[29] And since, according to China, not just the South China Sea but the East China Sea is all Chinese, and has been since historical times—even parts Japan claims to own—it declared China well within rights to open fire there as well.

Beijing has also been working on a SCS Code of Conduct with ASEAN for over twenty years. A recent proposal by the PRC would give it a veto on ASEAN nations doing military training with outside nations (that is, the United States, and maybe Japan).

These aren't a joke. They are meant to be a framework for justified aggression. And China is, as it is wont to do, starting to test the limits. In May 2022, a PLAAF fighter jet launched chaff and flares in front of a Royal Australian Air Force P-8 patrolling in international airspace above the South China Sea. It could have been deadly.[30]

The Chinese government referred to its own laws to justify its actions. Of course, it didn't mention its claims had been rejected almost completely by the Permanent Court of Arbitration's 2016 ruling, in a case based on UNCLOS—a convention that China helped draft, had signed, and had agreed to follow. It should have inserted a "some conditions apply" clause. That, at least, would have been more honest.

Bilateral Agreements

We've seen that Beijing doesn't care about the law, but loves lawfare. Another way lawfare can be deployed is by getting countries to sign opaque bilateral agreements.

For example, in early 2022, news broke that the PRC had signed a security agreement with the Solomon Islands. The terms were kept secret, including from the Parliament of the Solomons. A PRC spokesman stated, without offering any proof, "[The agreement] is normal cooperation in law enforcement and security, and consistent with international law and international customary practices."[31]

The spokesman added that the security cooperation between the two countries is open and transparent and does not target any third party. It proceeds in parallel with the Solomon Islands' existing cooperation with other partners and regional mechanisms and conforms to the common interests of the Solomon Islands and the South Pacific region.[32]

Prove it.

But they won't. And that itself is a lawfare win, because the opacity of the deal and its implementation creates distrust and division within the Solomons, and between the Solomons and other partners. That makes the authoritarian leader who signed the deal, Prime Minister Manasseh Sogavare, more isolated internationally and internally, and so more reliant on his new best friends in Beijing.

Remember entropic warfare? This is how you use lawfare to speed along domestic disintegration and vassal statehood. You can see elements of it in Sri Lanka, Pakistan, Kenya, Uganda, Zambia, and elsewhere. Beijing uses it because it works.

Getting the Law in Place to Attack Taiwan

The most ominous example of Chinese lawfare is the CCP's use of domestic law to justify an attack on Taiwan—and get the law-abiding United States to back off when China attacks.

One key element of this is China's 2005 Anti-secession Law. The key provisions in Article 8 read:

> In the event that the Taiwan independence secessionist forces should act under any name or by any means to cause the fact of Taiwan's secession from China, or that major incidents entailing Taiwan's secession from China should occur, or that possibilities for a peaceful reunification should be completely exhausted, the state shall employ non-peaceful means and other necessary measures to protect China's sovereignty and territorial integrity.
>
> The State Council and the Central Military Commission shall decide on, and execute, the non-peaceful means and other necessary measures as provided for in the preceding paragraph and shall promptly report to the Standing Committee of the National People's Congress.[33]

A former diplomat who has long experience with and in China explained, "China has always contemplated how it could construct pretexts of Taiwan Independence for military action against Taiwan which would deter the United States from getting involved. The major thrust of China's 2005 Anti-secession Law was how to make whatever

Taipei does look like independence and thereby give the U.S. a pretext for inaction."[34]

This is what Chinese lawfare in the region has been building to. But it's not where it will end. If the United States uses spurious Chinese laws as an excuse not to defend an independent democratic ally from invasion, it's over for the United States in the Indo-Pacific—and maybe the whole world.

In a May 26, 2022, speech on Washington's strategy to deal with Beijing, Secretary of State Antony Blinken said the United States would not hinder China's economic development, but wanted it to abide by international rules. The United States will not change China's political system, but will defend international law and institutions that maintain peace and security and can make countries coexist.[35]

Two comments: Good luck with China following international rules. And Secretary Blinken, you've got your work cut out for you.

If Chinese lawfare keeps working, China will eventually get around to passing a law making it illegal for the United States to disobey Beijing.

CHAPTER 7

Changing—or Undermining—
Global Rules and Norms

In some ways, China is trying to do just that by changing and shaping international rules and norms. China routinely complains that the United States and its friends are trying to contain it. One of the tools allegedly used to hold down the PRC is the array of international rules governing how nations behave, both on their own and toward each other.

China's argument is that since they were not involved in setting up the rules, the rules are therefore unfair. This isn't entirely accurate—and, even if it were, it is somewhat akin to claiming a personal exemption from the Ten Commandments since one was not present on Mount Sinai.

The Republic of China certainly was involved in the rule-making. It was practically the only independent country in Asia after World War II. It had a hand in the founding of the United Nations. But it wouldn't make any difference, really. The Chinese Communist Party only obeys rules when the rules are in the CCP's interest.

A university professor and former U.S military officer described a conversation with a Beijing University professor at an international symposium in the United Kingdom in 2007.

> She told me that the Taiwan Strait was Chinese territory. I told her that I know of no case of international law or article of UNCLOS (United Nations Convention on the Law of the Sea) that would support her view. She responded by noting international law was shaped during the period of European imperialism and anything based on power can be changed by power. That conversation has stayed with me ever since.[1]

In other words, to the PRC, the rules are at best advisory, and at worst whatever the CCP says they are.

When you can choose the rules, your various types of political warfares all work better.

Also, there are some areas where rules are still being made. In those cases, Beijing is trying to take over or influence the procedures for setting up new international rules and norms, including in cyber and space, and in setting new telecommunications standards—particularly for 5G and 6G networks.

There are obvious commercial advantages that come from setting the rules in such cases. Any self-respecting surveillance state can also see obvious advantages to shaping and governing networks norms. It helps you create and exploit vulnerabilities.

But in most cases, the rules are already set.

Rewriting the rules is hard. You've got to get a lot of nations to agree with you (even ones you've not got in your pocket), and that takes time.

So the Chinese employ work-arounds. These look familiar. They are related to some of the things we see in lawfare.

Just Make Stuff Up

For example, the PRC wants in on the Arctic. It's a strategic part of the globe—with natural resources, a shorter transport route to Europe, and it's useful from a military perspective.

Beijing's problem is that China is far away from the Arctic and has no more claim to an interest than would, say, the Netherlands.

So China has declared itself a "near Arctic state,"[2] even though the expression has never existed in international law. Chutzpah will get you a long way—especially when Westerners are afraid to challenge you, either because it's too hard or because they think they are getting rich off you.

The "near Arctic" phrase, since it was first uttered around 2015, is a classic example of how China builds concepts, principles, vocabulary, and justification for pursuing its interests in shaping global rules and norms.

A Western observer with many years in China and a good sense of humor—let's call him "The Professor"—explains how this works:

Step 1: A term appears in an obscure Chinese academic journal. Measure responses and continue…

Step 2: Term appears in a regional Chinese newspaper. Measure responses and continue…

Step 3: Term is used at a Chinese national conference or seminar. Measure responses and continue…

Step 4: Term is used in Xinhua and *China Daily* articles. Measure responses and continue…

Step 5: Term is used at international conferences and academic exchanges held in China. Measure responses and continue…

Step 6: China frequently refers to the term in international media and at international conferences. Measure acceptance and continue...

Step 7: China issues policy white paper stating its position, its implied right, and an implied threat to defend this.[3]

Dr. June Teufel Dreyer of the University of Miami adds another step:

Step 8: China maintains this has "always" been China's policy, and that nothing has changed.[4] (Translation: Get used to it, barbarians.)

The Professor explains that it usually starts with the discovery of ancient maps, admirals' journals, artifacts being dug up, and so on.[5] Dr. Dreyer has her own theory, noting only half tongue in cheek that, "Somewhere in the bowels of Zhongnanhai is an office marked 'Department of New Ancient Documents.' Inside are calligrapher scribes with stacks of paper chemically identical to whatever dynasty's claim is to be re-asserted, and authentically reproduced brushes and ink, churning out definitive proof of whatever."[6]

However, The Professor notes that "near Arctic" did not follow this path, but shortcut the process. That may be so, given the country's success in establishing de facto control over the South China Sea in the last several years, and its trend of going unscathed when ignoring rules and promises.

Why, it's even possible that Beijing might claim the Native Americans got to America second—or perhaps they are, in actual fact, Chinese themselves. The Professor remarks that China is currently building the case for having had a historical presence in Alaska. The near-Arctic campaign has its own objectives but also serves as a runway toward claiming historical, cultural, and civilizational contributions to our forty-ninth state and beyond.

The Professor explains how a look at the world map highlights the audaciousness, if not the absurdity, of Chinese arguments. China's northernmost land point is Mohe County, 53/29 North. By implication, other near-Arctic cities within a degree or two of 53 N, are: Dublin, Ireland;

Liverpool, England; Calais, France; Amsterdam, Netherlands; Frankfurt, Germany; Prague, Czech Republic; Warsaw, Poland; Kiev, Ukraine.

Once China is done with the Arctic region, The Professor says he anticipates the first mentions of China as a "near-*Antarctica* state."[7] Dr. Dreyer, meanwhile, expects "proof," one day, that Admiral Zheng He arrived in Antarctica before the penguins. "Or perhaps that the penguins, given their similar color, evolved from pandas who arrived in Antarctica over a now-disappeared land bridge from China."[8]

As is par for the course, while the PRC insinuates itself into the Arctic region—to which it has about as compelling a claim as Iraq, Morocco, or the Philippines—it loudly warns the United States to keep its nose out of the South China Sea, since it is far from U.S. territory (conveniently ignoring Guam).

If one doesn't mind hypocrisy, such claims and concrete efforts to occupy territory that isn't one's own may well succeed. But only if they go unchallenged. Real Arctic-contiguous nations are worried about what the PRC is doing, but they aren't likely to complain. China wouldn't listen, anyway—except perhaps to President Xi's friend, Vladimir Putin. Putin still reckons he has something to gain from cozying up to China. And after invading Ukraine, Putin doesn't have much choice, no matter what.

As usual, it's down to the United States. China's claim over the Arctic is the chance for the world to say: "No, you are not a near Arctic state. You are a state proclaiming its interest in the Arctic. Your rationale is militarily and economically motivated, not geographical."

But China has reason to think it will get away with it. It has before.

Getting Exceptions to the Rules

This worked when China elbowed its way into the World Trade Organization (WTO)—with U.S. help. The PRC was allowed in despite not meeting the requirements for market economy, state subsidies, non-discrimination, intellectual property protection, and the like. Think of it as a near-WTO state.

Once inside WTO, the Chinese have run wild, throwing their political weight around without coming into line with any of the rules as they promised to do.

Since 2013, China's companies have listed on the New York Stock Exchange and other U.S. exchanges—with a *waiver* of accounting disclosure requirements that American and every other countries' companies must follow.[9]

Even better for the CCP, in 2016 the International Monetary Fund (IMF) included the Chinese yuan into its basket of currencies (U.S. dollar, euro, yen, and British pound) used for Special Drawing Rights purposes.[10] This was the equivalent of the IMF giving Chinese currency (and the PRC government) its stamp of approval.

Inclusion in the basket is supposed to require a currency to be freely usable—which the partially convertible yuan was not, and still isn't, despite Beijing's promises to allow it to trade freely.

IMF managing director Christine Lagarde granted the waiver for reasons that remain unclear.[11] Or, at least, the real reasons remain unclear.

Ignore the Rules

Besides obtaining exceptions and not living up to actual or implicit promises made when the exceptions were granted, the PRC finds that ignoring rules also works well. Especially when the United States and others decline to do anything about it.

Case in point, our old friends Scarborough Shoal and the South China Sea takeover. They are contrary to international law and specifically the United Nations Convention on the Law of the Sea—that the PRC negotiated and signed on to.

Yet Beijing has paid no real price. And this abrogation has a knock-on effect—both encouraging more bad behavior and also discrediting the rules themselves. It's hard for smaller nations, say in the Pacific, to take seriously fisheries laws when the Chinese fishing fleet shows up in their territory and starts vacuuming up fish. Who is going to enforce them? If a law isn't enforced, is it still a law?

What's the best that can be hoped for? Furrow-browed expressions of concern by U.S. State Department press officers? Yes. But more than that? Rare.

World Health Organization requirements to notify and cooperate in the event of a serious disease outbreak such as COVID? Beijing didn't follow the rules, and almost nobody seriously talks of holding China liable. Just look at the wrath of tariffs and bans—all completely against the rules—that China visited upon Australia for just having the temerity to ask for an inquiry into the origin of COVID.

Indeed, China remains a WHO member in good standing. There was even a recent effort to change WHO rules to authorize the organization to declare health emergencies and dictate responses in affected countries. A violation of sovereignty, but also a neat tool to disrupt adversaries for the PRC, given that it appears to call the shots at the World Health Organization.

The Biden administration was prepared to go along with this and only pulled back owing to domestic political opposition.

One former Trump administration official remarked that "it's easy to write rules, but nobody wants to enforce them."[12] And with WHO, you just had to enforce the existing International Health Regulations when COVID came along.

The PRC can be forgiven for feeling assured that if it comes across a rule it doesn't like, it can get a waiver or just ignore it—and nothing will happen, even when a cyber attack on the United States steals millions of personnel files of government employees.[13]

That's certainly against the rules, but the Obama administration did nothing, and would not even identify the PRC as the culprit.

Working the Rules

Sometimes the PRC can even get agreements making it official that rules apply differently to China.

Remember the 2015 Paris Climate Agreement to reduce carbon emissions? It asks a lot less of the People's Republic of China than of the United States and the Western nations. Here's one big way:

Sometimes the PRC pleads that it is just a developing country and needs special treatment. Using this line during the Paris Agreement negotiation, China promised to reach peak emissions by 2030, and to end all carbon emissions from fossil fuels by 2060.[14] That means it can go all-out burning coal or other petrochemical fuels until 2030. China has over 1,058 coal plants, half the world's capacity. And it is building more.

Meanwhile, the agreement obligated the United States to start cutting carbon emissions *immediately*. Not surprisingly, President Trump pulled the United States out of the Paris deal. President Biden's first move on taking office was to lock America back in.[15]

So China has worked the rules to give it fifteen years and then some before getting serious about carbon reduction. Assuming it ever does—and that's a tall assumption—or that such rules can be enforced. Meanwhile, its main enemy agreed to rules that require disrupting its economy straightaway. Furthermore, China can leverage the American legal system and environmental NGOs to try to make sure it complies.

One U.S. official stated things correctly: "Beijing isn't interested in being bound by Paris or any other agreement that impacts its economic growth. Hope (that they will follow the rules) is not a strategy."[16]

Undercutting Ideals

The PRC also tries to undermine the ideals behind the rules.

Notably, its diplomats and officials aggressively sell the idea of democracy and human rights with Chinese characteristics. They offer a People's Republic of China alternative to commonly accepted standards of governance and individual freedoms.

The basic argument is that the PRC system is more efficient and better suited to Chinese culture and current conditions. Also, you'll hear talk of the need for improved balance between individual and collective rights, and that democracy is just too messy.

The PRC does have a constitution that includes many of the elements we would recognize. It also has a criminal code that looks familiar. In actual practice, of course, it's not so nice.

It's easy to laugh off Chinese efforts to sell their governance system. It's communist, after all. No elections. No protections from a government or its officials that want to hurt you or take your property. Judges reach decisions based on what the Communist Party tells them. You can only be as free as the Party allows you to be. They can kill you if they want. And then sell your organs.

But in a lot of the world, that sounds pretty good for ruling elites—or people who think they have a shot at becoming a ruling elite. Chinese arguments might need less selling than we imagined.

The rules, China seems to be saying, are for suckers.

for International Organizations

CHAPTER 8

Capturing International Organizations

Beyond just trying to shape the rules, the CCP is attempting to fully capture the organizations that make and enforce those rules.

If you read the press releases, China has a lot of friends. There is the China and Pakistan "Iron Brotherhood,"[1] and the China and Russia "no limits" partnership,[2] and the China and Iran "Comprehensive Strategic Partnership."[3] But China isn't very good at being a long-term partner. It is more comfortable having compliant concubines and eunuchs.

As it stands, China may not have as many real allies as the United States. In fact, it doesn't have any true friends, as U.S. officials sometimes boast. But that may not matter much. While the PRC doesn't have U.S.-style allies—each nation promising to defend the other in the event of a war—it has plenty of countries that vote its way at the United Nations—nations that provide cover and support for China's positions, behavior, and objectives, including its push to reshape rules and norms.

At the United Nations and most international organizations, the rule is "one nation, one vote." A group of small nations can often out-vote the few big ones.

China's influence in international organizations is the result of successful grassroots political warfare, country-by-country, over decades.

The PRC accumulates small and not-so-small nations that will vote its way at the UN and other international organizations, or at least that will not challenge Beijing. Many of these nations still have ties with the United States, but the ties have softened. This is what political warfare is about: eroding American influence and power while increasing China's. All done without shooting.

It just took some effort—and paying attention to the leaders and political dynamics of these other, often less developed nations. Some of them may have an affinity for China's hard-edged form of government. But a payment to a Pacific Island nation's trust fund, a new house for the speaker of parliament, or a stadium and a highway is sometimes all it takes, and is the first step towards gaining a vote for China in international forums. If that results in those leaders getting a stern lecture from a Western diplomat, all the better. It creates the sort of resentment that Beijing can feed—creating an even bigger divide. Remember entropic warfare?

This stable of friends keeps the enemy (the Americans and other democracies) from ganging up on China, and can shift local and global power balances. The Chinese communists hate alliances or groupings that pose resistance to PRC objectives.

What's the advantage to Beijing of capturing the international organizations? Ashok Malik, an Indian Foreign Ministry policy advisor, said it well in the *Wall Street Journal* in 2020: "If you control important levers of these institutions, you influence norms, you influence ways of thinking, you influence international policy, you inject your way of thinking."[4]

Instead of receiving criticism, sanctions, or being ostracized for its behavior, Beijing gets outright support or the tacit acceptance that comes of nations keeping their mouths shut to avoid offending China and ensure the goodies keep flowing their way. As an aside, it's notable how many countries seem more afraid of the Chinese than they are of the Americans, including countries we've let into our most important alliances, like New Zealand.[5]

Softening Up the International Community for the Invasion of Taiwan

What this means is that when the time comes for kinetic warfare, China has set things up to its advantage.

Suppose Beijing makes its move against Taiwan, either setting up a blockade or launching an outright assault and invasion.

China's influence over international organizations has managed to keep Taiwan out of organizations such as the World Health Organization, ICAO, INTERPOL, and many others—and of course the United Nations. Even as observers.

And Beijing keeps peeling off the pitifully few—currently around a dozen—countries that have diplomatic ties with Taiwan.

This is effective psychological warfare, demoralizing the Taiwanese and potentially affecting their will to resist Chinese pressure or a future kinetic attack. But it also suggests to many nations that the United States (and its allies and friends) are unable—indeed, too weak—to back up Taiwan in the face of Chinese pressure.

We've already seen China get away with illegally claiming ownership and militarizing large sections of the South China Sea—and the United Nations doing nothing to stop it. When the Permanent Court of Arbitration ruled against Chinese claims in 2016, Beijing declared the court's ruling a "piece of waste paper."[6] Nobody said much in response. The international community and its organizations are being conditioned to look the other way. Talk about encouraging aggression.

So, when China moves on Taiwan, many countries might stay neutral and wait to see how things turn out. Given PRC influence, the

United Nations likely won't do much beyond a few bland statements from the General Assembly. As for the UN Security Council, the PRC has a veto, and that's enough. The Russians will likely abstain, and it will be interesting to see what the French do.

The Americans may try to impose broad sanctions against China outside the United Nations, but Washington may be surprised with how many countries don't participate. We saw this with Russia after it invaded Ukraine in February 2022.

The United States, the European Union nations, Canada, Australia, Japan, Singapore, and a few others came out against Russia. But the majority of nations—including China—did not.

We will see something similar should China attack Taiwan—while arguing it is just an internal dispute.

How Deep Is the Rot?

Is it really that bad at the United Nations?

Let's recall some history.

In 1944 (this was during World War II), the International Red Cross convinced the Germans to allow a Red Cross visit to Theresienstadt, a ghetto in the Czech town of Terezín where Jews were collected and imprisoned prior to onward transportation to the death camps.

Mindful of appearances, the Germans "embellished" (their word) Theresienstadt into a model town with schools, a post office, a swimming pool, an orchestra, sports, and a local Jewish administration. The Red Cross officials (two Danes and a Swiss) came on the appointed day, June 23, 1944, and were shown around. They went along with the charade. The Swiss representative, Maurice Rossel, even seemed to believe that it was a normal Jewish town: "SS police gives [sic] the Jews the freedom to organize their administration as they see fit" and "[the]

Terezin camp is a final camp from which no one who has once entered the ghetto is normally sent elsewhere."[7]

In the fall of 1944, the eighteen thousand Jews in Terezín were sent from Terezín to Auschwitz. Almost none survived.

In 2022, the United Nations Human Rights director general Michelle Bachelet visited China and Xinjiang, where upwards of a million Muslim Uighurs are in prison camps as the Chinese communists carry out what is being called genocide.

The Chinese put on a show. And Madame Bachelet went along with it, saying things the Chinese wanted to hear. She referred to communist "efforts at vocational training," "de-radicalization," and not a mention of genocide. She repeated Chinese claims to have shuttered re-education centers, and complimented her hosts on reducing poverty, saying her access was "pretty open, pretty transparent."[8]

What Madame Bachelet did *not* do was challenge the PRC, but on the day she left office, the UN finally put out a report criticizing China for human rights violations. This apparently was a hard-fought effort.[9]

If Beijing can pull off anything close to a Theresienstadt, it has the UN by the snout. Even now, most countries say nothing about Xinjiang, and the PRC remains a member in good standing of the UN Human Rights Commission.

Indeed, in 2020, the PRC made it onto the UN Human Rights Council five-member panel that approves United Nation rapporteurs on human rights misconduct.

The rapporteurs are the official investigators for the UN. It helps to have friendly ones if worried about being called to account over Uighur vocational training camps in Xinjiang. And it's not just Xinjiang that Beijing is worried about.

The PRC arranged and helped fund a UN rapporteur in 2021 to report on U.S.- and allied-driven sanctions against North Korea. The rapporteur, a "human rights expert" from Belarus (a dictatorship closely allied to Russia), concluded sanctions against the North Korean regime were unwarranted.[10]

This is all part of stymieing American and allied efforts to apply economic pressure on the PRC's protégé and proxy, that nation-state prison called North Korea.

To demonstrate China's reach, at around the same time, the United Nations appointed North Korea as the head of the UN Conference on Disarmament. Think that would have happened without Beijing making a few calls?

It was further evidence of the PRC's success at using international organizations as proxies that provide a veneer of respectability and legality—no matter how ridiculous it might look. And if it ultimately undermines the legitimacy of the UN, all fine with Beijing. The more weakening and entropy in international systems, the more Beijing thinks it will become the default center of power.

And, if necessary, China has no issue playing rough to silence criticism. One rapporteur who cited Chinese communist oppression of its Muslim population was fiercely attacked by a Chinese UN diplomat for "wantonly spread[ing] false information, lack[ing] minimum professional ethics, and serv[ing] as a political tool for some Western countries and anti-China forces."[11]

When cautioned by UN officials, the Chinese diplomat amped it up, charging that the rapporteur had "misbehaved," and demanding he be "[held] accountable," and that the UN's system for producing such reports should be reformed.[12]

Total Impunity and Immunity for the PRC?

Beijing may not act with total impunity and immunity, but sometimes it seems like it does.

China has its citizens in place at the top of many UN organizations. And others have CCP-compliant foreigners running things or in positions of influence. The Chinese officials behave like Chinese officials rather than global civil servants—and that's how Beijing views them.

That was clear when, in 2018, Meng Hongwei, the Chinese citizen who became director of INTERPOL (the International Criminal Police Organization, closely associated with the United Nations but not formally a part) was summoned to China and disappeared. Beijing later announced he was arrested for corruption—though it was no doubt something else.[13]

The fact a PRC national was even allowed to head up INTERPOL, an organization with access to deeply sensitive intelligence, is clear enough evidence of Chinese influence in the organization. Remember that, according to China's 2017 National Intelligence Law, every Chinese citizen is required to assist in PRC intelligence operations if asked. One can assume he was asked.

Besides access to INTERPOL intelligence resources allowing China to go after its enemies and likely obtain information useful for leverage operations, during Meng's tenure, INTERPOL reportedly issued red notices for suspects on the CCP's enemy's list. His wife now lives in France under political asylum—and was for a period under French police protection.[14]

The institutional response to this incident was noteworthy. A few nations complained, but for most it was just a shoulder shrug, if that.

And in 2021, Hu Binchen, a Chinese law enforcement official, was elected to INTERPOL's executive committee that oversees the group's operations.[15] Fifty politicians—including U.S. senator Marco Rubio and congressman Mike Gallagher—from twenty countries objected that Hu's election would "be giving a green light" to China's government "to continue their misuse of Interpol and would place the tens of thousands of Hong Kongers, Uyghur, Tibetan, Taiwanese and Chinese dissidents living abroad at even graver risk."[16]

But INTERPOL has 194 member nations. China's strategy of using the little fish to control the pool, and ultimately the big islands, worked once again.

There are myriad situations like INTERPOL. While Chinese influence in the World Health Organization is now widely known owing to the compliant way Beijing's WHO puppets acted during the COVID-19 pandemic, that's far from the only control node where the PRC has its nationals in charge, quietly fulfilling their National Intelligence Law duties, ready and waiting to be more active when required.

This includes at the International Civil Aviation Organization (ICAO), Food and Agricultural Organization (FAO), International Telecommunications Union (ITU), and United Nations Industrial Development Organization (UNIDO).

These organizations are more important than they might seem. ICAO, for example, is a central component of civil aviation. Gain access to its systems, and you might be able to find out not only whatever it has about its staff and finances, but also use ICAO's connections to national systems worldwide to worm into the networks of a whole set of countries' domestic civil aviation systems.

Which was exactly the concern (among many others) when, in 2016, ICAO experienced the worst hack in its history. According to an internal ICAO email, "patient zero" for the infection was Maxim Aliu (the son of Olumuyiwa Benard Aliu, Nigeria's representative on the council in 2010, and later council president).[17] Maxim's laptop had become infected in 2010 when he was on a trip to the agency's regional office in Beijing. The hack was attributed to cyberespionage group Emissary Panda, which is known to have links to the Chinese government.[18]

But it didn't stop there. Once the hack was uncovered in 2016, then ICAO secretary general, Chinese citizen Fang Liu, ignored internal recommendations to investigate ICAO's IT team and their boss, James Wan.[19] The full breadth of the damage caused by the hack is unknown, and Fang Liu stayed in office until 2021.[20]

But that's nothing compared to the degree of vulnerability the International Telecommunications Union (ITU) is setting us up for. The head of the ITU has supported Huawei against U.S.-led efforts to rein in the company as a security threat. He has always promoted a new internet protocol that appears aimed at facilitating Chinese surveillance and censorship, according to some observers.[21]

And it's not just telecoms infrastructure China wants to control. Thirty United Nations agencies and bodies, including UNIDO, have signed formal support agreements for the PRC's Belt and Road Initiative, thus giving a UN imprimatur for the physical embodiments of China's flagship global political warfare effort.[22] BRI and related political warfare efforts help bring nations "on side" for China. It's literally an "all (belt) roads lead to China" approach.

Of course, the failure in too many cases by the United States and friends to work with countries to deliver much needed basic infrastructure has just made it easier for China.

China also nearly got its candidate placed at the head of the UN-affiliated World Intellectual Property Organization (WIPO) in 2020. The Americans stopped it—with considerable effort and some luck. Intellectual property theft is a recognized technique of Chinese economic warfare. In 2020, then director of national intelligence John Ratcliffe described the goal of China's economic espionage as a process of "rob, replicate, and replace."[23] WIPO would have been a useful place for the CCP to have its guy. The CCP will keep trying.

And then, as we've seen, there's the World Health Organization. In my opinion, the WHO let China get away with murder—via COVID-19.

The WHO director general, Tedros Adhanom Ghebreyesus, who is not a medical doctor but a former official of a Marxist political group in Ethiopia, covered for the PRC from the beginning of the COVID outbreak.[24] Beijing stonewalled and obstructed efforts to learn what happened, and still does.

It has, by and large, gotten away with it, and not just at the World Health Organization. China's accumulated fish show no interest in the matter. It doesn't matter how much the United States and the handful of countries it can draw together complain. All that does is show Beijing who they should be hitting harder—that is, which countries need a bit more entropy to weaken their ability to complain.

China's post-SARS control over the WHO is so thorough that a senior advisor, Dr. Bruce Aylward, panicked at a press conference in March of 2020 when a Hong Kong journalist asked a question about Taiwan's possible membership in the World Health Organization. Dr. Aylward appeared to pretend he did not hear the question, and then apparently cut off the phone connection.[25] Now *that* is influence.

Perhaps not surprisingly, the PRC was recently elected by consensus to the World Health Organization's executive board.

And in what looked like a calculated insult, in May 2022, the PRC Academy of Sciences named the Wuhan Bio Lab as a candidate for its Outstanding Science Achievement Award—for research on coronaviruses.[26]

The next time the PRC deploys a biological weapon—whether for real or opportunistically—it will be well positioned to deflect criticism or punishment, and shape our response. Again.

What about the NGOs?

On a range of issues from climate to Israel to refugees, it sometimes seems as though opaquely funded non-governmental organizations—the NGOs—are driving the UN policy train.

China has been successful at keeping inconvenient NGOs from interacting with the United Nations, thus avoiding awareness, criticism, and loss of support over Beijing's questionable labor and environmental practices and human rights abuses. China's fishing fleet, for example, scours the high seas and other nations' Exclusive Economic Zones, and yet criticism from the vast majority of NGOs is muted or non-existent. The United Nations itself doesn't do much, either.

This cover from international organizations plays out nicely for China's political warfare strategy.

Chinese logging activities in Southeast Asia and the Pacific Islands go unchecked and largely uncriticized. This builds PRC's economic power and creates political influence—while fracturing local societies. It is an ideal vector for entropic warfare.

The same thing plays out with the Chinese fishing industry in this region, as economic influence leads to political influence, and as we are seeing now, the beginning of the PRC's military presence in the region.

NGOs that should be leading the charge are not allowed into the UN—to the extent they speak up at all. UN agencies are not saying much. And doing even less.

Meanwhile, favored groups such as Extinction Rebellion that effectively preach economic warfare against the West, are allowed into the United Nations and listened to.

One, of course, can scoff that the United Nations and its agencies don't matter. Maybe so. But it is a political warfare battlefield, and many smaller and developing countries take it very seriously. For some with small foreign ministries, the UN might be one of their few diplomatic missions. It is a demonstration of China's Comprehensive National Power to have so many nations voting on its side. And they notice when the U.S., and democratic criticism of China's dictatorship and human rights abuses, too often lose when it comes to a vote.

This feeds the narrative that China is being picked on by the West. And that China's system of governance and its versions of democracy and human rights are an acceptable alternative that most of the world's nations must tolerate, if not approve of. And anyway, Beijing has the votes, "so whaddyagonnadoaboutit?"

It's Not Just the UN

Beijing uses the same playbook, with the same goals, anywhere it can. Three more examples.

International Monetary Fund

In 2018, the PRC pressed to have the managing director of the International Monetary Fund (IMF), Kristilina Georgieva, apply pressure on World Bank analysts to improve China's ranking in the bank's annual Doing Business report.[27] The report rates countries' ease of doing business based on local rules and regulations.

The PRC had been assessed to fall from number 78 to number 85. But it was bumped back up to 78 following Ms. Georgieva's intervention.[28] Beijing was concerned a worse rating might have affected foreign investment coming into China, among other issues.

This example of Chinese influence over an important international organization is impressive, considering that the PRC is not a market economy, does not have a freely convertible currency, and is—after twenty years—still noncompliant with World Trade Organization rules despite promises to reform.

Not surprisingly, Ms. Georgieva kept her job.

One shouldn't be too surprised. Remember that Ms. Georgieva's predecessor, Christine LaGarde, approved the inclusion of the Chinese yuan into the IMF's basket of currencies along with the dollar, euro, yen, and pound.[29] Ms. LaGarde handed this major economic and financial warfare victory to Beijing despite the yuan not being convertible as IMF rules require.

She accepted Chinese promises to make the yuan convertible. That, of course, has not happened. And don't hold your breath. It would mean the Chinese Communist Party giving up control of a key element of the Chinese economy.

That's not really China's thing.

Don't Forget Davos

Speaking of economic control...Davos? The World Economic Forum that meets yearly in Davos, Switzerland, may not be an international organization of the United Nations sort. But to the elites who attend, it is *the* international organization. It's easy to dismiss the Davos crowd as self-important gasbags, but they do have power and influence. And they like Xi Jinping. There was plenty of oohing and aahing in 2019 when Xi spoke in Davos, using the magic words "globalization" and "win-win," and saying that China was all in with whatever the Davos men and women were selling.[30] So maybe it's not surprising that the World Economic Forum also holds an annual get-together in the PRC.

The Roman Catholic Church

The Chinese communists have even gotten the Roman Catholic Church—the original multinational organization—to come on board. A couple years ago, the Vatican agreed with the CCP to only appoint cardinals and bishops that had Beijing's approval.[31]

This might not have taken much effort given the liberation theology leanings of Pope Francis. But the effect is that the Vatican is providing cover for the Chinese Communist Party's efforts to strangle opposition—actual or potential—to its control.

Beijing will adroitly use this religious support for its system in its engagements with other nations, such as Latin America, where the Roman Catholic Church is influential. What happens when Beijing-anointed, Vatican-approved priests head out to South America to tend the flock?

And what happens to unapproved people of faith? Well, the Tibetans and Uighurs know, and now so do Catholics. When, in early 2022, the PRC arrested ninety-year-old Cardinal Joseph Zen, the senior cleric in Hong Kong and a stalwart defender of freedom, religious and otherwise, the Vatican's response was muted.[32]

Even the United States didn't have much to say. There was a pro-forma calling for his release, and Kurt Campbell, President Biden's Asia czar, when asked to comment on Cardinal Zen's arrest, said: "All I can tell you is that I think we're increasingly troubled by steps in Hong Kong to pressure and eliminate civil society."[33]

That's pretty much it. China must be quaking.

So what's the real payoff for China's capture of international organizations?

It allows the PRC to present its system of authoritarian dictatorship as an equal, if not superior, alternative to U.S. consensual government based on rule of law. It erodes its enemies and their will—even their faith—while demonstrating that U.S. influence and the United States itself are in decline. China can argue that a majority of countries agree with them, even support them. At the same time, the organizations themselves are weakened, and less able to resist more Chinese pressure. China's Comprehensive National Power goes up, America's goes down, and everyone knows it's happening.

One sad aspect of China (and Russia) assiduously attempting to weaken all the post–World War II institutions built by that jaded, cynical victorious greatest generation, who were intent on building structures and institutions so it would happen "never again"—the UN, the World Bank, the IMF, NATO—is that all of them were to serve as impediments to totalitarian governments.

This organizational subversion contributes to give the CCP tangible operational advantages on the ground in other facets of political—and possibly kinetic—warfare as well.

CHAPTER 9

Biological Warfare: China Sickens America

N ot surprisingly, the People's Republic of China has been conducting biological weapons research for many years. But at least
it doesn't much publicize what it is doing (not on purpose, anyway).

In 2015, a dozen facilities—identified as part of the Chinese government's defense establishment, and another thirty locations connected
to the People's Liberation Army—were said to be involved in biological
weapons development activity.[1] The U.S. Department of Defense
believes the People's Liberation Army has both biowarfare capabilities
and delivery systems. The PRC admits this, but claims that its research
and whatever it has in the arsenal are for defensive purposes only.

Notice that under China's doctrine of Military-Civil Fusion, not to
mention that pesky National Intelligence Law, civilian facilities conducting biological research are required to share know-how and
resources with military counterparts.

So, what are they thinking? We have had some troubling glimpses. For example, in 2015, eighteen Chinese "military scientists and weapons experts" wrote a paper: "The Unnatural Origin of SARS and New Species of Man-Made Viruses as Genetic Bioweapons." The paper reportedly describes how coronaviruses can be "artificially manipulated into an emerging human disease virus, then weaponized and unleashed in a way never seen before," possibly even causing "the enemy's medical system to collapse."[2]

The Biological Weapons Convention requires signatories to reveal past and present activities related to biological warfare programs. For the last two years, the PRC has refused to meet with U.S. officials to discuss worries about PRC biowarfare. And, as we covered, after SARS, the PRC worked to neuter the World Health Organization so it can't interfere again.

That said, as far as we know, the People's Republic of China has not intentionally launched a bioweapon attack. It can be argued, however, that by closing off Wuhan once the coronavirus outbreak couldn't be hidden in late 2019—while still allowing Chinese to travel throughout the world—the CCP opportunistically seeded the rest of the globe with the COVID-19 virus.

I'll steer clear of the debate over where the COVID-19 virus came from. But we know it came from Wuhan, China, in late 2019. Even the Chinese government called it the Wuhan flu when it first hit.[3] The main competing theories are that the virus came from an animal market or from a nearby virology lab—probably the Wuhan Institute of Virology (WIV). The WIV is known to have done research work on coronaviruses and is the PRC's only Level 4 biosafety lab—where the most dangerous work is performed. *Washington Post* columnist Josh Rogin reported that in 2018, U.S. diplomatic officials had, in fact, expressed concern over safety protocols after visiting the Wuhan Lab.[4]

Regardless, the Chinese government's behavior from the time of the outbreak until now suggests the communists are hiding something.

It's been a continuous series of lies and obfuscations, and a total lack of meaningful cooperation with international efforts to investigate the origins of the disease.[5]

Intentionally launched or otherwise, the ensuing COVID-19 pandemic over the next two years (and counting) gave Chinese biowarfare researchers a good look at the effects of a biological attack on an enemy. They may like what they're seeing—with a few bugs worked out.

Consider the damage to the United States, and all without firing a shot. Also consider the effects of China's ongoing political warfare campaign.

For starters, COVID-19 was a powerful piece of economic warfare. It brought the United States economy that was humming along to a standstill. In fact, the virus threw the economy in reverse, as the U.S. government shut down business and left millions jobless as a result.

When Senator Tom Cotton suggested the virus might have come from the Wuhan Institute of Virology and that basic inquiries were warranted, he was savaged by the *Washington Post*, the *New York Times*, most of the media, and America's pundit class.[6] They accused him of peddling debunked conspiracy theories. A year later, when the possibility of a lab leak was accepted by elites, the *Washington Post* apologized—in part.[7]

President Trump was similarly condemned as a racist and xenophobe for pointing out the obvious—that the virus came from the People's Republic of China. Such was the hatred that it became nearly impossible to handle the normal business of running the country—as Trump's opponents made sure they did not let the crisis go to waste.

As previously mentioned, the pandemic likely cost Donald Trump a second term as president—to Beijing's advantage. The Trump administration was the first one in fifty years to take effective action against the PRC's aggressive and predatory behavior against the United States and its allies.

The PRC's longstanding elite capture efforts further paid off during the COVID pandemic. Dr. Anthony Fauci, the director of the National Institute of Health and President Trump's lead medical advisor, was the public face of the administration's pandemic response. He was curiously uninterested in the virus's origins and outright dismissed the idea that WIV was the source. He was later shown to have more connections to Chinese virology research institutions than he first let on.[8]

Also running cover for the PRC was Peter Daszak of the EcoHealth Alliance. He repeatedly insisted the virus couldn't have come from the lab.[9] Why? Because the Chinese said so. He was not exactly a disinterested party, having worked with Wuhan Institute of Virology for sixteen years on bat research.[10] The U.S. National Institutes of Health (Dr. Fauci's group) funded him.[11]

Even better for the Chinese, the director general of the World Health Organization, Tedros Adhanom Ghebreyesus, had deep connections with the PRC, as we saw in the international organizations chapter. He provided cover as well, particularly in the early days of the outbreak. He praised Chinese cooperation with the WHO and rejected the idea of a lab leak.[12]

President Trump took on the World Health Organization since it provided cover for the PRC instead of insisting that Beijing cooperate and live up to its obligations under WHO rules. Trump threatened to halt U.S. funding and suspend America's membership in the WHO.

The chattering class, of course, vilified him—because he was Trump. Max Boot from the Council of Foreign Relations published a *Washington Post* opinion piece, complaining, "Threatening to leave the WHO during a global health crisis is the geopolitical equivalent of injecting Clorox as a coronavirus remedy."[13]

It was all about Trump: get rid of Trump, and everything would be fine, at least for the Chinese. The CCP also saw no end of Americans who, for their own reasons, wanted the same outcome as Beijing.

COVID-19 was immensely effective as psychological warfare in other ways, too.

The psychological effects of COVID-19 on Americans—not just the illness, but the responses to it—were astonishing. The Wuhan-originated COVID-19 virus created such terror that Americans, who saw themselves as the freest people on the planet, submitted to so-called lockdowns in the name of public health.

Students and preschoolers went to remote learning. The harmful effects of two years of this anti-socialization on young (and not so young) children are now being recognized: lockdowns have hurt children's cognitive and social development. This was another COVID-19 win for America's enemies that will play out years from now.

Unemployment and enforced idleness were similarly harmful, ushering in attendant psychological and mental problems and increasing alcohol and drug abuse. Additionally, in the summer of 2020, there was an indirect connection between COVID-19 and the widespread rioting and attacks on government buildings that followed the unfortunate death of George Floyd while he was in police custody. As any warden knows, keeping people in lockdown can breed a riotous response.

America's gaping political divide widened even further during the pandemic. The extreme leftist fringe—think Representative Alexandria Ocasio-Cortez—had always existed in American politics, but now came to have real influence on the nation's governance.

The U.S. military was similarly hamstrung—and frightened—by the virus. Training and exercises were particularly affected. As mentioned earlier, one of the U.S. Navy's aircraft carriers dropped off its normal patrol in the Western Pacific and pulled into Guam, its skipper afraid of a COVID outbreak.

The controversy over emergency-approved vaccines caused still more disruption in the U.S. forces and led to the forced separation of many troops who refused to take the vaccines. The irony of all this is the COVID virus is not very harmful to service members, given that most of them are young and fit. But that's the psychological clout we've given COVID-19.

COVID-19 also was potent as financial warfare. It led to massive U.S. government spending to counter the effects of the economic downturn. This further debased the U.S. dollar and ultimately led to the highest inflation in forty years—making life difficult for all citizens. It also threatens the dollar's role as the world's reserve currency, something China has been angling to overcome for many years.

So you see how it works: biological warfare ties into other warfares—such as financial warfare, economic warfare, psychological warfare, international organization warfare, media warfare, etc., and all are mutually reinforcing. The cumulative effect wears down the opponent and creates entropy, affecting their ability to resist or to conduct kinetic operations. It took decades to destroy Baltimore. Many other locations were pushed as far in just two years—restaurants run by the same family for generations were closed, storefronts boarded up, people fled the downtowns, addiction and dropping out of school increased, all problems created in the name of public health.

The COVID case study, or test run, depending on how you look it, had a global effect as well. It hit America's allies (and every other country) just as hard. It shook alliances as nations closed borders—and started to see neighbors as frightening instead of friends. The PRC's biological warfare experts (and the CCP leaders) were no doubt taking notes.

The lesson: before making your move, hit your enemy with a bio-attack that is amplified by tame media, international organizations, and local elites—and your forces (already vaccinated with the right drugs) will have a much easier time. Indeed, COVID suggests that even just making the enemy think he is under biological attack might be enough.

Another big advantage of bio-weapons: you have plausible deniability if you do it right—for example, by releasing it in another country. You might also have friendly enemy citizens willing to obfuscate on your behalf. We just saw it happen for two years with COVID-19. Things got so insane that it was forbidden in many quarters to even say or write that the coronavirus came from China.

As one observer noted at the time regarding the taboo of suggesting COVID came from the Wuhan laboratory, "If you see a giraffe walking down the street, you might at least check at the zoo to see if they had a giraffe that's gone missing."[14]

COVID Is Just One Item on the Biological Warfare Menu

In recent years, so-called gene editing research and experimentation in the PRC has been reported and has gotten overseas attention. This is because a Chinese scientist claimed to have created genetically modified human babies, or CRISPR babies—a reference to the specific gene-editing technique.[15]

Reportedly, this technique has a dual use for potential biological warfare—to include plagues that destroy certain crops or designing diseases that can target a specific race based on genetic makeup.

According to Bill Gertz, a U.S. official speaking anonymously in 2020 expressed concern over Chinese biological testing on ethnic minorities. Gertz cites a 2017 book in which a Chinese general said that, owing to biotechnology advances, "specific ethnic genetic attacks" could happen in future warfare.[16]

PLA super-soldiers are rumored. Former DNI Ratcliffe said that China is conducting experiments on PLA soldiers to create soldiers with "biologically enhanced capabilities."[17]

And so, there's plenty to worry about.

Yes, but...

But certainly, the Chinese communists would never use biological weapons. That would be too awful to contemplate.

Well, given they seem to be in the "anything that works" business, maybe not. n other words, if it weakens the enemy, it's good for Beijing. It increases China's relative Comprehensive National Power.

But surely, the PRC signed the Biological Weapons Treaty?

Remember the lawfare section? The PRC has signed a lot of treaties and agreements. And it's hard to name one they have scrupulously obeyed when it was not in Chinese communist interests.

But the PRC doesn't want to harm its reputation?

That ship has long since sailed. And anyway, it values fear more than a genial pat on the back from the international community.

But isn't the PRC is afraid of potential casualties?

Up to a point, maybe, but only if the casualties are the top people in the Chinese Communist Party and their relatives. Remember that the CCP is responsible for the deaths of at least fifty million of its own citizens—in peacetime and good weather—since taking over in 1949. It may be willing to take its chances, especially if it ends up with its main enemy, the United States, on the ropes.

With the Chinese Communist Party, it is all about power, dominance, and ultimately control. If a weapon contributes to that, it's worth having in the arsenal.

If you need to calibrate on PRC willingness to use biological weapons, consider this May 2022 *Global Times* headline, and remember that the virus came from China: "200,000 U.S. Children Orphaned by COVID-19 Grill Washington's Conscience: Global Times Editorial."[18]

Beijing does not appear to have a conscience. That which it has done, and works, it might do again.

CHAPTER 10

Chemical Warfare:
Killing Americans by the Tens of Thousands

The PRC's incredibly effective biological and psychological warfare assault—the COVID-19 pandemic—raised alarms that America is deeply vulnerable on the chemical warfare front. As the response triggered frantic efforts to secure personal protective equipment, medicine, medical equipment, and more, it seemed that many—in some cases, all—roads led to China. In particular, it became clear China had the power to withhold the drugs (chemicals, really) we needed through its control over the supply chains of key elements required to manufacture essential pharmaceuticals.

This didn't happen by accident.

Starting around 2000, the U.S. pharmaceutical industry began moving its manufacturing overseas, chasing cheap labor and weaker safety and environmental controls. Much of this capacity ended up in China, helped along by China's expanded access to global markets following its accession to the World Trade Organization in 2001.

Things are now at the point, to cite just one example, that about 80 percent of the U.S. supply of antibiotics is made in the PRC. The pharmaceutical reliance includes about 95 percent of imports of ibuprofen, 70 percent of acetaminophen imports, and 40–45 percent of penicillin imports.[2]

During the height of the COVID pandemic, Robert Lighthizer, the Trump administration's lead trade representative, noted (with China in mind) that "over-dependence on other countries as a source of cheap medical products and supplies has created a strategic vulnerability."[3]

Echoing this, an official with the U.S. Defense Health Agency, the organization responsible for medical preparedness for the U.S. forces, warned that "[t]he national security risks of increased Chinese dominance of the global API [active pharmaceutical ingredients—that are an essential component of many drugs] market cannot be overstated."[4]

The logic is intuitive. It is unwise to rely for medical supplies (or anything else of importance) on an adversary that is already conducting political warfare against you—and has on eye on the regular kind of warfare.

The Chinese know this. In 2020, Huang Sheng, a financial commentator and nationalist author, wrote in China's state-owned news service Xinhua:

"If China wants to retaliate against the U.S. at this time...it could also announce strategic restrictions on the export of medical product to the U.S."[5]

So while we were put on notice that China has a card to play on the chemical warfare front by withholding essential pharmaceuticals from the United States, China hasn't played it yet. The United States has time to reconfigure drug supply chains—if it has the will to do so.

But the United States has a more immediate problem involving Chinese chemical warfare. Instead of the PRC threatening to keep needed drugs out of America, they are shipping us drugs we don't want—drugs that are killing us in massive numbers.

Here's how this front in China's political warfare scheme is producing results akin to an all-out shooting war. It is grim reading.

First, a Little History...

Foreigners have been buying—or at least renting—America's ruling class since the republic was founded. Just over 225 years ago, in his 1796 Farewell Address, George Washington warned against "the insidious wiles of foreign influence," adding that "foreign influence is one of the most baneful foes of republican government."[6]

In modern times, everyone who can, including the Saudis, Japanese, Canadians, South Koreans, and Israelis, to name a few, have all tried to purchase influence. Rival powers typically try this through buying off the "right" people. Sometimes this is direct, and sometimes it is via the legal, if parasitic, industry set up for the purpose: the lobbyists. The practice is so overt, the lobbyists are often simply referred to by the street in Washington where so many of them have offices, K Street. The usual goal of these activities is for each nation to gain its own advantages. What we are seeing now is something much more dangerous: using influence to corrode the United States from within and wage entropic warfare.

The People's Republic of China is pouring highly addictive and unpredictable illicit drugs into the American bloodstream—killing tens of thousands a year, destroying families and communities, and cities like Baltimore. The American elites are doing absolutely nothing about it. Now *that* is influence.

Yes, I'm talking about fentanyl.

Fentanyl, cheaper and thirty times more powerful than heroin, mostly originates in China, often moving via Mexico (and Mexican drug gangs) into the United States. The Chinese are also into the money laundering part of the business, helping drug gangs launder (or recycle) their massive earnings. Talk about a "win-win," as the Chinese communists like to say.

Casualties

The deluge started around 2013 and has picked up steadily since then. The numbers are staggering.

In 2017, 47,600 Americans died of opioid overdoses, many involving fentanyl.[7]

In a 2018 meeting with President Donald Trump, China's leader, Xi Jinping, pledged to restrict all fentanyl-like substances.[8] Trump declared this a "gamechanger."[9] Not surprisingly, the fentanyl and drugs kept flowing.

In 2019, around 70,000 Americans died from drug overdoses—about half from fentanyl.[10] That's nearly five times the number of American troops killed in the wars in Iraq and Afghanistan.

In 2020, the U.S. government reported 92,478 American residents died from a drug overdose, the majority from fentanyl poisoning.[11] The COVID-19 lockdowns helped bump up the already horrific death totals.

And it is getting even worse. In 2021, the death count was 107,573, the biggest number from fentanyl, according to the U.S. Centers for Disease Control and Prevention.[12] Law enforcement officials note that an alarming portion of the overdoses involved counterfeit pills laced with fentanyl and purchased via social media by teenagers and young adults.

For Americans aged eighteen to forty-five, drug overdoses are the main cause of preventable death. That outpaces suicide, guns, and auto accidents.

Yet, even as the death toll mounts, U.S. businesses and financial titans almost never mention it. The think tanks are mostly silent. Academia? Can't be bothered. The U.S. media often downplay or ignore the fentanyl bloodbath, and even more so its source, as they're seemingly afraid to mention the C-word: China.

On Capitol Hill—where there's bold, blustery, "bipartisan" talk about taking on the Chinese regime—when it comes to fentanyl and

China, and especially doing something that would get the PRC's attention, one hears little. There are indeed representatives and senators who are outraged and would like to act, but there is something in the water in D.C. that keeps anything from happening. Especially if it's not in the donor class interest.

Excuses

Even the Trump administration—the firmest yet in standing up to China—didn't make much of the fentanyl issue, though Mr. Trump raised it directly with Xi, and others tried.

One senior U.S. State Department official suggested calling the "fentanyl scourge" the "Third Opium War," a reference to the nineteenth-century wars between Britain and the Qing Dynasty that were fought, ostensibly, over British demands to import opium into China—which created a drug problem. There was more to it than that, but that is the perception.

Regardless, the response from inside the Beltway to the State Department official's suggestion was immediate and visceral: "You can't say that!" (When it comes to China, there are all sorts of things "you can't say.")

In this case, the response was particularly curious as, in some quarters (including in China), there is indeed a tendency to excuse Chinese non-cooperation on fentanyl as payback for the Opium Wars of the nineteenth century.

Payback to whom? The Opium Wars were 180 years ago, and the United States wasn't involved. By that logic, slave labor in Xinjiang is "payback" for the pre–Civil War plantations. How does creating new despair and death rectify old despair and death?

American elites also have plenty of other "insider" excuses for why the Chinese regime can't (or, better said, won't) stop the illicit drug flow. These are three of the most common:

1) The Chinese regime is in a legal bind as fentanyl producers keep jiggering the formula to avoid the "illegal list." Therefore, the producers are always one step ahead of a government that can't revise laws fast enough, try as it might.

A nice excuse, but in China the law is what Xi and the Chinese Communist Party say it is, as billionaire Jack Ma and any number of other powerful, well-connected Chinese tycoons and officials have discovered the hard way. If Beijing wants to shut down fentanyl producers and exporters, the law is no obstacle.

2) Chinese local authorities, supposedly outside of Beijing's reach, won't stop fentanyl production since they want tax revenues and employment—and are also thoroughly corrupt.

True enough on the wanting money and corruption fronts. But local officials are also frightened of being caught crossing Beijing. Everyone knows what happened to Jack Ma.

3) Chinese authorities can't locate the illegal drug producers. China is a big place with a lot of people, you know.

The CCP is creating a surveillance state that even George Orwell couldn't have imagined. Draw a mustache on a poster of Xi Jinping and see how long it takes to be arrested and imprisoned. Post on social media that Xi resembles Winnie the Pooh, and you'll have Ministry of State Security agents at your front door in minutes.

The CCP police can do whatever they want. "Disappear" people, arrest starlets, intimidate tennis players, and kidnap billionaires and booksellers. Even take foreigners hostage and lock them up? No problem. The only restraints come from Zhongnanhai—the very top of the CCP.

The fact the Chinese regime doesn't ban fentanyl entirely—much less go after producers the way it goes after Uighurs, Christians, Falun Gong, or Hong Kongers—suggests the CCP is glad America is awash in fentanyl.

When Trump told Xi to knock off the fentanyl flow back in 2018, Xi reportedly replied: "We don't have a drug problem in China."[13] That means Xi can control the drugs domestically and is channeling the chemical warfare agents—in true "unrestricted warfare fashion"—towards his number one rival and greatest enemy. Most things involving the CCP just aren't that hard to figure out.

But they are apparently too hard for the U.S. Drug Enforcement Administration (DEA). The DEA can't quite parse the fact that the drugs are coming from the PRC with the approval—actual or tacit—of the Chinese government.

In the DEA's most successful case to date involving the PRC, the Americans provided intelligence about the "Diana" drug gang to the Chinese Narcotics Control Bureau. Chinese authorities eventually convicted nine members in 2019. Both sides claimed this was a great success.

According to RealClearInvestigations, "while China has made several more fentanyl-related arrests, it doesn't appear to have convicted any major traffickers in the two years since the Diana case."[14]

The report goes on: "Some former DEA agents question how far China is willing to go in enforcing its bans since the U.S. would be the main beneficiary."[15]

Really.

A former American intelligence officer who operated successfully in Asia for many years offered some insights:

> The DEA and the rest of the U.S. government (U.S.G.) live in a bubble, and the Chinese and others simply tell them what they expect to hear.... The feedback loop time and again confirms their false assumptions. Of course, we start by mirror imaging: assuming the Chinese services have the same objectives—fight the scourge of drugs and other criminal businesses—which is simply not true.

But the Chinese tell us this all the time, and we believe them despite the overwhelming evidence to the contrary. The U.S.G. simply doesn't take the time and effort to really delve into Chinese motivations and interests. They also don't—and never will—understand how criminal businesses work in authoritarian societies or failed or near-failed states.

The businesses simply don't exist without the direct cooperation and protection of the state security services. The police, etc., are the mafia. They have the absolute monopoly over the use of violence and can make anyone disappear. The traditional, brand-name organized crime, such as the Big Circle and various [Chinese] triads, are nothing. They only exist with the acquiescence of the security services.

These names persist mainly because the likes of the DEA need to cite them to make their cases look impressive. They're press conference material, nothing more.[16]

The Effects of China's Chemical Warfare

The carnage can't be overstated. Fentanyl is ravaging all parts of American society, and the youth are particularly badly hit. About half of the deaths attributed to fentanyl are young people of military age. As it is, only around 23 percent of seventeen-to-twenty-four-year-olds meet the standards for military service.[17] The deaths, disabilities, and social destruction caused by the fentanyl epidemic are shrinking the already small candidate pool.

As one former U.S. government official noted, this is the equivalent of removing five or six divisions of Army or Marines off the rolls every year. And that's just the "KIA." Don't forget the "battlefield casualties" who survive but can no longer function as productive members of society—with health problems, poor education, diminished intelligence, and inclination to committing crimes.

One estimate is that for every drug death, there are ten addicts. Then there's the burden and expense of caring for them, and the devastated families left broke and broken—not to mention the drain on local first responders, emergency services, hospitals, and local economies.

One hears elites who should know better say that victims are just "druggies" and wouldn't have joined the military anyway. That's malicious and wrong. Young people have been misbehaving for centuries, and that includes many who join the U.S. military. But a six-pack or a joint is one thing; a difficult-to-identify drug, one that is often mislabeled and unpredictably kills or permanently disables in minuscule quantities, is quite another.

And it's not just military recruitment that is affected. Private sector employers, including manufacturers trying to reestablish themselves, often have trouble finding workers who can pass a drug test or are otherwise unaffected by addiction.

This is indeed having an effect on America.

From China's perspective, what's not to like? You're weakening your avowed enemy—whom you plan to dominate by mid-century. And, even better, the CCP makes a lot of money from the drug trade and in convertible currency. Buy fentanyl and you pay in dollars.

The dollars fund the People's Liberation Army's buildup, as well as everything the Chinese government needs to obtain from overseas that requires real money. This includes buying companies and farmland overseas, Belt and Road projects, and, of course, the bribes and under-the-table grease to local politicians and officials that are part of the deal. Even the American participants in the Chinese Thousand Talents Plan, who quietly (and often illegally) provide technology know-how to the communist regime, only accept payment in U.S. dollars.

Accomplices

While China is ultimately to blame, it is America's ruling class that refuses to do anything for fear of "offending" China. Or, more accurately, for fear of not being able to feed its own addiction to Chinese money. Money that, in some small part, may have come from selling fentanyl to Americans in the first place.

Maybe overlooking seventy thousand-plus dead countrymen—and exponentially more left in the wreckage—in exchange for Chinese cash is easier when you think only deplorables and Neanderthals in fly-over country are dying.

It can't be helped if these people were too stupid and lazy to "learn to code" or to get a Wharton MBA when their jobs, livelihoods, and communities were shipped overseas from the 1990s onwards—mostly to China—by those same political and business elites.

There's a sickening maliciousness to it all.

Countering "the Most Baneful Foes"

Watching America's elites do nothing—or, worse, call for unrestricted engagement with the Chinese regime—one concludes that the Chinese have indeed gotten their money's worth from America's ruling class.

Just listen to the head of the U.S.-China Business Council, or the CEOs of Boeing, Nike, or Apple if you need some examples.

And how about the luminaries who signed the "China Is Not an Enemy"[18] letter in 2019? Not a word in there about fentanyl.

Here is an alternate letter they might consider signing:

> To the President of the United States of America:
> You have sworn to protect American citizens, not to ensure Wall Street and U.S. industry can take advantage of

Xi's umpteenth promise to "open up." By now, you should have figured out the Chinese Communist Party is conducting chemical warfare against us.

We, the undersigned, call on you to do one, or ideally more, of the following:

First, suspend all Chinese financial institutions from the U.S. dollar network. Start with the People's Bank of China—the PRC's main financial institution.

Second, require government approval of all U.S. investment, financial and business, in the PRC.

Third, immediately de-list every Chinese company from the New York Stock Exchange and other exchanges—and do it now, not three years from now as you are thinking about doing. They should not have been listed in the first place.

Fourth, revoke the Green Cards and visas and place liens on the properties and bank accounts of the top five hundred CCP members' relatives in the United States.

Yours sincerely,

The American People

Here's another idea: require prospective graduates from elite MBA and International Relations programs, as well as the denizens of K Street, congressional staffers—and maybe even members of Congress themselves—to spend a couple of weeks in the so-called "Rust Belt" that's been hit both by fentanyl and the carnage caused by the pedigreed classes when industries and jobs were shipped off to China.

Try Youngstown, Ohio; Uniontown, Pennsylvania; Buffalo, New York; or East Cleveland, if you need some ideas. The list could be much, much longer. Of course, if they don't want to travel too far from their Tesla charging stations in D.C., they can just head up to Baltimore.

Put them up in a local motel and require them to be outside on the streets from 8:00 a.m. to 10:00 p.m. "soaking in the atmosphere."

And maybe, for a break, accompany the EMTs (better called war medics) out on drug overdose calls. Or stop off at the local high schools and sit in with the guidance counselors—just to get a sense of things and the bright futures too many of these kids face.

Is this likely? No.

One gets the impression America's Best and Brightest just don't care. They have become willing accomplices to the "baneful foes."

This is particularly infuriating because we *can* fight back. China is not invulnerable. They are hitting us where it hurts—in our families and communities. We need to hit them where it hurts—in their elites.

So, what's the plan of our leaders? As fentanyl kills tens of thousands of us a year and poisons our society, Secretary of State Antony Blinken laid out the plan in his long-awaited China Strategy speech of May 26, 2022: "To counter illegal and illicit narcotics, especially synthetic opioids like fentanyl that killed more than 100,000 Americans last year, we want to work with China to stop international drug trafficking organizations from getting precursor chemicals, many of which originate in China."[19]

That's all.

The Chinese Communist Party can stop pushing drugs into America. It just needs a reason to do so. And we need to give it one. At the same time, we need to break our most "insidious" addiction, the addiction of our elites to Chinese money.

Fentanyl has been one hell of success for Chinese political and entropic warfare. It's even easier when the opponent doesn't fight back—and doesn't want to.

The deluge will continue. Unless we stop it.

CHAPTER 11

Economic Warfare:
Putting America out of Business

Americans know economic competition can be bruising and can cause companies to fail. But they don't think of it as a way to cause a country to fail.

China does.

Beijing sees its economic, trade, and commercial activities as feeding into a broader fight to the finish with the United States—a core element of China's Comprehensive National Power.

The CCP actively works to destroy the U.S. manufacturing and commercial sectors. It tries to lure companies to China, where it is easier to steal technologies, techniques, and clients. It focuses on dominating key elements of the global supply chain to make China the world's center of economic gravity.

This isn't normal economic competition. This is economic warfare. And we are arming our enemy to their teeth.

The Original Sin of the WTO

We're two decades into the trade front of the economic war, and it has gone well for the Chinese. Foreign trade is the oxygen fueling the PRC's growth. The money it earns allows the Communist Party to fund its military and pay for the Belt and Road Initiative—and just about everything else China needs from overseas. That includes buying up American and foreign companies with useful technologies for civil or military purposes—and often both. Given China's military fusion doctrine, it's a moot point.

Foreign trade also keeps Chinese people employed, no small thing for a dictatorship where citizens can't vote the bums out (as they can in a democracy), and may string them up instead.

Washington gave Beijing the go-ahead to attack on the trade front in 2001 when it let the People's Republic of China (PRC) into the World Trade Organization (WTO)—despite China not meeting the qualifications.[1]

Joining the WTO requires a nation to be a market economy and to follow some basic rules that everyone else has to follow, such as:

- Respecting intellectual property and not stealing or strong-arming it from companies wanting do business in your country
- No government subsidies
- No dumping—in other words, no selling products over-seas at less than it costs to make them, and so driving your competition out of business
- Treating foreign companies like your own domestic companies
- Controls on state-owned companies (SOEs) that, by defi-nition, have an advantage over a private company (at their

most basic, SOEs don't have to make money. No small advantage when running a business).

Those factors, however, nicely describe key components of the CCP business model.

So Beijing, knowing there was no way it could comply, bought itself a runway to launch a serious assault, promising to meet WTO standards, if just given a little time to get things in order. And there were plenty of Americans urging that we give Beijing time.

The stated thinking was that by accommodating China—letting it into WTO and ignoring its behavior—the PRC would gradually play by the rules and even liberalize.

It required the U.S. government to pretend the People's Republic of China was not a threat and had no harmful intentions. There were many in and around government who knew better.

But plenty more were willing to pretend otherwise, and some actually believed China could be turned into a liberal play-by-the-rules member of the international community. Especially once its economy developed, and Chinese people got richer. According to the theory, China's new middle class would demand its rights.

And so, China was admitted to the WTO. From a global economic standpoint, this was an original sin.

Instead of becoming a big version of Canada, the Chinese communist rulers just solidified their hold while muscling up the military—and the citizenry, by and large, went along with it. Many were happy to have decent enough jobs (or at least the hope that their children would have better ones) and were proud enough at China's development to come across as nationalistic, and not a little bit anti-American.

It didn't take a strategic genius to know what would happen. It's not as if following international rules is a Chinese Communist Party

strong point. In 1988, a Chinese official came by a United States consulate in a European nation. He hoped he and his wife might get visas
to America or, in other words, to defect. The local CIA guy met with
him. This was while China was trying to join the General Agreement
on Tariffs and Trade (GATT) agreement.

To interest the Americans, he brought along a stack of official (and
"secret") Chinese Trade Ministry pamphlets that explained how to get
around GATT rules—with pamphlets for specific products like tennis
shoes and or bath towels. Beijing was preparing to undermine GATT
while lobbying to join it.

Similarly, with China's entry into the WTO, the PRC was allowed
access to other countries' markets while keeping its own mostly
closed—only allowing restricted access while weaponizing its state-owned
enterprises against foreign companies that had to make a profit.

So the PRC got stronger and caught up. Its rivals (or its enemies, as
Beijing saw them) lost relative advantage and even, as a result of targeted
maneuvers by Beijing, became increasingly dependent on China.

South America is a good example of China's impressive economic expansion and attendant
influence building over the last twenty years. To compare the U.S. and China's economic
influence in each country, this adds: (A) foreign trade (imports and exports), (B) the stock
of foreign direct investment, (C) the sum of credits granted by political and commercial
banks, and (D) official development aid. This trend is seen worldwide, particularly in the
developing world. *Map courtesy of Research and Design by the Center for a Secure Free
Society (SFS). Originally published in the* VRIC Monitor 28, October 2022.

What has this meant in the real world? Let's look at what happens when businesses go to China, when Chinese businesses come to the United States and when goods and services travel the world on CCP belts and roads.

Welcome to China: Here Be Dragons

Setting up in China is building your own competition, and it always has been. The WTO accession just made it worse.

When I worked at Motorola in the 1990s, I watched one of America's most respected companies fail.

The company went all out in China, building factories, handing over technology, employing thousands of locals, demonstrating its commitment to the market, and ingratiating itself to the communist leadership.

All was good for a while, but Motorola was really committing suicide and unwittingly helping Chinese telecom manufacturing and operators get on their feet. While I tried to help Motorola hang on to its technology, the Chinese government talked about doing what was necessary—including stealing trade secrets—to speed up industrial development by leaping over stages.

Today, Chinese electronics company Lenovo owns a good chunk of what was once Motorola.

As mentioned earlier, former director of national intelligence John Ratcliffe called this pattern "rob, replicate, and replace,"[2] and it is standard operating procedure in China.

Beijing is open about it. In 2020, Xi Jinping said, "[We] must forge some 'assassin's mace' technologies. We must sustain and enhance our superiority across the entire production chain . . . and we must tighten international production chains' dependence on China, forming powerful countermeasures and deterrent capabilities based on artificially cutting off supply to foreigners."[3]

Former National Security Council deputy director Matthew Pottinger correctly assessed that Xi's deterrent capability is better viewed as an offensive capability.[4]

Developing that capability is one of the drivers behind the CCP's strategic and industrial policy Made in China 2025, officially adopted in 2015.[5] The CCP regularly issues Five Year Plans that give insight into its goals—and Made in China 2025 is that, on steroids.

The idea of Made in China 2025 is, well, to make *everything* in China—at least the good stuff. It's a new name for the idea of milking foreigners of their technology and secrets and replacing them with a Chinese company. It's no idle boast.

The goal of Made in China 2025 is to upgrade industry writ large—especially sectors with military/strategic applications. The plan highlights ten priority sectors:

1. New advanced information technology
2. Automated machine tools and robotics
3. Aerospace and aeronautical equipment
4. Maritime equipment and high-tech shipping
5. Modern rail transport equipment
6. New-energy vehicles and equipment
7. Power equipment
8. Agricultural equipment
9. New materials
10. Biopharma and advanced medical products

American companies have seemingly fallen over themselves to help Made in China a success. Convincing themselves they had to be in the China market was easy. There was the dream—never requited—of selling one of something to every person in China. Or it was the allure of cheap labor—and no labor unions and weak environmental standards.

Also, if you move manufacturing to China and bump up revenues and share price, there's a nice bonus awaiting. "Score" just once, and you're set for life. Who cares what happens to the company itself—you'll be sipping sangria on a beach somewhere as creditors pick over its bones.

Or take the easy route: sell the entire company to a Chinese buyer, and top executives make off with a bundle. If you needed more justification, there were the three magic words that made Chinese economic warfare even more effective: Maximizing Shareholder Value.

This mantra asserts that management's sole duty is to "maximize shareholder value"—and it provided excellent cover for the Great Decoupling of U.S. industry *from* the United States and *towards* China of the last four decades.

Yet "maximizing shareholder value" is essentially a *theory* that took on a life of its own, serving as a convenient excuse so CEOs and CFOs can better look after their own interests. Nobody quite knows where it came from, though Milton Friedman often gets credit.[6]

One only has to find a country where somebody will work for next to nothing (compared to Americans), and one can make a killing—at least long enough to pad his bank account before running for the hills or the beaches.

As for the effects on your own workers and local communities in the United States?

"Can't be helped. Shareholder value, you know."

Among much of the managerial class, an unspoken, get-rich-quick "I got mine" or "*Après moi le deluge*" approach to China took hold—especially since long-term prospects were, well, "long-term."

As a result, with China, an entire generation of MBA grads have spent their entire working lives de-industrializing the United States in favor of quick profits to themselves—and longer term profits for China.

One American executive recently said that, looking back, "The business guys became amoral when stock analysts became more important than God."[7]

The Americans were also often naïve and even condescending from the start. Tech transfer was the entry ticket to the China market since it opened in the late 1970s—and it still is. Many Americans are willing to pay the price.

The president of a well-known American aviation electronics firm stated in the early 1990s that he didn't mind giving technology to the Chinese—since his company would always be ahead of them.

The voluntary handovers, strong-arming, and theft for China's economic (and military) advantage were not taken as seriously as they should have been. They were regarded as the cost of doing business with the PRC.

It was often said (and still is) that the Chinese can't innovate, so they have to steal. Thus, nothing for us to worry about, since we are smarter and have a better system. The British applied the same thinking to nineteenth-century Americans who had lifted key technologies from British factories.

We called it Yankee ingenuity to take someone else's technology and improve on it. In our case, doing so powered the Industrial Revolution that caught us up to the British, and eventually we overtook them. Perhaps they didn't see us coming. Many Americans similarly seem not to realize a shift may be coming, and that *they* are helping it happen.

Around the early 1990s, the aerospace firm Loral Corporation had a retired U.S. Marine general on the payroll insisting the PRC posed no threat. Loral (they claimed unintentionally) helped the Chinese communists master MIRV technology, used for launching multiple satellites from a single missile.[8]

The Chinese put it to use for ballistic missiles—launching one missile and multiple warheads from a single missile instead of one missile and one warhead. Intercepting one incoming missile is much easier than trying to stop a half dozen.

Around 2017, when understanding of the nature of the CCP became more widespread, more foreigners started to wonder if they were targeted for extinction.

So the CCP ordered state media to stop talking about Made in China 2025, but it didn't go away. And a new term came to the fore, "Dual Circulation."

"Dual Circulation" aims to create an independent economy inside China. China manufactures and consumes internally, making its economy less dependent on exports—and less vulnerable to external pressure or sanctions. That's useful if China expects to go kinetic (start a shooting war) someday in the not-so-distant future.

Even then, the American companies have kept coming. Just look at Boeing.

Boeing Down to the Chinese Market

Boeing is America's premier aerospace company and provides essential aircraft and aerospace systems for the U.S. military (and its allies). But Boeing is also love-struck by the China market. In 2018, it set up a finishing plant for 737s near Shanghai.[9]

China is Boeing's second largest market, and a cut of an estimated $1.2 trillion demand for over 7,690 new aircraft[10] in the Chinese market over the next twenty years is alluring for any company.

Jumping into the PRC is, of course, risky, given Chinese economic warfare objectives and the CCP's track record for stealing or strong-arming technology, lack of an honest legal system, and discrimination against foreign companies—especially successful ones.

But it's even riskier for Boeing. The PRC sorely wants into the commercial airliner market. Aerospace technology is on the CCP's

Made in China 2025 top ten list—both for civilian and military applications.

China has done well developing military aircraft—partly from stealing other nations' technologies—though it still lacks state of the art engine technology. The PRC also bought a chunk of America's general aviation industry and its technology early on. Teledyne-Continental Motors was sold to the Chinese company AVIC International in 2010, and Cirrus Industries was bought by China Aviation Industry General Aircraft in 2011.[11] But building reliable commercial airliners to compete with Boeing and Airbus is tough. It's one key industry the Chinese haven't mastered—yet.

Boeing's move into China puts it squarely in the crosshairs of PRC industrial policy and on Chinese turf.

In the China market, things have a way of turning out differently than one expects. Ask Motorola, Microsoft, Google, and Apple. Why does Boeing think it will be different?

By the way, as for Boeing's plans to sell thousands of planes in China's domestic market, in 2022 Chinese newspaper headlines announced the launch of the Chinese-built C919 aircraft.[12]

Also known as: "The Boeing 737 Killer."

Energy

The PRC's success at getting U.S. industry hooked on China has been breathtaking. And we've helped them. Just look at the renewable energy sector.

Solar energy. The United States was originally the leader, but China purloined the technology and undercut rivals, driving most of them out of business. Now installers are demanding the United States lay off cheap Chinese imports. Environmental groups are backing them up.

Wind power. The same thing. A retired U.S. intelligence officer noted: "China's wind sector industries are notorious for IPR theft, industrial espionage, dumping and market manipulation to drive foreign competitors out of business. Google American Superconductor and China for one case study. End comment."[13]

Electric vehicles (EVs) are another technology the Chinese are keen to dominate—to include getting a lock on the mineral supply chains needed to produce EV batteries. A major Congo cobalt mine belonged to an American company, Freeport McMoran, until the company ran into financial difficulties and looked to sell in 2016. They asked the U.S. government for help. No interest. Not from the U.S. ambassador in Congo, the State Department, the Department of Commerce, or the National Security Council.[14]

A PRC firm, China Molybdenum, stepped in and bought it for $2.6 billion.[15] In case you were wondering how the PRC puts to good use the foreign exchange it earns from your Walmart shopping and others, this is it.

Even more maddening, the U.S. government knew the importance of cobalt in laptop and cellphone batteries—and that demand would skyrocket in coming years along with demand for clean-energy raw materials. It knew the U.S. supply of cobalt is scant. It knew most cobalt comes from Congo. It knew China was aiming to corner the market.

An American diplomat commented that the Freeport McMoran Congo cobalt story "points up the crux of the problem: two systems and two different games. The separation between the U.S government and business is no match for China's unchallenged government-business fusion. The few tools the U.S. government has only help on the margins and within the U.S. system (for example, government guarantees of commercial loans, lent in a manner our system allows)."[16]

We know there is a problem. The U.S. Department of Energy publicly reported Chinese dominance of solar power and rare earth mineral mining vital for modern technology.

Throughout the pandemic, it has become widely known, as mentioned earlier, that generic drug supplies are similarly China dominated—including, according to Commerce Department data, 95 percent of U.S. imports of ibuprofen, 91 percent of hydrocortisone, 70 percent of acetaminophen, over 40 percent of penicillin, 40 percent of heparin, and 80 percent of the U.S. supply of antibiotics.[17] We know this because Chinese state media threatened to choke off our supply as retaliation for asking about the origins of COVID, causing us to be "plunged into the mighty sea of coronavirus."[18]

By drawing American and other foreign businesses into the PRC, Beijing made its rivals and enemies dependent on the China market, thus ensuring the foreigners would continue to supply necessary inputs (money, technology, manufacturing) to bolster CCP rule.

This, in turn, restrains Washington's willingness to challenge Chinese behavior—for fear of being shut out of the China market or being cut off from key products (such as medicines) that only China provides. Chinese political influence has grown apace, and that's useful for fracturing U.S. alliances and peeling off America's friends, capturing international organizations, and further isolating Taiwan.

Ask yourself: How tough would you be on the country that makes the pharmaceuticals that keep you healthy? Or the batteries for your military? Or provides the raw and rare materials your industries need?

Coming to America

The WTO accession also turbocharged the CCP's entry into the U.S. market.

It had a hell of run, and largely unchecked.

Between 2002 and 2016, Chinese state-owned or state-linked companies spent $120 billion buying up assets in the United States.

Here are a few:

Smithfield Foods—bought by Shuanghui International in 2013 for $4.7 billion.[19] As of 2021, Smithfield was the world's largest pork processor, a useful holding to have if, like China, you might be concerned about food security.

AMC Theatres—bought by Dalian Wanda Group in 2012 for $2.6 billion;[20] Legendary Entertainment also bought by Dalian Wanda Group in 2016 for $3.5 billion.[21] Useful to have for influence and propaganda aspects of political warfare.

GE Appliances—bought by Qingdao Haier Co., Ltd. in 2016 for $5.6 billion.[22] The owner, Zhang Ruimin, was also a party delegate to the 19th Chinese Communist Party Congress. He described an Internet of Things with Chinese Characteristics, saying, "Imagine by touching the screen on your fridge, you online shop. By using apps on your cellphone, you can check which laundry room close to you has washing machines available."[23] (What could possibly go wrong?)

Motorola Mobility (my old company)—bought by Lenovo in 2014 for $2.91 billion.[24] Lenovo became one of the world's biggest cellphone makers.

Henniges Automotive—acquired by CCP state-owned Aviation Industry Corporation of China (AVIC) for $600 million in 2015.[25] It is a precision parts manufacturer and, according to Peter Schweizer, AVIC sits at the heart of the Chinese military-industrial complex.[26] Given it was in a sensitive sector, the deal required Committee on Foreign Investment in the United States (CFIUS) approval. And John Kerry's State Department gave it.

It Wasn't a CFIUS One-Off

As one high-tech executive noted, "I couldn't believe that U.S. government allowed the (semiconductor) industry to leach away from the U.S. to Taiwan and China—but whenever I asked, the answer from the senior management was always: 'We asked.... Congress, the White House, and CFIUS don't consider it important.'"[27]

That was all the cover U.S. business needed.

The dangers were clear early on. In 2013, an American trade lawyer and former government official described the dynamic during this period and how China's successful trade warfare affected U.S. government policy towards the People's Republic of China:

> Basically, (the Chinese) were sitting on the mountain of U.S. currency foreign exchange earned through Chinese exports of everything U.S. consumers wanted to buy—but not build themselves in sweatshops. Next, Federal Reserve went into printing money (quantitative easing 1 & 2...) by the billions and billions of dollars per month.
>
> The Chinese government leaned on the U.S. government to relax CFIUS' (Committee on Foreign Investment in the United States) review of their "foreign" purchases of U.S. domestic industry. Armed with mountains of cash of diminishing value, during the most recent recession, they have now gone on a buying spree of crown jewels of American industry and business from U.S. shareholders/executives eager to maximize quarterly profits.
>
> Including the crown jewels of American general aviation. The sale of this priceless technology is now being hailed as "China, the Savior of U.S. General Aviation"—fools.[28]

In 2018, nearly twenty years after China was allowed into the World Trade Organization, the respected American economist Marvin Feldstein noted, "What is needed is a change in Chinese behavior to conform to rules Beijing accepted when it joined the WTO in 2001."[29]

Good luck with that.

I'll Have What She's Having

What American companies didn't give away, the Chinese stole—and still do. The damages: $225–$600 billion in losses every year.[30] But it's not just the immediate monetary loss. We also lose the market, all future earnings, and R&D development. It's easy enough to steal from other companies inside China, but the scouring also goes on overseas for anything of value. Some of it is state-directed, as legitimated by the 2017 National Intelligence Law. But some is on speculation, as private Chinese steal IP and know-how with the aim to get hired back in China or set up competing businesses.

For example, in 2012, Tze Chao, who had worked at DuPont from 1966 to 2002, pled guilty to conspiracy to commit espionage.[31] According to his plea agreement, he had "learned that the PRC government had placed a priority on developing chloride process TiO_2 technology in a short period of time and wished to acquire this technology from western companies."[32]

Tze put in a bid to design a TiO_2 facility with the Pangang Group that included "secret" DuPont information.[33] He didn't get the bid. But he was later asked to review the design work by others, and provided yet more DuPont trade secrets to Pangang Group.[34]

FBI director Christopher Wray said in 2021 that the FBI opens a new case every ten hours involving Chinese and CCP sponsored theft—from consumer goods to satellite technology to agricultural seeds to military hardware.[35]

A Few Examples

Often it is old-fashioned espionage, not involving computer hacking. In 2021, Yanjun Xu, a Chinese Ministry of State Security (MSS—like the CIA or FBI) officer was convicted of attempting to recruit an employee of General Electric to provide the company's proprietary jet-engine technology.[36] It was a classic recruitment effort: spot, assess, and gradually reel in the target.

The FBI got wind of it. They arranged to arrest the MSS spy in Belgium, and he was extradited to the United States. He was tried, convicted, and sentenced to twenty years in prison in a rare win for the Americans.[37]

China's ongoing Thousand Talents Program is another scheme to identify Chinese and foreigners working in key technology areas and offer them a lucrative side-gig to share what they know. And, in some cases, to bring them entirely into the fold.

It's not always stealing, but often it is or is close enough. Since everything is done quietly, it does suggest something is not quite right.

In a high profile case, a Harvard University professor, Dr. Charles Lieber, was convicted in 2020 of receiving millions in project funding from the Chinese government and concealing the point. He denies having provided any protected information.[38]

Nick Eftimiades, who literally wrote the book on Chinese espionage, keeps a database of PRC-related economic espionage cases. He is at *seven hundred* and counting.[39] And those are just the ones who have been caught.

This is nothing new.

The Chinese military and Huawei put Northern Telecom (Nortel) out of business in the mid-2000s. Northern Telecom was Canada's biggest company. That's akin to putting AT&T out of business (back when it was America's dominant telecom company). And in the process, Huawei and ZTE flourished.

How did they do it?

Through computer hacking, planting bugs and spies inside Nortel, reportedly making use of Chinese Ph.D. students working for Nortel to steal information, and efforts to compromise Nortel managers by CCP and PLA agents.[40]

The implications are far-reaching, and far from over. According to Anders Corr:

> It appears that Huawei hacked Canadian and UK telecom companies (Nortel and Marconi) to steal their IP and pricing data, and then underbid them for contracts in their own countries, putting them out of business. Nortel was at the time Canada's biggest company and had its technology facilitating 70 percent of the world's internet traffic.
>
> I think a reasonable person could conclude that we need to rip out not only Huawei components from our systems and Huawei bids from our bidding processes, but all of China's companies (e.g., civil nuclear companies, which are on the rise), which likely systematically benefit from stolen pricing data and government subsidies, thus can underbid their rivals and destroy their businesses.
>
> Once these businesses go, it is difficult, if not impossible, to reinvent them given the increasing competition from China. And as China's companies step into our critical infrastructure and key nodes of our economies, they have increasing control of all of our systems, and leverage over our political leaders who will never want to admit the grave mistakes they made.[41]

Xi and Obama agreed in 2015 not to engage in cyber economic espionage. The Americans don't do it, in any case. But presumably, Xi had his fingers crossed.

And anyway, the Chinese embassy in Washington denied it all: "China's achievements in scientific and technological development have come not from stealing or robbing, but from the hard work of the Chinese people."[42] There you have it.

According to a study by Brookings, this well-funded, targeted, and persistent hollowing out of America's economy has resulted in millions of lost jobs. Much of the steel and semiconductor business has disappeared, the U.S. textile industry and furniture industries are mostly gone.

In once-thriving sectors like manufacturing, it's not as if suddenly those who lost their jobs are learning to code. The study found that "regions experiencing larger trade-induced reductions in manufacturing employment saw neither differential reductions in labor supply—due, for example, to out-migration—nor greater absorption of workers by nonmanufacturing sectors. Manufacturing job loss translated nearly one for one into declines in the employment-population ratio."[43]

You can see the effects for yourself in Baltimore; Erie, Pennsylvania; or East Cleveland. Remind yourself that what used to be there mostly went overseas, and most of that to China. There's a big difference between the kind of life one can have making things versus being a Walmart greeter—working at it as a living, not a retirement booster.

And it gets worse.

Military-Civil Fusion

The idea that all this might have military applications is, of course, Chinese government policy. It is called military-civil fusion, and is a cornerstone of how China sees its Comprehensive National Power.

To Beijing, military-civil fusion means to take civilian technologies, R&D, and know-how and apply them to military use. It can also work in the other direction—for example, using military-grade spying to gain commercial advantage. The idea is to make the People's Liberation Army (PLA) the world's best by 2049—the one hundredth anniversary of the founding of the People's Republic of China.

To accomplish this, the PLA is expected to obtain the technologies and techniques from wherever they exist—including overseas—and by any means, fair or foul.

Here's an example of how it works in practice, and why we should worry. Both in terms of sophistication and scale, China's shipbuilding has become a dominant, world-class industry over the last three decades. And it's just as easy to build a civilian cargo ship as it is to build a naval warship.

U.S. shipbuilding? It has languished along with U.S. Navy ship numbers. Over the last decade, China launched five warships for each ship America has launched. The PLA Navy is already larger than the U.S. Navy. At this rate, by 2030 it will be half-again the size of the American fleet.

The Chinese military has reached a point where in certain circumstances—say, a fight close to the Chinese mainland or in the South China Sea—it could hammer American forces.

Even if the United States decided to rebuild its fleet (beyond just talking about it), it's not clear if we have the shipyards or the trained workers to do so (a by-product of China killing our manufacturing sector is that it also obliterates the know-how). So what happens in a war when ships get sunk and you need to build new ones, or to repair damaged ships but don't have the capacity to do so? You can't, so you don't.

The enemy usually doesn't wait around and let you rebuild your industry.

Adding insult to injury, foreign companies—Taiwanese, Japanese, European, and American—have helped the PRC shipbuilding industry develop by placing orders with Chinese yards. These Chinese yards set up with military-civil fusion in mind. We are killing our own capacity while subsidizing theirs. Or, in other words, exporting more of our Comprehensive National Power to China. China got us to make ourselves vulnerable. How bad is it?

It's bad.

A 2022 Department of Defense (DOD) report about the Chinese chokehold over key materials needed for the U.S. military is grim reading.

The report describes the U.S. military as dependent on Chinese suppliers in multiple areas including batteries, microelectronics, and metal casings (think bullets).

Just looking at batteries, China supplies finished batteries, but even more of the components to make batteries: 94 percent of lithium hydroxide, 76 percent of electrolyte, 70 percent of lithium carbonate, and 65 percent of anodes. And the United States' and U.S. military's shift to become green will, according to the report, "inadvertently grow Chinese dominance."[44]

The PRC is also aiming to strengthen its grip on microelectronics. The DOD report cites Chinese "purchases of key microelectronics companies and technology, IPR theft, and aggressive talent recruitment."[45] And worse, "Counterfeit microelectronics components have been identified in multiple DoD systems."[46]

China also has a lock on the metal casting industry. DOD admits to buying certain large cast and forged products from China, as well as "many machine tools and manufacturing systems on which the DoD is reliant."[47]

It's anybody's guess who thought such reliance—indeed, dependence—on a country that sees the United States as the enemy was a good thing.

It would be a good first step if we were just clear about the problem. One U.S. official commented a few years ago: "It would be a great improvement if we simply coordinated U.S.G. efforts under a common strategy and understanding. Instead, we have contradictory efforts within the U.S.G., if not the same department. Department of State demarches the PRC in the morning and gives its scientists a grant and visa in the afternoon."[48]

While the DOD issues a report about China's chokehold on critical materials, it also funds small start-ups and other companies through the Small Business Innovation Research (SBIR) program. There are cases of companies taking that DOD-funded technology and know-how to China—in some cases, working with outfits that support the People's Liberation Army and China's defense industry.

For example, Solarmer Energy, Inc., a U.S. developer of polymer solar cells, received SBIR and then dissolved its U.S.-based businesses and transferred its research, development, and intellectual property to a Beijing-based subsidiary. That subsidiary reportedly works with a Chinese government-run lab and has undertaken research with defense applications.[49]

We do make it easy. And so have the Japanese, Europeans, and others.

The PRC's success on the economic front and its massive economic growth over the last thirty years has, in turn, made possible the People's Liberation Army's stunning military growth. The Chinese communists did not have to choose between guns and butter. They could have both thanks to the United States (and others) willingly, and sometimes even eagerly, providing much of the necessary funds and technology the PLA needed.

And when you look beyond what's happening to U.S. businesses in China and Chinese activities in America, you can see things are even worse than they might seem.

BRI: Belt and Road Initiative or Bribery and Repression Initiative?

I have focused on China's direct economic warfare against the United States. But the PRC sees the fight against America as global, extending to every corner of the planet. That's where the Belt and Road Initiative comes in—as part of the PRC's attempt to translate economic power into political power—and eventually military power.

The Belt and Road Initiative (BRI), officially announced by the CCP in 2013, started as a strategy for Chinese infrastructure and commercial investments outside of China—everything from railways to ports to power plants and dams throughout much of the Indo-Pacific and in Latin America, Africa, Central Asia, and Europe.

The belt refers to land-based infrastructure and the road to maritime-related projects. There is now a digital component as well. Give Beijing time, and it'll find a way to justify lunar infrastructure as part of the BRI. It was incorporated into the constitution of China in 2017 and is intended to be completed in 2049. Remember that date?

It's basically a catchall, benign-sounding justification for engineering a world in which "all (belts and) roads lead to Beijing."

The BRI plays a prominent role in the CCP's effort to gain economic, political, and military dominance. It has both financial and strategic angles. If projects can make money and put otherwise idle Chinese labor (including prisoners) to work, that's good.

But if China can gain access, political influence, and create dependency in BRI nations—just like it does with the Americans—that is priceless, and financial results don't matter much.

As a small example, BRI investment in Greece may have played a role in the Greeks blocking a European Union resolution on China's human rights violations.[50]

Many of the BRI projects—ports and airfields, for example—have a "dual-use" aspect. They work just as well for commercial purposes as for military purposes. Look at where the CCP has developed port and airfield access around the globe, and the military "power projection" usefulness is obvious. Chinese officials and military officers regularly talk about it—it's not hidden.[51]

And often, there is a third use as well: illicit activity that pulls in local corrupt actors, tying them in even more closely with Beijing.

A good example of the Chinese regime successfully using BRI investment (and the promise of more) to gain strategic advantage is seen in the countries of Solomon Islands and Kiribati—known to Americans of a certain age as the sites of the bloody World War II battles of Guadalcanal

CHINA'S PORT-FOLIO
IN LATIN AMERICA

ENSENADA PORT

VERACRUZ PORT

MEXICO

FREE PORT

MANZANILLA PORT

SANTIAGO DE CUBA

LÁZARO CÁRDENAS PORT

EL SOMBRERO SATELLITE TRACKING STATION

CRISTOBAL PORT

VENEZUELA

LUEPA SATELLITE CONTROL GROUND STATION

COLOMBIA

BALBOA PORT

PERÚ

BRAZIL

CHANCAY PORT

AMACHUMA GROUND STATION

TUCANO GROUND STATION

BOLIVIA

LA GUARDIA GROUND STATION

PARANAGUÁ PORT

ATACAMA LARGE MILLIMETER ARRAY

ARGENTINA

CHINA-ARGENTINA RADIO TELESCOPE

SAN JUAN SATELLITE LASER RANGING

ESPACIO LEJANO STATION

SANTIAGO SATELLITE STATION

RÍO GALLEGOS GROUND STATION

ANTARCTIC LOGISTIC POLE USHUAIA

CHINA'S STRATEGIC INFRASTRUCTURE THROUGH PRC STATE-OWNED OR CONTROLLED COMPANIES

🌐 **CHINA PORT** CONSTRUCTION PROJECTS

✵ **CHINA SATELLITE** GROUND STATION

The data does not depict all of China's port projects or satellite stations but shows a snapshot of some of the major potential dual-use infrastructure in Latin America that could have military applications.

Advancing **freedom** and **security worldwide**

Research and **Design by the Center for a Secure Free Society** (SFS). Originally published in the VRIC Monitor No. 28 - October 2022

China's broad involvement in South American port development is nominally for commercial purposes but has obvious military uses as the PLA expands its power projection capabilities. Similar graphic depictions can be made in all parts of the world. *Map courtesy of Research and Design by the Center for a Secure Free Society (SFS). Originally published in the* VRIC Monitor *28, October 2022.*

and Tarawa. In 2019, as a result of opaque promises from Beijing, both nations de-recognized Taiwan.

Less than three years later, the PRC and the Solomon Islands government signed a deal that allows the People's Liberation Army (and People's Armed Police) to come and operate in the Solomons almost at will. This was a first and potentially installs the Chinese military in a location that threatens Australia and New Zealand and undercuts Washington's entire defense scheme in the Pacific.

Meanwhile, in Kiribati (1500 miles from Pearl Harbor) moves are afoot for China to refurbish an old American airfield on Canton Island. Officially, it is for tourism, but nobody really believes that. These BRI-inspired initiatives are worth any price to Beijing—and have gotten attention in Washington and Canberra. Not that they've figured out what to do about it.

China's BRI is often criticized as predatory or so-called "debt-trap diplomacy." And indeed, the deals usually are opaque, stacked in China's favor, way overpriced beyond what is fair or affordable, and rife with bribery of local officials and politicians.

But get closer, and the locals will often tell you: "What else are we supposed to do?" The president of a Central Pacific nation with close ties to the United States was overheard several years back wistfully commenting, "We don't do this by choice, but by necessity."[52]

And China takes time to lay the groundwork. Since long before BRI, Chinese commercial activity was literally everywhere out to the far ends of the Indo-Pacific region—even down to the corner shop level. For example, at least 80 percent of retail businesses in Tonga are run by recent Chinese arrivals.[53]

This general pattern is predictable if you pay attention.

Typically, the economic-to-political-to-strategic progression creates dependency and influence, especially among the elites—and no little resentment in the general population. Remember entropic warfare?

But by then, it's too late and hard to turn things around without great effort. And if the population gets too restive, the pro-PRC elites can look to their friends in Beijing, as the prime minister of Solomon Islands did, and ask for protection—from their own people. That's why, in many cases, the BRI can also stand for the Bribery and Repression Initiative.

There is an aggregate effect as well, as neighbors see what is going on and perceptions are shaped. China's economic clout not only reinforces its defense buildup, but it also helps feed the perception that China is a powerful country on the rise—the country that's destined to dominate. At the same time, America is projected as in decline or, worse, Americans just don't care.

This spurs some other nations to want to get closer—some to attach themselves to the future winner, some for self-preservation. Meanwhile, China's adversaries are worried and even intimidated.

One may not like what China has done on the economic warfare front but, you've got to admire their efforts. And to their credit, the Chinese are willing to go "out there" and do the hard work of commerce the way the Yankee trader of old used to. These days, U.S. businesses (and many diplomats as well) seem uninterested in places where the living isn't so easy (not enough five star hotels) and returns aren't guaranteed or big enough.

China's Belt and Road Initiative is another economic, political—and eventually military—windfall for the PRC that would have been impossible without waging successful economic warfare against the United States.

And Then Came Donald Trump

Trump and his team got Beijing's attention with tariffs, intellectual property theft prosecutions, and pressure on major Chinese companies such as Huawei and ZTE. Trump also tightened CFIUS restrictions on Chinese investment in the United States.

This crimped Chinese economic warfare strategy and cut the flow of life-blood foreign exchange (that is, U.S. dollars) to the CCP.

This was a sea change from when American companies and executives (and governments at all levels) were falling over themselves to attract Chinese money or to sell their corporate birthrights at a nice premium. Remember Chimerica and Chinafornia?

Just as importantly, more than a few Europeans, Indians, Australians, Japanese and others were quietly cheering Trump on.

Not surprisingly, both Xinhua and the Communist Party publication People's Daily ran an editorial declaring a "people's war" against the United States' efforts to fight back against China's economic warfare. Xi Jinping told his countrymen to prepare for a "new long march."[54] China's defense minister vowed at the Shangri La Dialogue to "fight to the very end" over Taiwan.[55]

Nearly every week, Chinese media produced a retired military officer or other commentators demanding Beijing skip the trade war and go straight to a real war with the United States.

Meanwhile, Wall Street, the U.S. Chamber of Commerce, and a constellation of the Great and Good (friends of China) also seemed to declare a people's war on Donald Trump—on China's behalf.

The Letter

By July 2019, the Trump administration's attempts to slow China's attack—and maybe even push back on Beijing—were starting to work. China felt threatened. And some in the United States didn't like it.

The *Washington Post* published a letter titled "China Is Not an Enemy."[56] It began:

> We are members of the scholarly, foreign policy, military and
> business communities, overwhelmingly from the United
> States, including many who have focused on Asia throughout

our professional careers. We are deeply concerned about the growing deterioration in U.S. relations with China, which we believe does not serve American or global interests.

It continued:

> We do not believe Beijing is an economic enemy or an existential national security threat that must be confronted in every sphere.... China's engagement in the international system is essential to the system's survival and to effective action on common problems such as climate change. The United States should encourage Chinese participation in new or modified global regimes in which rising powers have a greater voice.

It was signed by over a hundred of the elite.[57]

Here are some of the ones who at some point were on the payroll of the American taxpayer: Jeffrey A. Bader (former senior director for East Asia on National Security Council), Dennis J. Blasko (former U.S. Army attaché to China), Bernard Cole (former U.S. Navy captain), James F. Collins (former U.S. ambassador to the Russian Federation), Robert Einhorn (former assistant secretary of state for nonproliferation), Thomas Fingar (former deputy director of national intelligence for analysis), David F. Gordon (former director of Policy Planning at the U.S. State Department), Philip H. Gordon (former special assistant to the president and coordinator for the Middle East and assistant secretary of state for European and Eurasian Affairs), Morton H. Halperin, (former director of Policy Planning Staff at State Department), Lee Hamilton (former congressman), Clifford A. Hart Jr. (former U.S. consul general to Hong Kong and Macau), Paul Heer (former national intelligence officer for East Asia), Ambassador Carla A. Hills (former United States trade representative), Mickey Kantor (former secretary of commerce, U.S. trade representative), Albert Keidel (former deputy director of the Office of East Asian Nations at the Treasury Department), Herbert Levin (former staff member for China on National Security Council and Policy Planning Council), Kenneth Lieberthal (former Asia senior director, National Security Council), John McLaughlin (former deputy director and acting director of the CIA), Michael Nacht (former assistant secretary of defense for global strategic affairs), Daniel W. Piccuta (former deputy chief of mission and acting ambassador, Beijing), Thomas Pickering (former under secretary of state for political affairs; former U.S. ambassador to the United Nations from 1989 to 1992), Charles S. Robb (former U.S. senator, chairman of the East Asia sub-committee of the Senate Foreign Relations Committee and governor of Virginia), J. Stapleton Roy (former U.S. ambassador to China), David Shear, (former assistant secretary of defense, U.S. ambassador to Vietnam), Anne-Marie Slaughter (former director of policy planning, State Department), James Steinberg (former deputy secretary of state), Strobe Talbott, (former deputy secretary of state), Susan A. Thornton (former acting assistant secretary of state for East Asian and Pacific affairs), Daniel B. Wright, (former managing director for China and the Strategic Economic Dialogue, Treasury Department).

They should all go serve a tour of duty as a guidance counselor at a public high school in Baltimore.

Shortly after the letter was published, a virus came out of China, large sections of the United States committed economic suicide, and Joseph Biden became president.

China Won't Stop

The Biden administration shut down the China Initiative that the Trump administration put in place to go after Chinese spying, after civil rights groups called it racist.[58]

Team Biden also released five Chinese government-related researchers in scientific and high-tech fields (with military applications) who'd been caught lying about their government ties.[59] Why they did so is a mystery.

And the Biden administration gave up on energy independence. It shut down pipelines, cancelled oil leases, and scared the hell out of the oil industry. That's all a good thing from China's perspective. It increases unemployment and inflation, as well as America's dependence on Chinese solar manufacturing and China's supply of key minerals needed for manufacturing green technologies.

Cheap oil and gas under Trump helped bring manufacturing back to the United States by lowering the energy component of manufacturing. Team Biden gave this up.

But that doesn't mean Beijing will play nice. On the contrary. Economic warfare is in high gear.

The PRC response to the U.S. Trade Representative's 2022 report on Chinese intellectual property violations included a *Global Times* editorial that stated: "To China, the U.S. special 301 report is essentially just a piece of paper filled with the same baseless claims that can be easily discarded as a piece of trash."[60]

China is putting out another message as well, an even more familiar one. The PRC is promising reforms and further "opening up" and that this time they really mean it. Really.

In May 2022, according to Chinese state media, Premier Li Keqiang

reiterated China's stance that it will unswervingly expand its opening-up and continue to make the country a big market for the world and a hot spot for foreign investment.... Li said China is ready to work with other countries to safeguard the rules-based multilateral trading system with the World Trade Organization as the core.

China will adhere to free and fair trade, advance trade
and investment liberalization and facilitation, and keep the
stability and smooth flow of the global industrial and supply
chains to maintain international and regional peace, stability, development, and prosperity.... China will continue
to deepen administrative reforms, make clear the regulatory
rules that are transparent, stable, and predictable, further
liberalize market access, guarantee equal access of foreign
enterprises to areas that have opened up under the law, and
strictly protect intellectual property rights.[61]

Li also said Beijing wants to be "a hot spot for foreign investment"
and will work closely with foreign companies to make sure its rules are
predictable.[62]

Just as Charlie Brown keeps thinking Lucy will hold the football
for him to kick, there's no shortage of Americans who believe—or say
they believe—whatever drivel the CCP spouts. In 2022, Craig Allen,
president of the U.S.-China Business Council, said, "American businesses that we talk to are reasonably optimistic about the future."[63]

He said this in the middle of COVID lockdowns, during an assault
on the so-called private sector, while China was arming for war when
it faced no enemies, while it is committing genocide in Xinjiang, and
as it was smothering Hong Kong.

A few people on the U.S. side or in American industry aren't convinced by Chinese promises on the trade front anymore.

One American businessman who has worked in the PRC for several
decades said a couple years ago:

The U.S. weekend-only edition of *China Daily* is distrib-
uted in my hotel. I picked up a copy yesterday. The bold
print headline: "Xi Pledges Greater Opening-up." I can tell

you with all seriousness, this same headline has been blasted out at least once a quarter ever since I started in China. I have been in China or doing business with China for a total of 133 quarters. This means China has made 133 pledges to "greater opening up." Each opening up results in "first-time-ever" streamlined procedures and new promulgations. The rules change, but the result is always the same...the "house wins."[64]

This fellow was prescient, if not clairvoyant. Experience will do that.

Chinese negotiators will also promise (sort of) to stop stealing technology—which they say they don't steal anyway. But such theft is part of the Chinese modus operandi, and a cultural imperative. It's worth noting that Chinese companies steal from each other with equal enthusiasm.

But even if the U.S. side is properly skeptical, it also requires enforcing the agreement. That's the hard part.

In fact, it's probably impossible. You see, the Chinese Communist Party cannot live up to its promises and survive.

Besides requiring behavioral changes that might threaten CCP control, China won't allow Americans to dictate Chinese behavior. In fact, take U.S. demands—or even full Chinese compliance with WTO requirements—to their logical extreme, and you have regime change.

The CCP will drive the Chinese economy over a cliff before voluntarily letting that happen. That gives a clear sense of the importance of economic warfare to the Chinese regime. The PRC never had any intention of living up to its promises. If it had, the CCP would have collapsed. And in China, it's all about the Party and ensuring it is in control.

Their system is not like ours. You must keep this in mind to understand the Chinese threat, particularly on the economic and trade front.

Everything is for the benefit of the Chinese Communist Party. It may seem haphazard and chaotic in practice, but in the end, it is true.

What happened to Chinese e-commerce billionaire Jack Ma is a good example. He seemed to have broken free of CCP gravity, but not even close. None of these tycoons have. He crossed a line, and the Party (or someone powerful in the Party) brought him crashing down.

Since 1950, there has been *no era* of unbridled capitalism in China. There is no privatization in CCP China as it is defined in open economies. China is like the mafia: the Don owns part of your company—sometimes more than one Don.

The CCP sees China's four factors of production—land, labor, capital, and management (entrepreneurism in the United States)—as their personal assets to fashion into an economy and culture that preserves the basic mission of the Party: the perpetual rule of China. Unbridled capitalism as we know it is the threat to fulfilling this mission, as is a strong—or even functional—U.S. economy.

Too many Americans, in the ruling class at least, never saw—or wanted to see—commerce as a war. Not surprising, since a lot of them got rich from China—or at least selling out to China.

Professor William Hawkins states it well:

> Beijing did not just build itself up to become a manufacturing giant dominating global supply chains. It tore down American industry and gutted the blue-collar middle class. It was like the U.S. heartland had been subjected to strategic bombing, but it was actually more like sabotage by Chinese collaborators among American capitalists who became "transnational" as men without countries (except they actually were servicing one country without thinking about it). Our government cannot be indifferent to anything that

moves across our borders (in or out), because it is these movements that shape the balance of power.[65]

Of course, the United States has not collapsed yet—and there is still a lot of manufacturing going on. Meanwhile, Xi Jinping hasn't fully sanctions-proofed the PRC economy—though he's trying with the Made in China 2025 and dual circulation schemes. Xi is not there yet, and has a ways to go, though more importantly, Xi himself might think otherwise.

And, America has lost its relative advantage over the PRC. Three decades ago, the United States was the unquestioned superpower. Not anymore—and the U.S. government now refers to China as a peer competitor.

This comes with attendant loss of American political influence worldwide—and diminished self-confidence. Americans can still kick this addiction, but the clock is ticking, and if we don't manage it, PRC military and economic clout may one day overwhelm U.S. capability to resist.

Chinese economic warfare against us (and our friends) has been very successful. Indeed, probably one of the easiest wars ever fought.

And it won't stop until we stop it.

CHAPTER 12

Financial Warfare:
Defenestrating the U.S. Dollar

Beijing's political warfare campaign against the United States has had a run of successes on many fronts, including economic, as we just saw. But here's the good news. China still has one huge disadvantage—practically an Achilles' heel—in its faceoff with America.

Is it the People's Liberation Army's lack of combat experience? Or that the Chinese Navy's submarines are too noisy and easily tracked? Maybe it's the inherent brittleness in any ruthless one-party dictatorship? Perhaps the onrushing demographic disaster owing to the Chinese Communist Party's one-child policy? Or maybe the threat of a U.S. embargo on technology exports to China?

These are all serious problems for the People's Republic of China, and we'll get to how to leverage them in order to defend ourselves. But China's biggest challenge is, in fact, a paper problem—that is, the Chinese currency, the yuan, also known as the renminbi (RMB).

Specifically, the yuan is not freely convertible. In other words, it is not very useful outside of China. So for almost anything the PRC needs to obtain from overseas, it has to pay in American dollars, euros, yen, Swiss francs, or some other convertible currency.

What is convertible currency? In simple terms, you can buy or sell any amount you want on the currency market at any time without needing permission from any monetary authorities. Bottom line—and the ultimate test—is, you can take it somewhere other than the country that issued the money, and people will accept it rather than ask you to change it into U.S. dollars.

Accept Chinese yuan for payment—say, of a house in Los Angeles—and the seller will find it hard to exchange it for U.S. dollars or the like. Holding yuan is a few steps removed from holding Monopoly money.

Another way to think of this is to consider the scrip at a school carnival. You can use it to go on the rides, play games, or buy popcorn. But leave school grounds and go to the nearest 7-11, and the cashier will want real money.

In 2005, Chinese official Bo Xilai remarked that if China wanted to buy a plane, it had to sell eight hundred million t-shirts to buy one Airbus A380.[1]

Bo was talking about an Airbus, but the same idea applies to the iron ore China buys from Australia to build PLA Navy ships. To buy the things it needs from overseas, the PRC has to earn foreign exchange—or get it some other way.

Not surprisingly, the Chinese Communist Party is desperately trying to displace the U.S. dollar as the world's reserve currency—the currency used by much of the world for international trade and finance. This is why the PRC goes to great lengths to talk up its own currency—and tries to to get other nations to accept it. Once that happens, it doesn't matter if the United States threatens to cut off access to U.S. dollars, or even if it *does* cut off the flow of dollars.

In some respects, the dollar is America's most, if not last, powerful tool for applying pressure against Beijing. Yet the Biden administration and previous administrations (with congressional help) have done their best to debase the currency. If the Chinese regime makes enough progress on this front, the United States will not even be able to fund its own defense.

Beijing is also glad to see the United States handling its own finances in a way that gives drunken sailors a bad name. China doesn't mind helping the U.S. government along.

To understand Chinese behavior and objectives when it comes to financial warfare, let's consider China's foreign exchange dilemma in more detail.

Foreign Exchange Dilemma

Here's Xi Jinping's problem: as explained, anything China needs from overseas—food, oil, iron ore, and technology—requires dollars, although convertible euros, yen, and sterling will do.

And that's only for the imported necessities. China's global ambitions also require convertible currency. So, to fund Belt and Road projects, buy foreign technology and companies, or even to buy foreign countries (or their leaders), Beijing must pay in currency somebody will accept.

The same goes for operating PRC embassies, paying off dollar bonds, or covering the debts of overextended tycoons. Harvard professors with under-the-table contracts with China's Thousand Talents Program demand payment in dollars—and certainly not the supposedly convertible "offshore yuan."[2] (The "offshore yuan" is a sort of foreigner-friendly yuan, but nobody is fooled.)

Don't forget that the Chinese domestic economy faces the same problems as any economy—even if some Westerners think China is exempt since the CCP plays the long game and possesses the wisdom of the Orient.

When people aren't working, and shops and factories are shuttered, that spells trouble just as much in China as in the United States of America.

Chinese authorities can print yuan, reduce bank reserve requirements, offer subsidies, lower interest rates, order repayment moratoriums, and the like. But even if Beijing gives money away, it still must worry about unemployment, inflation (too much money chasing too few goods), and too much debt at all levels, from individuals to the central government.

If this gets out of control, people lose confidence in the economy, which translates into loss of confidence in Chinese Communist Party leadership and the system itself. Lose enough confidence, and public unrest becomes likely. In the last few years, that discontent has already been stoked by the brutality, dishonesty, and incompetence of the CCP response to the Wuhan virus outbreak and more, including an imploding domestic real estate market.

That's all bad enough. But without a convertible currency, it's even worse. Beijing can't just print dollars or euros (legally, at least). It has to earn them. So how does China earn foreign exchange (FX)?

The main ways: It exports products and gets paid in convertible currency. Or it attracts foreign direct investment as foreigners pour money (convertible currency) into the country to invest or to set up businesses. Some of those that have helped China with both are Apple, Nike, Boeing, General Electric, Volkswagen, Dell Computer, and Microsoft, and a very long list of others. Beijing also pretends that it's still a developing country—making it eligible for preferential treatment and the equivalent of financial aid from other countries and international organizations.

Other methods of earning foreign exchange include buying foreign companies or setting up businesses overseas—and getting paid in convertible currency. These seem like win-wins, but many Chinese businessmen earning dollars overseas are keen to keep their money out of China and out of the hands of the CCP.

So one sees Xi's problem: if China isn't exporting, it's not earning dollars (or other real money). And if the PRC looks chaotic, vindictive, or prone to future biological disasters, foreign businesses will move out, fully or partially. Or they will avoid future investment in China. All this adds up—and Beijing is left without enough foreign exchange to buy what it needs—or to do what it wants.

This does make the draconian zero-COVID crackdowns in China and Hong Kong look like an act of economic self-harm by the CCP. Foreign business leaders can overlook just about any CCP affront or atrocity, but for some, like Apple,[3] zero-COVID was a bridge too far.

Too Little FX

But doesn't the PRC have plenty of foreign exchange?

No, it doesn't. Beijing's $3 trillion in foreign exchange holdings isn't much. It used to have $4 trillion, but it blew through a trillion overnight in 2015 when the Chinese stock markets—using the term "markets" loosely—crashed.[4] One more such disaster and China's foreign exchange cushion will disappear.

There have always been telltale signs of Beijing having too little foreign exchange.

For example, Chinese citizens can only legally export the equivalent of fifty thousand U.S. dollars a year. Exchange limits aren't surprising given that moving one's wealth out of the country—by hook or by crook—has been a national sport in China for the last thirty years. If Beijing removed exchange controls, China's foreign exchange vault would soon empty out.

Even, or better said, *especially* as the ruling elite are leading the pack in trying to move their money out of China. Indeed, it might help if the top one hundred Party leaders sold their overseas real estate, emptied their bank accounts, and brought it all home.

It's estimated that the Chinese have $20 trillion stashed overseas, where the CCP can't get it.[5]

A notable feature of the PRC's Belt and Road Initiative and the Asian Infrastructure Investment Bank is Beijing's efforts to have other countries provide the funding—not exactly what a country flush with foreign exchange does.

Furthermore, foreign companies in the PRC cannot exchange their earnings into dollars without permission from the Chinese government—the State Administration of Foreign Exchange (SAFE)—a point routinely overlooked by people who should know better. (All currency going into China goes via SAFE, where it is turned into yuan. And all yuan going out of China also goes via SAFE, where it is turned into foreign currency. SAFE decides who gets what.)

As an American businessman with four decades in the China market noted to me, "China does not have nearly the pool of FX available to make good if 50 percent of the foreign investment community wanted to cash in their investments in 2020. As long as China's currency is a controlled currency and not freely convertible, investing in China is contributing to a Ponzi scheme."[6]

Indeed, it's not at all unusual for a foreign company to be denied permission to remove its money from China (in currency the company wants, at least).

In theory, Beijing should have to make some tough choices. The CCP can have the world's largest navy and rocket force *or* a string of bases around the world *or* money-losing Belt and Road projects *or* a world-class health care system and flush toilets for the five hundred million citizens currently lacking them. Or it can do something about the five hundred million Chinese who live on five dollars a day.

"Beijing pretends to be richer than it is," a long-time China analyst commented. "They've been taking the fake-it-'til-you-make-it path. China's GDP simply doesn't support the totality of the enormous projects they've committed themselves to."[7]

"They can't afford it all at once," the analyst explained, "and that's what they tried to do on the theory that it would all work itself out once they commanded the world. They are on a thin string, and the Wuhan virus is wickedly expensive."[8] And zero-COVID policies that disrupt the economy are making things even worse.

When you're not exporting, you're not earning. And when foreign companies are having second thoughts at last, that's even more reason to worry about the FX flow.

Things would be a lot grimmer for the Chinese Communist Party on the foreign exchange front, and the CCP would be forced to change its behavior for the better, were it not for longstanding help from an unlikely source.

First, Western financial firms are rushing to pour money—other people's money, at least—into China, and have been for decades. A few recent examples show how it works.

In early 2019, before the Wuhan virus struck, Morgan Stanley Capital International (MSCI) increased its weighting of Chinese stocks.[9] Tens of billions of dollars worth of overseas money—convertible currency—flowed into PRC coffers.

The Bloomberg Barclays Global Aggregate Index did something similar for the Chinese bond market, and the PRC got another $100 billion-plus in convertible currency.[10] This is a lot of money, and also "real" money. There is always more on the way.

In 2021, BlackRock's research unit advised investors to boost their exposure to China by two to three times—and this after a government stilettoing of major Chinese tech firms that reduced their value by $2 trillion, and relations between Washington and Beijing turned nasty.[11]

The chief investment strategist of BlackRock Investment Institute remarked, apparently without irony: "Think of this journey as one step forward, half a step back.... It's not about eliminating risks, it's about, are you being rewarded for the risks? We believe we are being compensated."[12] (It is unclear who the "we" are.)

It's perhaps no coincidence that BlackRock, the largest asset manager in the world, had recently been approved as the first foreign asset manager to start a wholly-owned mutual fund operation in the PRC.[13]

But consider the financial benefits and risks to investors in the China market—and the payoff from providing the Chinese Communist Party with foreign exchange that it deploys against the United States.

Between its inception at the end of 1992 and August 31, 2021, the MSCI China stock index has returned an average of 2.2 percent annually, including dividends.[14] Over the same period, the MSCI Emerging Markets index grew 7.8 percent annually; the S&P 500, 10.7 percent.[15] That covers a nearly thirty-year period in which China's economy often grew by at least 10 percent a year.[16] Nevertheless, you would have earned much better returns on U.S. Treasury securities than on Chinese stocks. Maybe China, which holds more than $1 trillion in U.S. Treasuries, knew something that Wall Street didn't.

Investing in the PRC gets you worse returns than super-safe Treasuries while having more risk than the worst junk bonds. Yes, somebody is making money in China, but it's never passive foreign investors, ever. It's a law of nature. To put that in perspective, if you had put $10K into the PRC when MSCI started in 1992, it would be worth $19K today. If you had put that $10K into a generic S&P 500 index fund, it would be worth $220K today. Think of the missing $200K as the CCP's tax on suckers.

Second, the government sector in the United States has piled on. At the national level, the Thrift Savings Program (TSP) has moved savings of retirees (many of them ex-military) into the China market. It was forced to pull back by President Trump a few years ago, but the financial gang is persistent, and they are still trying to get TSP money into China.

At the state level, in California, CalPERS, the country's largest public employee retirement system, has gone into China. CalPERS even dispatched a top executive to work with the PRC's State Administration of Foreign Exchange (SAFE) for several years. The executive quietly resigned from CalPERS after a fuss was raised.[17]

When U.S. senators and representatives challenge the wisdom (and the morality) of funding the CCP—an aggressive, capricious dictatorship that seeks to displace, if not dominate, the United States—the financial industry responds with the rhetorical equivalent of an extended middle finger.

U.S. commercial firms, big and small, have flocked to China for supposedly cheap manufacturing for export back to the United States. Others believe they will succeed in selling their products and services in the China market, even over the long-term. This all provides the Chinese Communist Party with convertible foreign exchange.

It's as if Wall Street and American commercial firms had done business with Hitler's regime, helping it develop into a powerful military that planned to attack our allies (and us). That's not even to mention the immorality of dealing with a regime whose barbarities included sending its citizens to concentration camps.

Unfortunately, Wall Street and U.S. industry did exactly that—right up until the Nazis declared war on the United States. Some presumably stopped only because they could no longer cash their checks.

The Americans and other foreigners pouring convertible currency into the PRC are allowing the Chinese Communist Party to paper over huge fissures in the PRC, its economy, and its society.

We are buying them time as they try to fix their weakness. Beijing recognizes the danger and is trying to do something about it.

For one thing, Beijing uses its influence to cheat. It persuaded the International Monetary Fund (IMF) to include the yuan in the IMF's basket of currencies that central banks are required to hold in 2016—and can claim to have gotten the IMF's seal of approval.[18]

A few years ago, S&P Global Ratings was giving high ratings to Chinese companies—in my opinion, so it wouldn't offend the CCP and lose the S&P business in China.[19]

And the New York Stock Exchange listed Chinese companies even though they didn't qualify under disclosure rules enforced for everybody else.[20] That raised foreign exchange for the CCP. A lot of it.

There has also been some success (or at least rumored success) at persuading the Saudis to accept payment for oil in yuan instead of U.S. dollars.[21]

The Russian ruble-yuan trade has boomed since the Russians invaded Ukraine in February 2022 and the United States imposed financial sanctions on the Russians, largely excluding the nation from using U.S. dollars.

The PRC has only made limited progress in internationalizing the yuan and removing vulnerability that comes with needing dollars and other convertible currencies to operate. This is largely because there simply isn't enough trust in the government behind the yuan—in other words, the Chinese Communist Party.

The Chinese have been pushing so-called digital yuan since at least 2014 and hope that it will expand use and acceptance of the yuan overseas. But there's more to it than that for the Chinese Communist Party—it will be one more tool of social control and intimidation.

A report by the Center for New American Security (CNAS) noted: "The [digital yuan] will allow for real-time or near-real-time financial surveillance of all users' transactions.... It is a giant leap for the CCP's control and influence in Chinese society."[22]

The report added: "Anyone using a digital yuan pretty much conceded his or her financial privacy directly to the Chinese government" and has allowed his or her movement to be tracked.[23]

Displease the Chinese Communist Party and your account freezes or disappears, of course. China would like to have the digital yuan someday link up with a digital dollar, though we aren't there yet. One imagines that certain parts of the American ruling class like the idea of a digital dollar for the same reasons the CCP likes the digital yuan.

Hurting the United States

Chinese financial warriors must like what they see the Americans doing to themselves. The COVID-19 pandemic out of Wuhan led to massive U.S. government spending that effectively debases the dollar.

Resulting inflation is officially 8 percent as of mid-2022, but probably higher. Inflation? The PRC loves it. Many historians argue that inflation was one of the things that brought down the Kuomintang (KMT) government in the late 1940s and aided the communist victory in the Chinese Civil War.

Inflation shrinks the U.S. defense budget. Eight hundred fifty billion dollars might seem like a lot of money, but it's not, and inflation takes a nice chunk from it, affecting everything from hardware and weapons procurement to training and exercise time. This all impacts the military's ability to fight an actual war.

Beijing is also glad to see (and encourage) America to relinquish its short-lived energy independence (after a brief period during the Trump administration) and move for green energies—before the bugs are worked out. This all adds to inflation, hurts the economy, and causes political unrest. And U.S. oil dependence on Saudis and other less-than-democratic suppliers, such as Iran and Venezuela, restrains Washington's political and military room for maneuver.

Nowadays, the United States has to spend money on imported oil. That's money that either adds to debt or doesn't go to things like the U.S. military.

China likes what it sees—and is glad to help move things along.

Global Times reported in 2021 that according to Fudan University professor Shen Yi, "the US does not have enough resources to engage in a full-scale collision with China on the Taiwan question, let alone a showdown—the high inflation in the US, soaring debt, and a hallow [sic] treasury that needs to be filled by stealing other countries money, all show that the US, if rational, has no reason to intensify contradictions with China."[24]

It's worth mentioning Chinese holdings of U.S. Treasuries. Sometimes they're brought up as a potential weapon China can use against the United States. Yes and no. They would be most effectively used if Beijing unloaded them suddenly in conjunction with the start of a kinetic war as part of the shock effect. And they might as well do that. Once the shooting starts, the United States isn't going to be paying the PRC interest on anything.

In the meantime, China can continue to count on the Americans to keep funding the CCP with its foreign currency needs.

A headline in *China Daily* shortly after the Russian invasion of Ukraine declared: "Global Investors Keep Big Bet on [Chinese] A Shares."[25]

One experienced American observer noted:

> There has been a noticeable uptick in these type of *China Daily* articles since [the invasion].... The propaganda lights must be on all night long pumping this stuff out to try and persuade American talking heads, some U.S. state governors, Wall Street

types, any academic at an American university founded before
1820, and retirement funds like the California Teachers
Association that China is a hot market, and [a] safe harbor for
USD investment…taken by the State Administration for
Foreign Exchange [SAFE] when their investment arrives at the
China border to be exchanged into RMB—that are then for-
warded to the intended investment target. What happens to
the USD SAFE has in its vault? It is used to purchase American
farmland in Iowa. Is this a wonderful world or what?[26]

Another headline in the *People's Daily* in late 2021 further sug-
gested China knows how to play to its audience and its foreign exchange:
"Bank of China Sustainable Bonds Valued at USD 2.2 Billion Listed in
London."[27]

Translation: China is playing to the greenies in their latest effort to
secure foreign exchange. For a lot of people around the world, a new
era of Green China is in, and a villainous America that gained its wealth
and power by plundering the environment is out.

China's currency problem is a major weakness. If we were smart,
that would be one for the places we'd hit. And hard.

CHAPTER 13

Cyber Warfare:
Hacking through American Defenses

The PRC has already gone to work, looting U.S. government and private industry networks of strategic data (including biometrics) and sector-dominating trade secrets. Yet the PRC has escaped almost entirely unscathed, even though the Americans know who did it—and still does it. At most, there's a stern talking-to and naming and shaming (as if that works with the Chinese Communist Party.)

Is it really that bad? Yes.

The U.S. government's Cybersecurity and Infrastructure Agency (CISA) laid things out clearly in 2021:

> The Chinese government—officially known as the People's Republic of China (PRC)—engages in malicious cyber activities to pursue its national interests. Malicious cyber activities attributed to the Chinese government targeted, and continue

to target, a variety of industries and organizations in the United States, including healthcare, financial services, defense industrial base, energy, government facilities, chemical, critical manufacturing (including automotive and aerospace), communications, IT (including managed service providers), international trade, education, video gaming, faith-based organizations, and law firms.[1]

That's pretty much everything.

And it is not just vacuuming up secrets and information: the Chinese Communist Party uses cyber as an offensive weapon.

The U.S. director of national intelligence noted in 2021, "China presents a prolific and effective cyber-espionage threat, possesses substantial cyber-attack capabilities, and presents a growing influence threat.... China can launch cyber attacks that, at a minimum, can cause localized, temporary disruptions to critical infrastructure within the United States."[2]

Quest for Virtual Dominance

This has all presumably been going on since Westerners started using computers. We could see that focus in the 1970s, when China was first opening up to larger educational exchanges with the West. With Canada, for instance, while many Canadians went to China to learn language and culture, the vast majority of the Chinese heading to Canadian universities were studying science and technology.

PRC cyber theft of trade secrets and proprietary information is one method to leap over stages and help the Chinese economy close the gap with advanced nations. But there's also an aspect of achieving commercial dominance that, in turn, leads to political dominance. Additionally, there's an aim to sanctions-proof the Chinese economy—and ideally allow the PRC to withhold technology and to sanction other nations.

In 2014, Xi Jinping spoke on this to a group of prominent scientists and engineers: "Only if core technologies are in our own hands can we truly hold the initiative in competition and development. Only then can we fundamentally ensure our national economic security, defense security, and other aspects of security."[3]

There's a long list of examples of Chinese cyber warfare for commercial and defense advantage, but I'll just give you a flavor of things.

Keep in mind that these are only cases where the hacker has been caught or exposed—the proverbial tip of the iceberg. Also remember that in 2015, President Obama and Xi Jinping agreed that neither side would conduct cyber espionage against commercial targets.[4] It's hard to imagine Xi didn't have his fingers crossed, or he would have had he not been pinching himself to keep from breaking out laughing.

Commercial (Often Dual-Use) Secrets

According to the FBI report *China: The Risk to Corporate America*, "The annual cost to the U.S. economy of counterfeit goods, pirated software, and theft of trade secrets is between $225 billion and $600 billion."[5]

What does that look like? It looks like the following:

Winnti (2022)

In 2022, Bill Gertz of the *Washington Times* reported on Operation Cuckoo Bee, in which the cybersecurity firm Cybereason exposed a Chinese government-backed commercial espionage operation that ran undetected from 2019 to 2021.[6]

The hacking group, Winnti, existed since at least 2010 and had earlier been implicated in attacks on U.S. companies including Google and Yahoo.[7]

Winnti is described as "an umbrella group comprised of multiple threat actors under the control of Chinese intelligence organizations, including the Ministry of State Security (MSS)."[8]

The hackers pilfered computer networks belonging to companies in North America, Europe, and Asia. They stole "hundreds of gigabytes from more than 30 global organizations" involved in defense, energy, aerospace, pharmaceutical, and biotech.[9] What was taken? Gertz says, "Sensitive documents, blueprints, diagrams, formulas and manufacturing-related know-how."[10]

The targeted technologies align with PRC government lists of priority technologies—as we previously saw, for example, in the government's Made in China 2025 scheme.[11] And some of the technologies are dual-use with military applications. Remember military-civil fusion?

Hainan State Security Department

In July 2021, the U.S. Department of Justice announced the indictment of four Chinese nationals (still in China) for cyber theft of trade secrets from U.S. companies (and several other foreign companies) as well as universities and government entities from 2011 to 2018.[12] Three of the suspects were Hainan State Security Department (HSSD) officers.[13] The HSSD is an arm of the PRC's Ministry of State Security.

The conspirators worked closely with Chinese universities and targeted a wide range of technologies (once again, potentially dual-use) in fields such as aviation, defense, health care, biopharmaceuticals, submersibles and autonomous vehicles, commercial aircraft servicing, and genetic-sequencing technology.[14] The hackers also stole proprietary information to give Chinese state-owned companies an advantage in bidding on contracts such as high-speed rail.[15]

MSS and the Microsoft Exchange Hack

In July 2021, the Biden administration, along with Canada, Britain, and the EU, publicly accused the People's Republic of China and the Ministry of State Security of carrying out a massive hack of the Microsoft Exchange email server.[16] In addition to intellectual property theft and espionage, the wrongdoing included ransomware attacks.[17] That surprised U.S. officials, but it demonstrated MSS's use of contract criminal hackers and giving them some leeway. Or as likely, splitting the take with the hackers.

True to form, when asked for comment, the Chinese embassy in Washington replied: "The U.S. has repeatedly made groundless attacks and malicious smear against China on cybersecurity. Now this is just another old trick, with nothing new in it." The embassy added that China is " a severe victim of the U.S. cyber theft, eavesdropping and surveillance."[18]

Also true to form, the United States did not announce sanctions against the PRC for the Microsoft Exchange hack. A forceful condemnation would do.

Chinese MSS and Coronavirus Vaccines

In July 2020, the Department of Justice indicted two Chinese hackers for a decade-long hacking operation that included reconnaissance against U.S. companies working on coronavirus vaccines and treatments.[19] According to the indictment, the two hackers cooperated with a Ministry of State Security agent from Guangdong.[20]

The hackers also allegedly obtained and provided the MSS officer with the email accounts and passwords of a Hong Kong protest organizer, a Christian pastor in China, and another pro-democracy dissident.[21]

People's Liberation Army versus U.S. Companies and a Labor Union

In 2014, the Department of Justice charged five Chinese People's Liberation Army (PLA) members with hacking U.S. companies and one

American labor union for commercial advantage from 2006 to 2014.[22] The hackers reportedly belonged to the Third Department, Unit 61398 in Shanghai—a PLA cyber espionage unit.[23]

Westinghouse, one of the victims, was doing business in China. The hackers stole technical designs and emails of the company's internal discussions concerning its local Chinese partner—a state-owned enterprise.[24]

Another well-known American company, U.S. Steel, was at the time involved in a dispute with Chinese steel companies, including a particular state-owned enterprise. The hackers aimed to access U.S. Steel networks and to make off with confidential information useful to the Chinese side. They succeeded.[25]

In 2012, the hackers targeted an American solar power manufacturer, SolarWorld, for destruction. At the time, the U.S. Commerce Department had determined that Chinese solar product manufacturers were dumping products in the U.S. market. The Chinese hackers went after SolarWorld's financial details, manufacturing secrets, costs, and attorney-client discussions related to the ongoing trade dispute over dumping. The indictment noted that a Chinese competitor would be able to attack SolarWorld's business operations using this information.[26]

Now, a decade later, Chinese companies dominate the global solar products manufacturing business—with just a few beleaguered American producers left. Adding insult to economic injury, U.S. solar installers are lobbying the U.S. government to play nice with Chinese manufacturers and drop investigations into their unfair trade practices.

As for the labor union, the Allied Industrial and Service Workers International Union had brought charges of unfair trade practices against two Chinese industries. The hackers broke into the union networks and stole emails detailing the union's strategies and discussions regarding the trade disputes.[27]

Hacking U.S. Military Technology

The People's Republic of China's computer hackers have also done well against U.S. military secrets.

Submarine Technology

In 2018, the *Washington Post* reported Chinese hackers penetrated a U.S. Navy contractor supporting the Naval Undersea Warfare Naval Center in Newport, Rhode Island, and, over the course of two months, made off with 614 gigabytes of material related to a sensitive program known as Sea Dragon.[28] The *Washington Post* even withheld some of the details about the Sea Dragon program—at the U.S. Navy's request.[29]

If even the *Washington Post* was willing to keep something secret, it gives a sense of how serious the matter was.

The program involved a new submarine-launched missile. According to the *Washington Post* story, the hackers obtained sensitive information about "signals and sensor data, submarine radio room information related to cryptographic system, and the Navy submarine development unit's electronic warfare library."[30]

The U.S. submarine fleet has long been America's ace in the hole, even as the People's Liberation Army has gradually closed the capability gap with U.S. forces. Senator Jack Reed (D-RI), a longtime defense stalwart in Congress, declared it "very serious."[31]

Indeed.

Aircraft: C-17 Transport

Starting in 2009, a Chinese aerospace consultant named Su Bin, living in Vancouver, Canada, worked with two Chinese military officers in China to carry out a sophisticated hacking scheme to obtain protected technical details about Boeing's C-17 strategic transport.[32] The C-17, with development costs estimated at $3.4 billion, is now a mainstay of the United States and allies such as Australia, Britain, and EU nations.[33]

The indictment charges that Su stole 630,000 files from Boeing's system, or sixty-five gigabytes worth of data. This included schematics, details of wings and fuselage measurements, wiring systems, flight test data, and other key information.[34]

An intercepted report written by the hackers stated that "experts inside China have a high opinion" about the stolen information and that it was "the first [time] seen in the country."[35]

It is perhaps no coincidence that the PLA Air Force's Y-20 transport resembles the C-17. And it was presumably developed for a lot less than $3.4 billion, in a much shorter time frame, and with less trial and error required.

Su also reportedly obtained information on U.S. F-22 and F-35 fighter jets. The hackers boasted of collecting information on a drone development project, too.

There is one big difference in this case from most others. The Feds got their hands on Su. He was arrested in Canada, extradited, and he pled guilty before trial. He was sentenced to (only) four years in prison. Presumably, he'll have something nice waiting for him when he gets out if he returns to China.

Stealth Technology: The F-35 Hack

The F-35 is the U.S. military's most advanced fifth-generation fighter and is considered the world's best.

Starting around 2007, Chinese hackers with the People's Liberation Army's technical Reconnaissance Bureau, a part of the PLA's Third Department, got into Lockheed's networks and stole classified information about the F-35 stealth fighter aircraft.[36]

The stolen information included the design and manufacturing techniques that give the aircraft its stealth characteristics. The Chinese appear to have used the hacked details to develop their own fighters—the J-20 and the J-31 (which particularly resembles the F-35). According to a Bloomberg report, Lin Zuomin, the chairman of AVIC, the Chinese company that builds the J-31—you might remember AVIC from the economics chapter and the description of it buying up important U.S. technology—chuckled that the J-31 is superior to the F-35.[37] That's debatable but nonetheless raises hackles.

Besides successfully exploiting the F-35, the PLA hackers are also thought to have obtained controlled details about the U.S. Air Force's F-22 fighter, B-2 stealth bomber, space-based lasers, missile navigation and tracking systems, and nuclear submarine and anti-air missile designs.[38]

Beyond the specifics of the hacking incidents, the magnitude of just this part of the PRC's cyber warfare effort is breathtaking.

A Department of Defense review, apparently conducted into the F-35 hack, also noted that Chinese hackers had gone after other programs as well. *The Diplomat* reports "at least 30,000 hacking incidents, more than 500 significant intrusions in DoD systems, at least 1600 DoD computers penetrated, and more than 600,000 user accounts compromised, in addition to over 300,000 user ID/passwords and 33,000 U.S. Air Force officer records compromised."[39]

The Defense Department report stated that the hacker got "many terabytes" of information—reportedly enough to fill up "five Libraries of Congress."[40] And this is only what Defense knew about.

Getting Ready for Kinetic Hacks: Gas Pipelines, Internet, and Satellites

From 2011 to 2013, Chinese hackers targeted 23 U.S. natural gas pipeline companies, of which "13 were confirmed compromises, 3 were near misses, and 7 had an unknown depth of intrusion."[41] In several cases, the hackers obtained supervisory control over the pipeline. In other words, they controlled them.

The U.S. authorities assessed that the PRC hackers were "Chinese state-sponsored actors" and were aiming to develop the capability to conduct attacks on U.S. gas pipelines in the future.[42] This was not a case of intellectual property theft according to the FBI and CISA.[43]

The Internet

In 2021, the U.S. Federal Communications Commission (FCC) ordered China Telecom (Americas)—a state-owned company despite claims to the contrary—to shut down its operations in the United States.[44] This should have happened sooner.

For over a decade, China Telecom had been periodically re-routing internet traffic to the People's Republic of China. This included traffic in the United States and traffic passing through the United States. The company also took over Canadian internet traffic.[45]

This was first detected on April 8, 2010, when China Telecom took over 15 percent of the internet traffic for eighteen minutes. This included U.S. government (.gov) and military (.mil) websites. According to experts, this was a test run for internet traffic manipulation.[46]

China Telecom's internet re-routing activities continued over the following years for "days, weeks, and months," according to researchers Dr. Chris Demchak and Dr. Yuval Shavitt. They explain, "While one may argue such attacks can always be explained by normal [internet] behavior, these in particular suggest malicious intent, precisely because of their unusual transit characteristics—namely the lengthened routes and the abnormal durations."[47]

Regarding one particular event that lasted for two hours, Oracle's head of internet analysis similarly concluded, "Two hours is a long time for a routing leak of this magnitude to stay in circulation, degrading global communications."[48]

What's the benefit of grabbing the internet, especially if much of the haul is encrypted? China can store it, examine it for vulnerabilities, and have it available in the future when new exploitation methods become available.

The U.S. government agreed with the private researchers. The FCC's revocation order cited Chinese government control over China Telecom and the national security risks posed by allowing the Chinese government to "access, store, disrupt, and /or misroute U.S. communications" for espionage and "other harmful activities against the United States."[49]

Satellites

In 2018, security researchers at Symantec reported that a hacking attack originating from computers in the People's Republic of China had burrowed deeply into satellite companies and defense and telecom companies in the United States and Southeast Asia.[50]

Particularly troubling, Symantec said the hacking effort seemed to aim at intercepting civilian and military communications. The hackers reportedly targeted computers that operated the satellites—and could have changed their positions and orbits.[51]

Symantec's technical director remarked that "[d]isruption to satellites could leave civilian as well as military installations subject to huge [real world] disruptions."[52]

That's putting it mildly, given the U.S. military's reliance on satellites for commutations, targeting, and surveillance—say, to give advance notice of a missile headed our way.

One notes fairly that there are a number of other parts of the U.S. energy, transportation, agricultural, communications, and financial infrastructures, and even the consumer "internet of things" that are similarly vulnerable to outside penetration and interference.

The Chinese Communist Party is getting ready for the day the shooting war starts.

One almost doesn't wish to think about it other than to hope the United States can do the same thing to them.

Once again, in the bad news category: around 2014, the U.S. Office of Personnel Management was hacked by the Chinese. The hackers made off with the personnel records of around twenty-two million Americans holding security clearances. The records included the Standard Form 86 that is filled out when applying for a clearance; it includes extremely detailed—and sometimes embarrassing—personal information.[53]

Some potential uses an unfriendly government might have for this information: targeting for recruitment or blackmail, or even identifying covert government employees of U.S. intelligence agencies. The director of national intelligence, James Clapper, stated that China was a leading suspect, but the Obama administration refused to declare that the PRC was behind the hack.[54] For Beijing, it was a good day's work. No punishment at all. One more example of the Americans acting out the battered wife syndrome: the victim stays quiet, and there is no downside for the perpetrator.

The United States is under incessant cyber attack from the PRC (and others who mean us ill).

It's best to look at this as one front in the broader political warfare—or unrestricted warfare that the Chinese have been conducting for decades.

Note how Chinese cyber efforts reinforce the PRC's economic and trade warfare while improving kinetic capabilities—not to mention cyber being a potent weapon in the event of armed conflict, when a millisecond delay in response can lose you the battle, if not the war.

There is a psychological warfare angle to cyber warfare as well. It is demoralizing, for example, when the United States introduces a new advanced weapon, and then, a short while later, the Chinese roll out something that looks like its twin, or at least a first cousin. It also creates a paranoia that the Chinese are reading everything.

Influence and Control

The use of the online domain for influence and control is clear within China. The Chinese Communist Party uses cyber warfare against its own citizens. There is the Great Firewall and thoroughgoing censorship of the PRC Internet and social media—to include the 50 Cent Army.[55] Punishment is rapidly meted out to citizens with incorrect thoughts.

This is made explicit in its 2017 Cybersecurity Law. For example, Article 12 says:

> Any person and organization using networks…must not use the Internet to engage in activities endangering national security, national honor, and national interests; they must not incite subversion of national sovereignty, overturn the socialist system, incite separatism, break national unity, advocate terrorism or extremism, advocate ethnic hatred and ethnic discrimination, disseminate violent, obscene, or sexual information, create or disseminate false information to disrupt the economic or social order.[56]

This is essentially what Beijing would like to accomplish worldwide. You can see the tendrils expanding by the way the PRC uses cyber warfare as a tool for penetrating anti-communist groups and democracy, human rights activists, and others it considers threats. Tibetan and Uighur groups are particular targets for monitoring and harassment, as are those in the diaspora who challenge the Party line.

Hong Kong Canadians such as Cherie Wong say that Ottawa's failure to bar Huawei from modern 5G networks is putting lives at risk.[57] Wong, executive director of Alliance Canada Hong Kong, an umbrella group for democracy advocates, says Chinese dissident groups are already tracked and targeted by the Chinese Communist Party in Canada through Chinese social media apps like WeChat and TikTok—and the threat of Huawei 5G Internet in Canada is much worse.[58]

While it cracks down on dissent at home, China seems keen to create social disruption abroad, aiding in its entropic warfare goals.[59]

Global Reach

As we've seen with everything from the ICAO incident to the way Chinese hackers targeted the American lawyer representing the Philippines in the Permanent Court of Arbitration South China Sea case, Beijing considers everything fair game in its unrestricted warfare approach to cyber.

What is happening to Americans cyber warfare–wise is happening to everyone else. There is mass scale espionage on global cellular networks and location-specific operations.

At the PRC-build headquarters of the African Union, China reportedly installed listening devices, and data was sent off to Shanghai every night between midnight and 2:00 a.m.[60]

As of 2021, the PRC had built at least 186 government buildings in Africa, and fourteen "sensitive information technology networks."[61] Convenient.

You

Have a LinkedIn account? Should you be useful to the CCP, they will look for you. According to a 2020 report in the *Washington Times*:

> William R. Evanina, director of U.S. counterintelligence, singled out LinkedIn...saying the networking platform could be weaponized by the members of the Chinese military

whom the U.S. indicted on charges of hacking credit reporting giant Equifax and stealing data of more than 145 million Americans in 2017.

"They have more than just your credit score; they have all of your data," Mr. Evanina said. That includes Social Security numbers and other personally identifiable information such as bank account numbers. He said the data can be used as leverage to target vulnerable Americans inside and outside of government who have access to sensitive information and who can be reached through LinkedIn. "When they get a LinkedIn from someone in China, they already know everything about that person."[62]

It is possible, of course, to collect too much and be unable to process it—as with the Stasi, East Germany's security service that had most of the population serving as informers on each other. It knew everything, but it knew very little. AI, artificial intelligence, offers the Chinese authorities a way around this dilemma.

One marvels at the breadth of Chinese hacking—both in terms of resources applied and the range of targets. It appears there is absolutely nothing that is off-limits, as long as it potentially provides the CCP with an advantage.

According to Winnona DeSombre, a research fellow at the Harvard Belfer Center, China's offensive cyber capabilities "rival or exceed" those of the United States, and "its cyber defensive capabilities are able to detect many U.S. operations—in some cases turning our own tools against us."[63]

In the meantime, it's important to remember that the PRC has basically gotten away with its cyber warfare attacks and hasn't suffered any real punishment. The Department of Justice indicts hackers but rarely has them in custody. The embarrassment of an indictment has little effect on the CCP. They have limitless capacity to absorb embarrassment—just as we seem to have limitless capacity for absorbing punishment.

One day, it will really matter. Power plants, food factories, nuclear facilities, ATMs, air-traffic control, the internet—all will shut down. Think of how antsy we get when the Wi-Fi is out for fifteen minutes.

We don't seem to realize we are already at war, and that the cell-phones in our pockets are someone else's weapon.

CHAPTER 14

Proxy Warfare: China's Warfare Outsourcing

There is a whole other set of attacks that have come via Beijing's proxies. Proxies? Those are surrogates or, in simple terms, getting someone else to do your work for you, whether they realize it or not.

The PRC touts its so-called principle of non-interference and insists it never interferes in other countries internal affairs. Indeed, Beijing likes to present itself as just minding its own business and leaving everyone else alone—while just desiring to trade and do some business.

That's not true. For many years, the Chinese Communist Party has used a breathtaking range of proxies—military, business, and political—throughout the world. And it still does. The proxies target America's allies and friends, or at least countries where the United States has an interest or there is something Beijing wants. Remember, with Comprehensive National Power, the goal is to weaken the enemy or strengthen yourself—either is a win.

Let's take a look at some examples, starting along China's borders, then moving farther afield.

Korean Peninsula

North Korea is the mother of all proxies. The Kim regime could not survive without Chinese oil, food, and money. In return, it serves Beijing's interest very nicely, not least by keeping American and Japanese attention and resources focused on the Korean Peninsula—attention and resources that then cannot be directed towards the PRC or earmarked to defend Taiwan.

By keeping North Korea intact and threatening—with its nuclear and missile programs moving forward while pretending nothing can prevent it—Beijing creates restraint on the part of the Americans.

Additionally, through adroit PRC political warfare, China has managed to portray itself not as the problem, but as an essential part of the solution. Successive U.S. administrations and a few generations of diplomats have convinced themselves that they must overlook Chinese bad behavior because they need Chinese cooperation to solve the North Korea problem.

That means when the PRC absorbs the South China Sea, bullies the Philippines and Japan, threatens to destroy Taiwan, and engages in cyber theft and trade cheating, the American response is too often muted or non-existent, because "we need China's help with North Korea."

Beijing is exceptionally good at pushing forward a problem that can be framed as bigger or more urgent than dealing with China, and convincing Washington that it needs China onside to tackle it. Look at Ukraine. Rather than sanctioning China for supporting Russia, American diplomats were pleading for China to help.[1]

Beijing will use anything as a proxy. Planetary climate change is one example, where China demands any measures that support its goals of global domination.

Of course, in almost all these cases, China has no interest in solving the problems—at least not the way Washington wants them solved. So, for example, if it comes to kinetic war in Asia—say, against Taiwan—expect North Korea and the PRC to cooperate.

The Chinese Communist Party also has proxies in South Korea—America's ally. Indeed, South Korean leftists are often pro-North Korean and pro-China—and they are not some fringe group in the country's political universe. They have run the country more than once.

The South Korean administration of President Moon Jae-in (2017–2022) was leftist. It saw the United States and the presence of U.S. forces as the reason the Korean peninsula is divided—and it saw North Korea as not so threatening.

Moon had remarked in his autobiography that he was euphoric when he heard that the Americans had lost in Vietnam. No telling what he felt when the Afghanistan debacle happened.

The Moon Jae In administration roiled the U.S.–South Korea alliance and put ROK-Japan relations at their lowest ebb ever. Beijing was pleased. If the Americans and South Koreans (or the South Koreans and the Japanese) aren't getting along, that is a good thing from Beijing's perspective.

Moon stated more than once while in office that he saw South Korea's place as subordinate to China.[2] There are things you say as a statesman and things you say when you are fawning. And things you say when you mean it.

For some of Moon's officials and close advisors, even the description far leftist isn't quite enough. Take Lee In-young, the unification minister appointed in July 2020. While in college, he was the number two person in the Anti-American Youth Association, the underground organization that provided leadership to Jeondaehyup, the violent, radical 1980s student organization based upon North Korea's Juche ideology. During Lee's National Assembly confirmation hearing, he was asked if his views had changed. He avoided a direct answer, and that said enough.[3]

As for the PRC, Moon was all-in on Chinese investment in South Korea and was pushing plans for several dozen Chinatowns to be built throughout the country.[4]

And after the United States deployed the THAAD anti-missile defense system in South Korea, the Chinese complained and put economic sanctions on South Korea. Not long afterwards, Moon offered up the "three no's" to Beijing: no additional THAAD deployments; no participation in an integrated U.S. missile defense network; and no trilateral alliance with the United States and Japan.[5]

That was a trifecta for Beijing.

Like a good proxy, every problem was turned into a solution—for Beijing. When COVID-19 broke out, President Moon said South Korea would suffer together with China, and he let Chinese visitors pour into the country.[6] Predictably, he didn't ask those who would actually suffer—the Korean people—for their thoughts.

There's a credible case to be made that South Korea's April 15, 2020, National Assembly election, which produced an unexpected and overwhelming victory for Moon's Democratic Party, was manipulated with Chinese help.[7] If you have a good proxy, you don't want to lose them. Especially not to something as repellent to the CCP as a free and fair election.

Among several allegations were claims that the National Election Commission's (NEC) electronic network was hacked and the vote manipulated.[8] That seems like the stuff of spy books. But it's maybe not as hard as imagined. The NEC network is basically a main server at NEC that connects to each polling site. It's not the decentralized system Americans are used to. And Chinese Huawei equipment is said to have been installed in the hardware.

If true, and given that PRC cybercriminals hacked the U.S. Office of Personnel Management in 2015—stealing the personal information of twenty-two million current and former federal employees—one imagines they could handle the South Korean NEC system without breaking a sweat.

But an important point about China's proxy warfare is that the proxies sometimes stumble, along with Chinese strategy. In South Korea's case, much of the public was turned off by Moon's excessive pro-China, pro–North Korea policy. Moon's leftist party lost the 2022 presidential election to the conservative party candidate, Yoon Suk Yeol.

Washington was relieved, even if the leftist Democratic Party still dominates the National Assembly—a consolation of sorts for the PRC. But you can be sure Beijing is looking for the next South Korean proxies to back.

India

The People's Republic of China had an actual war with India in 1962, and they have been at a sort of war ever since—including, from China's side, proxy war.

The most obvious proxy is Pakistan. Aiming to cause New Delhi problems along its entire land border, the PRC works with Pakistan to keep pressure on India. Beijing's support includes helping Pakistan to train, equip, and dispatch terrorists against India, such as the Lashkar-e-Taiba and Jaish-e-Mohammed. And it uses its United Nations Security Council veto to protect Pakistan-based terrorists.[9]

China also provides aid to Indian insurgent groups operating in India's northeastern districts, as well as rebel groups in Myanmar that, in turn, provide support to Indian insurgent groups.[10]

The Indian government even indicted a Naga insurgent group's chief arms procurer in 2011 for buying weapons directly from NORINCO

(China North Industries Corporation)—and going to NORINCO's headquarters in Beijing to do the deal.[11]

American analyst Christopher Booth writes that "these methods provide a low-cost, high-deniability, asymmetric tool for China's intelligence services and military to harass India in their ongoing gray-zone conflict."[12]

Signals intercepts, captured insurgent interrogations, and journalist reports verify PRC supports to the separatist insurgents—and this has been going on since at least the 1960s. Chinese intelligence officers and People's Liberation Army personnel train and arm the guerrillas, including from bases in Myanmar.[13]

The United Wa State Army, which at over twenty-five thousand strong is the most powerful of the Myanmar insurgent groups, is also a Chinese proxy. It's a match for the Myanmar military.[14] China provides weapons to other Myanmar insurgent groups even as it maintains diplomatic ties with the government, as well as deep economic and commercial links. This allows Beijing to apply pressure on the Myanmar regime from multiple directions.

It is also reported that the PRC is the main backer of the Myanmar insurgent Arakan Army (AA).[15] Probably not by coincidence, the AA often attacks Indian-funded development projects in Myanmar, leaving untouched the Chinese construction activities that look to cross Myanmar and connect China to the Indian Ocean.

Chinese support for Nepal's Marxist guerrillas, starting in the 1960s and continuing into the 2000s, ultimately led to Beijing-allied groups dominating the Nepal government.[16] For years, Nepal was considered India's turf. No longer.

Global Proxies

Almost everywhere you look, you can find carefully cultivated CCP proxies. It's a fact of life in the Philippines that a good chunk of the elite class acts as Beijing's proxies, Filipino financial motivations combining with political-warfare-fueled resentment of the United States. They are doing Beijing's bidding and giving the Americans headaches—while eroding longstanding U.S. alliances.

In Japan, in just one example of Chinese proxy warfare, the ruling Liberal Democratic Party's coalition partner, Komeito, had top officials that used to be quietly tracked by Japanese police while meeting with PRC Embassy officials in out-of-the-way *ryokans*, or inns.[17]

There is a long list of Australian politicians, business magnates, and a huge number of academics who were, and still are, Chinese proxies. After reporter John Garnaut and academic Clive Hamilton covered the topic, the Australian government took steps to crack down on the worst of it.[18] They had some success, but the problem has not gone away.

Venezuela, Cuba, and Iran are effectively proxies for China. In particular, they are willing to make life difficult for the United States in any number of ways. Iran alone distracts U.S. attention and keeps the Middle East in turmoil. In the event of the PRC taking things kinetic, Iran is likely to cause trouble and prevent the United States from concentrating its resources elsewhere.

In Canada, Chinese organized crime groups—Beijing's proxies— have had a large presence in British Columbia and the port city of Vancouver—where, apart from other functions, they serve as a money-laundering conduits and drug merchants.[19] Beyond the Triads, certain prominent Canadian politicians and officials have met the definition of Chinese proxy.[20]

Speaking of Chinese organized crime, it is best regarded as an operational and enforcement arm of the Chinese communist government and its security services. Besides savagely attacking Hong Kong freedom protesters, China's organized crime machine is operational in Taiwan—potentially serving as a fifth column when the time comes and, meanwhile, operating impressive smuggling routes into and out of Taiwan.[21] Anywhere there is a Chinese presence overseas, there is Chinese organized crime. It is one more tool in the Chinese Communist Party's tool kit.

China has any number of proxies working in Africa on its behalf, and this goes back decades. The PRC armed Robert Mugabe's insurgent army, ZANLA, during the Rhodesian War and kept a close relationship with him throughout his rule in Zimbabwe—in exchange for access to the nation's mineral wealth.[22]

When Mugabe, after thirty-seven years of thuggery and corruption, finally got to be too much even for his associates (it had long since been too much for most Zimbabweans), Beijing switched proxies. It gave the go-ahead to Zimbabwe's chief of the army and ended up with Emmerson Mnangagwa, a former Mugabe associate.[23] Different proxy, same idea.

That is standard for Beijing. When one proxy is no longer serviceable, the PRC adroitly finds another one—and is often cultivating several at a time.

Over in Angola, something similar played out. Beijing was close to the ruling Dos Santos family for decades after independence. When the public tossed him out, China then reestablished itself with Angola's new rulers.[24] The benefits? Mineral wealth and potential access to the country's ports, with an eye toward the PLA Navy setting up shop in the not-so-distant future.

This proxy warfare plays itself out all over Africa and the rest of the developing world—and the developed world as well.

We saw it recently in the Solomon Islands, a strategic nation in the Southwest Pacific. The prime minister, a Chinese proxy, signed a deal that allows the PRC and its military easy access to the country, including setting up military facilities.[25] Most citizens oppose this, but by using a local proxy and the cover of the government, China gets its way.

Chinese Proxies in the United States

Before we get to the U.S. mainland, spare a moment for Chinese proxy warfare on Saipan in the Commonwealth of Northern Mariana Islands (CNMI)—a strategic U.S. territory in the Central Pacific. In the 2010s, a Chinese casino company serving as a CCP proxy turned Saipan's governor into a proxy as well.

Casino developers funded several candidates in the 2018 elections, and Saipan's governor also announced a $20.8 million special funding measure described as being generated by casino tax payments. The money appeared right before the election and included $3.5 million for CNMI retiree fund member bonuses and a $150,000 grant for the Marianas Political Status Commission, a body created solely to decide how to become independent from the United States—something that would suit Beijing and, even if not successful, sow domestic discord. Standard PRC win-win.[26]

But being a proxy doesn't always mean Beijing has total control or forever. When the FBI took an interest in the governor, and also in the Beijing-approved casino that was funding the proxy activity, things hit a brick wall.[27] For now. You can bet that Beijing's local agents are sniffing around for new openings.

Now Let's Head to the Mainland

China's hunt for sympathetic allies in the United States goes back decades. For example, on the entropic warfare front, in 1963, Mao—not generally concerned for those fighting for more representation—made a speech denouncing racism in the United States.

From there, China started a focused and funded outreach program that resulted in, among other things, Malcolm X talking positively about Mao and Black Panther founder Huey Newton visiting China in

1971 to meet Zhou Enlai.[28] The Black Panthers, Young Lords, and other revolutionaries even set up an "acupuncture collective" staffed by "barefoot doctors" in the Bronx.[29]

At least one of those involved in the clinic later served, according to Snopes, "as vice chair of the board of directors for Thousand Currents, an organization that provides fundraising and fiscal sponsorship for the Black Lives Matter Global Movement."[30]

Black Lives Matter turned American society upside down in summer 2020. They call themselves Marxists, and China treats them and speaks of them like a proxy.

China has equally spent decades developing its many proxies in America's business, financial, education, civil society, and political classes—though they will all fiercely deny it and may genuinely believe they are not.

But look at what they do and say, and one fairly thinks their interests and activities coincide with the Chinese Communist Party's, to the point it's hard to find another word besides proxy—even if unwitting. And that is maybe the best kind of proxy—one who believes what they are doing is right and even moral.

In the meantime, let's take a look at President Biden's family members who made a fortune from the People's Republic of China. Even during the 2020 presidential campaign, then candidate Biden dismissed talk of the PRC threat with these remarks: "China is going to eat our lunch? Come on, man."[31] And: "I mean, you know, they're not bad folks, folks. But guess what? They're not competition for us."[32]

Henry Kissinger also deserves special mention—he'd insist he was not a proxy, but look at his body of work since putting out his shingle as China consultant nearly fifty years ago. It's hard to find anything that China wouldn't like. Kissinger is influential, maybe less so these days, but for many years, he was the Delphic Oracle of all things China-related.

Large swathes of America's financial class are proxies that would make third-world dictators blush—and envious.

When the Trump administration was just getting started on reversing America's five-decades-long appeasement of the PRC, Beijing's Wall Street proxies fought it tooth and nail. They had their influence inside the administration, with Secretary of the Treasury Steve Mnuchin, a former Goldman Sachs executive, arguing for not upsetting things with Beijing.[33]

According to one participant, when President Trump first traveled to Beijing with a combative mindset, Goldman Sachs CEO Lloyd Blankfein and some others practically forced their way onto the airplane.[34]

And then there are the financial masters of the universe—the Ray Dalio, Steven Schwartzman, Larry Fink, and Jamie Dimon sort—who run, or once ran, vast hedge fund operations, huge banks, and the like.

All have been loath to say anything bad about the Chinese communists or the China market, and all have insisted that investment in China is a business—if not a moral imperative.

They are experts at explaining away the obvious. In 2021, after the multibillion-dollar wipeout when the CCP went after the not-compliant-enough Chinese tech companies, Goldman Sachs and others were saying things like: "The uncertain trading environment wasn't likely to hurt the case for buying Chinese equities too much" and "China has strong economic and earnings growth potential in a global context."[35]

Apparently, the Chinese Communist Party intervening in China's financial markets, throttling so-called private Chinese companies and costing investors (including foreign ones) massive losses, is just an "uncertain trading environment."

Ray Dalio, founder of Bridgewater Associates hedge fund, a major player in China, dismissed China's torment of its Uighur population and Beijing's brutal snuffing out of freedom in Hong Kong. He explained it is just the understandable outcome of the CCP's "sacrosanct" desire for sovereignty.[36] After Xi Jinping grabbed near-total power at the 20th Communist Party Congress in November 2022, Dalio offered the comforting assessment that none of Xi's new leadership team appear to be "extremists."[37] Tell that to Taiwan.

Hank Paulson, the former CEO of Goldman Sachs and former secretary of the treasury during the Bush administration, seems like another proxy. He played a leading role in helping the PRC build its economy that, in turn, funded its military buildup and broader global clout.[38] Yet Paulson seemed less concerned with the Chinese communists' horrific human rights record. He ought to know better. He was raised to know good from evil.

I asked a friend who knows about such things what the story is with these intelligent people who serve as frontmen for a totalitarian, genocidal regime that also harvests organs—and is hell-bent on kicking the Americans out of Asia, and then some. His reply:

> In China, persons are CCP assets to be directed to the point of attack to whatever issue the Party is attacking.
>
> Dimon, Schwartzman, and Fink are all in the same category: they have reached a narcissistic plateau where they each believe in the righteousness of their respective causes as the central force for the betterment of humankind.
>
> Anyone of these three could easily embrace a papal appointment and be really good at it.
>
> So through the righteousness of its cause, the CCP nourishes these three narcissists by encouraging (and inflating) each to think *he* can be the one to unite humankind by bravely—with immense foresight, singularly and remarkably—knitting humankind together by funding a big part of humankind: China.[39]

We may sometimes laugh at these people and their self-importance. But they are powerful and often influence national policy towards China or domestic policies that can benefit the PRC. Some of them get U.S. government appointments—which gives them even more influence and usefulness from Beijing's perspective. Indeed, in June 2022, Michael Bloomberg became chairman of the Pentagon's Defense Innovation Board.[40]

American Academia

Rather than list prominent and not-so-prominent academics who are witting or unwitting Chinese proxies, I propose the reader try to find academics who are *not* proxies.

I can only think of maybe a dozen who aren't. One prominent academic of my acquaintance, who is definitely not a proxy, claims there are "only three."[41]

Regardless of the actual number, one can ask: How many Perry Links can you name? Professor Perry Link is a renowned China scholar, yet he has been effectively banned from China for years owing to his clear stance on human rights.[42]

Professor Link made a choice that many other China studies academics don't, or have been made to think that they can't. Imagine you spent years learning Mandarin, studying Chinese culture and language, and have colleagues in China, but you know that if you say or write something that offends the Chinese communists, your next visa application to visit China will be denied, possibly putting the breaks on your research and your career. Additionally, invitations to attend seminars (often with nice honoraria) in the PRC may dry up. Or suddenly, there will be no more funding for your, or your university's, "China Studies Center."

This is especially relevant for up-and-coming academics without tenure.

To complicate things, what actually offends Beijing is a vague standard. Many academics err on the side of caution and self-censor before they can be censored by the Chinese.[43]

Many university administrators similarly walk on eggshells. When Chinese student groups at George Washington University complained about posters on campus highlighting the PRC's humans right record in connection with the Beijing 2022 Olympics, the university president declared himself "deeply saddened' and promised to track down the culprits—the ones who put up the posters in the United States, not the ones torturing people in China. He backtracked a bit when it was pointed out that a university ought to have some interest in freedom of expression and human rights.[44]

A lone example? Hardly. Invite the Dalai Lama or a Chinese desiring freedom to speak at your university and see what happens.[45]

U.S. Military: Proxy-Free?

Certainly, the U.S. military is proxy-free, right? It is the military's job to defend America, after all.

If only.

Case in point: retired admiral William Owens, former vice chairman of the Joint Chiefs of Staff. He has been unabashedly pro-PRC and is said to be handsomely compensated.[46]

He's not alone. There's always been a long list of very senior officers who've been keen to engage with the PLA and the PRC.[47] And especially for some of the retired ones, it often doesn't take much to buy their services—and get them to see the Chinese Communist Party as just friends they haven't made yet.[48]

Sometimes, it's just an invitation to the Sanya Dialogue with a first-class plane ticket. Sanya is an annual get-together put on by the PRC since 2008 (with a break for the Wuhan virus shutdowns.)

Participants include many high-ranking retired U.S. flag officers. They head to Sanya, a city on China's Hainan Island, for glorious days and fun-filled nights, getting to know their Chinese counterparts and discuss issues of importance to the PRC—all in the name of dialogue and engagement.[49]

The Chinese side's sponsor is the China Association for International Friendly Contact. That's another name for the PRC's intelligence and propaganda services.

The well-respected U.S.-China Economic and Security Review Commission explained it in 2011:

"[This] is a front organization for the International Liaison Department of the People's Liberation Army's General Political Department, which is responsible both for intelligence collection and conducting [PRC] propaganda and perception management campaigns, particularly focused on foreign military forces."[50]

It can be debated which is better for Beijing: a proxy who does it for money only, or a proxy who is convinced he (or she) is not a proxy but is simply doing the right thing—what the Soviets used to call a useful idiot.

From Beijing's perspective, it's presumably results that matter. And results they are getting.

Bottom line: China has plenty of proxies and, at least in the United States, there's probably a waiting list.

CHAPTER 15

The Chinese Military:
No One Is Laughing Anymore

When it comes right down to it, what does the PRC have militarily, and what can it do with it? Let's look first at China's military size and capability, and then its ability to project power.

Military Size and Capability

In 2000, if you suggested the People's Liberation Army (PLA) would one day be a threat to U.S. forces, you'd have been laughed out of the room. These days, however, nobody is laughing.

The U.S. Department of Defense 2018 assessment of Chinese military power described China's ambitions for a global military presence and the prospects of PLA operations far from the Chinese mainland:

"China's military strategy and ongoing PLA reforms reflect the abandonment of its historically land-centric mentality [as] PLA strategists envision an increasingly global role."[1]

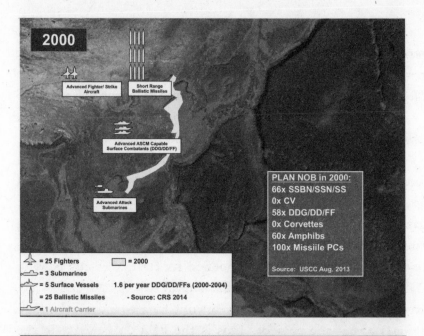

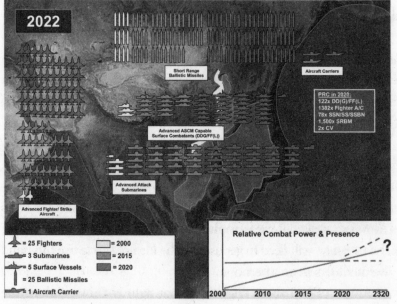

Two pictures are worth two thousand words. This shows the Chinese military's rapid development between 2000 and 2020 and its current ability to project power in the Indo-Pacific region. This build-up took place in plain sight. *Maps courtesy of James Fanell.*

This hasn't changed. The 2022 Department of Defense assessment notes: "The CCP has tasked the PLA to develop the capability to project power outside China's borders and immediate periphery to secure the PRC's growing overseas interests and advanced its foreign policy goals."[2]

The PLA has set out to have the same basic capabilities as the U.S. military in terms of both what it can do and where it operates.

To that end, the Chinese military has developed into a modern force, capable of operating in all domains (sea, undersea, ground, air, outer space) along with excellent cyber and electronic warfare capabilities, and a powerful rocket force with thousands of cruise and ballistic missiles. It conducts training, exercises, and operations around the globe and opened its first overseas base in Djibouti, in 2017. As of late 2022, a naval base is under construction at Ream, Cambodia, after years of Chinese (and Cambodian) denials about the project. This is the PLA's first base in the Indo-Pacific.[3]

As of now, in a large-scale, conventional global fight, the People's Liberation Army would not fare well against the Americans (and their allies). The PLA's power projection warfighting capabilities drop off rapidly once it operates beyond the so-called First Island Chain. This will probably be the case for another five or ten years.

But in a fight closer to the Chinese mainland, in certain circumstances, the PLA could even now bloody the U.S. military—and badly. As covered earlier, in 2018, a four-man U.S. Special Forces team was ambushed and killed in Niger by insurgents. It was front-page news and almost a national catastrophe.[4] In a fight with the Chinese, the American public will need to get used to the idea of losing five thousand service members in an afternoon.

The most talked about trigger for that fight is Taiwan, along the First Island Chain and only ninety miles across the Taiwan Strait from the Chinese mainland. Analysts differ, but in my opinion, the People's Liberation Army is capable of launching a full-scale invasion. U.S.

forces attempting to come to Taiwan's rescue would need to tread very carefully. If the fight were largely confined to the area around Taiwan, China would have considerable advantages.

Also, keep in mind that a military sometimes just has to be good enough to do a certain thing, at a certain time, at a certain place.

It's also worth keeping in mind how far the PLA has come in a relatively short time.

Some History

Until well into the 1990s, the PLA was an Army-dominated, infantry-heavy military with limited mobility, unable to conduct effective joint operations (in other words, combine air, sea, and ground forces.)

The 1991 Gulf War, during which United States and allied forces made short work of the Iraqi military, was a stark reminder of PLA shortcomings, as was the American performance in Bosnia several years later.

It took the PLA time to improve its capabilities. The Chinese Army's outsized influence within the PLA and its considerable political power was a huge obstacle. Moreover, the PLA's extensive business interests and attendant widespread corruption further hampered military reform efforts.

In 1998, China's civilian leadership ordered the PLA to divest its commercial enterprises.[5] This had limited effect. Indeed, rooting out corruption in the PLA was a priority for Xi Jinping when he took power in 2013.

Despite the obstacles, the early-mid 2000s and onwards have seen rapid, if imperfect, progress in turning the PLA into a more modern, balanced, high-technology force capable of joint operations and expanded maritime and air operations.

Some analysts highlight President Hu Jintao's military reform efforts as a turning point and cite a 2004 speech in which Hu called for the PLA to protect China's overseas interests—implicitly requiring a different type of People's Liberation Army.[6]

This led to the PLAN (People's Liberation Army Navy) and PLAAF (People's Liberation Army Air Force) being prioritized over the Army for funding and hardware. Over the last decade and a half, the PLA's mobility—particularly within China's borders—and ability to operate beyond the Chinese mainland has improved markedly.

President Xi Jinping built on Hu's reformation momentum (and pushed through serious reforms of his own) that have moved the PLA even further from the old ground-centric force. These reforms have emphasized joint training and more realistic exercises that often incorporate civilian transportation resources.

The Army even took the brunt of the PLA's three-hundred-thousand-man reduction in 2015, to about nine hundred thousand troops.[7] This had the effect, however, of improving both mobility and capability.

To recap, currently, the PLA consists of the:

- People's Liberation Army (PLAA)
- People's Liberation Army Navy (PLAN)—with PLA Marine Corps (PLAMC)
- People's Liberation Army Air Force (PLAAF) and PLAN Aviation (Naval Air)
- People's Liberation Army Rocket Force (PLARF)—all the missiles
- PLA Strategic Support Force (SSF)—space, cyber, electronic warfare, psyops, political warfare

There are also the China Coast Guard—which is big and has ships that are combatants—and the maritime militia, which is composed of thousands of fishing boats that are double-hulled, fast, armed, and crewed by trained militia.[8] This, of course, doesn't include anything civilian China wants to press into action under its military-civil fusion doctrine.

Xi Jinping has set two major deadlines for the PLA: to complete its modernization process by 2035 and to become a "world class" military by 2049, the centenary of the establishment of the People's Republic of China. It is worth noting that China has typically developed capabilities some years before Western experts predicted they would.

Paying for What's Important

A good way to get a further understanding of the PLA is to look at the numbers and what the Chinese leaders spend on defense.

The CCP always ensures the PLA is well funded, regardless of China's overall economic performance—and regardless of a COVID-19-induced economic slowdown.

It has officially announced a 7.1 percent increase in defense spending in 2022. The year before, the increase was 6.8 percent. The year before that it was 6.66 percent. The one before that was 7.5 percent.[9] It's been that way for many years.

This shows just how serious the Chinese Communist Party is about building a powerful military. Keep in mind that China has no enemies—other than the ones Beijing declares as its enemies.

Let's Look at the Numbers

The official military budget was 1.45 trillion yuan (CNY) or $230 billion (USD) in 2022.[10]

One fairly doubts the accuracy of this figure. It is probably far too low.

Why would the Chinese government hide the true figure? For one thing, there is absolutely no reason for China to provide a correct number.

Indeed, it works in China's favor to issue a low number so it can claim it poses no threat to anyone and spends only one third or one quarter of what the Americans do. So, naturally, it's the American warmongers who are to blame for trouble around the region and the globe. More than a few American experts will accept and echo this argument.

The actual figure of China's defense budget is debatable—and perhaps not worth fixating on. More important is to consider what Beijing gets for its money. A few useful data points:

- It pays its troops a fraction of what the Americans spend on personnel
- In 2021, it launched seven naval warships for every one the U.S. Navy launched, and for the previous decade, the average ratio was five to one
- It also incorporates civilian transport and logistic capabilities into its military far better than just about any other country—all off the books, as far as official military expenditure is concerned

There's another problem with the $230 billion USD figure: the Chinese leadership is not bound by congressional appropriations as is the U.S. Department of Defense. For local yuan expenditures, the Chinese can and will print any amount necessary.

Who is going to tell Xi Jinping no?

What Kind of Military Does China Need?

It comes down to the kind of military China *thinks* it needs. The People's Republic of China is building a military that can do two main things (apart from being a backup to crush domestic "unrest"): 1) Defeat the U.S. military; 2) protect China's global assets and interests—for instance, ports, factories, farmland, and Chinese citizens overseas—which it currently cannot do very well, if at all.

The Chinese leaders will spend whatever it takes to achieve these two objectives.

As mentioned earlier, if a fight were near to the Chinese mainland, the People's Liberation Army (PLA) could inflict serious damage on U.S. forces. Beyond the First Island Chain, the PLA's punch weakens, but after five to ten years, things may be different.

In what military branches and capabilities is China prioritizing investment?

All of them.

As mentioned, the Chinese are investing in the areas needed to defeat the Americans and to increase power projection overseas. These areas include:

- A modern Air Force (both regular and naval)
- A modern Navy, Coast Guard, and maritime militia
- Anti-submarine warfare
- Long range missiles
- Cyber
- Electronic warfare
- Outer space capabilities
- A more modernized ground force able to conduct joint/combined arms operations
- Logistics capabilities
- Long range aerial transport
- Amphibious forces
- Airborne forces
- Large numbers of modern nuclear weapons

There is one big limitation, however. That is the need for foreign currency to buy certain things that must be procured overseas. Since the Chinese yuan is not freely convertible, China has to earn dollars, euros, and the like.

This should put a limit on the People's Liberation Army's capability advances, in theory at least. However, as we've seen, Wall Street and Western businesses are providing the Chinese Communist Party with billions of dollars in foreign exchange every year, along with access to the high technology the PLA needs. And as Moscow moves even closer to Beijing, it may have more access to Russian advanced technologies as well. The Russians may accept payment in Chinese currency—especially after Russia's invasion of Ukraine.

It's obvious why the PRC is so keen to get over the considerable barrier that is the U.S. dollar.

But money is only part of the solution for improving People's Liberation Army capabilities.

In fact, spending money is probably the easiest part of building up a military. The bigger challenge is figuring out how to create, equip, and train a military that can conduct effective operations, especially once the shooting starts.

Many Western observers even discount the People's Liberation Army's capabilities. They point out problems with the actual conduct of joint operations, officer and troop quality, lack of a solid non-commissioned officer corps, and difficulties mastering amphibious operations, for example. The Chinese themselves complain about these shortcomings.

Regarding the idea that the Chinese military "just isn't good enough" yet, a retired U.S. Navy officer with decades of experience in the Indo-Pacific region commented,

> The fact the PLA is discussing [its] problems suggests the mistakes are being studied and lessons learned. The PLA now does multi-day exercises at its OPFOR training area inside Inner Mongolia. Unlike their Russian counterparts,

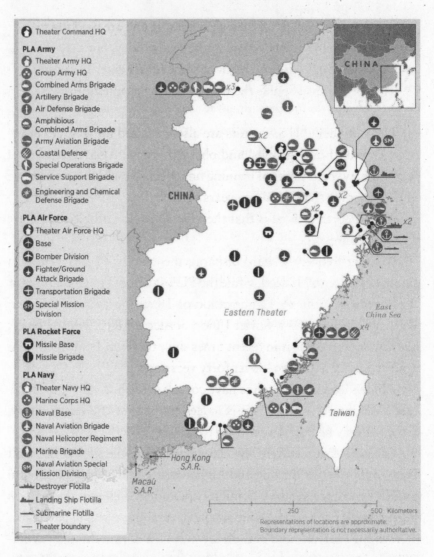

This map from the U.S. Department of Defense 2022 *China Military Power Report* gives a clear sense of the massive PLA forces arrayed against Taiwan. *Map courtesy of U.S. Department of Defense,* Military and Security Developments Involving the People's Republic of China, *2022, online version: https://media.defense.gov/2022/ Nov/29/2003122279/-1/-1/1/2022-MILITARY-AND-SECURITY-DEVELOPME NTS-INVOLVING-THE-PEOPLES-REPUBLIC-OF-CHINA.PDF.*

PLA leaders recognize their shortcoming and are working to overcome them. They may not be ready today, but they are taking the actions to be ready at some future date. The more important question: Is the U.S. preparing as intensely?

He continued: "U.S. recruits are also criticized for lack of knowledge, critical thinking skills, and physical fitness. Also, the extent of non-military socio-political training now occupies a higher percentage of U.S. training than it did five years ago."[11]

The important thing is that they recognize the problems and are trying to address them.

Another frequently heard disparagement of the PLA is its lack of combat experience. Indeed, while the PLA saw some tough fighting in the Korean War, its 1951 annexation of Tibet, the 1962 Sino-Indian War, and the 1969 Sino-Soviet Union border conflict, it really hasn't had any serious combat in recent times since the short but bloody fight against Vietnam in 1979—over forty years ago.

China's leaders themselves have complained about the "peace disease" afflicting the PLA. This is indeed an issue with every military, though it may be less of a problem than imagined.

Consider that relatively few U.S. personnel at the start of the Gulf War (1990–1991) or the Iraq and Afghanistan conflicts had meaningful combat experience, yet the U.S. military performed well once the conflicts began. And if Chinese forces are simply operating overseas in peacetime, performing exercises and anti-piracy patrols and peacekeeping operations, lack of combat experience is even less of a disadvantage.

The aforementioned U.S. Navy officer noted, "Combat provides valuable experience, but [experience] gained fighting light infantry insurgents may not be readily applicable to fighting a high-technology combined arms force. Many battles are lost by the side that makes a mistake at a critical moment or applies the wrong lessons to a fight."[12]

The Chinese are persistent and intelligent and have come a very long way in twenty years.

They have said where they intend to end up, and that includes taking territory that currently belongs to other countries, by force if necessary.

They should be taken seriously.

Operating Globally—and Projecting Power

Another key measure of a nation's military strength is power projection capability.

That means "the capacity of a state to deploy and sustain military forces outside its territory."

In other words, can a military move beyond borders, conduct operations, and stay for a while? Operations can range from exercises to humanitarian assistance to warfighting.

The ability to use violence raises a country's power projection rating. But being able to fight your way across a beach or to bomb something isn't all there is to power projection. In fact, it's rare to use force. Being perceived as able and willing to do so is usually enough.

Power projection is as much about influence, intimidation, deterrence, and even reassurance.

The United States can do power projection better than anyone. China wants to do what the Americans can.

The People's Liberation Army fought wars across its land borders in Korea in the 1950s, against India in the 1960s, and against Vietnam in 1979. It conducted amphibious assaults against Taiwan's offshore islands in the 1950s,[13] and there were several short skirmishes to seize Vietnamese islets in the South China Sea in the 1970s and 1980s.[14]

But the PLA's offshore power projection, such as it was, centered on developing and maintaining an amphibious assault capability intended to seize Taiwan. This was not nearly enough to successfully invade Taiwan. Well into the 1990s, U.S. officers would joke about the PLA conducting a million-man swim to get across the Taiwan Strait.

It was even widely believed that the People's Republic of China had no interest in power projection—that is, no blue water Navy—or would never have it within anybody's lifetime, at least.

This misread and underestimated Chinese intentions and abilities.

The Chinese Communist Party wanted a military that could match U.S. forces both in combat and in terms of global power projection.

It's perhaps no coincidence that China's military buildup also picked up speed around the same time the PRC was allowed into the World Trade Organization. This provided the Chinese regime with the financial, technological, and manufacturing wherewithal needed to build out the PLA, the PLAN, and the PLAAF into a far more formidable force than otherwise would be the case.

From the early 2000s, the PRC systematically set about building a Navy and Air Force able to operate well beyond China's borders. And the PLA ground forces (Army and Marine Corps) were reconfigured and revamped to perform offshore missions as well. It is well on its way.

PLA power projection had (and still has) two main objectives: 1) Taiwan; and 2) the rest of the world.

Power Projection Objectives

Some observers cite President Hu Jintao's 2004 speech calling for the PLA to be able to protect China's overseas interests when Chinese power projection improvements started in earnest.[15] Less mentioned is that Hu's predecessor, Jiang Zemin, wanted the PLA to be able to "solve the Taiwan issue" by 2020.[16]

CHAPTER 16

Objective: Taiwan

The threat to Taiwan—a so-called "big island target" in Chinese terms—is now deadly serious, and has been since the early 2010s. While it is a work in progress, the PLA has assembled most pieces of the puzzle—naval, air, amphibious, missile, surveillance, logistics, cyber, and so forth—that the effort would require. The PLA has also gone about trying to master the joint combined-arms requirements that an opposed assault mandates.

Analysts reasonably differ on whether the People's Liberation Army can conduct a successful amphibious assault on Taiwan.

The 2019 DOD report on Chinese military power claimed a successful amphibious assault on Taiwan was beyond PLA capabilities. However, it noted that "[w]ith few overt military preparations beyond routine training, China could launch an invasion of small Taiwan-held islands in the South China Sea such as Pratas or Itu Aba. A PLA invasion of a medium-sized, better-defended island such as Matsu or Jinmen is within China's capabilities."[1]

The 2022 DoD report says basically the same thing—that a full-scale invasion of Taiwan is still out of reach for the PLA. However, it describes a formidable array of exercises and broader capabilities on the PLA's part, leading one to suspect the conclusion about an amphibious assault (much less in the context of an all-out / all-domain attack) on Taiwan being too hard is not entirely heartfelt.[2]

I think PLAN, operating with other PLA services and civilian resources, is indeed capable of landing ground forces (projecting power) to seize or occupy most small island features or to establish lodgments in coastal areas in much of the first-island chain, if it accepts the risks—military, political, and economic.

But Back to Taiwan

Skeptics of PLA power projection capabilities point to a lack of lift (ships needed to get across the Taiwan Strait); inadequate joint capability (the ability to combine PLA air, sea, and ground forces—essential for this kind of operation); and inadequate logistics capabilities.

While Xi Jinping would prefer to bully Taiwan into submission or wait until an election (manipulated or otherwise) returns a compliant leader, I think the PLA has the capability to conduct an assault on Taiwan—and for both Xi and the PLA to think it will succeed. Let's look at each of the capabilities in turn.

Lift

China has over fifty purpose-built amphibious ships. Some are older models, but they work fine. The Chinese also have hundreds of commercial vessels, container and RORO (roll-on/roll-off) ships, and thousands of ferries and barges. If the objective is to get troops and hardware across the strait, then these will suffice. There is enough maritime lift to land three Army divisions and a Marine brigade in an initial assault, according to some analysts. In other words, to move at least several tens of thousands of troops across the strait in a single day. And there is no shortage of military and civilian aircraft to drop airborne troops. "Vertical envelopment" (i.e., helicopters) will also be part of the mix, with civilian ships as platforms serving as "helo-relays" to shrink the one hundred–mile wide Taiwan Strait.

Joint Capabilities

Joint capabilities are a challenge for all militaries, but the PLA has identified this requirement and it trains to improve them. And don't forget that Taiwan has been the PLA's main objective for decades, so it's gotten plenty of funding, attention, planning, procurement, and practice—including amphibious assaults and necessary air, naval, and fire support coordination.

Logistics

The PLA's logistics capabilities may not up to U.S. military standards, but they may be good enough, especially if you consider military-civil fusion and China's proven mastery of global supply chain management.

It's worth noting that the rapid construction of railways, highways, and airfields within China over the last several decades has improved China's ability to move PLA forces and equipment swiftly across the country. It also has made it easier and faster to position forces, equipment, and logistical support for an assault on Taiwan—without necessarily being observed or recognized by U.S. and other reconnaissance assets. In other words, it makes a no-notice (or very-limited-notice) assault feasible.

Keep in mind that an assault will very likely take place in the context of missile barrages, cyber attacks, electronic warfare, space operations

to blind Taiwan and U.S. satellites, and naval and air forces swarming
the island and its environs—at least. Also, there is a "fifth column" of
saboteurs and agents in Taiwan that China has had sixty years to put
in place.[3]

One can also expect coordinated attacks by some of China's proxies
(North Korea, Pakistan, Iran) in other theaters for their own benefit as
well as to distract and divert the focus and forces of Taiwan's
allies—particularly the United States and Japan—and to keep South
Korea from getting ideas about stepping in to help Taiwan.

This, by any measure, is a power projection capability. That is not
to say it will necessarily succeed. But compared to 2000, the PLA's
improvements are breathtaking. Nobody jokes about the million-man
swim anymore.

Objective: The World

The PLA's move to develop global power projection capabilities
might have happened on its own due to Beijing's natural desire to assert
itself militarily as a major global power. But the PRC's extensive commercial and economic overseas activities—particularly in Africa,
Southeast Asia, the Middle East, and the Indian Ocean region—and
the perceived need to dominate vulnerable sea lanes required the PLA
be able to protect it all.

The Belt and Road Initiative, launched in 2013, further increased
the scope of potential military coverage for China's overseas interests.

In many respects, the commercial has laid the physical, political,
and psychological groundwork for the PLA's overseas military
presence—whether temporary or permanent.

The most notable feature of Chinese power projection development
is the PLA's expanding global reach over the last decade and a half,
driven by a rapidly built-out People's Liberation Army Navy operating

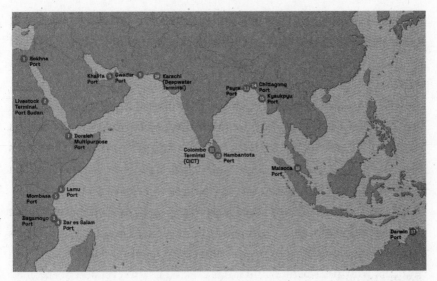

This depiction of PRC port positioning in the Indian Ocean is typical of what is happening worldwide. Under China's military-civil fusion doctrine, it is believed this is taking place with future military uses in mind. *Reproduced by permission from Saeed Faridi, Debarpan Das, Gateway House, India, https://www.gatewayhouse.in/wp-content/uploads/2021/08/CHInvstPorts-04.png.*

worldwide. This includes aircraft carriers, amphibious ships, and a full range of support and combatant ships.

Professor Andrew Erickson of the U.S. Naval War College states things succinctly: "China is building a blue-water Navy for the long term: not just the aircraft carriers themselves but the auxiliary ships to supply them and the warships to protect them. . . . Other ships built or under construction include a new type of supply vessel, as well as four cruisers suited for escorting a carrier."[4]

Since the early 2000s (and probably earlier), China wanted to build aircraft carriers. These are prime power projection platforms—as America has demonstrated since the 1940s.

Since 2012, the PLAN has launched three aircraft carriers. Most recently, in June 2022, it launched the eighty-thousand-ton CNS

Fujian.[5] It is similar to the largest American aircraft carriers, and it is the largest warship any Asian nation has built.

The PLAN carrier fleet is not yet fully operational and not a match for the U.S. Navy, but it is moving fast. Far faster than most people thought it could—including some INDOPACOM commanders.

In the meantime, imagine a Chinese aircraft carrier showing up anywhere in the Indo-Pacific with a complement of fighter aircraft. That would get any country's attention, and few, except for Japan or India, could do much about it.

By any measure, this is power projection—though of the coercive military diplomacy sort.

Besides aircraft carriers, the PLAN also studied how the U.S. Navy and U.S. Marines operate, and it has created its own version of the U.S. Navy / U.S. Marine Expeditionary Unit / Amphibious Ready Group (the MEU/ARG). Along with the U.S. aircraft carrier strike groups, the MEU/ARGs are on constant standby for power projection and continuously "float" in designated parts of world.

A MEU/ARG is typically composed of three amphibious ships with upwards of two thousand Marines along with their equipment, transport, and aviation assets.

If they wanted to do so, the People's Liberation Army Navy and the PLAN Marine Corps could form and deploy their own "MEU/ARGs" for roughly six months deployments—essentially anywhere on earth.[6] Extended combat operations against a serious enemy would still be a challenge, but they could manage just about everything else an American amphibious force could do. In fact, the Chinese Marine Corps mission list mirrors that of the U.S. Marine Expeditionary Unit.[7]

Before long, when natural disasters strike in, say, the Indo-Pacific region, or local Chinese populations are targeted in riots somewhere, it will be a PLAN amphibious force coming to assist. Indeed, after the January 2022 volcano eruption and tsunami hit Tonga, the Chinese Navy immediately dispatched two ships, including one amphibious ship and a Y-20 transport aircraft, to assist.[8] They outshone the U.S. Navy, which had mostly outsourced its response to the Australians, and the Tongans noticed.

Or suppose, for example, the pro-PRC Solomon Islands' government calls in the PLA Marines under the guise of "peace-keeping" to put down demonstrations in one of the provinces protesting against Chinese influence in the country? Not unthinkable.

How did the PLA figure it all out? Study and practice. For example, the Horn of Africa's anti-piracy patrols allowed mastery of the skills required to deploy naval task forces (with Marines) thousands of miles away from China—and to sustain them while handling the intricate political requirements to deploy forces into foreign countries.[9]

The PRC amphibious power projection capability has developed at a striking speed. This is important to keep in mind when assessing overall Chinese progress towards global power projection presence that seems more limited by political will than anything else.

The PLAN only received its first modern amphibious ships in 2008. They were about eight modern, but smaller, Type 071 "amphibs" (equivalent to U.S. San Antonio class ships) that could embark a battalion of six hundred Marines with helicopters.[10]

Since then, the PLAN has received three modern Type 075 amphibious ships—equivalent to the U.S. Navy's forty-thousand-ton Wasp class ships—able to handle aircraft and nine hundred or so Marines. More are on the way, and a more advanced Type 076 is reportedly in the works.[11]

Importantly, Chinese shipbuilding capacity exceeds American shipyards by far. The Chinese launched their three Type 075s between 2019 and 2021.[12] It took them about six months to build each ship. That's fast. During that period, the U.S. Navy launched one large amphibious ship while another, U.S.S. *Bonhomme Richard*, burned up pier-side in San Diego.[13]

Not Just the PLA Navy

So far, we've only talked about the People's Liberation Army Navy and the Chinese Marines. But China's Air Force, the PLAAF, has also built up its power projection capabilities and is rapidly adding long-range transport aircraft to the inventory.

In 2016, the PLAAF introduced new Y-20 transport aircraft (equivalent to the U.S. Air Force's C-17, whose schematics the Chinese stole). There are important power projection assets. Don't forget that the Boeing and Airbus commercial airliners sold to China work just as well as troop transports.

Often overlooked, PLAAF Airborne forces are sizeable and now have expanded range and lift capacity. This will increase even more as new Y-20 transport aircraft with 4500-kilometer range are introduced—with extended range once refueller variants are built.

China's sizeable airborne forces have an obvious role in a Taiwan invasion scenario. In one well-publicized exercise in 2015, paratroopers dropped on and assaulted a mock-up of Taiwan's presidential office at a western China training area.[14]

Commercial Access = Military Access

Power projection requires access to places overseas where military forces can organize, rest, replenish, and operate.

The PRC cannot yet replicate America's worldwide network of bases and military support facilities that allow global operations. But that may not be a serious impediment.

Chinese commercial interests (all state-tied to some degree, either formally, or on order) offer potential access worldwide—and support for PLA operations—air, sea, and ground.

Starting long before China's Belt and Road Initiative was announced in 2013, the Chinese began building a worldwide network of dozens of ports and airfields that it owns, operates, or has access to for commercial purposes. A port and an airfield are decidedly dual-use and just as easy to use for military purposes as for civilian. So, when the PRC announced it is funding a huge fishing port on Papua New Guinea's south coast, just across from Australia, you can imagine why people worry.[15]

China also has a worldwide network of logistics and shipping companies that provide support for Chinese business and shipping. COSCO, the global Chinese shipping company, has nearly four hundred large container ships, for example.[16] There is no reason it cannot provide the same support for PLA operations. Under the Chinese doctrine of military-civil fusion, it is expected to do so.

With some more effort, these could work just as well as a support infrastructure for PLA operations worldwide, and with still more effort (and financial grease in the right pockets), they may serve the PLA, or even become full-fledged bases.

For years, the People's Republic of China (PRC) swore it wouldn't have overseas bases. Indeed, over a decade ago, a U.S. Marine commander in Djibouti warned of what was coming from the PRC. He was told by the U.S. State Department to "stay in his lane," and that the Chinese were not "serious" and "had no long term intentions."[17]

Sure enough, in 2017, the PRC established a military base in Djibouti, garrisoned by a PLA Marine battalion and its armored vehicles, with the added role of carrying out missions throughout the broader region. They call it a logistics support base.[18]

The PRC may only have one military base for now. But another is under construction in Cambodia, and, on the current trajectory, it is only a question of time until the PLA has a base—or at least a "forward operating location"—in the Solomon Islands. And they are rumored to be "biding their time" at any number of locations around the world—both sides of Africa, Pakistan, Latin America, the Azores.

Indeed, look at any map sometime and see where Chinese-owned or operated ports and airfields are located.

With some effort and imagination, if current trendlines continue, tying up the Atlantic and the Indian Oceans, and even the Pacific, is not unthinkable. Just look at the ports China has in the Indian Ocean—and imagine the view from India.

The Chinese sequence for establishing power projection access is easy to understand and easy to spot.

It's starts with years of commercial presence, infrastructure investment, foreign aid, and building political influence (if not dependence) while insisting China has no military interests in the country.

"Mask ambition, expand influence while avoiding direct challenge and confrontation (with the Americans)" until the time is right. We saw it in Djibouti. We saw it in Cambodia. We saw it in the Solomon Islands. It's not that complicated. And it is very effective.

This is lightning fast progress for just twenty years. The PLA is not yet a match for the United States in terms of global power projection if one has kinetic warfare in mind. But in terms of influence power projection, it is perhaps a match (or more) for the Americans, owing to Chinese commercial activities worldwide and effective political warfare at the local level—where Americans are either absent or ineffective.

This is laying the groundwork for adding in the military part of power projection. It may take a while, but the PRC is making the effort and testing—and pushing—limits.

But what's so bad about China's global power projection? The Americans do it, after all.

Fair point. Except that the two countries are not remotely comparable. One is humane and democratic, for all its shortcomings. People are literally dying to get in. The other is an aggressive, expansionist totalitarian dictatorship that does not have an illegal immigrant problem.

CHAPTER 17

Will China Launch a Kinetic War?

China would like to get what it wants without kinetically fighting for it. Who wouldn't? Getting what you want through political warfare and gradually subverting and wearing down your target is easier, costs less, doesn't kill as many of your own people, is less likely to result in third party intervention, is less likely to trigger effective resistance within the target country, and is a little easier on the reputation. But make no mistake: the Chinese will go kinetic if—by their own calculations—they think they need to *and* believe they can get away with it.

There is no moral constraint. Chinese communist leaders have gone kinetic against other Chinese plenty of times. Such regimes prefer to intimidate and selectively kill their own citizens to keep them in order, but they will kill on large scale if necessary.

To the Chinese communist regime, political warfare and kinetic warfare are part of the same continuum, and it will seamlessly transition from one to the other, and back, to achieve its goals of expanding its Comprehensive National Power.

If Beijing (or better said these days, Xi Jinping) thinks going kinetic is the most effective way to accomplish its goals, there are no internal philosophical, moral, legal, or political restraints stopping it. Just ask Tibet, Vietnam, India, or any of the others it has attacked—directly or via proxies—over the years.

The CCP doesn't see a distinction between war and non-war in the way we do. In its world view, China should naturally dominate the world. This was made explicit by Mao. As Gordon Chang explained:

> [Mao] had hoped to establish "an Earth-management com-
> mittee in the future to carry out a united planning for the
> whole Earth." A year after starting the Cultural Revolution,
> he had even charged assistants with drafting a plan "for the
> whole humankind." Tellingly, in 1950 he replaced the ritu-
> alistic "Long live the central people's government," which
> had been carved on the Gate of Heavenly Peace in Beijing,
> with "Long live the grand unity of the people of the world."
>
> "Grand unity" sounds benign, but Mao was evoking
> *tianxia*, the notion that the world was united and that the
> Chinese ruled it, presiding over "all under Heaven."[1]

This world view means the communists are in a constant struggle for domination against those that would hold down or hold back communist China from taking its rightful place as the ruler of the world (in China-speak, those who would "contain" China).

This is both a Chinese view of things and a Marxist view of the constant and inevitable struggle between rival and implacably opposed systems. Only one can survive. That one is communism, according to Marx—and Xi Jinping—as embodied by the Chinese Communist

Party. This fits in well with the Chinese expression: "You die, I live" that long pre-dates the Chinese Communist Party.

Marxist-Leninist regimes are always at war with everyone, especially countries that can hurt them. It's also the nature of regimes that have many of the characteristics of an organized crime gang. Using intimidation and outright violence when the threats don't work is natural—if not common sense.

It's also tied in to the *tianxia* concept: you deserve to run the show, so using force to either get to the top or stay there is simply a statement of fact.

But Mao died in 1976, and maybe Xi Jinping is less of an "extremist," as Ray Dalio might suggest?[2] That's unlikely. Just pay attention to "Xi Jinping thought."

Ian Easton describes a passage from a textbook used at the National Defense University where senior PLA officers are trained. The textbook, aligned with Xi Jinping thought, states: "Xi Jinping has emphasized that our state's ideology and social system are fundamentally incompatible with the West. Xi has said, 'This determines that our struggle and contest with Western countries is irreconcilable, so it will inevitably be long, complicated, and sometimes even very sharp.'" The textbook elaborates: "To use war to protect our national interests is not in contradiction with peaceful development. Actually such is a manifestation of Marxist strategy."[3]

However, this hasn't stopped those wanting to wish away the very real ambitions of the Chinese communists from putting forward predictable statements that function to downplay the threat. Let's look at some of the most common ones.

"Economic Interests Will Restrain the Kinetic Option—Trade Ties and Investments Are So Deep That a War Is Unthinkable"

This idea has been around for a long time. One newspaperman insisted that economic intertwining between the European nations made a European war impossible—shortly before World War I erupted. He achieved lasting notoriety.[4]

We hear the same thing today about U.S. and PRC economic ties somehow restraining Chinese kinetic actions. And Taiwan's role as the world's leading semiconductor manufacturer—essential to modern economies—somehow will stay Beijing's hand for fear of destroying Taiwan-based factories.

Don't bet on it. For Beijing, chips or no chips, the military benefit of taking Taiwan, by force, if necessary, and the political humiliation of the United States (not to mention ensuring Xi's status as one of the Great Ones for "reunifying" China) are enough. You can always rebuild a semiconductor industry—and remember Comprehensive National Power. You might not have chips, but neither will your enemy

"The CCP Elite's Personal Interests Restrain a Kinetic Move"

This is the phenomenon over the last twenty to thirty years, as Chinese—especially the most successful—are trying, by hook or by crook, to move their wealth out of the country (away from the potential grip of the CCP) and to put it somewhere secure. The money doesn't go to Moscow or Pyongyang, but rather to the free world: the United States, Great Britain, Australia, and Canada. In other words, the countries the Chinese communists view as enemies.

But it's more than moving one's loot out of China. It's better for a family to send out a relative who gets a green card or residence permit, staking out a foothold for other family members—just in case.

It's hard to think of another historical example when a powerful, rising nation is arming itself to the teeth and looking for a fight while, at the same time, its most successful people are hedging their bets and setting up bolt holes in the nations that they declared enemies—where conditions are safe and sound under local systems or property rights and rule of law.

It wasn't as if well-connected Nazi-era German elites were buying up real estate in London, Paris, and New York and angling to live there—just in case. But Chinese elites? That's a different story.

Even supreme leader Xi Jinping's daughter is rumored to have a green card, and she attended Harvard.[5] Xi went to great lengths a decade ago to suppress *New York Times* and Bloomberg stories about his family's (and other Chinese leaders') overseas wealth.[6]

In some ways, this is a futures market—with the people at the top of the heap in communist China and benefitting most from the system having some real doubts about its future prospects. In other words, they are going "short" on the PRC.

Presumably, Chinese elites would be putting this at risk by starting a war with the United States—as seen by how Russian oligarchs and their wealth have been targeted after Vladimir Putin's invasion of Ukraine in March 2022 as a way to pressure Putin. But it could be the CCP leaders might be willing to write it all off. Or they might consider their prospects of victory so bright that overseas holdings might remain intact. They will expect to get them back. Xi Jinping recently issued orders for Communist Party officials and their relatives to dispose of overseas assets and return the proceeds to China.

Ultimately, this is an interesting phenomenon, but is it enough to keep the PRC from going kinetic? It is best not to plan as if it is.

"What about Chinese Public Opinion?"

Won't public opinion matter and tend to restrain the CCP? Michael Bloomberg might think so, having said Xi isn't a dictator and has to consider public opinion.[7]

But in these sorts of regimes, any real talk back is intimidated, controlled, or silenced—either literally or figuratively. What are you going to do, write to your congressman? Protest outside the White House?

And anyway, "reunifying" Taiwan *does* seem to resonate with many Chinese of all sorts.

The broader public in China, like the public anywhere, is susceptible to manipulation, including capitalizing on resentments and historical wrongs, as well as claims China is being harassed and threatened, or even supposedly disrespected.

So a large chunk of the population might think a kinetic fight is just the thing.

If it hits the Japanese, too, that's even better. Crudely racist anti-Japanese movies are staple fare on Chinese TV and have been for years.[8]

The CCP has no trouble putting together protest mobs—violent ones, too—to go after the Japanese (or even the U.S.) embassies. Japanese-owned businesses have been targeted when needed.[9]

And not just the Japanese. In 2021, a movie on the Chosin Reservoir battle during the Korean War, in which Chinese forces overwhelmed U.S. forces in an epic fight, was a huge success, earning $600 million.[10]

In 2017, the *Wolf Warrior 2* movie, depicting noble Chinese squaring off with American villains in Africa, was another blockbuster. Its message resonated.[11]

Furthermore, if the CCP goes kinetic, Beijing can burn off excess capacity—manufacturing and human. It's estimated China has thirty million single males (a result of sex selection and the one-child policy): so-called bare branches who have little chance of ever finding a wife. They might potentially blame the Chinese Communist Party for their plight.

Regardless, won't a war mean that a lot of young men die? It might. But who will complain, and how does the anger coalesce in such a society? Even when shoddily made school buildings collapsed in an earthquake in 2008, and thousands of youngsters (many only children) died, the ensuing anger did not rock the CCP.[12]

Indeed, the resentments and a conditioned population (at least enough of it) just might create a population that says, why not? Foreign reporters and on-scene observers in Argentina in 1982 noted that most Argentinians were overwhelmingly in favor of a war to erase the perceived humiliation of Britain occupying the Falklands (Malvinas) Islands—as long as the Argentinians were winning.

Also, if you haven't been in a real war for a couple generations or more, and the government has talked up past battles and glories, you might find that martial ardor refreshing. A population just might like the idea of a war to help rejuvenate the nation.

In 1996, even then secretary of state, Madeline Albright, berated then chairman of the Joint Chiefs of Staff Colin Powell, who was reluctant to deploy American troops without a good reason and U.S. national interest. Albright said, "What's the point of having this superb military you are always talking about if we can't use it?"[13] One imagines such thinking is even easier to have in the PRC. A Colin Powell wouldn't last long.

So the CCP may not have to coerce too many people to go along with a kinetic campaign. Note that the maritime militia is already pitching in, strong-arming (and sometimes sinking) Vietnamese, Philippine, and other fishing boats in the South China Sea.[14] China's fishing fleet is a willing adjunct to CCP efforts to dominate with promises of plunder and free gasoline.

Perception of an easy fight creates band-wagoning effects.

"China Has Never Attacked Anyone"

This one is pretty common among "experts." You'd also hear it all the time in the Marine Corps, including from graduates of Command and Staff College who had read Henry Kissinger's book *On China*. The implication being, since (as declared in the face of evidence to the contrary) the PRC has never attacked anyone, we are conjuring up a phantom enemy.

China's neighbors might disagree with the idea that China doesn't do kinetic. Indeed, in its surrounding area, the PRC has regularly used kinetic force to strengthen its position while weakening its rivals and enemies. Some examples:

Vietnam. China attacked Vietnam in 1979 to teach it a lesson in a short, bloody war. Earlier in 1974, when China saw the opportunity and knew the South Vietnamese and the Americans were too preoccupied to respond, it grabbed South Vietnamese-held islets in the South China Sea. In 1988, the PRC seized more Vietnamese-held islands (communist Vietnam this time). In the process, the PRC gunned down eighty or so helpless Vietnamese sailors and Marines standing knee-deep in the water.[15]

The Chinese were so pleased with themselves that they publicized it—and the video—to help with recruiting. You can find the footage on YouTube.[16]

This typified the formula for the Chinese going kinetic: capability + opportunity + nobody will do much about it.

India. I've heard perplexed Indian generals and admirals say, "We've been at war with China since 1962. Why can't you Americans figure out that you are as well?"

The PRC launched a full-out assault on India in 1962, and the two nations' soldiers have been jostling on the border ever since.[17] China keeps trying to move the boundary deeper into Indian territory. In

2020, twenty Indian soldiers and likely more PLA soldiers died as a result of a Chinese ambush of Indian troops.[18]

The PRC is expanding its military infrastructure of roads, railways, and airfields to allow rapid movement and reinforcements for a major war on India's northern border. The PRC continues to claim and encroach on Indian territory. Once again, Beijing is building capability while looking for opportunity—and gauging when the time is right.[19]

Additionally, China has been using, supplying, advising, and assisting proxies against India for years. Insurgents in eastern India's Nagaland and Assam provinces have been getting plenty of direct Chinese help, as mentioned earlier.

Nepal. Nepal's Maoist insurgents got direct Chinese aid, weapons, training, and advice. As part of a broader political warfare effort, Maoist political factions have come to dominate the country.[20] Nepal was earlier considered under India's influence.

Burma. Burma's United Wa Army receives weapons (modern and sophisticated ones), training, and funding from the PRC. The guerrilla army is a rival for the Burmese Army, a situation that allows China to exert influence as it likes—both over the government and the insurgents.[21]

Tibet. Tibet was an independent nation until 1949. Mao's PLA invaded that year and has had it ever since. This allows the PRC to dominate the high ground and potentially use water as a weapon: six major rivers on which India, Thailand, Laos, Cambodia, and Burma depend flow out of the Tibetan Plateau. In recent years, China is moving to dam these rivers.[22] Once again, both actual and psychological domination are on display. Richard Gere? The once-famous Hollywood actor. Haven't heard much from him or anyone else who supports the Tibetans in a while. The media seems to have accepted China's takeover of Tibet as a *fait accompli.*

Cambodia. China supported the Maoist Cambodian Khmer Rouge when they fought against the Lon Nol government. After taking over the country in 1975, the Khmer Rouge killed a third of the population to establish its utopia.[23] People's Republic of China's support continued unabated.

Thailand. China backed Thai Communist Party guerrillas in a decades-long insurgency against the government from the late 1950s through the 1980s. With immense U.S. support, the Thai government defeated the guerrillas, but only after the CCP finally cut off their support. Yet, in a remarkable political warfare victory for the CCP post-insurgency, the Thai government now gives most credit to the PRC—not the United States—for the end of the civil war.[24]

So, China *has* gone kinetic. And, for Beijing, there doesn't seem to be a Western-style "red line" between political and kinetic warfare. In fact, political warfare is used to up the requisite conditions for China to conduct kinetic warfare in many, if not most, of China's international interactions. To Beijing, military-civil fusion doesn't stop at China's border. Indeed, it's not intended to.

As one example, and as mentioned before, if the People's Liberation Army is to project power worldwide, it needs access to ports and airfields, just as the U.S. military does.

Chinese political warfare (commercial and diplomatic in particular) has systematically funded the construction or refurbishment of a global network of ports and airfields. In some cases, political warfare has ensured that Chinese-linked companies were the lowest bidders on management contracts of existing facilities. Just one China-linked company, Hutchinson Port Holdings (HPH), manages fifty-two ports in twenty-six countries.[25] This is relevant because of military-civil fusion and the National Intelligence Law. If China wants something from HPH, it will get it.

And China wants control over ports. Everywhere you look, under the putative excuse of the BRI, China is investing in locations that might not make economic sense but are strategically important.

When Greece's economy went into crisis in 2008 and the state was forced to sell its prized port of Piraeus, it was a Chinese company that grabbed it.[26] A Chinese company helped build the Walvis Bay port in Namibia.[27] Debt trap financing gave China a ninety-nine-year lease on the Hambantota Port in Sri Lanka.[28] And the China Pakistan Economic Corridor ends in the Pakistani port of Gwadar, which is starting to look a lot like a Chinese naval base.[29] The examples go on and on. All over the world.

China's political warfare influencing over the last few decades has created constituencies in many countries—particularly in less developed parts of the globe, which is most of it—that potentially welcome the Chinese presence. It's all worrisome for the United States, but Chinese commercial, diplomatic, and political inroads throughout the Pacific Islands are worth paying special attention to.

The Pacific Island region is *terra incognita* to most Americans, and even U.S. military officers often have to consult a map to remind themselves where things are. The expression 'benign neglect' was, in fact, coined years ago to describe the United States' approach to dealing with the Central Pacific nations and territories.

Unfortunately, the PRC knows the area very well and understands its strategic (not to mention economic) importance. Most of the Pacific Islands, with their militarily useful locations, ports, and airfields, are only an election away from shifting into the PRC camp. This includes the three Freely Associated States—Palau, the Federated States of Micronesia, and the Republic of Marshall Islands—with which the United States has treaties guaranteeing military access.[30] Try enforcing those treaties if you're told to "get lost."

In a foretaste of things to come, the Solomon Islands (where the World War II battle of Guadalcanal was fought) signed an agreement with the PRC that likely will lead to the PLA establishing a permanent presence in the country.[31] Washington rightly fears that more of these deals will be signed throughout the region—the center of U.S. defenses in the Pacific.

And Beijing is trying hard. Starting a few days after the Quad leaders meeting in Tokyo on May 24, 2021, China's foreign minister Wang Yi started an eight-nation Pacific Island tour and met virtually with three other island nations. The foreign minister offered a package of enhanced economic and security ties with the countries, both as a group and bilaterally.[32] The group response was varied, giving Beijing a better read on whom to support and whom to attack. The bilateral deals were kept secret, pulling those leaders deeper into the Chinese way of doing things. So, while the Quad issued press releases, Wang worked on the ground to build China's own "island chain"—in the middle of existing U.S. defenses and astride key lines of communication between the United States and Australia.[33]

You can see how the two approaches—political and kinetic—are mutually reinforcing. And the political doesn't stop once the shooting starts. Look at how both Russian and Chinese political warfare was deployed after Russia invaded Ukraine in order to confuse and weaken the response from the wider international community.[34]

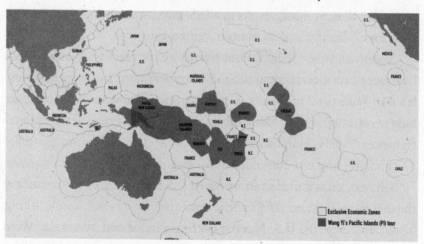

The eight Pacific Island nations Chinese Foreign Minister Wang Yi visited in May and June 2022 are small in land mass but have huge maritime territories—right in the middle of U.S. Pacific defenses. *Map courtesy of Pavak Patel and Cleo Paskal.*

There is also a deliberately blurred intermediate space between what we think of as the political and kinetic, in which China thrives.

The "Not-Quite-War" War

The element of surprise is considered an important component in military strategy, but the Chinese communists have gone one better. Suppose you could start a war without the enemy believing you'd started one? That's what the People's Republic of China has done—to its considerable advantage.

The Chinese communists understand their main enemy rather well.

They figured out long ago that the Americans can't, and won't, believe they are at war unless someone shoots at them *and* issues a government proclamation on official letterhead that states: "We are at war as of 0700 this morning."

Everything else, even if Americans and others are imperiled, get hurt, or even killed, is just a "misunderstanding" or "unprofessional behavior" that, at most, results in a U.S. government official expressing "concern." Or, if it's really serious, "grave concern."

Some examples? For the last twenty years, the PRC has harassed U.S. ships and aircraft operating in international waters and airspace. It's a miracle no Americans were killed in 2001 when a Chinese jet fighter rammed a U.S. Navy EP-3 surveillance plane in international airspace off of Hainan Island.[35]

The pressure has continued ever since.

Chinese ships and aircraft menaced U.S.S. *Bowditch*, a Navy survey ship, in 2001 and 2002.[36] In 2003, it was rammed by a Chinese fishing boat.[37] In 2009, the U.S. Navy ships *Impeccable* and *Victorious* were roughed up.[38] In 2013, PLA Navy ships attempted to ram the U.S. Navy destroyer U.S.S. *Cowpens*.[39]

In 2016, the U.S.S. *Bowditch* deployed an underwater drone in the South China Sea. It was stolen by Chinese ships nearby.[40]

These are just a few examples. A U.S. Navy report cited eighteen examples of "unprofessional" Chinese behavior from 2016 to 2018.[41]

America's friends in the region get the same treatment, or worse.

In 2022, a Chinese jet fighter launched chaff in front of a Royal Australian Air Force plane over the South China Sea.[42] It could have easily downed the plane and killed Australians. PLA jets also dangerously harassed Royal Canadian Air Force planes that were helping enforce UN sanctions against North Korea—something which the PRC had signed up for and was supposed to enforce.[43]

There is plenty more. China has occupied and seized terrain—terrestrial and maritime—belonging to India and Southeast Asian nations—or just "international waters."

Chinese Coast Guard and maritime militia have intimidated Japanese fishermen and pushed them out of their traditional fishing grounds in Japanese waters. Vietnamese[44] and Filipino ships[45] have been rammed and sunk by Chinese maritime militia, and crewmen have disappeared.

The PLA has ambushed and killed Indian soldiers on India's northern border. It used its military to intimidate and threaten Taiwan—while launching missiles into Japan's Exclusive Economic Zone and near Japanese islands. It has taken hostages, too, both American and allied, and locks them up in China.[46]

The United States' muted response is puzzling. Normally, it excuses its restrained behavior as wanting to "deescalate" and avoid "provoking" China. Nothing to worry about, politicians and military leaders say, it's just some local military commander acting without orders, or a rogue pilot, or a corrupt judge. Poor Xi Jinping doesn't know. We need to give him an off-ramp.

But ask yourself, in the communist system, what is the upside of doing something "the center" doesn't want or tell you to do? Not very much. What's the downside? A long prison stay or a 9mm round in the back of the head. You do the math.

Maybe it's an American character trait to desperately wants foreigners to like us. Indeed, Americans are often thoroughly puzzled when they don't, and we reckon it must be because of something we're doing wrong.

It seems like too many American academics and political, business, and military leaders just can't, or won't, believe that to China, the United States is an enemy to be subdued and defeated—by force if necessary.

So China does things that objectively, at least, look warlike, and that might achieve the same results as an actual "full-scale" war of the sort Americans understand, including getting Americans to withdraw and cede control of large strategic (physical, economic and political) areas to the PRC.

The PRC sometimes even seems exasperated that the United States is not taking this seriously, to the point that in 2018, Chinese rear admiral Lou Yuan said that China might have to sink a couple U.S. carriers and kill ten thousand Americans. He added, "What the United States fears the most is taking causalities.... We'll see how frightened America is."[47]

All this unacknowledged war allows the PRC to test and size up the enemy. It even "conditions" the opponent—us—to this aggressive behavior, making us even less ready for when the big-time shooting starts. It also puts China in a better operational position when the "regular" war starts, as it is already dominating strategic territory and has expanded the People's Liberation Army's operational reach.

Bottom line: while America insists it is not at war and is just "competing" with China, it is on the way to ending up in the same position it would be if it lost a "regular" kind of war.

We Call It "Gray Zone"—but Had Better Start Calling It "War"

The aforementioned Chinese activities are taking place in something called "the gray zone."

One definition of gray zone is "the contested arena that lies between routine statecraft and open warfare."[48]

American policy makers seem to think that means it's not war, so it is sort of okay, rather than thinking this isn't routine or statecraft, so it's not okay. Gray zone has the effect of kryptonite on us. We can't figure out what to do, and the Chinese know it.

They behave aggressively because they think they can get away with it. Apparently, they have good reason to think so.

China benefits from a belief in U.S. quarters that the Chinese don't know what they are doing—that they just don't know the rules of the "civilized" world, but with a little more patience (always just a little more), they'll catch on. This was one of the reasons for inviting the PLA to the premier Rim of the Pacific naval exercise in Hawaii in 2014 and 2016, and otherwise "engaging" with the Chinese military.[49]

Maybe we should start to think that people doing (or setting up to do) things that can hurt or kill us is warfare and not some mysterious gray zone. We should look at it the way they look at it. But we don't. We primly avert our gaze, hoping they'll suddenly read a copy of Hoyle and start to act "properly."

As a result, the PRC gets the advantage of a trial war in which they can test limits and probe for weakness. And when Beijing decides to move forward—it is already in a better position. It has developed entire gray-zone fleets to help this happen.

China's Gray-Zone Vanguard: Maritime Militia, Fishing Fleet, and Coast Guard

China has a large maritime militia.[50] According to Chinese military expert Lonnie Henley, in the case of attack on Taiwan, People's Liberation Army sources have ascribed these tasks[51] (among others) to the maritime militia:

- Delivery of forces
- At-sea support (logistics)
- Over-the-shore logistical support
- Medical support
- Obstacle emplacement and clearing
- Engineering support
- Reconnaissance, surveillance, and early warning
- Deception and concealment
- Helicopter relay platform

Meanwhile, China's fishing fleet, often with embedded or accompanying maritime militia and Coast Guard, goes around taking other people's property and fish.[52] Indeed, fishing fleets, which are ultimately an extension of the Chinese government and its coercive power, are a perfect cover for expansion, surveillance, and intimidation. They give the appearance of being non-military and less threatening (and given their commercial component, they even cover some of their own costs).

You get the same results—taking over territory and subduing people who might resist—as you do with a shooting war, but without all the headline-grabbing violence and destruction.

South China Sea: China Takes It Over via the "Gray Zone"

The Chinese have taken full advantage of America's unwillingness to consider anything short of a shooting war as "war," as well as Washington's paralysis when dealing with gray-zone activities.

The South China Sea (SCS) is legally a combination of international waters and claims by multiple countries that, together, are one and half times the size of the Mediterranean Ocean. Over the last decade, the PRC has gained effective control of the region, largely through gray-zone activities.

It seized the Scarborough Shoals from the Philippines, a U.S. ally, in 2012. Then it carried out an aggressive campaign to construct several artificial islands, three with major military airfields and all with significant naval facilities—despite Xi Jinping's agreement with the White House in 2015 not to militarize the islands.[53]

And Beijing didn't just use the military to expand control.

It moved an oil-drilling rig into Vietnamese waters in 2014—backed up by the China Coast Guard with the PLA Navy nearby.[54] The rig moved out eventually, and Westerners claimed, "China blinked." No, they'd demonstrated they can go and occupy any part of the South China Sea, and nobody could, or would, do anything about it.

By 2015, the Chinese had effective control of the South China Sea. These seem like warlike acts. Yet China has gotten away with them.

During the Obama administration, China's encroachment in the South China Sea was never really challenged. President Obama even prohibited the U.S. Navy from conducting Freedom of Navigation Operations (FONOPS) in the South China Sea from 2012 to 2015, before allowing some poorly conducted patrols in 2016 (a year before leaving office).[55]

Instead of admitting that the PRC was already at war with the United States, China's military buildup and expansion never seem to evoke a consistent sense of threat on the U.S. side. One U.S. Indo-Pacific Command chief, Admiral Samuel Locklear, was thought to have considered global warming his biggest challenge.[56] His successor, Admiral Harry Harris, dismissed Chinese submarines as Model Ts while the American versions were Corvettes.[57]

And a previous commander, Admiral Dennis Blair downplayed Chinese island-building to take over the South China Sea, noting it would take only ten to fifteen minutes to neutralize Beijing's man-made islands in the South China Sea—the so-called "Great Wall of Sand"—if a real war happened.[58]

He didn't notice that it was already happening.

China's Navy, Coast Guard, and maritime militia continued to bully Vietnam, the Philippines, Malaysia, and Indonesia.

Japan, America's main ally in Asia, is under incessant harassment and pressure from Chinese ships and aircraft in the East China Sea looking to carve off Japanese territory. In the late 2010s, Japan Maritime Self-Defense Force officers quietly admitted they were being "overwhelmed."[59]

These days, the United States conducts exercises in the South China Sea that include aircraft carrier strike groups. America makes a show of being able to go wherever it wants.

But there is a sense that the United States is there at China's sufferance. It's roughly the equivalent of the New York Police Department sending a squad car through Times Square in the bad old days before Mayor Giuliani.

The human flotsam would part as the squad car went through, only to flow back in and continue illegal antics once the police cruiser was gone.

Meanwhile, the PRC keeps solidifying its hold and dominance. For every ship the United States puts into the South China Sea, China can deploy ten ships. So it kind of looks like it is escorting the Americans. And before long, Beijing will require permission to enter areas it controls—if not from the Americans, from others.

What China has accomplished in the South China Sea is not quite the same as launching a missile into Washington, D.C. But it got similar results. China's gray-zone activities in the South China Sea are also about conditioning Americans. At first, Beijing just "warned" the Americans about the South China Sea. Then it established a zone defense. Now it's man-to-man, but with a lot more men. Meanwhile, on the lawfare front, it has continued passing laws establishing the South China Sea as China's internal waters. Eventually, the SCS will be no-go, and Beijing will enforce it.

Special Military Operations

Similarly, in mid-2022, Xi Jinping issued an order allowing Chinese troops to engage in Special Military Operations abroad.[60]

Special Military Operations? It sounds a lot like fighting a war that "really isn't a war."

Calling warlike activities by another name works well. Too many Americans will contort themselves to believe it. State Department lawyers will fret over what Xi intends and the "legality" of it.

But one might fairly consider this as "war" and not some "gray zone" behavior that must not be challenged. One observer explained it:

> Special Military Operations becomes a long preplanned policy "excuse" to engage the PLA in far-flung corners of the world, bypassing the traditional branding of such actions as "an invasion" or "war." Putin has utilized this concept with the Russian citizenry. This "non-invasion" propaganda works nicely for the Party domestically as nobody panics. It also works nicely for the naïve outside the country who buy into this nomenclature and false distinction. Think about the 140 or so countries that are directly involved with China under its BRI (Belt and Road Initiative). Each investment, each project, and each loan is then a potential PRC asset that will require or may require PLA "Special Military" defensive protection in the future. I anticipate that we will see the extensive use of the Special Military Operations excuse in the near future, for example, the Solomons and selected African countries. Presumably, anywhere China has "overseas interests"—either physical, economic, or human.[61]

And China has a lot of overseas interests.

This is all part of a continuum: sizing up reactions, getting practice and experience, influencing and conditioning, and getting infrastructure and presence in place for the day the "real" shooting starts, if that's necessary.

China sees itself as at war. Americans can't imagine it, even if we know this isn't good.

But we've been conditioned to think we can't do anything until "war" starts.

Call it gray zone if you will, but if we don't deal with it forcefully and prepare to fight, we can expect to lose.

But maybe there's a deal to be cut to ensure "peace in our time"? Probably not, despite the American conceit that everyone wants to be us, and if we can just talk, we can transform behavior.

To show how dangerous this approach is when dealing with a nation that sees the United States as an enemy to be vanquished, an experienced American China hand (of the good sort) noted: "There is no acceptable 'act of good faith' that can be offered as an intermediate step while trying to settle a larger-scale contentious relationship. What we call 'good faith' only delays what the (Communist) Party believes should be the inevitable outcome: complete recognition and acceptance of the wisdom, guidance, and leadership of the Party. In English, this would often be referred to as capitulation."[62]

Talking for talking's sake also allows the PRC to better size us up and buys it time to calculate what it needs to develop militarily—so it can take us on or deter us from backing up our friends in Asia.

How do you compete with that sort of opponent? They have different objectives and different rules than us, and are not interested in guardrails for the relationship. But they are glad to see us erect self-imposed "guardrails" on ourselves.

Let this "not-quite-war" activity continue unchecked, and the United States might awaken to find itself in a stranglehold it can't get out of, except at too high a price.

We've watched the lead-up to kinetic war and haven't recognized it for what it was. But at some point, the PRC may decide it's time to go from "not quite war" to "real" war—of the sort the Americans recognize.

The Taiwan Question

The combination of political warfare, gray-zone actions, and the potential for kinetic warfare come together most clearly around Taiwan, which offers the most immediate prospect of China going on a major kinetic offensive.

Taiwan remains *the* key objective for the Chinese communists, and Xi's declaration at the 20th CCP Congress in November 2022 that China would use all possible means (i.e., force) to seize Taiwan got loud applause from the audience. It's presented as unfinished business from the Chinese civil war. But even more, Taiwan is key to Chinese communist domination of Asia, the Pacific, and ultimately the United States.

Taiwan is where China is getting ready for a war of the sort of the Americans will recognize.

It conducted a dress rehearsal in August 2022. The PLA established "live fire exclusion zones" around Taiwan following Speaker of the House Nancy Pelosi's visit. The Chinese fired missiles bracketing both Taiwan and southern Japanese islands and conducted a range of naval and air maneuvers towards Taiwan.[63]

Was this an act of war?

The U.S. administration apparently doesn't think so, and the Chinese communists are glad to let it think that. To the Chinese, however, it is war. Or at least a test run.

One American observer described it as follows:

> This is not an infantile reaction to the denial of Beijing's narrative about Taiwan. This is what the Chinese call a "demonstration

project" to test how Taiwan and its allies and friends respond to these aerial (and naval) incursions (and missile launches). It gives the PLA the opportunity to measure and evaluate the aggregate Taiwan-U.S. defense umbrella performance from satellite over-head to sub-surface activity under the sea. It's a tabletop (and field training) exercise in real-time, 3D, to access certain capabili-ties of the Taiwan-U.S. defense umbrella.[64]

At the same time, Beijing intimidates Taiwan (as well as the Ameri-cans, the Japanese, and everyone else) and tests the response. If the response is weak or frightened, it advances China's thinking and makes it more likely Xi Jinping will issue the "go" order.

Even before the August 2022, Chinese test blockade of Taiwan, PLAAF aerial incursions were a regular feature in the airspace around Taiwan.

A U.S. Marine pilot described how one particular incident ties in with an eventual war:

> This appears to be an armed electronic warfare reconnais-sance team sniffing out Taiwanese aerial defense radars, locations, and arrays. Simultaneously conditioning the Taiwanese and the world to larger and larger intrusions, until one day that lead intrusion package initiates hostilities and takes out a meaningful wedge of [Taiwan's] anti-access aerial denial systems in an entire sector. [This creates] a breech for the main assault package to enter and attack the remaining radar sites and missiles from the rear. This is not good, nor is it the action of a respectful neighbor.[65]

The PLA has been preparing itself for an attack on Taiwan for the last fifty years. Since 2016, when Taiwan elected President Tsai Wing-en (who, unlike her predecessor, was unwilling to kowtow to Beijing), Chinese military pressure on Taiwan has steadily increased.[66] PLA aircraft and ships routinely encroach on Taiwan's territory and space, and the PLA has laid the infrastructure for an assault on Taiwan—should Taipei not concede peacefully.

As mentioned, Beijing is also looking at America's political condition and strength—domestic and global. This directly affects America's ability to respond effectively to a Chinese kinetic move against Taiwan. So, disruptions caused by activists burning down American cities, and half the country and much of America's elite class (including Republican Never Trumpers) afflicted with Trump Derangement Syndrome, weigh in favor of going kinetic.

The United States economic and financial conditions also weigh into Beijing's calculations. American supply chain dependency is in China's favor. This works both ways, but less so if China is sanctions-proof, as it has been trying to make itself. U.S. manufacturing, especially the defense industrial base, has diminished to the point it cannot produce weapons or build ships and aircraft fast enough (much less repair them) to fight a serious war against a serious opponent that is willing to roll the dice.

From China's perspective, America's heavy indebtedness, high inflation, and out of control entitlement (social) spending choking out defense spending are another favorable sign for Chinese planners.

The United States may find itself simply unable to afford to deploy forces to respond. Combine this with an assault on the dollar and China dumping its U.S. bond holdings at just the right time.

Fentanyl and other China-sourced drugs ravaging the U.S. and killing tens of thousands of Americans a year, many of military age, further alter the balance in Chinese communist favor.

And as important from China's perspective, there is the question of will on the part of the U.S. government.

The Trump administration was the first American administration since 1972 that seemed to have the will to resist the PRC, and Beijing sensed this. During President Trump's visit to China in 2017, Chinese officials tried to rough up members of the visiting American delegation. Chief of Staff John Kelly (a retired Marine general) reportedly got physical with them.[67] This perhaps set the tone for the Chinese treatment—hesitant, almost deferential—of the Trump administration.

But the successor administration seems to be less willing to fight—although it has not entirely rolled over for China as some previous administrations had, both Republican and Democrat.

U.S. secretary of state Antony Blinken stated in a speech laying out the Biden administration's foreign policy vision: "Our relationship with China will be competitive when it should be, collaborative when it can be, and adversarial when it must be. And we will engage China from a position of strength."[68]

However, the U.S. Secretary of State's high-sounding statement may not convince Beijing. It perhaps underestimates Chinese intentions to have one winner and one loser in the PRC-U.S. fight. It also potentially backs the Americans into a corner. Often, U.S. administrations have believed they must have China's cooperation on various issues: climate change, North Korea, transnational crime, and so forth. And that translates into overlooking all sorts of Chinese misbehavior.

America's Allies?

China also considers the state of the United States' relations with its allies (and potential allies). It is keeping score and trying to bring more into the China column.

Japan seems solidly with the United States at the end of the day—assuming the Americans are serious about fighting—and the

Japanese Navy is a problem for China. The other parts of the Japan Self-Defense Forces, less so.

Australia, even the Labor governments, have shown backbone in standing up to China since 2015 when reporter John Garnaut and Professor Clive Hamilton came along and took the lead in exposing PRC influence (political warfare) in Australia.[69]

New Zealand is very much in play from China's perspective.

South Korea was pro-China under the Moon Jae-in administration, but the current conservative administration has arrested the shift towards the PRC, and most South Koreans have no great love for the Chinese anyway.

ASEAN nations are a mixed bag, and even nominally "pro-U.S." Singapore is trying to avoid choosing sides in a fight between China and the United States over Taiwan—or over anything else.

The Philippines have proven harder than expected for China to bring on board. Philippine-U.S. defense cooperation has proven more resilient than Beijing might have expected after President Duterte was elected. And things have shifted in Washington's favor following the election of President Marcos in 2022.

At the same time, the PRC has had considerable success in developing friends throughout Latin America and Africa, to the point nearly every government in South America is now leftist and tilting towards China.

And until the COVID pandemic hit, Europe (including the United Kingdom) was heavily leaning towards China. As an example, British prime minister David Cameron (a conservative) welcomed unchecked Chinese investment into the country and the sensitive nuclear industry, not to mention resisting warnings about Huawei. Cameron set up a China-focused investment fund shortly after leaving office.[70] (You'd think he was an Australian politician before 2015.)

However, the Ukraine war and China's support for Russia have shifted European thinking strikingly. Most European nations now see

China as a threat, having doubts about the economic relationship with the PRC, though to varying degrees, with Germany being a case in point.[71]

So the PRC's scorecard tends to fluctuate as it calculates prospects for getting away with something kinetic.

When Will China Go Kinetic?

"When the time is right."

In 1974 after the Portugal Revolution, the new Portuguese government offered to give Macau back to the PRC. The reply: "Not now. When the time is right."[72] This fits in with Deng's "bide your time" admonition.[73]

The Chinese are opportunistic. They will move when there is an opening that allows them to take what they want with the enemy (or enemies) unable or unwilling to respond effectively.

But being opportunistic doesn't mean the Chinese are not on a timeline. Nor does it mean the Chinese are infantile. They are just as smart as we are.

Retired U.S. Navy captain James Fanell, formerly the head of intelligence at the U.S. Navy's Pacific Fleet, was the first to lay out this timeline in the mid-2010s as it related to a kinetic attack to seize Taiwan.

Captain Fanell assessed that the decade starting in 2020 would be the "Decade of Concern." This is when China would think it had the military capabilities to attack Taiwan, seize the self-governed island (a country in all but name), and still have nearly two decades for the free world to get used to it before 2049—the hundredth anniversary of the founding of the People's Republic of China. Thus, the men in Zhongnanhai could claim that China's "great rejuvenation" was complete.[74]

So it's perhaps fair to say that within this general time frame, China is watching for opportunity to move. Meanwhile, it continues its political warfare efforts to soften up potential opposition—and even brings together some nations that will either support Beijing, or at least stay mute—which are fundamentally the same things.

Meanwhile, China's main enemy—the United States—seems off-balance. Society is fractured. People are at each other's throats. The economy is vulnerable. Even the U.S. military isn't what it used to be. Financial matters aren't in much better shape. However, the U.S. dollar is still powerful owing to there being no serious alternative—yet.

From Beijing's perspective, it has the capabilities for a fight, and its main opponent seems confused and distracted. Wait too much longer, say, five years, and the Americans (and their friends, especially the Japanese) might collect their wits and become more able and willing to fight.

Taiwan shows no sign of surrendering.

So, if it's to be kinetic, move fast, hit hard, and present your enemies with a *fait accompli*.

Section Three

WHAT IT LOOKS LIKE
WHEN WE LOSE

CHAPTER 18

China Attacks: The Political and the Kinetic Combine

The Chinese communists will calculate the odds and strike when they think they have the best chance of winning. This isn't to say they will win. But they at least believe they will, and that's what matters.

We covered this in the introduction, but let's look at it again. Here's how I see Chinese thinking and events playing out.

The PRC will not try for an all-out crushing of the United States—at least in the sense of occupying U.S. territory. That would be too hard—and domination of the Americans and their submission will be fine for Beijing.

It's also unlikely the Chinese will launch an all-out "Pearl Harbor" sort of assault on U.S. bases in Japan or the Pacific, including Hawaii or the U.S. West Coast, even though they could.

However, the People's Republic of China will aim for an attack that bloodies the Americans and discredits and humiliates them in the eyes of America's allies and friends, and every other country that looks to the United States for leadership and protection—even if they won't say so publicly.

It's equally important to the Chinese that America's ruling class and government are discredited in the eyes of its citizens.

PRC strategists aim to give U.S. leaders a choice between 1) the United States as a smoking ruin with tens of millions dead or 2) the option of accepting Chinese suzerainty.

Owing to decades of successful Chinese political warfare, plenty of Americans would accept the latter choice—especially those in the ruling class. The Cold War 1.0 slogan was "Better Dead Than Red." The Cold War 2.0 slogan will be "Better Red Than Dead."

Beyond delivering a physical, psychological, and political hammering to Americans, China will aim to put the People's Liberation Army in a better operational position. Taking Taiwan would do that. Such improved positioning would permit freer access for PLA operations throughout the Indo-Pacific and globally—as more locations open up to receive Chinese ships, planes, and troops.

This also provides additional political leverage for the Chinese communists. Note how economic and political warfare have already laid the groundwork for these advances, as well as making eventual kinetic activities more effective.

China Will Assess the U.S. Domestic Situation When Deciding Its Course of Action

One analyst told me that if China strikes Taiwan between 2022 and 2030, it will be because China perceives America is decisively weak and has no will or ability to resist, not because China is decisively stronger.[1]

Perhaps. But Beijing will, in any event, calculate America's ability to put up a serious, unified defense. That makes all the difference. Remember the CCP's benchmark Comprehensive National Power is a relative matrix.

The Chinese communists will carefully calculate the then-administration's will and competence, and which officials are already friendly towards the PRC—or can be made friendly with some persuasion.

Beijing will like its chances even more if the United States is tearing itself apart politically, with half the nation seeing the other half as enemies to be destroyed. Social and racial unrest will be another plus from Beijing's perspective—and it will continue to stoke it via media warfare and use of proxies.

China will also count on Wall Street and other "friends of China" to counsel caution and negotiation to resolve differences and lower temperatures—and if necessary, give the PRC what it wants to avoid further war. Fear of blackmail may also shape the behavior of certain American elites.

Adding to the PRC's confidence is the perception that the U.S. military's will, condition, and capacity for fighting are in question after having been unsuccessful in the Iraq and Afghanistan campaigns—and against far less formidable opponents than the Chinese. At the same time, senior leaders are seemingly as interested in critical race theory and understanding imaginary white rage in the ranks as in fighting wars.

Additionally, America's finances—out of control spending, debt, and inflation—weaken U.S. defenses and ability to focus on external threats. Inflation in particular eats away at away at military readiness by reducing training opportunities, hardware procurement, and even the nation's ability to finance a war. An $850 billion defense budget is 10 percent less when you consider inflation.

Beijing will also closely watch (and try to influence) U.S. elections. There's always the chance of civil unrest and rioting. Both are not conducive to a proper defense against China. If the Democrats win, that's good for the PRC—given their majority focus on climate change and social justice. If the Republicans prevail, that's less good for China, as at least some Republicans talk a good game about national defense.

But either way, the PRC has a window of at least three or four years before the U.S. can even begin to get its financial house in order, rebuild, and reconfigure its military so it can fight a war. Regardless of electoral outcomes, American society looks to remain divided for a long while, especially if the influence operations of the PRC (and others) aren't shut down.

It's often claimed that there is bipartisan agreement on Capitol Hill about the need to get tough with the People's Republic of China. Maybe. Maybe not. Strong language often comes out of Congress, but it doesn't always translate into concrete actions. Taiwan still has not been invited to the RIMPAC exercise—despite congressional resolutions calling on the administration to do so.[2] Nor was Taiwan included in the administration's Indo-Pacific Economic Framework plan.[3] Apparently, fear of the PRC is too great.

And the truth-teller: Chinese-origin fentanyl kills over seventy thousand Americans a year—and nobody does anything. China might fairly think that even if it goes kinetic, Americans might take it—the way they do the fentanyl assault.

The point is, Chinese decision-making on whether and when to go kinetic will be shaped by America's domestic situation as much as anything. The stomach of the administration counts. If it is seen as weak and distracted, and there are fractures and unrest in U.S. society and politics, as well as messy government finances, it makes a go decision more likely.

It's also important to note that, for at least two decades, the PRC has been working to sanctions-proof itself. It just might be thinking it can absorb the financial and trade sanctions the United States will likely impose in the event of a Chinese attack. After all, Vladimir Putin did after he invaded Ukraine, albeit with considerable strain. And if the Russians could do it, certainly the Chinese can do it better, Beijing might think.

What Would an Attack Look Like?

As described at the start of this book, the main focus of the direct kinetic action will probably be close to home—i.e., within range of the Chinese mainland. PLA power projection capabilities are improving rapidly, but classical Chinese military power drops off beyond the First Island Chain. This will be the case for the next five years at least.

However, China may conduct, or arrange for, gray-zone activities and proxies to launch supporting efforts well beyond the First Island Chain, in different parts of the globe. But the primary effort will likely be closer to home.

Chinese planners will aim for a fight in a setting and location where the PLA has the clear advantage in terms of ability to mass forces and supporting fires (particularly its huge missile force), and to ensure logistical support.

Keep in mind that a military just has to be good enough to do a certain thing at a certain time and at a certain place. And, while the U.S. has had to build a military able to handle a range of threats around the globe, the PRC has had the luxury of being able to hone a force primarily designed to counter and defeat a single enemy—us

Two likely candidates for the main effort: the South China Sea and the Taiwan Strait (though don't discount either a simultaneous or opportunistic hit on the Indian border).

China already has de facto control of the South China Sea. Attacking U.S. Navy ships transiting or exercising in the South China Sea would likely achieve surprise, but it would not be a decisive blow against the United States. Nor would it improve PLA operational positioning, as it would still be at risk of being hemmed in within the First Island Chain.

Plus, Americans would have time to catch their breath and get ready—and try to rally allies and partners and implement harsh sanctions. This would also be the case if China attacked, say, Japanese, Australian, or some other U.S.-friendly nation's ships.

By elimination, this leaves Taiwan.

China has studied the Russian assault on Ukraine and aims to avoid Vladimir Putin's mistakes.

The main lessons learned from Ukraine for an assault on Taiwan?

Do it fast and use everything. Do not skimp on missiles or violence. No gradual build up—either before the attack or once it has begun.

And block Taiwan's communications. Cut the internet and undersea cables connecting Taiwan to the outside world. Do not allow Taiwan's president or other surviving leaders to have a microphone with which to rally the citizenry or the world.

Any Taiwanese satellites will be shut down. And the PLA will hit American satellites just enough to make the United States back off—though not totally blinding us, so we don't panic and actually decide to fight.

Fifth columnists and maritime militia will pay a major role. Pre-invasion insertions of special forces and saboteurs will ramp up—having already been in place for years, to include via almost regularly scheduled smuggling routes between Taiwan and the Chinese mainland. Turncoats, quite possibly plentiful, within the Taiwan Armed Forces will also make their presence felt.[4]

And the invasion fleet, much of it civilian ships (remember military-civil fusion) will be employed from dispersed locations. Meanwhile, the American strategists will have been waiting for signs that the fleet was coming together in centralized coastal locations in preparation for setting off for Taiwan.

Helicopters and airborne troops will be used in large numbers. Getting across the Strait is more than just boats.

Taiwan's largest port, Kaohsiung, has a substantial COSCO presence—the Chinese state-owned shipping company. Even more, the port is said to have been under organized crime control for many years. This was my area of expertise for over a decade. In my experience,

Taiwanese and Chinese organized crime are pretty much blood brothers and are ultimately under Chinese Ministry of State Security control. One more check in the attack box.

China will do a better job with narrative control than Russia did with Ukraine.

In this case, it will be:

"Taiwan secessionist forces were about to declare independence."

"We told you what we would do."

"This is a domestic issue."

"Wasn't Secretary of Defense Lloyd Austin listening to our defense minister when they met in Singapore in June (2022) and then again in Cambodia in November?"[5]

These sorts of messages will resonate with many Chinese, especially if the battle is going well. And those with second thoughts know to keep their mouths shut.

The message might also work with the many nations that want to hold off and wait to see how things play out. This is especially so with other Indo-Pacific nations—many of which are penetrated by their own pro-PRC fifth columnists.

Expect a simultaneous (or precursor) virus outbreak in the United States, maybe near a U.S. military base. The PRC liked what it saw from COVID-19 panicking and paralyzing the U.S. government, and presumably will have worked out the kinks for the next run. An outbreak in Taiwan is equally likely.

Nuclear weapons? Beijing will loudly threaten, and just might use, nuclear weapons. A couple of options: a tactical nuclear weapon detonated in the ocean east of Taiwan—the route the American relief force would take. Or perhaps a small nuke fired at Taipei itself to soften up the population and break government resistance.

China claims it has a no-first-use policy for nuclear weapons. But does anybody care to bet that will not go by the wayside? Remember the promise not to militarize the (illegally occupied) islands of the South China Sea? And anyway, using the PRC's own logic, Taiwan is a part of China, and there is no legal barrier to nuking your own country.

The message from employing nuclear weapons—or threatening to do so—is clear: United States…stand back. And maybe we will. Trading New York for Taiwan may be too steep a price for a president—no matter who it is. Just the threat of thousands or tens of thousands of casualties, even without nuclear weapons being used, is no less daunting.

Americans will find that we really should have talked to the Taiwanese about a combined defense beforehand—rather than expecting to wing it when the time came. (Amazingly, in fifty-plus years, the Americans have done only two small—platoon sized—exercises with Taiwanese forces.)

And so, the PLA will have breached the First Island Chain—the American, Japanese, and partners' main defense line. And from Taiwan, the PLA Navy and Air Force then range easily into the central and south Pacific Oceans, and will be in a position to surround Japan. Australia can also be cut off from Southeast Asia and the U.S. West Coast.

Americans will find ourselves with plenty to think about. Not least domestically.

The United States: A Shock to Our System

The Americans public (most of it, at least) will be shocked, scared, and furious when it discovers the United States is unprepared for a war like this one. They won't like that Chinese cargo ships and fishing boats have sunk U.S. Navy ships, and that the U.S. Navy didn't have enough ships to start with. We only have 295 (including Littoral Combat Ships that aren't really fighting ships) to cover the entire globe,[6] while the Chinese have 350 PLA Navy combatants—700-plus ships if you count China Coast Guard and other ships that work well for combat, too.[7]

The PRC fishing fleet and militarized maritime militia add thousands more ships to the Chinese fleet.

The American public will also be distressed to learn that the United States can't replace its sunk ships and can't repair damaged ones nearly as fast as is needed, because, in spite of warnings, America has let its shipyards die.

The U.S. Navy and Air Force do get in some shots—via submarine and air launched long range cruise missiles—and sink dozens, and maybe a lot more, PLA ships. But China made the first move and set things up right, so the United States suffers plenty of damage and casualties.

Some pundits assume that an attack on Taiwan, and even killing Americans in the process (there are seventy-five thousand of them living in Taiwan, not to mention American service members dying in large numbers), would unite America the way the 9/11 terrorist attacks did.

Twenty years ago, I would have said: "100 percent sure."

A decade ago: "80 percent sure."

These days: "Maybe 50 percent, and that's being optimistic."

Nobody under ninety years old has any real memory of America being in a serious war and suffering thousands of casualties in a single day. And nobody has any memory of the American mainland being hit. And we still aren't even talking about the hundreds, maybe thousands, of Americans left behind—with some likely killed—during the catastrophic withdrawal from Afghanistan.[8] Weren't we the country that leaves no one behind?

Maybe 40 percent.

There'll be no shortage of American elites—business, political, academic, and financial—saying it was America's fault. Nothing to do now but negotiate a deal.

Expect one hundred scholars and foreign policy mandarins to sign a letter calling for a cease-fire—and, if the administration is Republican, to blame the president for either starting the war or not winning it.

Wall Street and the business community will push hard to end hostilities. Taiwan just isn't worth it, it will be argued once again. And Beijing's offer of a special Free Trade Agreement with the United States as part of the PRC's new co-prosperity sphere will have some takers among the Quisling class.

Congress (at least part of it) may even call for the president's head—or at least impeachment.

If we don't immediately fall to our knees, economic and financial chaos will grow with cyber-attacks and power grids and ATMs no longer working. Not having enough gas and oil since we've gone green will exacerbate matters.

The United Nations? That's a good one.

Canada, Mexico, Latin America, and Africa might just sit it out and wait to see what happens. And there might be plenty of quiet satisfaction that the Americans are suffering.

Even our longtime ally, Japan, will take its lead from a hesitant, stumbling United States and do the bare minimum—appearing to provide support and saying the right things, while in fact, not really joining the fray and committing the Japan Self-Defense Force.

Australia will try, but will realize Taiwan is harder to reach than it thought, and Canberra's bigger worry is protecting Australia itself, which is dangerously exposed.

The Southeast Asian nations? They've said for years that they don't want to have to choose between the United States and China. So they don't. Not even our friend, Singapore. The Philippines doesn't, either.

After a couple of months (probably sooner), it will be clear that the United States is losing—or has lost. Taiwan is gone, having asked for terms from Beijing. The United States has pulled back.

Of course, it is possible that the United States may decide at this point that nuclear weapons are an option.

Expect the PRC to call for talks in that case. But it will not give up anything it has taken, and it will not apologize.

Instead, Beijing will issue a list of demands for the United States to comply with to restore "mutual respect," "mutual cooperation," and "respect for China's core interests," which was all the PRC and the Chinese people wanted in the first place, of course.

The Americans may be lucky enough to retain independence and even cobble together a free nation bloc and try to rebuild defenses.

Or the United States may, under threat of Chinese nuclear attack, and even a conventional overmatch, accept suzerainty status. In other words, allowed a degree of internal self-governance, but foreign affairs are de facto controlled by the PRC, perhaps via reconfigured and compliant international organization. And when China says it wants Washington to do something, it does it. What sorts of demands are likely?

A social credit score system implemented. The Chinese currency, the RMB declared legal tender in the United States, and whatever China buys from America will be paid for in Chinese currency—possibly digital currency for increased surveillance and control.

The United States will end its containment policies towards China, reduce the size of its military, and withdraw from all bilateral and multilateral treaty commitments—if its allies haven't already done so. It will withdraw from all overseas bases unless the PRC allows otherwise.

Insulting commentary and statements about the PRC and the Chinese Communist Party will be prohibited. The free press and media are finished. Academia, however, won't need to change very much. It was already pro-PRC. The United States will hand over people on lists provided by the PRC. A Hong Kong-style approach to government and law and elections will be implemented, all approved by Beijing, with court verdicts subject to review by China's Supreme Court.

All property belonging to Chinese citizens that was seized or frozen by the U.S. government will be returned with compensation.

China will insist certain Chinese companies have access to the U.S. market with no competition, and there will be import quotas of food-stuffs, raw materials, and energy for America to provide. And U.S. companies will enter the China market by invitation only.

What will daily life look like in the United States? On a good day, post-crackdown Hong Kong. On a day we "misbehave"? COVID-lockdown Shanghai (or COVID-lockdown Canada).

There will be no shortage of Quislings who will make the best of things. And as we saw in the case of COVID lockdown dissent controls, some states will gladly go along with an authoritarian approach to governance. That sort of power is intoxicating for certain sorts of bureaucrats, managers, and politicians—and they can pretend (even to themselves) it's all just to be "efficient" and "effective," without having to provide proof.

The White House will issue executive orders suspending the Constitution, declaring martial law, and federalizing state National Guards.

But some states might not go along.

Expect fighting to break out throughout the United States if an armistice and overt suzerainty status is agreed to.

Some states may attempt to form another country—a free one. The central government in Washington will try to prevent it. Hard to imagine? Consider the events of the COVID-19 rule-by-fear experience, and the state-by-state actions and reactions that you never thought would happen.

The United States breaking apart? Maybe even ruled by an emperor—by whatever name? Not impossible.

Regardless, the United States as we know it will be finished.

Final note: the United States won't have the benefit of time to recover or become a safe haven from which to organize and operate as it did in World War II. How much time do we have to get things in order?

Not much. At most, a few years. And that's being (very) optimistic.

How to Win

CHAPTER 19

How to Defend and Counter

The PRC is attacking us on many fronts, and now we know how. So what do we do?

It's not complicated. We must defend and counter where necessary, going on the offensive where the Chinese communists are vulnerable to our strengths.

As the Chinese have shown with their political warfare campaign against us, there's plenty of damage to be done without (or before) using actual violence. Fortunately, this strategy works both ways—and the People's Republic of China can both be countered and attacked where it is vulnerable. We just have to want to do it.

The United States needs its own political warfare strategy that systematically combines diplomacy, propaganda, and economic, financial, and technological strengths with military power and alliances, thus forming a proper campaign plan. The strategy needs to last beyond a single administration and needs direction—in other words, somebody in charge—and with real authority, and with some sort of punishment for failure.

The attack on the United States has been, to use Beijing's term, comprehensive. To win, we have to be just as comprehensive—and a bit more so.

One starting point is a simple word: reciprocity. Don't let them do anything in the United States that we can't do in the PRC. And maybe let them do even less, given the nature of the Chinese communist regime and what it intends to do to us. We should begin by giving as good as we get. What does that mean in practice? Let's go through some of the ways we saw the PRC attacking us through the course of this book and see how we can fight back.

Psychological Warfare

On the defensive side, we must start with the right mindset, get the noise out of our heads, and look at the situation clearly.

Among other things, that means recognizing and admitting that the United States is already at war with the People's Republic of China. It may not be an American version of war, but it is a Chinese version of war—and that's what matters. Be grateful that it's not yet a shooting war and there's still some time to get organized. But it is a war.

Then admit that we might lose—as hard as that is for Americans who grew up in the post–World War II era to imagine. Don't assume that a humane system of consensual government based on individual liberty and freedoms will always win out. As Benjamin Franklin was reported to have said, we have "a republic, if you can keep it."[1]

We should also make it clear what happens if we can't keep it. This must include teaching about the nature of communist and totalitarian regimes. What does that look like? In 2022, Florida governor Ron DeSantis signed legislation requiring public schools to teach about "atrocities" committed by communist regimes while declaring November 7 "Victims of Communism Day." DeSantis was clear about his motivation: "Honoring the people that have fallen victim to communist regimes and teaching our students about those atrocities is the best way to ensure that history does not repeat itself.... While it's fashionable in some circles to whitewash the history of communism, Florida will stand for truth and remain as a beachhead for freedom."[2]

These kinds of reminders are necessary since most Americans under forty have no real sense of communism, and certainly not of its depredations and bellicosity. There is little recognition today that there were regimes in Eastern Europe, Africa, and Southeast Asia—not forgetting the Soviet Union and PRC—enslaving and murdering their own citizens and looking to *destroy* us.

With generational change and little education on the topic, societal understanding fades. When I was young, it was the Great Depression that we'd hear about from parents and others with firsthand experience. But we still couldn't quite understand it.

That's how you end up with Cadet Spencer Rapone taking a photo at his West Point graduation in 2016 that shows "Communism will win" written inside his hat.[3]

He's not just one nut—he was living in a sympathetic ecosystem of nuttiness. A key incubator for that ecosystem are the education systems, which is why the PRC and others try to influence our curricula. It's also why the Florida initiative is important. No, imperative.

Liberating academia will be hard. Just within the universities, the subversion is often thorough, and the addiction to full-tuition Chinese students great.

But it can be done. We've seen glimmers. The Trump administration's China Initiative had a component that went after some of the more egregious Thousand Talents Program participants, and it made a difference.[4] Confucius Institutes were also hammered—that is, universities were told they could get government research contracts or have a Confucius Institute, but not both.

This showed we can fight, but we need to stick with it. The Biden administration dropped the China Initiative.[5] Without oversight, the Confucius Institutes seem to be renaming and reconfiguring.[6]

What would help is to go even bigger. If a university is caught facilitating Chinese-government-linked espionage or IP theft (for example, through Thousand Talents), or pushing a CCP-approved line (for example, maps that show borders that only the CCP a recognizes), take away the school's tax exempt status. Or just do it immediately for the universities with billions in endowments. Why should U.S. taxpayers subsidize the CCP-friendly indoctrination of students and transfer of knowledge to China?

Similarly, we should launch a national initiative to further limit Chinese access to American universities in key science and engineering areas and subsidize a quadrupling of American enrollment in the same programs. In the past twenty years, America has gone from enjoying a five to three advantage over China in the number of STEM graduates to now seeing China graduate four times as many STEM students as the United States, and three times as many computer scientists.[7]

One long-service U.S. intelligence official lamented:

"Whenever U.S. universities or labs work on Chinese state priority research topics (e.g., Made in China 2025; new battery technology, etc.) PRC researchers are ALWAYS involved, if not leading."[8]

We should also make it a lot less desirable for American STEM students to go to China after graduation. During the Cold War, if a promising young nuclear scientist at an American university was offered a job at a Soviet lab and said yes, he or she would be considered a traitor. Today, young scientists envy their classmates who get highly paid jobs in well-equipped labs in China.[9]

There should be much more awareness on campuses that taking knowledge to China means American students will contribute to a system seeking the destruction of the free world and committing genocide against its own people. If that doesn't work, the students should be told that, if they work in China, they will no longer qualify for any job in the United States that is funded by government money or requires a security clearance.

As for whatever the Confucius Institutes are now called—campus-linked organizations that can act as CCP-indoctrination and monitoring hubs—be clear that these are outposts of a foreign, malign power, publish the MoUs, and send the supervisors home. Make sure Confucius Institutes don't reappear in other guises. Crack down on Chinese Student and Scholars Associations and other arms of the CCP's intimidation network operating in the United States.[10]

This will also help the Chinese diaspora. Chinese emigrants are among the primary influence and intimidation targets of United Front organizations. Most came to the United States to get away from CCP. And now, we let MSS terrorize them and use them against our society and government.[11]

In October 2020, FBI director Christopher Wray announced charges against eight people for participating in China's Operation Fox Hunt, an initiative described in these terms:

> A sweeping bid by General Secretary Xi and the Chinese Communist Party to target Chinese nationals here in the United States and across the world who are viewed as threats to the regime…. The target had two options: Return to China promptly or commit suicide. And what happens when Fox Hunt targets do refuse to return to China? Their family members, both here in the United States and in China, have been threatened and coerced; and those back in China have even been arrested for leverage.[12]

Wray added: "Simply put: It's outrageous that China thinks it can come to our shores, conduct illegal operations, and bend people here in the United States to their will."[13]

Yes. And what's more outrageous is, we let them.

Even worse, it has recently been revealed that the PRC has set up overseas police stations in over fifty foreign countries, including one in New York City. The PRC calls them "service centers" where Chinese nationals can get drivers licenses renewed and the like. In reality, they provide platforms for the CCP to control and intimidate Chinese people—and Chinese Americans—living overseas. Can you imagine something similar being allowed in China? Of course not.

FBI director Wray noted he was "very concerned."[14] Really.

In December 2022, hopefully starting a trend, the FBI arrested a Chinese citizen studying at Berklee College of Music in Boston on charges of harassing and threatening another Chinese national who posted a flyer near the school that called for freedom and democracy in the PRC.[15] The suspect also claimed to have informed Chinese law enforcement so the victim's family in China could be punished.[16]

Fighting back effectively will mean doing something about America's Quisling class (from Wall Street, to K Street, to Silicon Valley, to Hollywood). It will probably take laws to get it under control—and in the meantime, we can start with proper enforcement of existing laws. Embarrassment works, but only up to a point. Punishment of the donor class is ultimately more effective.

It also helps to make sure there's no money to be had. You can do business with China, or you can do business with the United States government.

The Department of Justice needs to seriously and impartially enforce the Foreign Agents Registration Act,[17] as well as expose all business dealings and consulting relationships—direct, indirect, laundered—of all U.S. officials and politicians. If they want to work for U.S. government, they have to put everything out on the table—unlike current disclosure statements that are hopelessly, and probably intentionally, vague.

We are focusing on China, but Russia, Iran, North Korea, and others are also causing serious damage, sometimes in collusion. We need systems that protect from all foreign (and domestic) enemies.

We should look around and learn from like-minded countries. For example, we should consider doing what the Australians did to shine light on the worst of Chinese political influence in politics and the media. The United Kingdom is also revamping its espionage legislation to tackle modern threats.

Ultimately, we have to up the odds of a Quisling getting caught. Quislings can do cost-benefit analysis. Fear of losing money, or, even worse, going to jail, seem to be a couple of possibilities that actually change their behavior.

During the Cold War, we were clear about who the enemy was—Rocky could fight Ivan Drago, and we were allowed to cheer the good guy (by extension, the U.S.A.) and boo the bad guy (by extension, the Soviet Union).

Try cheering the U.S.A. or booing the Chinese Communist Party on a university campus (or on Wall Street, or Silicon Valley, or Hollywood) today. I'm not sure what reception you'll get. Just the fact of being not sure can cause people to self-censor, which gives a win to the CCP.

That has to stop. We have our faults, but we *are* the good guys. We need not apologize for that.

We need to start punching the bad guys and get cheered for it.

Taking It to Drago

As we clear our own heads, we need to look for weaknesses in China's psychological defenses.

We want to hit the enemy where he is weakest. Chinese communist leaders often helpfully tell us what they are most afraid of—where they are most vulnerable. As a general rule, when the Chinese communists demand America stop doing something, it is a good idea to do more of it—because it is working.

So, for example, after a virtual meeting between President Biden and Xi Jinping in early 2022, the PRC produced an official readout that offered, probably inadvertently, helpful targeting guidance for the U.S. side.[18]

System Fragility

Xi Jinping stated that nobody should try to change another country's system.[19] This suggests that, despite its bluster, Beijing is concerned the stability of its regime is vulnerable to attack. So, hit them there. Launch a well-run political warfare campaign (including media and information warfare), backed by economic and financial pressure and (ideally) unassailable U.S. and allied militaries.

For example, we've seen that many Chinese have been trying for decades, by hook or by crook, to get their wealth out of the PRC and away from CCP. This is a political warfare advantage—as it's evidence that the people most benefitting from the Chinese Communist Party system don't have enough confidence in its future prospects to keep their money inside the country. This should be trumpeted from the rooftops by U.S. officials.

It can also be used against Wall Street and those saying we just have to be in the PRC market. If the Chinese who have a choice choose not to be in their own market, what is it they know that America's best and brightest don't? I can't think of a similar example in history when the elite and not-so-elites of a rising, powerful nation were hell-bent on getting their money into countries that they said were their biggest enemies.

Certainly, this is something worth mentioning. Loudly. Repeatedly. And make sure everyone in China knows what the Chinese Communist Party elite are doing. It's only one of many messages that could shake the CCP to its core.

It's also vulnerable to the right messenger. The Trump administration knew it. So, what did it do on the strategic messaging front? Deputy National Security Advisor Matt Pottinger made speeches in Mandarin, telling the Chinese that they deserved more than a boot on the neck from the CCP.[20] It drove Beijing crazy that an American might be able to speak directly to the Chinese people. The Americans had the PRC reacting for once—instead of vice versa.

But that was the exception. If we are going to conduct information warfare, we'd better know what we are doing. And except for a brief few years of effort by parts of the Trump administration, the U.S. government neither reacts well nor has any offensive messaging worth mentioning. Notice how Chinese vitriol, propaganda, and blatant lies so often go unchallenged—and are sometimes even explained away or, worse, defended.

There is a Global Engagement Center at the U.S. State Department that allegedly does propaganda and strategic communications. But it seems to be more effective at explaining to congressional committees why it needs continued funding rather than changing anybody's minds beyond Capitol Hill.

We need to bring back the United States Information Agency and United States Information Service (competently run). We also need to rebuild the Foreign Broadcast Information Service that offered English translations of what the Chinese communists were saying in Chinese—that is often very different from what they release in English.

If remedial study on effective propaganda is required, U.S. government types might consider the excellent China Uncensored programs. These are informative, produced on a shoestring budget, have nearly two million subscribers, and the Chinese government hates them. Google and YouTube routinely censor, demonetize, and impose age-restrictions on China Uncensored's shows covering topics such as Chinese protests against zero-COVID lockdowns. Presumably, the help from Google and YouTube pleases the CCP.

One expert on propaganda I talked with suggested the United States ought to get beyond sophomoric strategic communication and develop a useful U.S. narrative. "In the absence of a clear national strategy for confronting the PRC's bullying behavior and expansionism, it's no surprise that what passes for U.S. strategic communication regarding the threat is not working," this individual observed. "There is no 'whole-of-government' communication approach to the threat, and a lack of useful synchronicity in messaging between the National Security Council, State Department, and Department of Defense. On this point, America should take bold action: it can tell the truth about the PRC."[21]

Indeed. *They* are the bad guys. We should jam human rights, hypocrisy, and corruption down Beijing's throat—and not stop.

Again, there are examples that show that we can do it, and it makes a difference. We need to speak up—like the U.S. government did during the Trump administration when it finally said the Permanent Court of Arbitration ruling against the PRC and PRC behavior in the South China Sea was important and mattered.

Former assistant secretary of state David Stilwell explained:

> Until Beijing demonstrates that they want to talk, we in the Free World would be foolish to chase after Xi Jinping just because he claims we're containing him. When Beijing's tone-deaf treatment of India pushed Delhi into the Quad, the original sin was obviously China's. Until our leaders start mocking Beijing's claims of containment (why is that assumed to be a bad thing? The main effort in dealing with a pandemic is containment so the evil doesn't spread) instead of denying the accusation, we'll always be stuck in defense. Time to go offensive.[22]

Speaking of the pandemic and system fragility, Xi also noted to President Biden that politicizing diseases does no good. He was talking about COVID. Not surprisingly, Beijing is hypersensitive on this point and has tried to distract attention from the question of COVID's origins since, well, it originated in China. (Remember that when the virus first appeared, the Chinese Communist Party referred to it as the Wuhan virus).[23]

We should keep this issue alive and push it. David Stilwell noted the importance of U.S. officials "[restating] that COVID began in Wuhan,

China, that Beijing covered it up, all but ensuring a global pandemic, and that Beijing has not cooperated with the World Health Organization to get to the bottom of the pandemic origins and learn what Beijing knows."[24]

Nicholas Wade, the respected former *New York Times* science reporter, points out that understanding COVID's origins has more importance than just pinning blame on Beijing:

> The COVID-19 epidemic first emerged in Wuhan, almost on the doorstep of the Wuhan Institute of Virology, where SARS-like viruses were being engineered for greater infectivity. That the two things could be connected is a possibility as plain as day. Yet for two years, people of influence gulled most Americans into believing the opposite of what common sense suggested. In whose interest was this colossal misdirection? Of course, in China's. The congressional committee should look into China's ability to influence the beliefs and actions of America's elites. . . . Did it lean on media companies with substantial sales in China? Did China exploit the close connections of its Western-educated health officials with their counterparts in the West? It matters a great deal whether American opinion leaders merely deceived themselves or were manipulated by others.[25]

We should also ask for reparations, even if it is unlikely Beijing will pay up. This puts the Chinese communists on the defensive and refutes Beijing's efforts to deny responsibility and shift blame. We could also back those countries now struggling to repay their BRI debts to China because their economies collapsed due to a virus from China. If they decide to stop interest payments to Beijing for, say, a decade, so that their economy can recover, we can ensure it won't affect their standing in other financial fora.

COVID isn't the only damage China has inflicted on the world and lied about. Everyone from senior U.S. officials down to the wide range of U.S. influencers should constantly challenge and expose false Chinese claims on a range of issues. Examples: the South China Sea being declared "historically Chinese," and transparently false statements of "non-militarization" of the islands.

We should go after China's willful ecological destruction of the reefs and natural habitat of the South China Sea.[26] And maybe we should find out why otherwise noisy environmental NGOs have voiced so few complaints (while amplifying the voices of those who have).

While we are at it, we should stop calling it the South China Sea—a term that uses language to legitimize China's illegal claims. The Philippines calls its part the West Philippine Sea. Indonesia calls part of it North Natuna Sea. Maybe we should go with the inclusive name some in India are using, the ASEAN (Association of Southeast Asian Nations) Sea. It would show support to our friends in the region while also showing we won't accept looking at the world (and its maps) through the eyes of Beijing.

In a similar approach, but on a larger scale, we should build on existing cultural exchanges and journalist programs, bringing emerging leaders, journalists, and other influential sorts from like-minded nations. They can examine such topics as the likely future impact of PRC hegemony on the Indo-Pacific region. Too often, the people invited by U.S. embassies to come on these programs seem to dislike America, and then they get placed in academic environments where the teachers are even more anti-American. We should bring on some individuals who are at least well-disposed to the United States and have them meet people who love America, warts and all.

While pointing out ways the CCP has damaged the world, the United States and its representatives should aggressively, unapologetically speak up for the system of rights, freedoms, and accepted rules of international behavior that has been largely responsible for peace and security for decades and has benefited most on the planet (and allowed the PRC's development).

Human Rights

Another thing Xi and the Chinese communists absolutely hate is the human rights issue. They try to get around it by arguing there is a Chinese version of human rights—presumably, one including concentration camps and removing and selling organs on-demand from religious and political prisoners. Human rights ought to be front and center in U.S. policy towards the PRC—not least as a matter of morality. But this also can hit Beijing on the economic and financial front.

Take a page from what was done to apartheid South Africa. Make corporate CEOs explain why investing in a market where the regime has black prisons, zero individual liberties, a "medical tourism" industry that sells freshly extracted body parts, concentration camps, and conducts genocide is a good place to invest. Not to mention, that regime has a market in which a contract means only what a capricious dictatorship says it does.

Use the Global Magnitsky Act (which sanctions human rights violators) aggressively against PRC entities and individuals. This may not decisive by itself, but it applies useful pressure.

And don't let up with this propaganda effort—that's "propaganda" in the original Jesuit meaning of the word: explain yourself and your ideas. Trumpet the other side's problems. That's not hard with a regime that, again, has black prisons, harvests organs from live people (for the crime of being religious), and has concentrations camps for ethnic minorities. One thought the world was done with such horrors in 1945. Never again? Hardly.

A good example of something that works is Representative Chris Smith's Tom Lantos Human Rights Commission hearings at Congress on forced organ-harvesting in China.[27] Ignore that, Xi.

And, in May 2022, the European Union passed a resolution condemning the Chinese communist regime's continuing forced organ removals. It called for member states to raise the issue of organ "harvesting" in China at every Human Rights Dialogue, publicly condemn the practice, raise awareness, and prevent citizens from going to China for "transplant tourism."[28]

Sometimes even the Europeans get it right on China.

Corruption

Public anger over corruption terrifies Xi and the rest of the Chinese Communist Party's leadership. The CCP has outdone the old pre-1949 KMT in terms of corruption. One may be fairly skeptical of Xi's selective efforts to punish corruption—until he arrests a relative or an ally. But even if he wanted to actually root out corruption, rather than use corruption as an excuse to root out his perceived challengers and enemies, the problem is too deep-seated in the nature of the communist system for Xi to fix.

The United States could explain with a straight face that it is just helping Beijing stop abetting the illegal capital outflows that constitute one of the biggest thefts in history. The CCP has tried to suppress the Panama Papers, reports that included evidence of leading Communist Party families' involvement in secret offshore companies.[29] The CCP's harassment of the New York Times and Bloomberg in the early 2010s for reporting ruling-class corruption, including Xi's family's vast overseas wealth, shows how this issue frightens the Chinese leadership.[30] Good. Another soft spot to hit.

The United States must expose ruling-class corruption, perhaps starting with the top five hundred CCP leaders and their families, and trumpet it repeatedly and widely. That corruption is the juice that speeds along the BRI and Chinese influence efforts in the Pacific, Africa,

Latin America, and elsewhere. Allies and partners would be grateful to know more about corrupt CCP-linked agents trying to operate in their countries.

The United States is aware of part of the problem, but it can uncover much more with proper effort. The CIA might even do its job (and if it doesn't, fire the director until it does). The truth can be spread with expanded media programs. Voice of America used to be respected everywhere. We can do it again.

Simply requiring Chinese investors in the United States to prove their money was lawfully exported from the PRC would be useful. For those already here, selectively place liens on real estate and finances. Suspend green cards until the green card holders provide a note from the Chinese government verifying and explaining how the money to make their grand purchases was lawfully exported from China.

The PRC routinely claims its actions are a response to mistreatment (past and present) by foreigners. This is debatable, but CCP corruption is unquestionably a homegrown phenomenon that's hard to blame on outsiders. Don't let them try.

Political Warfare 101

These are simply a few strategies and tactics. There is much more that should be done. Meanwhile, in the existing vacuum, Beijing's narrative is heard repeatedly from multiple channels as if playing on a loop. The PRC's claims may be nonsense, but if they are unchallenged or inconsistently opposed, the relentless claims tend to reinforce the Chinese position and create a sense of inevitability.

The United States must quickly get beyond its often confusing, timorous statements suggesting "grave concern" from State Department spokesmen or other U.S. government officials whenever China does

something that offends sensibilities. The United States must begin to
speak firmly, clearly, and consistently.

We must realize that there is presently no deal to be cut with the
Chinese Communist Party. If keeping the peace is the primary objective, as it was for Neville Chamberlain in 1938 at Munich, we can
expect trouble.

Even Henry Kissinger got this right: "Whenever peace has been the
primary objective, the international system has been at the mercy of its
most ruthless member."[31]

This means we must make the Foreign Service a priority (more staff
in more places), and making sure they do their job—not just write lov-
ingly crafted cables about what is going on. As one observer wrote:

> If every attending country took half of their in-house diplo-
> matic and military desk officers or country analysts devoted
> to looking at the Indo-Pacific and actually had those billets
> forward-based *in* the Indo-Pacific, a tremendous amount
> could be realized. But doing that would take these desk war-
> riors away from their local cafes, pubs, and comfort zones.
> And we shan't have that![32]

But the fact is, we need that. The world is complex and dynamic.
If we are going to make policies that work, we need to be there to
understand it. As an ex-pat business executive whom I spoke with said
about the creation of a U.S. trade agreement with the PRC:

> It was a unique experience to be on the front-end of the
> agreement's formation and then have to live with the agree-
> ment after all the negotiators went home. It has led to my
> belief every government negotiator who is instrumental in
> building agreements with the other side should remain

in-country after the agreement is signed to live and work five days a week, 8:00 a.m. to 5:00 p.m., for three years in one of the subject fields contained in the agreement to understand the differences (or sometimes similarities) between what was intended during negotiations and what in fact was the practice after the agreement was signed.[33]

This is a corollary to the Baltimore Guidance Counselor Principle: everyone who had a hand in shipping U.S. jobs overseas for an ephemeral quarterly bonus should have to go to the community that lost those jobs, sit in the office of a guidance counselor at the local high school, and advise graduates on what they realistically can now do with their lives.

Rule of law is supposed to be one of our strengths. We need to live up to what we say we believe in and show others, through our actions, why we are right.

Fundamentally, we need to know, value, protect and build the strengths of the United States of America, and shed the light of truth on the corruption, in every sense of the word, of the Chinese Communist Party.

That could mean in discussions with family, community, at school or wherever that understanding needs bolstering. The tools are out there. One is Kerry Gershaneck's groundbreaking 2020 book *Political Warfare: Strategies for Combating China's Plan to "Win without Fighting."* Gershaneck lays out a five-day training course in PRC political warfare.[34] Any decision-makers who work with China, including university administrators, members of Congress (and their staff), military, regulators, border agents, and more, should be required to take it.

It is basic mental self-defense, which is an essential starting point if we are going to fight back.

Taiwan Strait Area

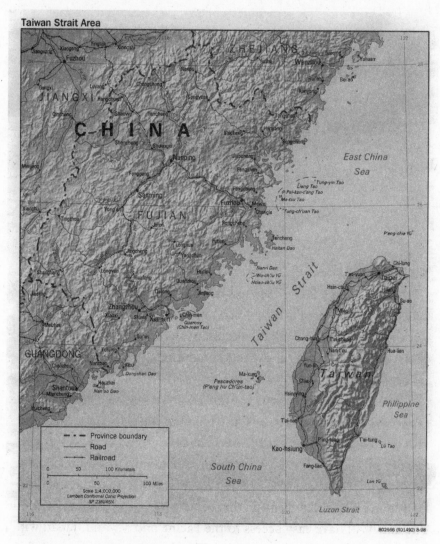

Map courtesy of the Central Intelligence Agency.

CHAPTER 20

Saving Taiwan

Where are we likely to have to fight? Chinese leaders have told us. At the 20th Party Congress in October 2022, Xi said of Taiwan (to loud applause): "There is no commitment to renounce the use of force, and the option to take all necessary measures is retained. . . . The complete reunification of the motherland must be realized and can certainly be realized."[1]

Beijing has long declared Taiwan a core interest and has vowed to take resolute measures (that is, use force) to seize Taiwan. The CCP says this all the time, and threatens to smash anyone who tries to stop them to smithereens. The PRC is serious about taking Taiwan.

If Taiwan comes under Chinese communist control, the so-called First Island Chain that hems in the Chinese military will be breached. The PLA will have easy access to the Pacific and beyond. Japan will find itself outflanked and surrounded. The blow to American credibility regionally and worldwide will be staggering.

Think about that again. Let it sink in: the world will have seen that the U.S. military couldn't save Taiwan, nor could U.S. financial and economic sanctions, nor could U.S. nuclear weapons deterrence. Who exactly is then going to trust American security guarantees—actual or implied? In short order, Asia will turn "red," except for maybe Japan and Australia, and they will both be skeptical about U.S. protection.

The lesson? The United States needs a military (either alone or with allies) that can defeat both the People's Liberation Army and any friends the Chinese communists can muster. Indeed, this really is the key to everything. Without the ability to prevail using military force, no combination of diplomacy, economic and financial pressure, and information warfare will succeed against a ruthless regime of the PRC sort.

The current U.S. trend is to talk of something called Integrated Deterrence. This seems to be an attempt to skimp on military power and spending and count instead on diplomacy, sanctions, and allies to make up the difference. It won't work. It is an excuse for spending more on a national dental plan than on national defense.

Given what's at stake over Taiwan, and the catastrophic ripple effects of a Chinese communist takeover, the United States needs to do everything possible to preserve a free Taiwan—and make it clear to Beijing that it will do so.

But isn't Taiwan one of China's core interests? China always claims to have core interests. The United States can have core interests as well. And a free Taiwan is one of them. The U.S. foreign policy and business elites need to overcome the paralysis caused by fear of what "China" will think. Remember, when they say that, they are really talking about what the brutal and repressive Chinese communist leadership will think—and if they don't like it, good. You are probably doing something right.

One thing we know they won't want is for us to break Taiwan and its military out of the more than forty years of isolation that have left it demoralized and dangerously vulnerable to a Chinese assault and psychologically primed to give up. So that's one of the first things we should do.

It's often said that Taiwan is indefensible since it is only a hundred miles from the Chinese mainland and the Chinese military advantage is overwhelming. It might be a daunting challenge, but Taiwan's prospects (and America's) improve considerably when the battlefield is expanded to target the PRC's overseas interests and assets that the Chinese currently have no way to protect—other than by threatening to use nuclear weapons, or maybe cutting off pharmaceutical shipments to the United States.

We can threaten and act right back at them. If a nation is at war with us, or a key ally, it should prepare to have its assets seized. That brings us to another Chinese weakness.

Trade Pressure and Technology Embargoes

China conducts economic warfare extremely well, but it doesn't like being on the receiving end. Xi complained to President Biden that the United States "should stop abusing the concept of national security" to suppress China's businesses.[2] Beijing is complaining because it hurts. Despite Beijing's successful economic and trade warfare and efforts to sanctions-proof itself to create a self-contained economy, it is still vulnerable on the trade front, not to mention the food, energy, and foreign exchange fronts, and it isn't used to being challenged because, well, we haven't really challenged it.

The United States' approach to dealing with China from the Nixon-Kissinger era onwards resembles a fifty-year science experiment.

The underlying hypothesis was that an accommodating approach to the PRC, including on trade, would inevitably lead to a more liberal China that followed the established rules of the international system.

It seemed logical, the hypothesis went, as China benefitted handsomely under that system.

This hypothesis was long ago proven incorrect, in part because the experiment was corrupted from the start. China never followed the established rules of the international system, and we didn't force it to. It came into the WTO, for example, under terms that it never met (and had no intention of meeting). What it actually benefitted from was tying us up in our rules while it did whatever it wanted.

Plenty of people today—usually because of some financial or reputational investment in the PRC—choose to ignore that the experiment failed. Saying, "I was wrong" is not exactly a common trait of the "must-be-in-the-China-market-business" crowd or the China Hand (more accurately, China Hand-Out) community.

Now and then, a few China Hands will grudgingly suggest that things haven't worked out as planned—but that nobody could have foreseen what would happen. And besides, since the PRC has nuclear weapons, well, there's no alternative to engaging with them. Fight back? That would mean thermonuclear war. And we don't want that, do we?

What they ignore is that we did start to fight back, and the Chinese didn't nuke us, though they did complain—and likely put in a lot of calls to their Hands. Notice how the Chinese wailed when Huawei and ZTE were sanctioned during the Trump administration and technology imports were curtailed.[3] China's demands that the United States remove relatively limited tariffs imposed by President Trump suggest that the sanctions work rather well, despite what Trump's critics claimed.[4] And, hypocrisy being the coin of the realm in Washington, the Biden administration has kept most of the Trump-era trade restrictions on China—and has even added a few.

Indeed, in December 2022, the Federal Communications Commission widened the ban on sales of Huawei and ZTE hardware in the United

States.[5] It also sanctioned ten other Chinese companies, including Hikvision that provides surveillance cameras for the PRC's gulags and cities.[6]

The companies' American lobbyists screamed bloody murder. One of them was former chief of staff for the late senator Harry Reid, in his day one of the most powerful men in Washington.[7]

President Biden also deserves credit for the CHIPS Act, which potentially bolsters and revitalizes American semiconductor development and manufacturing capabilities. Among other features, the CHIPs Act targets China's dependence on imported semiconductors, imposing restrictions on chip exports and, as importantly, the chip-making equipment and U.S. skilled labor working for Chinese companies, on which the PRC depends.[8]

The United States has an excellent hand to play (both offensively and defensively) on the economic warfare front—and from many directions, if it chooses to play it. It's one that would reinforce any American moves on the financial warfare front.

How so? Trade sanctions and potential human rights boycotts threaten to cut PRC access to foreign exchange, including through foreign direct investment in China, exports, or limits on Chinese companies operating overseas. As mentioned earlier, Beijing doesn't have anywhere near enough convertible currency to cover its needs, and if the flow dries up, the Chinese regime will have to make tough decisions about guns for the PLA or better lives for its citizens.

This is why one of the most important things the United States has to do, if not *the* most important, is defend the U.S. dollar's dominance as the world's reserve currency at all costs. This is something Capitol Hill and the White House directly control. Stop spending like morons. Just doing that will be worth one thousand destroyers and one thousand F-35s. At the same time, go after the legitimacy of the RMB, including the digital yuan. Show it for the Monopoly money that it is.

Economic Article 5

In that previously mentioned call readout between Xi and Biden, Xi tipped us off to another Chinese communist vulnerability. He referred to groupings and divisions.[9] He may have been talking about AUKUS—the U.S., Australia, and UK alliance intended to provide Australia with nuclear submarines and cooperate on other technologies.

This highlighted Beijing's fear of the United States and other like-minded countries banding together to present a unified front against Chinese pressure—and combining to direct reciprocal pressure against Beijing. The Chinese communists much prefer taking on countries one-by-one, when they usually have an overwhelming advantage.

Like any bully, the PRC hates when its targets work together. Americans should do everything possible to bolster alliances—and create new ones, military and political, but also economic.

The PRC uses trade and economic pressure against its rivals, whom it likes to isolate and overpower one-on-one. As part of a defensive measure and political warfare measure of its own, the United States can establish and implement a so-called Economic Article 5. This refers to Article 5 of the NATO Treaty, which declares that a military attack on one country is an attack on all nations and that mutual assistance will be forthcoming.[10] Instead of a military attack, make it an economic attack. When China applies sanctions or trade pressure on America's friends, as it has done recently to Australia, South Korea, the Philippines, Palau, and Japan, America should step in and help. This can include direct economic support and concessions.

Remind friends of why they like (or should like) the benefits of being connected to America, and that China is not where their economic futures lie. This can work with *potential* friends, too, and is an excellent way to build alliances—again, something that the Chinese communists hate.

At the same time, to send a message, take quiet but commensurate action on Chinese investment in the United States. Just create a little more pain and friction for them—just as the Chinese do to foreign companies in China. However, in the case of the U.S. actions, there are real reasons for closer investigations given Chinese military-civil fusion, lax safety standards, IP theft, and more.

U.S. government officials serving any administration should remember that it is better to be in a country where the people, the Congress, and the executive all believe that allies should be supported. We act on it generously and without hesitation. And economics and security are not two separate things.

Inbound and Outbound CIFIUS

Reviews by CIFIUS—the Committee on Foreign Investment in the United States—of inward Chinese investment should be tightened up. Presumption against approval should be standard unless a compelling case is made that an investment is unobjectionable from both national security and human rights standpoints (even if Wall Street and American industry prefer to ignore both).

An outbound CIFIUS is a new idea, as such outbound investment has almost been considered a human right by the U.S. business and financial class. However, a bill that's working its way through Congress would require review and approval if investments into the PRC would potentially benefit the Chinese military or involve key technologies that China aims to dominate—and use against us commercially and militarily. With this bill, investments that pose supply chain risks, making us dependent on the PRC, are similarly frowned upon.[11]

Not surprisingly, Wall Street, China's Washington lobbyist, and other "interested parties" are fighting this tooth and nail.[12] More coverage on the money flows behind the campaigns would be helpful.

Disentangling—Especially the Supply Chains

Chinese political warfare has effectively created a dependence on the PRC for manufacturing and for supply of key materials and products in America and other nations.

It is insane to depend on an avowed enemy to provide our economic wherewithal and finished products and manufacturing. And giving the PRC a stranglehold on essential lifesaving pharmaceuticals and military necessities such as ammunition components, batteries, magnets and rare earth materials is beyond insane. It's more of a death wish.

And don't forget that investment in the PRC funds the Chinese military that seeks to kill Americans.

The United States can defend against this economic warfare—while in effect conducting its own. It isn't complicated. The USA should not be dependent on the PRC for anything that matters.

And don't forget that investment in the PRC funds the Chinese military that seeks to kill Americans.

Are there impediments to decoupling or, as David Stilwell puts it, "disentangling"?[13] If there are, they are no greater than when U.S. business decoupled millions of Americans from their jobs and lives over the last decades, affecting both their families and generations yet unborn.

When the elites and Wall Street say we can't decouple from China, well, they themselves sure as hell decoupled from America, from places like Baltimore, Youngstown, Pittsburgh, and a thousand other places.

The excuses sound like pure laziness, avarice, or the spurious reasons for staying in an abusive relationship.

You don't have to be that old to remember when the China market didn't matter, and yet, the world was still a decent and prosperous enough place. It can be once again—without China. Indeed, Walmart used to crow about being Made in America until it caught the China cheap labor disease in the 1990s.

At the same time, we should prioritize working with like-minded and—in the case of sensitive technologies, trusted—partners. You'd think this would already be the case, but clearly, it's not. There have been some moves in this direction, with the Clean Network[14] and the 2021 U.S.-EU Trade and Technology Council.[15] This needs to continue, expand, and intensify.

If they do, where will it lead? We might end up with a world with two separate blocs: a free one and an un-free one. And if the free one stops effectively supporting and subsidizing the unfree one, let's see how long it will last.

Extracting ourselves from this pathologic dependence on Chinese manufacturing and materials won't be easy or fast, but once it begins, it will gather steam. Instead of having unbounded globalization as we have known it, we probably will end up with two distinct and separate technology and economic systems, represented by the U.S./EU/Japan bloc on one side and the China/BRI bloc on the other side. If that happens, it will be important that major growing economies, such as India, are part of the free bloc.

This could mean developing different sets of global rules and norms and might compromise international organizations. So be it. If they are hopelessly subverted and have no chance of reform, we should leave. That includes the World Health Organization, UN Human Rights Commission (that includes human rights stalwarts such as Iran and Cuba), and maybe even the United Nations itself.

Currently, the money we are pouring into the international organizations that are acting as proxies for Beijing is being used to subsidize Chinese influence operation to the detriment of ourselves and the rest of the free world. That doesn't make sense.

If this happens, it might be time to set up free nation alternative organizations. We could take the money we would have spent on the legacy organizations and instead use it to achieve something useful—and in line with what the organizations are supposed to be doing.

In the process, we could give free countries a real alternative.

Shareholder Lawsuits

The Chinese Communist Party's announced objective is to replace foreign companies with Chinese ones. And there is the problem of reputational harm from doing business in a country that is committing atrocities against its citizens. So corporate shareholders might decide not to tie their fates to the opaque, mercurial dictates of the CCP. Instead, they might file lawsuits charging malfeasance for investing in a national market that is entirely at the whim of a ruthless, capricious dictatorship. It's astonishing that lawsuits are not already daily fare for companies doing business with the PRC.

Energy Supplies

In the readout of the Xi-Biden call, Xi let slip another of the PRC's huge economic vulnerabilities: energy. He mentioned the need for China, the United States, and the international community to jointly protect global energy security.[16] This highlights a huge PRC vulnerability: not having enough energy resources, including fossil fuels, to power the country. This is an advantage for us. Play it. America has enough energy (oil and gas) to last forever. For a brief period during the Trump administration, we were independent.[17] Now we are begging Saudi Arabia, the Russians, Iran, and Venezuela to pump more oil.[18] The United States needs to get its energy independence back, and fast.

Adding to the madness, the Biden administration is trying to force Americans to go green despite current technologies being inadequate and the PRC positioning itself as the main supplier of our so-called green energy products. Quite a trick to get a potentially energy independent country (us) to distort its energy market to the point it becomes dependent on a hostile country that is itself an energy importer. Well played, Beijing.

Better to have our friends rely on us for energy than have to rely on our (and their) main enemy, the PRC, for energy. Do we really need to say these things out loud? Apparently yes. Vociferously.

Developing Power Leverage

In spite of his reference to global energy security (which essentially means fossil fuels), Xi also invoked the magic words "climate change" as a way of trying to ensure that China continues to receive billions through these accords (without having to make any real concessions).

That flow is justified by, as Xi said, China being *the largest developing country in the world*.[19] Despite China's undeniable economic strength, which it touts in other venues, it continues to use the even more important word "developing" in these sorts of international fora, because that word is worth trillions to Beijing.

In the case of climate change, deploying "developing country" terminology traps developed countries into going first and giving concessions, hobbling their economies to achieve carbon reductions. That all works to China's Comprehensive National Power advantage.

It has to stop. China must be forced to pick a lane and stick to it, or be called out loudly, legally, and repeatedly for hypocrisy. Since simple embarrassment has its limits with the PRC, sanctions will need to be employed in many cases.

Chemical Warfare

Speaking of which, one specific front in China's political warfare campaign against us demands an urgent counterattack. That's China's chemical warfare assault using the drug fentanyl. The attack started in earnest around 2013 and is now killing over seventy thousand Americans a year.

The White House and Congress must treat this as they would a direct kinetic attack. We must use the tools we've discussed before.

First, suspend all Chinese financial institutions from the U.S. dollar network. Start with the People's Bank of China.

Second, immediately de-list every Chinese company from the New York Stock Exchange and other exchanges. They should never have been listed in the first place.

Third, place strict controls on U.S. outward investment into the PRC. For example, no investment by government entities and companies that hold U.S. government contracts.

Fourth, revoke the green cards and visas—and place liens on the properties and bank accounts—of the top five hundred CCP members relatives in the United States.

There simply cannot be business as usual while we are being slaughtered chemically.

Military

The military component of the to-do list is in some ways the easiest part to get right. When Americans think of war, they think of having weapons and an Army, Navy, Air Force, and Marines to solve our disputes with enemies. And the United States has a powerful military.

So just telling the armed forces to take care of things seems easier for many administrations than hard, complex diplomatic, economic, psychological, and propaganda efforts, not to mention marshaling the necessary political support that's required to deal with violent adversaries.

What's needed hardware-wise? Enough troops, ships, submarines, aircraft, weapons (including nuclear ones), missiles, sensors, satellites, and so forth—and with the right capabilities, and in the right quantities, to take on and defeat any enemy (or enemies) on land, in outer space, in cyber space, and on, above, and below the oceans.

You also have to pay for it. Eight hundred fifty billion dollars might seem like a lot (and it's not as if defense contractors give Uncle Sam a break), but compared to entitlement spending, it's not much. One might try putting a price on how much losing a war and our freedoms will cost Americans. A lot more than $850 billion.

What does the U.S. military need? Defense contractors, of course, will say, "More of what we make," and their congressional representatives will agree. But if you really want to know what's needed to win a war, ask some good war planners. That's more useful than listening to any number of foreign affairs experts.

Some Things That Really Matter

Having the right hardware is essential, of course. It's hard to win without it. But it's not just what you have, it's what you *can* do with it, it's what you *do* with it, and it's what you are *willing* to do with it.

The enemy needs to know he has no chance.

Ask yourself, does the PRC think it can take on the U.S. military? Twenty years ago, and maybe even a decade ago, it didn't. Now it might like its prospects in certain conditions, and Beijing might like the trend line.

Remember What a Military Is For

Our military is for one thing only: fighting and winning battles and defeating America's enemies. And that includes the People's Liberation Army.

Find officers who understand this—and are willing to say so in public.

And hold them responsible for success or failure. The campaigns in Iraq and Afghanistan were not exactly rousing successes, despite the

U.S. military leadership having unlimited budgets and solid congressional and public support.

Yet, was any senior officer held responsible? No. It was end-of-tour awards and upward promotions for everyone. Fail to produce? No problem.

And, at the same time, to the extent the Indo-Pacific region even got any attention, the U.S. military basically stood still while China closed the gap and, in some cases, surpassed us. Really? Chinese anti-ship cruise missiles (ASCMs)—a key weapon for naval warfare—outrange and are faster than U.S. Navy versions. And the Navy poured billions into the wretched, easily sinkable Littoral Combat Ship (LCS)—expecting it would play a major role in U.S. naval presence in the Pacific. And the Zumwalt frigate fiasco blew more billions for three ships—without working guns or engines.

Who was responsible? Leprechauns, apparently.

So is the current crop of senior officers the right ones? One wonders. And the Chinese probably do, too. Where is today's Nimitz, Halsey, Spruance, or Burke? Presumably, out there somewhere. But possibly not in the military. If they are, we need to find them and let them do their jobs.

Two Other Things to Be Done Now

First, end wokeness in the military. Service seems to sometimes resemble a Chinese Communist Party struggle session. It's not surprising many young Americans are declining to join the military. The Chinese must have been delighted with Secretary of Defense Lloyd Austin launching the equivalent of a snipe hunt for extremists in the ranks when he ordered a service-wide stand down shortly after taking office.[20] That sent quite a message to many servicemen and servicewomen: "We don't trust you" and "snitch on your buddies."

The PLA must have been even happier to hear Chairman of the Joint Chiefs of Staff general Mark Milley's incoherent defense of critical race theory before the U.S. Congress.[21] Not to be outdone, Chief of Naval Operations admiral Gilday included racist "anti-racist" Ibram X. Kendi on the CNO's recommended reading list.[22] This all seemed to suggest that some racism is good—if it's the right kind—and is directed against the types of Americans who have joined the military in large numbers and for whom service is a multigenerational affair. If we keep it up, we'll have an early 1970s-style U.S. military—demoralized, undermanned, ill-disciplined, and plagued with gangs and race riots.

I've only mentioned the U.S. Navy, but the other service chiefs and senior officers also seem to be the go-along-to-get-along sort. Some are seemingly so busy seeking to understand White Rage and learning how to be an Antiracist that they've forgotten to read about how the Chinese are getting ready to kill us and how, in order to do it, they are turning out around five new warships for every American ship that is launched.[23]

Lose a war and the social justice demands won't matter. Just ask any of the women in the Chinese Politburo. Oh, wait. You can't. There aren't any.[24] Why isn't anyone protesting that?

After the wokeness virus is eliminated from the military, there's one more distraction to be dealt with: climate change.

Climate change is not what the military should be focusing on. Yet top commanders insist it is as urgent—or more so—as taking on the PLA. The Chinese will agree and are glad to see us keep on making mistakes, but nobody interested in winning a war against the PRC will.

Useful Partners

America is a global power, so it needs to watch the entire globe, but that has become a stretch, as the capabilities of the PRC (and its allies and proxies) have waxed in recent years.

The United States thus needs its own allies and their militaries more than ever.

But America has lots of allies and friends, doesn't it? It does. But how many of them can U.S. forces actually conduct real-world operations with—as opposed to scripted exercises requiring months of planning conferences? Not so many.

The Cobra Gold exercise in Thailand, for example, is practically a giant block party.[25] Even the PLA is invited.[26] A few years ago, one of the participating nations, supposedly a main beneficiary of the Cobra Gold exercise, quietly asked: "Can't we do something besides VIP landings?" In other words, can we do something useful rather than charging ashore for the cameras and the distinguished guests in the bleachers?

The United States and Japan

If America is going to win in the Indo-Pacific, the U.S.-Japan military alliance is the key to everything. In theory, combine U.S. and Japanese capabilities, and the PLA will have no end of trouble.

Unfortunately, the Japan Self-Defense Force (JSDF) is not built, equipped, organized, or capable of fighting a war against a serious opponent. And the Chinese are a serious opponent.

Japan's Navy is something of an exception. It has some excellent niche capabilities along with a good working relationship with the U.S. Navy's 7th Fleet. It is unfortunately about half the size it needs to be.

The JSDF as a whole is barely able to conduct joint operations between its own services, much less with U.S. forces—despite the alliance being over sixty years old.

This needs to be addressed now. Start with a Joint Operational Headquarters in Japan where U.S. and Japanese forces carry out the defense of Japan.

You mean one doesn't exist? Nope. Not yet.

Japan is showing signs of waking up to its inadequate defenses. The Japanese have announced plans to double defense spending by 2027 and procure an array of new hardware and weaponry, including long-range missiles that can reach China and North Korea.[27] As important, Tokyo promised to transform the JSDF into a joint force—at long last—but not until 2027.[28]

That's not fast enough. Time is short.

Taiwan

Everyone talks about how important Taiwan is to the United States—and to Japan as well.

But Taiwan's military has been isolated and has had no meaningful contact—such as joint training—with U.S. forces for more than forty years. As a result, it's something of a Galapagos military. And the Americans and Taiwanese apparently have not done the planning necessary for a joint defense of Taiwan, when the time comes.

Such is the fear of provoking the PRC that has handcuffed U.S. policy toward Taiwan—and towards China as well—for almost half a century.

It's time to treat Taiwan like a friend and take some risks—while ignoring Beijing's inevitable temper tantrums. If we do, we may find Taiwan taking its own defense more seriously. If we don't, it doesn't matter what sort of hardware it acquires to turn itself into a porcupine.

The Quad

In a bit of good news, there's the Quad (Quadrilateral Security Dialogue). The Quad is a loose security-focused arrangement between four countries—the United States, Japan, Australia, and India—intended to promote a "free and open Indo-Pacific," i.e., not dominated by communist China.[29]

The Quad has made strides in recent years. It has the potential to deepen security (and attendant political and economic) cooperation between the four nations. This sort of joint defense alignment concerns Beijing. It prefers to take on its victims one at a time.

The late Japanese prime minister Shinzo Abe deserves credit for raising the Quad idea in 2007, and to plenty of derision.[30] But he brought it to fruition during his second term as prime minister in 2017.

China's Xi Jinping also deserves credit—for scaring the four nations into deciding the Quad was a splendid idea.

Within the Quad, there are overlapping, growing bilateral and trilateral ties. For example, Japan and Australia are deepening defense ties to include a recent agreement that JSDF will become more active in northern Australia training grounds and in bilateral and joint exercises with other Quad nations.[31] This was unthinkable just a few years ago.

The United States is also setting up a strategic hub in northern Australia and is enhancing bilateral defense capabilities, beyond even what the AUKUS deal (Australia, UK, U.S.) envisions.[32]

The Australians are as game an ally as there is. It would be good if there were more Aussies. They, like the other Quad nations, are still figuring out how best to defend their country in what has become a rough, and getting rougher, neighborhood.

The Indians? They're responsible for the "left half" of the Indo-Pacific; it's good to have them even loosely joined with the Quad. One should take the Indians on their own terms, offer support where it is desired, and not try to force them into a particular niche or behavior. The Indians know they've got a problem coming from the PRC, and they are willing to fight.[33] You could say this about India long before you could about most other countries.

Ultimately, the Quad offers a lot of opportunity. It takes deft handling, a vision of the entire Indo-Pacific, and compromise to make it work. But it's worth it. The four nations will get out of it what they put into it, and the region will be better off for it.

An Asian NATO?

This is not likely. But there are a few countries in the region and outside it that might combine conventional forces to counter Chinese expansion and intimidation—but only if they think the Americans are serious, committed, and are likely to win.

We have already seen the QUAD and its potential. With some effort, South Korea, Vietnam, France, Canada, the United Kingdom, and maybe Singapore and the Philippines will join in, even informally. The political effect of this even exceeds the military advantages. Have some success, and maybe a few other countries will want to participate.

If so, Beijing will have some serious thinking to do.

Spread Out

To fight in the Pacific and do the influencing that improves our positioning and creates or keeps friends, we'll need to be present throughout the entire Indo-Pacific. Vacuums get filled, and it's the Chinese who have been filling it.

Too often, U.S. military activities have resembled the Harlem Globetrotters: showing up, putting on a good show, and then going home. A three- or four-star officer flying in for a high-level visit is supposed to be enough to ensure we have friends and access. If only.

Instead, USINDOPACOM needs to actually show up and stay—even small teams will do.

And we shouldn't squander opportunities that come along. Too often, when the local governments practically beg us to set up shop, we have been too busy or too uninterested. A few places over the last decade where U.S. force could have gotten into on a long term, permanent basis:

Timor Leste, Vanuatu, Solomon Islands, Palau, Federated States of Micronesia.

The Chinese have their eyes on all these places, have their claws in most of them, and signed a deal in 2022 that will let the PLA into Solomon Islands.

Message to USINDOPACOM and Washington: if you're not there, you're not interested.

Missile Defense

China's Strategic Rocket Force and its thousands of missiles—ballistic and otherwise—are indeed the threat they are claimed to be. And U.S. bases in Japan, Guam, and South Korea are potential missile sponges should the war develop a certain way.

Missile defense systems are thus an urgent requirement. Raytheon, Lockheed, and others will vouch for that.

But the United States will do well to be able to give as good as it gets on the missile front. One thing that deters an enemy is the certain knowledge that if he uses his own weapons, he will receive much more in return. In other words, we must see to our own offensive missile capability—and then some. There is much work to be done on this front.

Nuclear Weapons

Despite its claims to the contrary, China considers nuclear weapons—especially tactical nuclear weapons—as a feasible option. China has gone on an all-out push to build its nuclear arsenal to match what the United States has, and might even be superior in terms of types of nuclear weapons and delivery systems. China's are all new, while the American arsenal is aging.

And there is reason to believe that the Chinese nuclear arsenal is much bigger than experts have assured us for years. The 2022 Department of Defense *China Military Power Report* notes that China is believed to have 400 nuclear warheads capable of reaching the United States.[34] The previous report (and the one before that), however, assessed that China had nukes "in the low 200's" and might double that by 2030.[35]

You get the point. When the Chinese double their warhead numbers in one year, it suggests our experts have a wildly imperfect understanding of China's nuclear weapons program and intentions. At least take Admiral John Aquilino, commander USINDOPACOM, and Admiral Charles Richard, commander of Strategic Command, at their word when they warn that China's nuclear weapons capabilities are in a state of "strategic breakout" akin to the Soviet nuclear buildup in the 1960s.[36] If these gentlemen are scared, we ought to be as well.

Even worse, we helped the Chinese get where they are. A private report issued in 2022 described how 162 scientists working at Los Alamos nuclear laboratory between 1987 and 2021 returned home to China and helped out with China's nuclear program, as well as hypersonic missile and submarine programs.[37] Yes, Chinese scientists were working at Los Alamos.

The Biden administration is reluctant to do what's necessary to modernize our nuclear weapons and to give America adequate delivery systems.

If the PRC is willing to use nuclear weapons, it must be aware that the United States is equally willing and equally capable. Ideally, even more capable and willing, if necessary, to defend itself and its friends.

Outer Space

If you can't see or hear, you can't fight. That's why our satellite networks are vital—and a prime target for the PRC. We must protect our outer space infrastructure, but also be able to shut down the enemy's satellites if necessary.

The Biden administration's unilateral suspension of anti-satellite weapons tests—done to show the Chinese and the Russians what responsible behavior looks like—was ill-advised.[38] Though Beijing and Moscow were no doubt pleased to see it.

Are there agreements and treaties to be cut with the PRC (and with Russia and likeminded regimes) to cool things down in space? That's hard to imagine. Remember that Xi Jinping promised President Obama he would not militarize the South China Sea...or steal America's trade secrets.[39]

The 2022 DOD *China Military Power Report* gets it right when it explains: "The PLA views space operations as a means to deter and counter third-party intervention during a regional military conflict. Moreover, PRC defense academics suggest that reconnaissance, communication, navigation, and early warning satellites could be among the target of attacks designed to 'blind and deafen the enemy.'"[40]

We've been warned.

Make Stuff Again

America's industrial base needs work, and fast. This includes shipbuilding and ship repair capabilities, but also all ammunition, missiles, bombs, aircraft, and the thousands of other things that you need to supply and fight a war—as the war in Ukraine has reminded us. If we don't have these, we'll probably lose.

It's not a question of whether we can make everything we need. Our manufacturing capabilities and potential are the world's best. It's more a question of wanting to do so.

The Gray Zone

This phrase refers to Chinese actions that are sort of like war (to the PRC, they *are* war)—but that don't seem to rise to the level that demands shooting back. The Chinese benefit from the American definition of war differing from the Chinese interpretation.

Some examples of gray-zone activities: harassing U.S. and allied aircraft and ships operating lawfully, shooting lasers at U.S. pilots, and firing chaff in front of Australian and Canadian aircraft, with potentially fatal results. There are also China's weaponized fishing fleet and so-called maritime militia that occupy and seize territory, vacuum the seas of other countries' fish, and intimidate.

Gray-zone actions seem to paralyze the Americans—while giving the PRC an advantage equivalent to regular warfare.

The answer to this isn't that hard: let the People's Republic of China know that these actions are, by our interpretation, war, and will be dealt with as such. In particular, notify them that we consider the People's Armed Police, maritime militia, the Chinese Coast Guard, and the fishing fleet to be part of the Chinese military. Because, due to the way the PRC operates, they are.

The United States does need to have the physical capacity (ships, aircraft, intelligence resources) and the actual presence to deal with gray-zone problems. Currently, it doesn't. It has partners who can help, however. This has to be more than just talking about dealing with the gray zone.

The Pacific Island nations, several of them with agreements for the United States to handle their defense, are basically helpless when Chinese fishing boats illegally enter their waters and vacuum up their fish—the one major resource most of these nations have. USINDOPACOM and the Department of Defense hold seminars and produce much bold talk about taking on "unregulated fishing" and helping our dear friends.[41] To date nothing much has happened to make the Chinese pirates worry. It's about time that changes.

But won't the Chinese be angry, and won't this escalate tensions? They *will* be angry. They always are when someone defends themselves. But they aren't going to stop until the cost-benefit analysis is changed. Currently, it's all benefit for Beijing.

The Will to Fight

As you can see, many of these recommendations have as much to do with how we use what we have—and our will to fight—as with the types of hardware we have.

If we're not willing to fight back, we might as well not bother.

One observer concisely told me the proper way to deal with the PRC from the military perspective, and it applies to other warfares, too:

"Deter PRC militarism by developing a robust combined capability to dominate them at war. Collectively protect what is ours. Never do anything to help them."[42]

CONCLUSION

It's Our Choice: Pushing Back and Winning

This book's opening is grim. Baltimore—and the dozens of other Baltimores, and the carnage inflicted on America's working class—didn't have to happen. And neither did the dead Marines murdered near the Bashi Channel. The United States doesn't have to be driven out of Asia, its reputation and global influence in tatters, left to cower in fear at what China might do next and meekly obeying Chinese Communist Party demands.

Demands such as having to hand over Chinese enemies for re-education. Allowing Chinese political advisors on Capitol Hill. Police advisors, too. Making certain that school curricula and faith services are approved by Beijing. And one day, allowing Chinese military bases in the United States.

This future is not unthinkable. We can already see it happening in areas that have fallen to China.

We don't have much time left.

If we lose the war with China, it will be because we want to lose.

And if we want to lose, it will be because the CCP and its proxies and fellow travelers have gotten into our heads and have made us forget what it is to be American. What it means to be free.

Make no mistake: their goal is to take away our freedom.

We often hear that China wants to "win without fighting." But the more literal translation of that Mandarin expression is "get the enemy to submit without fighting." That is a big difference. A nation can win a war, and then the two sides move on, eventually work together, and even reconcile. Take it from me, a Marine who worked to help the Japan Self-Defense Force develop its first amphibious capability since World War II.

Submission is different. It's a permanent state of subjugation. We won't move on from submission. If we try to stand up, we will be smacked down again.

That is what the Chinese Communist Party wants to do to the United States of America. Make us submit. Forever.

So, what's at stake? The United States as an independent nation—or even a unified nation—is at stake. But ultimately, it's our freedom that is at risk—from the Chinese communists and even from other Americans working for them, knowingly or not.

Go to Hong Kong if you want (and if you dare) to see what Chinese communist domination looks like—and how fast it can happen. Or talk to someone from Eastern Europe back when the communists were in control.

In the past, when America has been hit, it has had time to catch its breath, recover, and go on the offensive. Our enemies couldn't get at the heartland or across the oceans. But these days, America is in range of enemy weapons—and even worse, it is being psychologically and economically eroded from inside through entropic warfare.

Chinese Comprehensive National Power (military, economic, psychological, and more) is potentially all-pervasive. Owing to technology, it can reach into our homes, offices, schools, and shops, and monitor and punish our actions, even our words and, in effect, our thoughts.

This has only happened because we have allowed it to happen over the course of fifty years, aiding and abetting (indeed, appeasing) China in the hopes the Chinese communists were somehow different from all other communists and could be changed. In the meantime, other totalitarians linked up with the PRC, making it even stronger. It seems like a powerful combination, and maybe an unstoppable force.

It isn't.

But first, let's consider some history.

The United States Has Been in Difficult Situations

In the 1860s, Americans hated each other so much they fought a war that cost seven hundred thousand lives. That hatred lived on for decades. Today's domestic hatreds sometimes seem equally bitter, but Americans got through it after the Civil War, and we can as well.

The 1930s Depression seemed hopeless, as though America and capitalism could never recover. Both of my parents were psychologically scarred by the experience. But we recovered.

In 1942, it seemed like we (and our allies) were losing everywhere— and it seemed like we might indeed lose World War II. We didn't.

We've seen all this before, and we still prevailed. Because we wanted to.

Defending Oneself Requires a Choice

"Either we embrace our survival instinct or we will end up being told how to live by the same bastards who are locking down tens of millions in China."—Captain Jim Fanell, U.S. Navy, retired

We have to want to defend ourselves and have to remember that we're defending an idea too: freedom. The same idea that has people (even from communist China) literally dying to get into the United States (and other free nations). Absolutely nobody is tunneling to get into China or Russia. Except maybe from North Korea.

We have to recognize that some things, even ideas, are worth fighting and dying for. Despite being a Marine, I never quite understood this completely until I was much older. Obeying orders was easy enough. It is what Marines do. But it never quite seemed that our own liberty was at stake.

These days, it does. The expression "better to die on one's feet rather than live on one's knees" resonates differently. Indeed, the three hundred Spartans make more sense these days. Or the Texans and Tejanos at the Alamo. Or the Marines at the Chosin Reservoir. Or the 101st Airborne at Bastogne.

Few Americans alive have been tested in this way. The Greatest Generation, the one that faced off against expansionist, totalitarian regimes and prevailed, is all but gone.

The several generations that have come since now have their chance to fight against something just as dangerous to America. The Baby Boom generation—or, correctly said, the part of it that sought political and business leadership (or, to run things) hasn't exactly proven the equals of its parents' generation. But there are a couple of other generations after them who may have the right stuff—if they can understand what's at stake.

Seeing an enemy on the horizon looking to enslave or kill you concentrates the mind. A defeat or a clout to the head concentrates it even more.

This was evident on December 8, 1941. Practically nobody would admit to having been an isolationist—even though there had been tens of millions of them. Nobody would admit to being among the twenty thousand who attended a Nazi rally in Madison Square Garden in 1939 either.[1]

People wake up—especially ones who have known freedom—and realize it may be slipping away. Perhaps more are realizing that now.

Americans

Chinese communists know the strength of the American people, of the American idea, and that's why China has launched so many warfares to try to weaken us, divide us, and get us to hate ourselves and each other. So, obviously, the way out of this is to rediscover why we are an exceptional country, get to know each other better, and fight side by side.

In some areas, that seems to be happening.

Some in the political class seem to be waking up. Support for Taiwan is bilateral, even if one wishes it showed more concrete outcomes. As China overreaches—and keeps clawing and threatening—it will persuade more politicians to admit there's a problem. Not least, there will be practically no votes to be had from being on China's side—even though a few politicians will claim there are.

America's business and financial classes? They funded the People's Republic of China and the People's Liberation Army. Once they see that they can't make money in China and that the CCP has them by the short and curlies—and was always planning to put them out of business—we might be surprised at how fast they remember what country's name is on their passports.

We are already starting to see movement out of China, especially at the smaller company level. Shareholders can make the bigger ones leave—though some will require Washington's help to lay down the law about funding and providing for the PRC.

American academia? They are a hard one. There's nothing stiffer than ideologues, especially ideologues with theories and with tenure. But given its lock on higher education (and even lower education) for at least a few decades now, it's remarkable how many Americans haven't been influenced to hate the United States—the Fourth of July is still celebrated with vigor. Most Americans still love their country.

What about the China Hands, many of whom got us into this mess? Some won't change, but they are opportunists if nothing else, so expect them to surf the wave, even if it means standing up to China. They'll claim they always were tough on China—or that nobody could have seen what was coming from the PRC. That's wrong, of course, but welcome to the fight.

Average Americans? When they are threatened, they fight. They are the least of our worries. In fact, they are the best of us.

Speaking of average Americans, America's political, business, and professional elites have to get out and see how they live. It's not hard to do. If they don't, they'll become easy prey to political warfare operations designed to rip the country apart.

The gap is vast. In July 2022, Bret Stephens, the *New York Times* sort-of-conservative columnist issued a mea culpa. He said he had no idea that tens of millions of Americans voted for Donald Trump because they felt ignored by the country's ruling class.[2] So here you had one of America's pedigreed elite, oblivious, if not contemptuous, of tens of millions of his fellow citizens. And he's just one who admitted it—though he didn't say he was sorry.

As we get to know each other again, we also need to get back to making more things in America. One of the deadliest blows inflicted by China was stealing our jobs—and along with them our self-respect, community, and independence. Those who say the United States has no choice but to send its manufacturing overseas ought to go to a Youngstown, Ohio, union hall and make their case. They never do.

The jobs might be different than they were thirty years ago, but muscular labor and so-called blue collar work should be valued. Enough with the contempt towards the so-called working class that didn't go to Wharton. One hopes to never again hear a politician's malicious talk of putting coal miners out of work, as if that's something to be proud of.

We need to be powerful and independent—which includes energy independence—so we can help our friends and use our influence for good purposes. Allowing ourselves to become dependent on a nation that wants to destroy us is insane.

The Enemy

And yes, China wants to destroy us. We need to know that, say that, repeat that. People who pump money into China, scientists who work for China, and media that ignore Chinese predations are aiding the enemy.

An enemy always looks formidable. We tend to look at the People's Republic of China as ten feet tall. They aren't ten feet tall. We've just been on our knees.

If you clear your head and look at things from the Chinese communist perspective, you'll see why we are so threatening to them that they feel they have to destroy us.

After more than forty years of unrestricted aid and accommodation from the United States, Europe, and Japan, China still has the per capita income of Mexico. At least five hundred million Chinese are still living on five dollars a day. Some success. Take away the unrestricted aid and accommodation, and the Chinese communists are in big trouble.

The Chinese leadership doesn't trust its people. China's government spends more on internal repression than it does on real defense. There's the Great Firewall, social credit, and black prisons. They all reflect the brittleness such regimes have—despite the apparent stability that comes from brute force and a police state.

Elections? Never. The Chinese Communist Party hasn't figured out a new way of running a country. It's always the same old thing.

If we take away foreign exchange and technology and require the CCP to play by the same rules as everyone else, we will see a very different China.

The PRC has been engaged in "fake it till you make it," and that game only lasts so long. This doesn't mean it can't do an enormous amount of damage in the coming years, including potentially fatal damage to America. It means that there are fundamental flaws in its system.

Even China's most successful people aren't convinced about the CCP's future. They are scrambling for green cards, foreign real estate, and the ability to put their money in the free democracies.

Furthermore, the PRC is unpopular worldwide. In many places, it can get only as far as its money (better said, the U.S. dollars that China collects) can take it.

This is why it is imperative that we let Beijing fend for itself. Don't try to change it. We tried, and that didn't work. Let the world see what it really is. Ultimately, this is a battle of systems. China needs to undermine and destroy ours, because ours is better. We just need to stop supporting theirs, and it will fail.

A Contest between Ideas

As Joel Kotkin wrote:

> Our response should not be to mimic the Chinese approach, but to show—as we did during the Second World War and the Cold Wars—that we can tap our nation's industrial might and resources without massive corporatist privilege or state-run companies. But we also have to do it in a way that reflects our own values and promises. We can never beat the Mandarins in

tyrannical control, whether over religion, political dissent, or lockdown policies, as we now see in Shanghai.... America's ideals may be abandoned by its elites, but the country still has the natural and human resources that, if husbanded, could prevent this century from becoming a springtime for autocracy.[3]

Former assistant secretary of defense for Asia-Pacific Security Affairs Wallace Gregson offers additional sound advice:

We've forgotten why we're the shining city on the hill for much of the rest of the world. We're not defending the idea behind America. And the challenge is, we need to remember who we are. We used to be very good at big things. We used to know how to organize our policies and strategies around a central organizing vector, or set of principles, that gained the support of our own people and those of other nations.

We need to remember who we are and act in accordance with our principles. Once we do that, the rest—the whole complex execution of policy and strategy—will be as fraught with human frailty and fallibilities as always, but at least our direction, our intended movement, will be clear and bright, and the world will be better for it. And so will we.[4]

So let's get our own house in order, and defend ourselves and our system—and stop seeing other Americans as the enemy. One of the great political warfare efforts of the CCP has been to try to get Americans to revive and relive the Civil War, when the historical period that is much more apt is the War of Independence.

We need to live within our means and according to law. And, above all, love our country and the ideals behind it. There's never been another one like it. Sometimes you've got to live a while to understand that, or have lived somewhere like China, Russia, or East Germany to appreciate what we have and what's at stake.

Maybe we should turn to the Bible for some guidance. Specifically, the story of Nehemiah rebuilding the walls of Jerusalem. He carefully went about his business. He resisted the temptations from his enemies and their plots to destroy him. He also had rows of archers ready to protect him while he focused on his work of rebuilding the defenses of Jerusalem.

Nehemiah knew engagement with Sanbalot and Gesham the Arabian was a trap: "They were all trying to frighten us, thinking, 'Their hands will get too weak for the work, and it will not be completed.' But I prayed, Now strengthen my hands" (Nehemiah 6:9 NIV).

All in all, not so different in some ways from what the United States faces from China today—the bribes, threats and other "engagements" designed to buy Beijing time as, distracted, we let our defenses crumble, and the glow of the shining city on the hill is systematically extinguished. It once again brings to mind James Lilley's comment about the Chinese communists: "First they try to bribe you, then they try to scare you, and after that, they are stumped."

That's sound guidance even now. Better to let the Chinese communists handle their problems on their own and worry about what we're going to do to them than vice versa. Oddly enough, we don't have to do much other than go about our own business—and be ready to defend ourselves and our interests. That requires work.

Communist systems always destroy themselves.

If the epitaph of the United States of America is written someday in the not-so-distant future, one hopes it doesn't say, "They knew what they needed to do, but just couldn't do it."

What happens now is our choice. And our chance.

Our chance to be Americans.

Acknowledgments

This book took ten months to write, but it was forty-plus years in the making. I'd like to thank the following people for their kind help and encouragement in bringing this project to fruition: Ian Easton, James Fanell, Kerry Gershaneck, Paul Giarra, Sean Killeen, and Cleo Paskal. The production of the book was made possible by Tony Daniel, Michael Baker, and Kurnica Bhattacharjee.

Whatever views I have developed about the matters covered in this book, as well the ability to express them in a hopefully coherent manner, have been shaped by many people—either directly or indirectly—since I first got interested in Asia in the late 1970s.

Naming a few: William Alford, Ross Babbage, James Belote, Gordon Chang, Dean Cheng, David Day, Andrew Erickson, Sam Faddis, "The Fish," Rick Fisher, Jonathan Goff, Chip Gregson, Robert Haddick, Hideki Kaneda, Yoji Koda, Michael Listner, Matt Pottinger, Warren Rothman, Nick Redondo, Scott Savitt, Carl O. Schuster, Richard Simcock, Keith Stalder, David Stilwell, Jeff Tennen, June Teufel-Dreyer, Robert Thomas, John Toolan, William Triplett, and Arthur Waldron, James Auer, and William Hawkins.

Several individuals who have provided the most important insights and understanding will need to remain unnamed. I am particularly grateful to them. There would be no book without them.

I also acknowledge the people who see things differently than I. They have been equally helpful in shaping my thinking.

Notes

Chapter 3: Witness to War: The Baltimore Battlefield

1. Personal correspondence.
2. Phil Davis, "A Record Number of Fatal Overdoses Ravaged Maryland in 2020, 'Exacerbated' by COVID Pandemic, Report Shows," *Baltimore Sun*, April 13, 2021, https://www.baltimoresun.com/health/bs-hs-drug-overdose-2020-report-20210413 -7c7e4owxfvaphkmxvjtox6uioy-story.html.
3. "Provisional Drug Overdose Death Counts," Centers for Disease Control and Prevention, September 9, 2022, https://www.cdc.gov/nchs/nvss/vsrr/drug-overdose -data.htm.
4. Brian J. Asquith et al., "U.S. Job Flows and the China Shock | Working Paper 24080," National Bureau of Economic Research, November 2017, https://www.nber.org /system/files/working_papers/w24080/w24080.pdf.
5. Isaac Stone Fish, "How Henry Kissinger Became an Asset of China," *The Spectator*, March 26, 2022, https://www.spectator.co.uk/article/how-kissinger-was-played-by-china.
6. Major Dan, "History Short: Sino-American Mutual Defense Treaty," History and Headlines, December 2, 2022, https://www.historyandheadlines.com/history-short -sino-american-mutual-defense-treaty.
7. Bernard Gwertzman, "U.S. Decides to Sell Weapons to China in Policy Reversal," *New York Times*, July 17, 1981, https://www.nytimes.com/1981/06/17/world/us -decides-to-sell-weapons-to-china-in-policy-reversal.html.
8. Ted Galen Carpenter, "George H. W. Bush's Shameful Kowtow to China: A Cautionary Tale," *American Conservative*, May 27, 2020, https://www .theamericanconservative.com/george-h-w-bushs-shameful-kowtow-to-china -a-cautionary-tale.
9. Peter Schweizer, *Profiles in Corruption: Abuse of Power by America's Progressive Elite* (New York: Harper Collins, 2020), http://peterschweizer.com/books.
10. Stephanie Condon, "Obama: 'We Welcome China's Rise,'" CBS News, January 20, 2011, https://www.cbsnews.com/news/obama-we-welcome-chinas-rise.
11. Laura Widener, "Video: Joe Biden Mocks China Threat—'They're Not Bad Folks,'" American Military News, May 2, 2019, https://americanmilitarynews.com/2019/05 /video-joe-biden-mocks-china-threat-theyre-not-bad-folks.
12. Matt Viser, Tom Hamburger, and Craig Timberg, "Inside Hunter Biden's Multimillion-Dollar Deals with a Chinese Energy Company," *Washington Post*, March 30, 2022, https://www.washingtonpost.com/politics/2022/03/30/hunter -biden-china-laptop.
13. Evan Medeiros, "The New Geopolitics of China's Rise: U.S.-China Tensions and China's Global Role," AmCham, November 20, 2019, YouTube video, 20:22, https://

www.amcham.org.hk/webcast-library-public/new-geopolitics-chinas-rise-us-china -tensions-and-chinas-global-role-evan.

14. Kinling Lo, "Beijing 'May Have to Wait for Change in White House,'" PressReader, May 17, 2019, https://www.pressreader.com/china/south-china-morning-post-6150 /20190517/281621014157781.

15. Koji Sonoda, "Ex-Diplomat: U.S. Must 'Figure out a Way to Work with China,'" *Asahi Shimbun* via Web Archive, November 6, 2018, https://web.archive.org/web /20200225040535/http://www.asahi.com:80/ajw/articles/AJ201811060015.html.

16. Ben Weingarten, "Biden Administration China Ties Reveal a Deeper Disturbing Truth," *Newsweek*, March 1, 2021, https://www.newsweek.com/biden -administration-china-ties-reveal-deeper-disturbing-truth-opinion-1572589.

17. Edwin Chen, "Feinstein Plays Unbilled Role in Taiwan Dispute," *Los Angeles Times,* March 22, 1996, https://www.latimes.com/archives/la-xpm-1996-03-22-mn-50059 -story.html.

18. "Details Surface about Sen. Feinstein and the Chinese Spy Who Worked for Her," CBS News Bay Area, August 1, 2018, https://www.cbsnews.com/sanfrancisco/news /details-chinese-spy-dianne-feinstein-san-francisco.

19. Glenn F. Bunting, "Feinstein, Husband Hold Strong China Connections," *Los Angeles Times*, March 28, 1997, https://www.latimes.com/archives/la-xpm-1997 -03-28-mn-43046-story.html.

20. Kevin R. Brock, "Eric Swalwell and the Spy: A Lesson in How China Is Undermining Us," *The Hill*, December 14, 2020, https://thehill.com/opinion/national-security /530008-eric-swalwell-and-the-spy-a-lesson-in-how-china-is-undermining-us.

21. Michela Tindera, "A $59 Million Will Sheds Light on Shipping Fortune Connected to Elaine Chao and Mitch McConnell," *Forbes*, June 10, 2019, https://www.forbes .com/sites/michelatindera/2019/06/10/million-will-sheds-light-on-shipping-fortune -connected-to-elaine-chao-and-mitch-mcconnell/?sh=202080c32eb2.

22. Daniel Lippman and Steven Overly, "China's ZTE Taps Joe Lieberman for D.C. Damage Control," *POLITICO*, December 13, 2018, https://www.politico.com/story /2018/12/13/zte-china-joe-lieberman-1031383.

23. Nicole Hao, "Chinese Company Hikvision Confirms It's Controlled by China's Military Industrial Complex," *Epoch Times*, May 30, 2021, https://www .theepochtimes.com/chinese-company-hikvision-confirms-its-controlled-by-chinas -military-industrial-complex_3836392.html; Bethany Allen-Ebrahimian, "What a Lobbyist's Remarks behind Closed Doors Tell You about Chinese Money in Washington," *Washington Post*, October 29, 2019, https://www.washingtonpost .com/opinions/2019/10/29/what-lobbyists-remarks-behind-closed-doors-tell-you -about-chinese-money-washington.

24. Kurt Tong, "Do No Harm in Hong Kong," *Foreign Affairs*, December 6, 2019, https:// www.foreignaffairs.com/articles/china/2019-12-06/do-no-harm-hong-kong.

25. Rowan Scarborough, "James Mattis Failed to Disclose his Role with Consultant Tied to China in Bombshell Column," *Washington Times*, November 25, 2020, https://www.washingtontimes.com/news/2020/nov/25/james-mattis-failed-disclose -his-role-consultant-t.

26. Alice Su (@aliceysu), "As seen on Weibo: Shanghai residents go to their balconies to sing & protest lack of supplies. A drone appears: 'Please comply w covid restrictions. Control your soul's desire for freedom. Do not open the window or sing.'" Twitter, April 6, 2022, 12:18 a.m., https://twitter.com/aliceysu/status/1511558828802068481?lang=en.

27. Junhua Zhang, "China's Social Credit System—a New Cultural Revolution," GIS Reports, October 11, 2021, https://www.gisreportsonline.com/r/china-social-credit-system.

28. Aldous J. Pennyfarthing, "Pillow Man Mike Lindell's Bank Drops Him to Avoid 'Reputational Damage,'" Daily Kos, January 14, 2022, https://www.dailykos.com/stories/2022/1/14/2074746/-Pillow-Man-Mike-Lindell-s-bank-drops-him-to-avoid-reputational-damage.

29. Amy Nelson, "Canadian Protestor's Truck Seized, Bank Accounts Frozen over Connection to Freedom Convoy," Fox News, February 21, 2022, https://www.foxnews.com/media/canadian-freedom-convoy-truck-seized-bank-account-frozen.

30. "'The Consequences Are Real': Freeland Says Action Has Begun on Cutting Off Convoy Funds," Global News, February 17, 2022, https://globalnews.ca/video/8627701/the-consequences-are-real-freeland-says-action-has-begun-on-cutting-off-convoy-funds.

31. Victor Morton, "Canada's Justice Minister Threatens to Seize 'Pro-Trump' People's Bank Accounts," *Washington Times*, February 17, 2022, https://www.washingtontimes.com/news/2022/feb/17/david-lametti-canada-justice-minister-threatens-se.

32. Nichola Saminather, "TD Bank Freezes Accounts That Received Money for Canada Protests," Reuters, February 12, 2022, https://www.reuters.com/world/americas/td-bank-freezes-two-accounts-that-received-funds-support-canada-protests-2022-02-12.

33. Ontario Superior Court of Justice, "Motion for an Interlocutory Injunction and Costs," February 7, 2022, https://www.ottawapolice.ca/en/news-and-community/resources/Li-Interim-Order---CV-22-00088514-00CP.pdf.

34. Jason Abbruzzese and Kevin Collier, "Biden Takes Big Step toward Government-Backed Digital Currency," NBC News, March 9, 2022, https://www.nbcnews.com/tech/crypto/us-government-digital-currency-rcna19248.

35. Helier Cheung and Christopher Giles, "Hong Kong Protests: Were Triads Involved in the Attacks?" BBC News, July 22, 2019, https://www.bbc.com/news/world-asia-china-49071502.

36. Sun Yu and Tom Mitchell, "Can Xi Jinping Vanquish Covid without Crushing China's Economy?" *Financial Times*, May 12, 2022, https://www.ft.com/content/69ac0449-c6f9-4b30-a346-bd6716e735e5.

Chapter 4: What's the Goal of the Chinese Communist Party?

1. USCC, "The China Model: Return of the Middle Kingdom," U.S.-China Economic and Security Review Commission, November 18, 2020, https://www.uscc.gov/sites/default/files/2020-12/Chapter_1_Section_2--The_China_Model-Return_of_the_Middle_Kingdom.pdf.

2. U.S.-China Economic Security and Review Commission, *Report to Congress of the U.S.-China Economic and Security Review Commission*, (Washington, D.C.: U.S. Government Publishing Office, November 2021) https://www.govinfo.gov/content/pkg/GPO-USCC-2021/pdf/GPO-USCC-2021.pdf.

3. U.S.-China Economic Security and Review Commission, "The Chinese Communist Party's Ambitions and Challenges at Its Centennial," in *2021 Report to Congress of the U.S.-China Economic and Security Review Commission* (Washington, D.C.: U.S. Government Publishing Office, November 2021), chapter 1, section 1, https://www.uscc.gov/sites/default/files/2021-11/Chapter_1_Section_1--CCPs_Ambitions_and_Challenges_at_Its_Centennial.pdf.

4. Zhong Wenxing and Liang Jun, "China Will Never Forget NATO's Bombing of Chinese Embassy: Spokesperson," People's Daily Online, May 7, 2022, http://en.people.cn/n3/2022/0507/c90000-10093385.html.

5. Lily Kuo, "Australia Called 'Gum Stuck to China's Shoe' by State Media in Coronavirus Investigation Stoush," *The Guardian*, April 28, 2020, https://www.theguardian.com/world/2020/apr/28/australia-called-gum-stuck-to-chinas-shoe-by-state-media-in-coronavirus-investigation-stoush.

6. Gordon G. Chang, "China Is an Existential Threat to the U.S.," *Newsweek*, August 24, 2021, https://www.newsweek.com/china-existential-threat-us-opinion-1622699.

7. Jian Yang, *The Pacific Islands in China's Grand Strategy: Small States, Big Games* (New York: Palgrave Macmillan, 2011), 47.

8. Michael Pillsbury, *Geopolitical Power Calculations: China Debates the Future Security Environment* (Washington, D.C.: National Defense University Press, 2000), https://fas.org/nuke/guide/china/doctrine/pills2/part08.htm.

9. Ibid.

10. Matthew Impelli, "Over 500 U.S. Scientists under Investigation for Being Compromised by China," *Newsweek*, April 23, 2021, https://www.newsweek.com/over-500-us-scientists-under-investigation-being-compromised-china-1586074; Associated Press, "Harvard Professor Found Guilty of Hiding Ties to China," December 21, 2021, https://apnews.com/article/charles-lieber-harvard-china-initiative-c509558b99785c0209b291b8944a8bb3.

11. Cleo Paskal, *The Strategic Importance of the Pacific Islands*, Washington, D.C.: Foundation for Defense of Democracies, October 20, 2021, docs.house.gov/meetings/FA/FA05/20211020/114157/HHRG-117-FA05-Wstate-PaskalC-20211020.pdf.

12. Cleo Paskal, "China Winning Entropic Warfare in Pacific Islands," *Sunday Guardian*, June 4, 2022, https://www.sundayguardianlive.com/news/china-winning-entropic-warfare-pacific-islands.

13. Ibid.

14. Qiao Liang and Wang Xiangsui, *Unrestricted Warfare: China's Master Plan to Destroy America* (Beijing: PLA Literature and Arts Publishing House, February 1999), 12, https://ia800201.us.archive.org/0/items/Unrestricted_Warfare_Qiao_Liang_and_Wang_Xiangsui/Unrestricted_Warfare_Qiao_Liang_and_Wang_Xiangsui.pdf.

15. Kerry K. Gershaneck, *Political Warfare: Strategies for Combating China's Plan to "Win without Fighting"* (Quantico, Virginia: Marine Corps University Press, 2020), https://www.usmcu.edu/Portals/218/Political%20Warfare_web.pdf.

16. Shea Donovan, "China's Militarized 'Fishing Fleets' Try to Wrest Control of Senkaku Islands from Japan," *Newsweek*, February 16, 2022, https://www.newsweek.com/chinas-militarized-fishing-fleets-try-wrest-control-senkaku-islands-japan-1679632.

17. Yanzhong Huang, *Learning from SARS: Preparing for the Next Disease Outbreak: Workshop Summary* (Washington, D.C.: National Academies Press, 2004), https://www.ncbi.nlm.nih.gov/books/NBK92479.

18. "China's Latest SARS Outbreak Has Been Contained, but Biosafety Concerns Remain—Update 7," World Health Organization, May 18, 2004, https://www.who.int/emergencies/disease-outbreak-news/item/2004_05_18a-en.

19. Joshua Rhett Miller, "BLM Site Removes Page on 'Nuclear Family Structure' amid NFL Vet's Criticism," *New York Post,* September 24, 2020, https://nypost.com/2020/09/24/blm-removes-website-language-blasting-nuclear-family-structure.

20. Ibid.

21. Brian Flood, "NY Times Ignores 18 Deaths, Nearly $2 Billion in Damage when Bashing GOP Bills Targeting Rioters," Fox News, April 23, 2021, https://www.foxnews.com/media/ny-times-ignores-18-deaths-2-billion-damage-gop-bills.

22. Richard Fisher Jr., "In Space, China Seeks Galactic Hegemony," Center for Security Policy, March 25, 2021, https://centerforsecuritypolicy.org/in-space-china-seeks-galactic-hegemony.

23. Personal correspondence.

24. Personal correspondence.

25. Dom Calicchio, "General Leaves National Security Council after Leak of 5G Telecom Memo: Report," Fox News, February 4, 2018, https://www.foxnews.com/politics/general-leaves-national-security-council-after-leak-of-5g-telecom-memo-report.

26. Mara Hvistendahl, "Films Financed by Steven Mnuchin Were Tailored to Appeal to China," The Intercept, September 22, 2020, https://theintercept.com/2020/09/22/films-steve-mnuchin-china-hollywood-censorship.

27. Zach Dorfman, "Alex Joske on China's Influence Operations Abroad," November 21, 2022, The Brush Pass, https://thebrushpass.projectbrazen.com/joskechinainfluenceoperations/.

28. Kurt M. Campbell and Ely Ratner, "The China Reckoning," *Foreign Affairs*, March/April 2018, https://www.foreignaffairs.com/articles/china/2018-02-13/china-reckoning

29. Personal correspondence.

30. "Law of the People's Republic of China on the Territorial Sea and the Contiguous Zone," Ministry of Ecology, People's Republic of China, February 25, 1992, https://english.mee.gov.cn/Resources/laws/envir_elatedlaws/200710/t20071009_109932.shtml.

31. Raul (Pete) Pedrozo, "China's Revised Maritime Traffic Safety Law," *International Law Studies* 97, no. 1 (2021), https://digital-commons.usnwc.edu/ils/vol97/iss1/39/.

32. Alex Wilson, "Chinese Mock-Ups of U.S. Carriers Send a Clear Message, Expert Says," *Stars and Stripes*, November 12, 2021, https://www.stripes.com/branches/navy/2021-11-12/china-carrier-mock-ups-indo-pacific-naval-war-college-3589732.html.

33. Liu Xuanzun, "Foreign Media Reports on China's Ship-Launched, Air-Launched Anti-Ship Ballistic Missiles 'Merely Speculative,'" *Global Times*, April 21, 2022, https://www.globaltimes.cn/page/202204/1259992.shtml.

34. Matt Pottinger, Matthew Johnson, and David Feith, "Xi Jinping in His Own Words," *Foreign Affairs*, November 30, 2022, https://www.foreignaffairs.com/china/xi -jinping-his-own-words.

35. Grant Newsham, "Defending Japan's Southern Islands from Chinese Osmosis," *Asia Times*, October 13, 2017, https://asiatimes.com/2017/10/defending-japans-southern -islands-chinese-osmosis.

Chapter 5: Psychological Warfare: How Communist China Does Your Thinking for You

1. Emily Jacobs, "Top Chinese Professor Boasts of Operatives in Top of U.S. 'Core Inner Circle,'" *New York Post*, December 8, 2020, https://nypost.com/2020/12/08/ professor-claims-china-has-people-in-americas-core-inner-circle.

2. Ibid.

3. Ibid.

4. Jonathan Guyer and Ryan Grim, "Meet the Consulting Firm that's Staffing the Biden Administration," The Intercept, July 6, 2021, https://theintercept.com/2021/07/06/ westexec-biden-administration.

5. Associated Press, "Japanese Troops to California," *POLITICO*, June 9, 2013, https:// www.politico.com/story/2013/06/japanese-troops-to-california-092452.

6. Joseph S. Nye Jr., "Work with China, Don't Contain It," *New York Times*, January 25, 2013, https://www.nytimes.com/2013/01/26/opinion/work-with-china-dont -contain-it.html.

7. Edward Luce, "'We Are Now Living in a Totally New Era'—Henry Kissinger," *Financial Times*, May 9, 2022, https://www.ft.com/content/cd88912d-506a-41d4 -b38f-0c37cb7f0e2f.

8. Lisa van Dusen, "The Tragic Legacy of Bill Clinton's China Doctrine," *Policy*, August 10, 2020, https://www.policymagazine.ca/the-tragic-legacy-of-bill-clintons-china -doctrine.

9. Personal correspondence.

10. David Harsanyi, "Tom Friedman's Warped Love Affair with Communist China," *National Review*, February 9, 2021, https://www.nationalreview.com/corner/tom -friedmans-warped-love-affair-with-communist-china.

11. George Calhoun, "Part 1: Beijing Is Intentionally Underreporting China's Covid Death Rate," *Forbes*, January 2, 2022, https://www.forbes.com/sites/georgecalhoun/2022 /01/02/beijing-is-intentionally-underreporting-chinas-covid-death-rate-part-1.

12. Mark Hemingway, "If Media Don't Want to Be Called Propagandists, They Need to Stop Publishing Chinese and Russian Propaganda," The Federalist, June 20, 2019, https://thefederalist.com/2019/06/20/if-the-media-dont-want-to-be-called -propagandists-they-need-to-stop-publishing-chinese-and-russian-propaganda.

13. Qin Gang, "Chinese Ambassador: Why China Objects to Pelosi's Visit to Taiwan," *Washington Post*, August 4, 2022, https://www.washingtonpost.com/opinions/2022/08/04/china-ambassador-op-ed-pelosi-taiwan-visit.

14. David Folkenflik, "Bloomberg News Killed Investigation, Fired Reporter, Then Sought to Silence His Wife," National Public Radio, April 14, 2020, https://www.npr.org/2020/04/14/828565428/bloomberg-news-killed-investigation-fired-reporter-then-sought-to-silence-his-wi.

15. Personal correspondence.

16. Rachelle Peterson, Ian Oxnevad, and Flora Yan, "China's Enduring Influence on American Higher Education," National Association of Scholars, June 15, 2022, https://www.nas.org/reports/after-confucius-institutes/full-report.

17. Dan Currell and Mick Zais, "The Confucius Classroom Conundrum," *Newsweek*, March 22, 2021, https://www.newsweek.com/confucius-classroom-conundrum-opinion-1577492.

18. Zhong Nan, "U.S. Companies Still See China as Top Market, AmCham Says," *China Daily*, May 17, 2022, https://global.chinadaily.com.cn/a/202205/17/WS62833b88a310fd2b29e5d333.html.

19. Personal correspondence.

20. Ibid.

Chapter 6: Lawfare: Rules for Thee but Not for Me

1. M. D. Nalapat, "PM Modi Strikes a Deadly Blow to China's Tech Ambitions," *Sunday Guardian*, July 4, 2020, https://www.sundayguardianlive.com/news/pm-modi-strikes-deadly-blow-chinas-tech-ambitions.

2. Ibid.

3. "Executive Order on Addressing the Threat Posed by TikTok," White House Archives, August 6, 2020, https://trumpwhitehouse.archives.gov/presidential-actions/executive-order-addressing-threat-posed-tiktok.

4. "Executive Order on Addressing the Threat Posed by WeChat," White House Archives, August 6, 2020, https://trumpwhitehouse.archives.gov/presidential-actions/executive-order-addressing-threat-posed-wechat.

5. Stephen McDonell, "China Social Media: WeChat and the Surveillance State," BBC News, June 7, 2019, https://www.bbc.com/news/blogs-china-blog-48552907.

6. Ibid.

7. Ibid.

8. William Nee, "China's 709 Crackdown Is Still Going On," *The Diplomat*, July 9, 2021, https://thediplomat.com/2021/07/chinas-709-crackdown-is-still-going-on.

9. Pak Yiu and Anand Katakam, "In One Year, Hong Kong Arrests 117 People under New Security Law," Reuters, June 29, 2021, https://www.reuters.com/world/asia-pacific/one-year-hong-kong-arrests-117-people-under-new-security-law-2021-06-30.

10. Primrose Riordan, "Davis Polk Asia Chair Withdraws from Hong Kong Security Law Forum," *Financial Times*, May 21, 2022, https://www.ft.com/content/f48bb3cc-24b3-4bdf-9677-350c8c357b7c.

11. "Global Financial Leaders' Investment Summit Agenda," Hong Kong Monetary Authority, November 1–3, 2022, https://www.hkma.gov.hk/media/eng/doc/key-information/insight/inSight-on-Investment-Summit-Summit-Programme.pdf.

12. "Beijing Loyalist John Lee Elected As Hong Kong's Next Leader," Associated Press, May 8, 2022, https://apnews.com/article/voting-rights-elections-beijing-hong-kong-f136ce684eaafab980800337dd9ef4c2.

13. "FBI Director Christopher Wray's Remarks at Press Conference Regarding China's Operation Fox Hunt," Federal Bureau of Investigation, October 28, 2020, https://www.fbi.gov/news/press-releases/press-releases/fbi-director-christopher-wrays-remarks-at-press-conference-regarding-chinas-operation-fox-hunt.

14. Ibid.

15. Personal correspondence.

16. Personal correspondence.

17. "National Intelligence Law of the People's Republic," adopted at the 28th meeting of the Standing Committee of the 12th National People's Congress on June 27, 2017, https://cs.brown.edu/courses/csci1800/sources/2017_PRC_NationalIntelligenceLaw.pdf.

18. John D. McKinnon, "Lawsuit Claims U.S. WeChat Ban Is Unconstitutional," *Wall Street Journal*, August 21, 2020, https://www.wsj.com/articles/lawsuit-claims-u-s-wechat-ban-is-unconstitutional-11598059765.

19. Ashley Gorski, "The First Amendment Fight against the WeChat Ban," American Civil Liberties Union, December 7, 2020, https://www.aclu.org/news/free-speech/the-first-amendment-fight-against-the-wechat-ban.

20. Louise Matsakis, "Biden Administration Pays Almost $1 Million in Legal Fees to End Court Fight over Trump's WeChat Ban," Business Insider, November 24, 2021, https://www.businessinsider.com/biden-administration-pays-900000-end-suit-over-trump-wechat-ban-2021-11?op=1.

21. Prashant Jha, "China against US' Plan to Boost Domestic Semiconductor Manufacturing: Biden," *Hindustan Times*, May 4, 2022, https://www.hindustantimes.com/world-news/china-lobbying-against-us-plan-to-boost-domestic-semiconductor-manufacturing-biden-101651683407599.html.

22. "China Remains against Restrictive Measures Targeting Russia," TeleSur, May 16, 2022, https://www.telesurenglish.net/news/China-Remains-Against-Restrictive-Measures-Targeting-Russia-20220516-0024.html.

23. Yang Zekun, "Agreement Will Help Boost IP Protection," *China Daily*, May 20, 2022, https://www.chinadaily.com.cn/a/202205/20/WS6286cd2ca310fd2b29e5dd8d.html/.

24. Ross Babbage, *Winning without Fighting: Chinese and Russian Political Warfare Campaigns and How the West Can Prevail*, Vol. 2, *Case Studies* (Washington, D.C., 2019), https://csbaonline.org/uploads/documents/Winning_Without_Fighting_Annex_Final2.pdf.

25. Hyun-Soo Kim, "The 1992 Chinese Territorial Sea Law in the Light of the UN Convention," *International and Comparative Law Quarterly* 43, no. 4 (1994): 894–904, http://www.jstor.org/stable/761006.

26. Congressional Research Service, *Arbitration Case between the Philippines and China under the United Nations Convention on the Law of the Sea (UNCLOS)*,

(Washington, D.C.: Congressional Research Service, July 6, 2016), https://www
.everycrsreport.com/reports/R44555.html.

27. Christine Pichel Medina, "Legal Victory for the Philippines against China: A Case
Study," Global Challenges, February 2017, https://globalchallenges.ch/issue/1/legal
-victory-for-the-philippines-against-china-a-case-study.

28. Christia Marie Ramos, "China Continues to Belittle PH Court Win in Sea Row as
'a Piece of Waste Paper,'" *The Inquirer,* July 13, 2021, https://globalnation.inquirer
.net/197649/a-piece-of-waste-paper-china-continues-to-belittle-ph-win-in-scs-row.

29. "Anti-Secession Law (Adopted at the Third Session of the Tenth National People's
Congress on March 14, 2005)," https://www.europarl.europa.eu/meetdocs/2004
_2009/documents/fd/d-cn2005042601/d-cn2005042601en.pdf.

30. Joshua Boscaini, "China Warns Australia to Stop 'Dangerous' Actions over the South
China Sea after RAAF Interception," ABC (Australia), June 7, 2022, https://www
.abc.net.au/news/2022-06-07/china-warns-australia-after-raaf-south-china-sea
-interception/101133128.

31. "Chinese Vice FM Defends China-Solomon Islands Security Agreement," Xinhua,
April 28, 2022, https://english.news.cn/20220428/5e2184274c16413ebe015c5837
953e9a/c.html.

32. Ibid.

33. "Anti-Secession Law."

34. Personal correspondence.

35. Anthony J. Blinken, "The Administration's Approach to the People's Republic
of China," transcript of speech delivered at George Washington University,
Washington, D.C., May 26, 2022, https://www.state.gov/the-administrations
-approach-to-the-peoples-republic-of-china.

Chapter 7: Changing—or Undermining—Global Rules and Norms

1. Personal correspondence.

2. Andrew Wong, "China: We Are a 'Near-Arctic State' and We Want a 'Polar Silk
Road,'" CNBC News, February 14, 2018, https://www.cnbc.com/2018/02/14/china
-we-are-a-near-arctic-state-and-we-want-a-polar-silk-road.html.

3. Personal correspondence.

4. Personal correspondence.

5. Personal correspondence.

6. Personal correspondence.

7. Personal correspondence.

8. Personal correspondence.

9. "Chinese Companies Listed on Major U.S. Stock Exchanges," U.S-China Economic
and Security Review Commission, September 30, 2022, https://www.uscc.gov
/research/chinese-companies-listed-major-us-stock-exchanges.

10. "IMF Launches New SDR Basket Including Chinese Renminbi, Determines New
Currency Amounts," news release no. 16/440, International Monetary Fund,
September 30, 2016, https://www.imf.org/en/News/Articles/2016/09/30/AM16
-PR16440-IMF-Launches-New-SDR-Basket-Including-Chinese-Renminbi.

11. Ibid.

12. Personal correspondence.

13. Brendan I. Koerner, "Inside the Cyberattack That Shocked the U.S. Government," *WIRED*, October 23, 2016, https://www.wired.com/2016/10/inside-cyberattack -shocked-us-government.

14. "China Headed towards Carbon Neutrality by 2060; President Xi Jinping Vows to Halt New Coal Plants Abroad," United Nations, September 21, 2021, https://news .un.org/en/story/2021/09/1100642.

15. H. J. Mai, "U.S. Officially Rejoins Paris Agreement on Climate Change," National Public Radio, February 19, 2021, https://www.npr.org/2021/02/19 /969387323/u-s-officially-rejoins-paris-agreement-on-climate-change.

16. Personal correspondence.

Chapter 8: Capturing International Organizations

1. Sushant Sareen, "China and Pakistan's 'Iron Brotherhood': The Economic Dimensions and their Implications on U.S. Hegemony," *ORF Occasional Paper*, no. 183, February 7, 2019, https://www.orfonline.org/research/china-and-pakistans-iron -brotherhood-the-economic-dimensions-and-their-implications-on-us-hegemony.

2. Tony Munroe, Andrew Osborn, and Humeyra Pamuk, "China, Russia Partner Up against West at Olympics Summit," Reuters, February 4, 2022, https://www.reuters .com/world/europe/russia-china-tell-nato-stop-expansion-moscow-backs-beijing -taiwan-2022-02-04.

3. Bradley Bowman and Zane Zovak, "Biden Can No Longer Ignore Growing Iran-China Ties," *Foreign Policy*, January 13, 2022, https://foreignpolicy.com/2022/01 /13/iran-china-biden-gulf-security-military.

4. Ken Thomas and Catherine Lucey, "Trump, Biden Trade Insults in Debate Full of Crosstalk," *Wall Street Journal*, September 30, 2020, https://www.wsj.com/public /resources/documents/bDZVZTvzOKzC7nUTHUWd-WSJNewsPaper-9-30-2020 .pdf.

5. "Don't Tolerate New Zealand Bowing to China," *Washington Examiner*, April 21, 2021, https://www.washingtonexaminer.com/opinion/editorials/dont-tolerate-new -zealand-bowing-to-china.

6. Christia Marie Ramos, "China Continues to Belittle PH Court Win in Sea Row as 'a Piece of Waste Paper,'" The Inquirer, July 13, 2021, https://globalnation.inquirer .net/197649/a-piece-of-waste-paper-china-continues-to-belittle-ph-win-in-scs-row.

7. Matěj Stránský, "Embellishment and the Visit of the International Committee of the Red Cross to Terezín," Holocaust.CZ, June 23, 1944, https://www.holocaust.cz/en /history/events/embellishment-and-the-visit-of-the-international-committee-of-the -red-cross-to-terezin.

8. FRANCE 24 English, "UN's Bachelet Defends Visit to China's Xinjiang amid Criticism from Rights Groups—FRANCE 24," YouTube, May 28, 2022, https:// www.youtube.com/watch?v=SiYpwO6bgno.

9. Yuan Yang and Henry Foy, "'Under Tremendous Pressure': The Battle Behind the UN Report on China's Xinjiang Abuses," *Financial Times*, September 14, 2022, https://www.ft.com/content/0d69e178-8f56-4153-84b2-7ca2d4fa80a4.

10. Stephanie Nebehay, "UN Expert Calls for N. Korea Sanctions to Be Eased as Starvation Risk Looms," Reuters, October 7, 2021, https://www.reuters.com/world /asia-pacific/exclusive-un-expert-calls-nkorea-sanctions-be-eased-starvation-risk -looms-2021-10-07.

11. Sophie Richardson, "China's 'Slanders and Smears' at U.N. Human Rights Council," Human Rights Watch, March 11, 2021, https://www.hrw.org/news/2021/03/11/ chinas-slanders-and-smears-un-human-rights-council.

12. Ibid.

13. Colin Dwyer, "Former Interpol President Sentenced to Prison in China for Corruption," National Public Radio, January 21, 2020, https://www.npr.org/2020 /01/21/798121397/former-interpol-president-sentenced-to-prison-in-china-for -corruption.

14. Aurelien Breeden, "Wife of Former Interpol Chief Seeks Asylum in France," *New York Times*, January 19, 2019, https://www.nytimes.com/2019/01/19/world/europe /interpol-chief-wife-asylum-france.html.

15. Linda Lew, "China's Nominee Wins Interpol Seat Despite Concerns of Human Rights Groups," *South China Morning Post*, November 25, 2021, https://www.scmp .com/news/china/diplomacy/article/3157409/chinas-nominee-wins-interpol-seat -despite-concerns-human.

16. "Parliamentarians Raise Global Alarm at PRC INTERPOL Election Bid," Inter-Parliamentary Alliance on China, November 15, 2021, https://ipac.global/ parliamentarians-raise-global-alarm-at-prc-interpol-election-bid.

17. Debra Arbec, "'Patient Zero' in Cyberattack on U.N. Aviation Agency Was Senior Official's Son, Email Reveals," CBC News, July 25, 2019, https://www.cbc.ca/news /canada/montreal/icao-patient-zero-cyberattack-whistleblower-1.5223883.

18. Ibid.

19. Debra Arbec, "Montreal-Based U.N. Aviation Agency Tried to Cover Up 2016 Cyberattack, Documents Show," CBC News, February 27, 2019, https://www.cbc .ca/news/canada/montreal/montreal-based-un-aviation-agency-tried-to-cover-up-2016 -cyberattack-documents-show-1.5033733.

20. Justin Ling, "The Election That Saved the Internet from Russia and China," *WIRED*, October 30, 2022, https://www.wired.com/story/itu-2022-vote-russia-china-open -internet.

21. Ibid.

22. "U.N. Agencies Belt and Road Initiative Involvement," U.N. Environment Programme, https://www.unep.org/regions/asia-and-pacific/regional-initiatives/belt -and-road-initiative-international-green-1.

23. John Ratcliffe, "China Is National Security Threat No. 1," *Wall Street Journal*, December 3, 2020, https://www.wsj.com/articles/china-is-national-security-threat -no-1-11607019599.

24. Anthony Ruggiero, "Biden Must Move Fast to Replace WHO's Tedros," *Foreign Policy*, September 9, 2021, https://foreignpolicy.com/2021/09/09/who-tedros-biden -election/; Jason Beaubien, "World Health Organization Elects First Director-General From Africa," NPR, May 23, 2017, https://www.npr.org/sections/goatsandsoda /2017/05/23/529712013/world-health-organization-elects-first-director-general-from -africa.

25. Helen Davidson, "Senior WHO Adviser Appears to Dodge Question on Taiwan's Covid-19 Response," *The Guardian*, March 30, 2020, https://www.theguardian.com/world/2020/mar/30/senior-who-adviser-appears-to-dodge-question-on-taiwans-covid-19-response.

26. Christina Zhao, "Chinese Science Academy Lists Wuhan Lab as Outstanding Prize Candidate for COVID-19 Research," *Newsweek*, June 20, 2021, https://www.newsweek.com/chinese-science-academy-lists-wuhan-lab-outstanding-prize-candidate-covid-19-research-1602381.

27. Jonathan Wheatley, "World Bank Inquiry Finds IMF Chief Pushed Staff to Boost China Rankings," *Financial Times*, September 17, 2021, https://www.ft.com/content/029b75dc-86a0-4ebb-956b-a3135b6c510d.

28. Ibid.

29. Keith Bradsher, "China's Renminbi Is Approved by I.M.F. as a Main World Currency," *New York Times*, November 30, 2015, https://www.nytimes.com/2015/12/01/business/international/china-renminbi-reserve-currency.html.

30. Xi Jinping, "President Xi Jinping's Message to the Davos Agenda in Full," World Economic Forum, January 17, 2022, https://www.weforum.org/agenda/2022/01/address-chinese-president-xi-jinping-2022-world-economic-forum-virtual-session.

31. Agence France Presse, "Vatican Renews 2018 Deal with China Allowing Beijing to Choose Bishops," *Barron's*, October 22, 2022, https://www.barrons.com/news/vatican-renews-2018-deal-with-china-allowing-beijing-to-choose-bishops-01666434906.

32. Gary Bai, "Hong Kong Police Arrest 90-Year-Old Cardinal Joseph Zen under National Security Law," *Epoch Times*, May 11, 2022, https://www.theepochtimes.com/hong-kong-police-arrest-90-year-old-cardinal-joseph-zen-under-national-security-law_4460156.html.

33. Ibid.

Chapter 9: Biological Warfare: China Sickens America

1. Dany Shoham, "China's Biological Warfare Programme: An Integrative Study with Special Reference to Biological Weapons Capabilities," *Journal of Defence Studies* 9, no. 2 (April–June 2015): 131–156, https://idsa.in/system/files/jds/jds_9_2_2015_DanyShoham.pdf.

2. Javin Aryan, "A Look at China's Biowarfare Ambitions," Observer Research Foundation, June 2, 2021, https://www.orfonline.org/expert-speak/a-look-at-chinas-biowarfare-ambitions.

3. Tim Morrison, "Controlling Chinese Weapons: The Wuhan Virus and Nuclear Weapons," Hudson Institute, April 2, 2020, https://www.hudson.org/national-security-defense/controlling-chinese-weapons-the-wuhan-virus-and-nuclear-weapons.

4. Josh Rogin, "In 2018, Diplomats Warned of Risky Coronavirus Experiments in a Wuhan Lab. No One Listened," *POLITICO*, March 8, 2021, https://www.politico.com/news/magazine/2021/03/08/josh-rogin-chaos-under-heaven-wuhan-lab-book-excerpt-474322.

5. Will Jones, "New Emails Chronicle Lab-Leak Coverup in Real Time," Brownstone Institute, November 29, 2022, https://brownstone.org/articles/emails-chronicle-lab-leak-coverup/; "H.R. 4080—China COVID-19 Restitution Act," Congress.gov, June 23, 2021, https://www.congress.gov/bill/117th-congress/house-bill/4080/text?format=txt.

6. Tom Cotton, "Cotton Op-Ed in the Wall Street Journal 'Coronavirus and the Laboratories in Wuhan,'" Tom Cotton: Senator for Arkansas, April 21, 2020, https://www.cotton.senate.gov/news/press-releases/-cotton-op-ed-in-the-wall-street-journal-and-145coronavirus-and-the-laboratories-in-wuhan-and-146.

7. Glenn Kessler, "Timeline: How the Wuhan Lab-Leak Theory Suddenly Became Credible," *Washington Post*, May 25, 2021, https://www.washingtonpost.com/politics/2021/05/25/timeline-how-wuhan-lab-leak-theory-suddenly-became-credible.

8. Ed Browne, "Fauci Was 'Untruthful' to Congress about Wuhan Lab Research, New Documents Appear to Show," *Newsweek*, September 9, 2021, https://www.congress.gov/117/meeting/house/114270/documents/HHRG-117-GO24-20211201-SD004.pdf.

9. Harriet Alexander, "British Doctor Peter Daszak Who Tried to Gag Wuhan Lab Leak Theory Is Fired from U.N. Commission Investigating COVID after He Was Exposed for Organizing Letter Denying Leak Claim in the Lancet Medical Journal," *Daily Mail*, June 21, 2021, https://www.dailymail.co.uk/news/article-9710875/Peter-Daszak-removed-COVID-commission-following-bombshell-conflict-report.html.

10. Paul Farrell, "Outcry as British Researcher Is Given Another U.S. Grant to Investigate COVID—Despite Fears His Initial Work at Wuhan Lab Triggered Pandemic: Peter Daszak Is Paid $650,000 to Study Bat Coronaviruses—and 'Assess their Ability to Infect Humans,'" *Daily Mail*, October 3, 2022, https://www.dailymail.co.uk/news/article-11273773/Outcry-British-researcher-given-grant-NIH-investigate-COVID.html.

11. Ibid.

12. Bradley A. Thayer and Lianchao Han, "China and the WHO's Chief: Hold Them Both Accountable for Pandemic," *The Hill*, March 17, 2020, https://thehill.com/opinion/international/487851-china-and-the-whos-chief-hold-them-both-accountable-for-pandemic.

13. Max Boot, "The WHO Has Been More Effective at Fighting the Coronavirus Than Trump Has. No Wonder He Hates It," *Washington Post*, May 19, 2020, https://www.washingtonpost.com/opinions/2020/05/19/who-has-been-more-effective-fighting-coronavirus-than-trump-has-no-wonder-he-hates-it.

14. Personal correspondence.

15. Jon Cohen and Nirja Desai, "With Its CRISPR Revolution, China Becomes a World Leader in Genome Editing," *Science*, August 2, 2019, https://www.science.org/content/article/its-crispr-revolution-china-becomes-world-leader-genome-editing.

16. Bill Gertz, "China Deception Fuels Fears of Biological Weapons Ethnic 'Experiments,'" *Washington Times*, May 14, 2020, https://www.washingtontimes.com/news/2020/may/14/china-deception-fuels-fears-biological-weapons-eth.

17. Adam Gabbatt, "China Conducting Biological Tests to Create Super Soldiers, U.S. Spy Chief Says," *The Guardian*, December 4, 2020, https://www.theguardian.com /world/2020/dec/04/china-super-soldiers-biologically-enhanced-john-ratcliffe.

18. "200,000 U.S. Children Orphaned by COVID-19 Grill Washington's Conscience: Global Times Editorial," *Global Times*, May 4, 2022, https://www. globaltimes.cn/page/202205/1264770.shtml.

Chapter 10: Chemical Warfare: Killing Americans by the Tens of Thousands

1. Guy Taylor, "'Wake-Up Call': Chinese Control of U.S. Pharmaceutical Supplies Sparks Growing Concern," *Washington Times*, March 17, 2020, https://www .washingtontimes.com/news/2020/mar/17/china-threatens-restrict-critical-drug -exports-us.

2. Ibid.

3. "Coronavirus Shows U.S. Too Dependent on Cheap Medical Imports, USTR Says," Reuters, March 30, 2020, https://www.reuters.com/article/us-health-coronavirus -trade-ustr-idUSKBN21I042.

4. Anna Edney, "Pentagon Sees Security Threat in China's Drug-Supply Dominance," Bloomberg UK, August 5, 2019, https://www.bloomberg.com/news/articles/2019 -08-05/pentagon-sees-security-threat-in-china-s-drug-supply-dominance.

5. Chuin-Wei Yap, "Pandemic Lays Bare U.S. Reliance on China for Drugs," *Wall Street Journal,* August 5, 2020, https://www.wsj.com/articles/how-the-u-s-ceded-control -of-drug-supplies-to-china-11596634936.

6. "The Address of General Washington to the People of the United States on His Declining of the Presidency of the United States," Mount Vernon, https://www .mountvernon.org/education/primary-source-collections/primary-sources-2/article /washington-s-farewell-address-1796.

7. Nana Wilson et al., "Drug and Opioid-Involved Overdose Deaths—United States, 2017–2018," *Morbidity and Mortality Weekly Report* 69, no. 11 (2020): 290–97, https://www.cdc.gov/mmwr/volumes/69/wr/mm6911a4.htm.

8. Jamie Ducharme, "China Has Promised to Crack Down on Fentanyl. Here's What That Could Mean for Overdose Deaths in the U.S.," *TIME*, December 3, 2018, https://time.com/5469231/china-fentanyl-controlled-substance.

9. Leandra Bernstein, "Is the U.S.-China Agreement on Fentanyl a 'Game-Changer'?" CBS Austin, December 15, 2018, https://cbsaustin.com/news/nation-world/is-the-us -china-agreement-on-fentanyl-a-game-changer.

10. Jesse C. Baumgartner and David C. Radley, "The Drug Overdose Toll in 2020 and Near-Term Actions for Addressing It," Commonwealth Fund, August 16, 2021, https://www.commonwealthfund.org/blog/2021/drug-overdose-toll-2020-and- near-term-actions-addressing-it.

11. "U.S. Overdose Deaths in 2021 Increased Half as Much as in 2020—but Are Still Up 15%," Centers for Disease Control and Prevention, May 11, 2022, https://www .cdc.gov/nchs/pressroom/nchs_press_releases/2022/202205.htm.

12. Ibid.

13.. Jamie Ducharme, "Trump Said China Doesn't Have a Drug Problem. The Data Tells a Different Story," *TIME*, February 15, 2019, https://time.com/5530597/trump-china -drug-problem.

14. Vince Bielski, "U.S. Ramps Up Fentanyl Counterattack on Chinese Mainland, as DEA Faces Troubles at Home," RealClearInvestigations, December 14, 2021, https:// www.realclearinvestigations.com/articles/2021/12/14/us_drug_agents_ramp_up _fentanyl_counterattack_on_chinese_mainland_-_as_dea_faces_its_own_troubles _at_home_807483.html.

15. Ibid.

16. Personal correspondence.

17. Courtney Kube and Molly Boigon, "Every Branch of the Military Is Struggling to Make its 2022 Recruiting Goals, Officials Say," NBC News, June 27, 2022, https:// www.nbcnews.com/news/military/every-branch-us-military-struggling-meet-2022 -recruiting-goals-officia-rcna35078.

18. M. Taylor Fravel et al., "China Is Not an Enemy," *Washington Post*, July 3, 2019, https://www.washingtonpost.com/opinions/making-china-a-us-enemy-is-counterp roductive/2019/07/02/647d49d0-9bfa-11e9-b27f-ed2942f73d70_story.html.

19. Anthony J. Blinken, "The Administration's Approach to the People's Republic of China," transcript of speech delivered at George Washington University, May 26, 2022, https://www.state.gov/the-administrations-approach-to-the-peoples -republic-of-china.

Chapter 11: Economic Warfare: Putting America out of Business

1. Phelim Kine, "China Joined Rules-Based Trading System—Then Broke the Rules," *POLITICO*, December 9, 2021, https://www.politico.com/news/2021/12/09/china -wto-20-years-524050.

2. John Ratcliffe, "China Is National Security Threat No. 1," *Wall Street Journal*, December 3, 2020, https://www.wsj.com/articles/china-is-national-security-threat -no-1-11607019599.

3. Xi Jinping, "Certain Major Issues for Our National Medium- to Long-Term Economic and Social Development Strategy," *Qiushi*, October 31, 2021, https://cset .georgetown.edu/wp-content/uploads/t0235_Qiushi_Xi_economy_EN.pdf.

4. Matthew Pottinger, "Testimony before the United States-China Economic and Security Review Commission," U.S.-China Economic and Security Review Commission, April 15, 2021, https://www.uscc.gov/sites/default/files/2021-04/Matt _Pottinger_Testimony.pdf.

5. Karen M. Sutter, "'Made in China 2025' Industrial Policies: Issues for Congress," Congressional Research Service, December 22, 2022, https://sgp.fas.org/crs/row /IF10964.pdf.

6. Milton Friedman, "A Friedman Doctrine: The Social Responsibility of Business Is to Increase Its Profits," *New York Times*, September 13, 1970, https://www.nytimes .com/1970/09/13/archives/a-friedman-doctrine-the-social-responsibility-of-business -is-to.html.

7. Personal correspondence.

8. "Loral Settles Charge It Gave China Data," *Washington Times*, January 10, 2002, https://www.washingtontimes.com/news/2002/jan/10/20020110-034757-8824r.

9. Josh Horwitz, "Boeing Opens First 737 Plant in China amid U.S.-Sino Trade War," Reuters, December 15, 2018, https://www.reuters.com/article/us-boeing-china/boeing-opens-first-737-plant-in-china-amid-u-s-sino-trade-war-idUSKBN1OE06C.

10. Ibid.

11. "AVIC International Acquires Continental Motors," Mergr, December 14, 2010, https://mergr.com/avic-international-acquires-continental-motors; "Cirrus Aircraft Was Acquired by China Aviation Industry General Aircraft on June 1, 2011," Mergr, n.d., https://mergr.com/cirrus-aircraft-acquired-by-china-aviation-industry-general-aircraft.

12. "China Eastern Takes Delivery of the World's First Made-in-China C919 Jet," Reuters, December 8, 2022, https://www.reuters.com/business/aerospace-defense/china-eastern-takes-delivery-worlds-first-made-in-china-c919-jet-2022-12-09.

13. Personal correspondence.

14. Eric Lipton and Dionne Searcey, "How the U.S. Lost Ground to China in the Contest for Clean Energy," *New York Times*, November 21, 2021, https://www.nytimes.com/2021/11/21/world/us-china-energy.html.

15. Ibid.

16. Personal correspondence.

17. Guy Taylor, "'Wake-Up Call': Chinese Control of U.S. Pharmaceutical Supplies Sparks Growing Concern," *Washington Times*, March 17, 2020, https://www.washingtontimes.com/news/2020/mar/17/china-threatens-restrict-critical-drug-exports-us.

18. Yanzhong Huang (@YanzhongHuang), "China's Xinhua News just posted a piece titled 'Be bold: the world owes China a thank you', which says if China imposes restrictions on pharmaceutical exports, US will be '"plunged into the mighty sea of coronavirus.'" Twitter, March 4, 2020, 3:24 p.m., https://twitter.com/yanzhonghuang/status/1235300037875335170.

19. Bill Chappell, "Smithfield Foods to Be Sold to Chinese Firm for $4.72 Billion," NPR, May 29, 2013, https://www.npr.org/sections/thetwo-way/2013/05/29/187029237/smithfield-foods-to-be-sold-to-chinese-firm-for-4-72-billion.

20. Terril Yue Jones and Denny Thomas, "China's Wanda to Buy U.S. Cinema Chain AMC for $2.6 Billion," Reuters, May 20, 2012, https://www.reuters.com/article/us-amcentertainment-idUSBRE84K03K20120521.

21. Michael Forsythe, "Dalian Wanda of China Buys Legendary Entertainment for up to $3.5 Billion," *New York Times*, January 12, 2016, https://www.nytimes.com/2016/01/13/business/dealbook/china-dalian-wanda-legendary-entertainment.html.

22. Xie Yu, "Haier Bought GE Appliances for U.S. $5.6 Billion. Now It's Working on Fixing It," *South China Morning Post*, October 23, 2017, https://www.scmp.com/business/companies/article/2116486/chinas-haier-has-plan-help-continue-turnaround-ge-appliances.

23. Ibid.

24. "Lenovo Completes Acquisition of Motorola Mobility from Google," Lenovo StoryHub, October 30, 2014, https://news.lenovo.com/pressroom/press-releases/lenovo-completes-full-acquisition-motorola-mobility-from-google.

25. "BHR and AVIC Auto Acquire Henniges Automotive," PR Newswire, September 15, 2015, https://www.prnewswire.com/news-releases/bhr-and-avic-auto-acquire-henniges-automotive-300143072.html.

26. Peter Schweizer, *Secret Empires: How the American Political Class Hides Corruption and Enriches Family and Friends* (New York: Harper, 2019).

27. Personal correspondence.

28. Personal correspondence.

29. Martin Feldstein, "The Next Step for Chinese Economic Policy," *Project Syndicate*, April 23, 2018, https://www.project-syndicate.org/commentary/china-wto-mandatory-technology-transfer-by-martin-feldstein-2018-04.

30. Mara Hvistendahl, "China's Theft of U.S. Trade Secrets Under Scrutiny," *Science*, February 28, 2017, https://www.science.org/content/article/china-s-theft-us-trade-secrets-under-scrutiny.

31. U.S. Attorney's Office, Northern District of California, "Former DuPont Scientist Pleads Guilty to Economic Espionage," Fedearl Bureau of Investigation, March 2, 2012, https://archives.fbi.gov/archives/sanfrancisco/press-releases/2012/former-dupont-scientist-pleads-guilty-to-economic-espionage.

32. Ibid.

33. Ibid.

34. Ibid.

35. Christopher Wray, "The Threat Posed by the Chinese Government and the Chinese Communist Party to the Economic and National Security of the United States," Fedearl Bureau of Investigation, July 7, 2020, https://www.fbi.gov/news/speeches/the-threat-posed-by-the-chinese-government-and-the-chinese-communist-party-to-the-economic-and-national-security-of-the-united-states.

36. U.S. Department of Justice, "Jury Convicts Chinese Intelligence Officer of Espionage Crimes, Attempting to Steal Trade Secrets," U.S. Department of Justice, November 5, 2021, https://www.justice.gov/opa/pr/jury-convicts-chinese-intelligence-officer-espionage-crimes-attempting-steal-trade-secrets.

37. U.S. Department of Justice, "Chinese Government Intelligence Officer Sentenced to 20 Years in Prison for Espionage Crimes, Attempting to Steal Trade Secrets From Cincinnati Company," U.S. Department of Justice, November 16, 2022, https://www.justice.gov/opa/pr/chinese-government-intelligence-officer-sentenced-20-years-prison-espionage-crimes-attempting.

38. U.S. Attorney's Office: District of Massachusetts, "Harvard University Professor Convicted of Making False Statements and Tax Offenses," U.S. Attorney's Office: District of Massachusetts, December 21, 2021, https://www.justice.gov/usao-ma/pr/harvard-university-professor-convicted-making-false-statements-and-tax-offenses.

39. Nicholas Eftimiades, *Chinese Intelligence Operations* (Oxfordshire, England: Routledge, 2016).

40. Tom Blackwell, "Did Huawei Bring Down Nortel? Corporate Espionage, Theft, and the Parallel Rise and Fall of Two Telecom Giants," *National Post*, February 24, 2020,

https://nationalpost.com/news/exclusive-did-huawei-bring-down-nortel-corporate
-espionage-theft-and-the-parallel-rise-and-fall-of-two-telecom-giants.

41. Anders Corr, Ph.D. (@anderscorr), "Long story short—it appears that Huawei hacked Canadian and UK telecom companies (Nortel and Marconi) . . ." (thread), Twitter, May 24, 2022, 2:42 p.m., https://twitter.com/anderscorr/status /1529171036062744579.

42. Kate O'Keeffe, "Pentagon's China Warning Prompts Calls to Vet U.S. Funding of Startups," *Wall Street Journal*, https://www.wsj.com/articles/pentagons-china -warning-prompts-calls-to-vet-u-s-funding-of-startups-11652014803.

43. David Autor, David Dorn, and Gordon Hanson, "On the Persistence of the China Shock," *Brookings Papers on Economic Activity* (Fall 2021): 381–447.

44. U.S. Department of Defense, *Securing Defense-Critical Supply Chains: An Action Plan Developed in Response to President Biden's Executive Order 14017* (Washington, D.C.: U.S. Department of Defense, February 2022), https://media .defense.gov/2022/Feb/24/2002944158/-1/-1/1/DOD-EO-14017-REPORT -SECURING-DEFENSE-CRITICAL-SUPPLY-CHAINS.PDF.

45. Ibid.

46. Ibid.

47. Ibid.

48. Personal correspondence.

49. O'Keeffe, "Pentagon's China Warning Prompts Calls."

50. Robin Emmott and Angeliki Koutantou, "Greece Blocks EU Statement on China Human Rights at U.N.," Reuters, June 18, 2017, https://www.reuters.com/article/us -eu-un-rights/greece-blocks-eu-statement-on-china-human-rights-at-u-n -idUSKBN1990FP.

51. Joel Wuthnow, *Chinese Perspectives on the Belt and Road Initiative: Strategic Rationales, Risks, and Implications, China Strategic Perspectives* 12 (Washington, D.C.: National Defense University, October 2017), Institute for National Strategic Studies, October 2017, https://inss.ndu.edu/Portals/68/Documents/stratperspective /china/ChinaPerspectives-12.pdf.

52. Personal correspondence.

53. Susanna Luthi, "Meth, Vanilla and 'Gulags': How China Has Overtaken the South Pacific One Island at a Time," *POLITICO*, August 29, 2021, https://www.politico .com/news/magazine/2021/08/29/tonga-china-south-pacific-influence-506370.

54. Alexandra Stevenson, "China Faces New 'Long March' as Trade War Intensifies, Xi Jinping Says," *New York Times*, May 21, 2019, https://www.nytimes.com/2019/05 /21/world/asia/xi-jinping-china-trade.html.

55. Sebastian Strangio, "Shangri-La Dialogue Concludes under Shadow of Ukraine, U.S.-China Tensions," *The Diplomat*, June 13, 2022, https://thediplomat.com/2022 /06/shangri-la-dialogue-concludes-under-shadow-of-ukraine-us-china-tensions.

56. M. Taylor Fravel et al., "China Is Not an Enemy," *Washington Post*, July 3, 2019, https://www.washingtonpost.com/opinions/making-china-a-us-enemy-is-counterp roductive/2019/07/02/647d49d0-9bfa-11e9-b27f-ed2942f73d70_story.html.

57. Ibid.

58. Ryan Lucas, "The Justice Department Is Ending Its Controversial China Initiative," NPR, February 23, 2022, https://www.npr.org/2022/02/23/1082593735/justice -department-china-initiative.

59. Aruna Viswanatha, "U.S. Drops Visa Fraud Cases against Five Chinese Researchers," *Wall Street Journal*, July 23, 2021, https://www.wsj.com/articles/u-s-drops-visa-fraud -cases-against-5-chinese-researchers-11627074870.

60. "GT Voice: U.S. 'Special 301' Report Just Another Piece of Trash Filled with Same Old Lies," *Global Times*, April 28, 2022, https://www.globaltimes.cn/page/202204 /1260617.shtml.

61. "Premier Stresses Expanding Opening-Up," State Council: The People's Republic of China, May 20, 2022, https://english.www.gov.cn/premier/news/202205/20/content _WS62877aadc6d02e533532b0d0.html.

62. Ibid.

63. "American Business Optimistic about Chinese Market," China International Import Expo, May 12, 2022, https://www.ciie.org/zbh/en/news/exhibition/focus/20220512 /32426.html/.

64. Personal correspondence.

65. Personal correspondence.

Chapter 12: Financial Warfare: Defenestrating the U.S. Dollar

1. "Bo: 800 Million Shirts for One Airbus A380," *China Daily*, May 5, 2005, https:// www.chinadaily.com.cn/english/doc/2005-05/05/content_439584.htm.

2. Marlo Safi, "Here's a List of Professors and Researchers at American Colleges Who Secretly Worked For China," Daily Caller, May 29, 2020, https://dailycaller.com/2020 /05/29/professors-academics-worked-china-college-campus/; Rich Edson, "Harvard Professor Charles Lieber Convicted of Hiding Ties to China," Fox News, December 21, 2021, https://www.foxnews.com/us/harvard-scientist-paid-by-china.

3. Yang Jie and Aaron Tilley, "Apple Makes Plans to Move Production out of China," *Wall Street Journal*, December 3, 2022, https://www.wsj.com/articles/apple-china -factory-protests-foxconn-manufacturing-production-supply-chain-11670023099.

4. Keith Bradsher, "How China Lost $1 Trillion," *New York Times*, February 7, 2017, https://www.nytimes.com/interactive/2017/02/07/business/china-bank-foreign -reserves.html.

5. Anjani Trivedi, "China's $20 Trillion Shadow Banking Business Won't Be Easily Tamed," *Wall Street Journal*, October 17, 2017, https://www.wsj.com/articles/chinas -greatest-challenge-1508137030.

6. Personal correspondence.

7. Personal correspondence.

8. Ibid.

9. "MSCI Will Increase the Weight of China A Shares in MSCI Indexes," MSCI, February 28, 2019, https://www.msci.com/documents/10199/238444/China _A_Further_Weight_Increase_PR_Eng.pdf.

10. "Bloomberg Confirms China Inclusion in the Bloomberg Barclays Global Aggregate Indices," Bloomberg, January 30, 2019, https://www.bloomberg.com/company/press

/
bloomberg-confirms-china-inclusion-bloomberg-barclays-global-aggregate-indices.

11. Sophie Kiderlin, "BlackRock Says Investors Should Triple Their Allocations in Chinese Assets Despite Increasing Regulatory Risks," *Markets Insider*, August 18, 2021, https://markets.businessinsider.com/news/stocks/blackrock-tells-investors -triple-exposure-chinese-assets-report-2021-8.

12. Steve Johnson, "BlackRock Calls for Investors to Lift Allocations to China's Markets," *Financial Times*, August 17, 2021, https://www.ft.com/content/f876fb63 -1823-4f4b-a28f-faa7797aa49c.

13. "BlackRock Becomes First to Operate Wholly Owned China Mutual Fund Biz," Reuters, June 11, 2021, https://www.reuters.com/business/finance/blackrock-wins -chinese-regulatory-approval-onshore-mutual-fund-business-2021-06-11.

14. Jason Zweig, "What the 'Smart Money' Knows about China's Evergrande Crisis," *Wall Street Journal*, September 24, 2021, https://www.wsj.com/articles/what-the -smart-money-knows-about-chinas-evergrande-crisis-11632495602.

15. Ibid.

16. Ibid.

17. Alexandra Alper and Aishwarya Nair, "CalPERS Investment Chief Steps Down at $400 Billion Pension Fund," Reuters, August 6, 2020, https://www.reuters.com /article/us-calpers-cio/calpers-investment-chief-steps-down-at-400-billion-pension -fund-idUSKCN2520V3

18. Shujie Yao, "China's Currency Gets the IMF Stamp of Approval as It Enters a New Normal," The Conversation, May 29, 2015, https://theconversation.com/chinas -currency-gets-the-imf-stamp-of-approval-as-it-enters-a-new-normal-42559.

19. Kinishka Singh, "S&P Affirms China Ratings, Says China to Maintain Robust GDP Growth," Reuters, June 25, 2021, https://www.reuters.com/article/us-china-ratings -s-p/sp-affirms-china-ratings-says-china-to-maintain-robust-gdp-growth -idUSKCN2E10SJ.

20. "U.S. Audit Requirements for U.S.-listed Chinese Firms Have No Teeth," *Asia Times*, December 17, 2020, https://asiatimes.com/2020/12/us-audit-requirements-for-us -listed-chinese-firms-have-no-teeth.

21. George Lei, Maria Elena Vizcaino, and Ye Xie, "Yuan Jumps after Report on Saudis Weighing Its Use in Oil Deals," Bloomberg, March 15, 2022, https://www.bloomberg .com/news/articles/2022-03-15/yuan-surges-after-report-on-saudis-accepting -currency-for-oil?.

22. Yaya J. Fanusie and Emily Jin, *China's Digital Currency: Adding Financial Data to Digital Authoritarianism* (Washington, D.C.: Center for a New American Security, January 2021), https://s3.us-east-1.amazonaws.com/files.cnas.org/backgrounds /documents/CNAS-Report-Chinas-Digital-Currency-Jan-2021-final.pdf.

23. Ibid.

24. "Democratic Govt Plays 'Taiwan Card' to Fill Vacancy of Competence, Achievement," *Global Times*, May 11, 2022, https://www.globaltimes.cn/page /202205/1265399.shtml.

25. Shi Jing, "Global Investors Keep Big Bet on A Shares," *China Daily*, March 19, 2022, https://www.chinadaily.com.cn/a/202203/19/WS62352f25a310fd2b29e51ee3.html.

26. Personal correspondence.

27. Wu Yidan, "Bank of China Sustainable Bonds Valued at USD 2.2 Billion Listed in London," *People's Daily Online*, November 12, 2021, http://en.people.cn/n3/2021/1112/c90000-9919099.html.

Chapter 13: Cyber Warfare: Hacking through American Defenses

1. "China Cyber Threat Overview and Advisories," Cyber and Infrastructure Security Agency, 2022, https://www.cisa.gov/uscert/china.

2. Office of the Director of National Intelligence, *Annual Threat Assessment of the U.S. Intelligence Community* (Washington, D.C.: Office of the Director of National Intelligence April 9, 2021), https://www.dni.gov/files/ODNI/documents/assessments/ATA-2021-Unclassified-Report.pdf.

3. Chris Buckley, "Xi Urges Greater Innovation in 'Core Technologies'," *New York Times*, June 10, 2014, https://archive.nytimes.com/sinosphere.blogs.nytimes.com/2014/06/10/xi-urges-greater-innovation-in-core-technologies.

4. Julie Hirschfeld Davis and David E. Sanger, "Obama and Xi Jinping of China Agree to Steps on Cybertheft," *New York Times*, September 25, 2015, https://www.nytimes.com/2015/09/26/world/asia/xi-jinping-white-house.html.

5. "China: The Risk to Corporate America," Federal Bureau of Investigation, 2019, https://www.fbi.gov/file-repository/china-risk-to-corporate-america-2019.pdf/view.

6. Bill Gertz, "Report Details Massive Chinese IP Theft," *Washington Times*, May 4, 2022, https://www.washingtontimes.com/news/2022/may/4/inside-ring-report-details-massive-chinese-ip-thef.

7. Jai Vijayan, "China-Backed Winnti APT Siphons Reams of U.S. Trade Secrets in Sprawling Cyber-Espionage Attack," Dark Reading, May 4, 2022, https://www.darkreading.com/attacks-breaches/china-winnti-apt-trade-secrets-us.

8. Ibid.

9. Ibid.

10. Gertz, "Inside the Ring: Report Details Massive Chinese IP Theft."

11. Vijayan, "China-Backed Winnti APT Siphons Reams."

12. "Four Chinese Nationals Working with the Ministry of State Security Charged with Global Computer Intrusion Campaign Targeting Intellectual Property and Confidential Business Information, Including Infectious Disease Research," U.S. Department of Justice, July 19, 2021, https://www.justice.gov/opa/pr/four-chinese-nationals-working-ministry-state-security-charged-global-computer-intrusion.

13. Ibid.

14. Ibid.

15. Ibid.

16. Eric Tucker, "Microsoft Exchange Hack Caused by China, US and Allies Say," Associated Press, July 19, 2021, https://apnews.com/article/microsoft-exchange-hack-biden-china-d533f5361cbc3374fdea58d3fb059f35.

17. Ibid.

18. Kate O'Keeffe, "Pentagon's China Warning Prompts Calls to Vet U.S. Funding of Startups," *Wall Street Journal*, May 8, 2022, https://www.wsj.com/articles/pentagons-china-warning-prompts-calls-to-vet-u-s-funding-of-startups-11652014803.

19. U.S. Department of Justice, "Two Chinese Hackers Working with the Ministry of State Security Charged with Global Computer Intrusion Campaign Targeting Intellectual Property and Confidential Business Information, Including COVID-19 Research," U.S. Department of Justice, July 21, 2020, https://www.justice.gov/opa/pr/two-chinese-hackers-working-ministry-state-security-charged-global-computer-intrusion.
20. Ibid.
21. Ibid.
22. U.S. Department of Justice, "U.S. Charges Five Chinese Military Hackers for Cyber Espionage against U.S. Corporations and a Labor Organization for Commercial Advantage," U.S. Department of Justice, May 19, 2014, https://www.justice.gov/opa/pr/us-charges-five-chinese-military-hackers-cyber-espionage-against-us-corporations-and-labor.
23. Ibid.
24. Ibid.
25. Ibid.
26. Ibid.
27. Ibid.
28. Ellen Nakashima and Paul Sonne, "China Hacked a Navy Contractor and Secured a Trove of Highly Sensitive Data on Submarine Warfare," *Washington Post*, June 8, 2018, https://www.washingtonpost.com/world/national-security/china-hacked-a-navy-contractor-and-secured-a-trove-of-highly-sensitive-data-on-submarine-warfare/2018/06/08/6cc396fa-68e6-11e8-bea7-c8eb28bc52b1_story.html.
29. Ibid.
30. Ibid.
31. "Reed Says Chinese Hack of Navy Contractor 'Very Serious,'" *Newport Daily News*, June 12, 2018, https://www.newportri.com/story/news/local/2018/06/12/reed-says-chinese-hack-of-navy-contractor-very-serious/11996078007.
32. U.S. Department of Justice, "Chinese National Who Conspired to Hack into U.S. Defense Contractors' Systems Sentenced to 46 Months in Federal Prison," U.S. Department of Justice, July 13, 2016, https://www.justice.gov/opa/pr/chinese-national-who-conspired-hack-us-defense-contractors-systems-sentenced-46-months.
33. "USAF Awards Boeing a $3.4 Billion Contract under the C-17 Programme," Shepherd Media, September 29, 2021, https://www.shephardmedia.com/news/air-warfare/usaf-awards-boeing-a-34-billion-contract-under-the.
34. Justin Ling, "Man Who Sold F-35 Secrets to China Pleads Guilty," *Vice*, March 24, 2016, https://www.vice.com/en/article/kz9xgn/man-who-sold-f-35-secrets-to-china-pleads-guilty.
35. Ibid.
36. "China's New Stealth Fighter Could Defeat F-35, AVIC Chief Says," Bloomberg, December 10, 2014, https://www.bloomberg.com/news/articles/2014-12-10/china-s-new-stealth-fighter-could-defeat-f-35-avic-chief-says.
37. Ibid.
38. Franz-Stefan Gady, "New Snowden Documents Reveal Chinese Behind F-35 Hack," *The Diplomat*, January 27, 2015, https://thediplomat.com/2015/01/new-snowden-documents-reveal-chinese-behind-f-35-hack.

39. Ibid.
40. Ibid.
41. CISA, "Chinese Gas Pipeline Intrusion Campaign, 2011 to 2013," Cybersecurity and Infrastructure Security Agency, July 20, 2021, https://www.cisa.gov/uscert/ncas/alerts/aa21-201a.
42. Ibid.
43. Ibid.
44. Federal Communications Commission, "FCC Revokes and Terminates China Telecom America's Authority to Provide Telecom Services in America," Federal Communications Commission, October 26, 2021, https://docs.fcc.gov/public/attachments/DOC-376902A1.pdf.
45. Chris C. Demchak and Yuval Shavitt, "China's Maxim—Leave No Access Point Unexploited: The Hidden Story of China Telecom's BGP Hijacking," *Military Cyber Affairs* 3, no. 1 (2018), https://digitalcommons.usf.edu/cgi/viewcontent.cgi?article=1050&context=mca.
46. Ibid.
47. Ibid.
48. Zak Doffman, "Russia and China 'Hijack' Your Internet Traffic: Here's What You Do," *Forbes*, April 18, 2020, https://www.forbes.com/sites/zakdoffman/2020/04/18/russia-and-china-behind-internet-hijack-risk-heres-how-to-check-youre-now-secure/.
49. Federal Communications Commission, "FCC Revokes and Terminates China Telecom America's Authority."
50. Joseph Menn, "China-Based Campaign Breached Satellite, Defense Companies—Symantec," Reuters, June 19, 2018, https://www.reuters.com/article/china-usa-cyber-idCNL1N1TL1K1.
51. Ibid.
52. Ibid.
53. Damian Paletta, "U.S. Intelligence Chief James Clapper Suggests China behind OPM Breach," *Wall Street Journal*, June 25, 2015, https://www.wsj.com/articles/u-s-intelligence-chief-james-clapper-suggests-china-behind-opm-breach-1435245782.
54. "U.S. Intelligence Chief—China Top Suspect in Hack of U.S. Agency: WSJ," Reuters, June 25, 2015, https://www.reuters.com/article/uk-cybersecurity-usa-china-idAFKBN0P525M20150625.
55. Joyce Lau, "Who Are the Chinese Trolls of the '50 Cent Army'?" *Voa*, October 7, 2016, https://www.voanews.com/a/who-is-that-chinese-troll/3540663.html.
56. Rogier Creemers, Paul Triolo, and Graham Webster, "Translation: Cybersecurity Law of the People's Republic of China (Effective June 1, 2017)," New America, June 29, 2018, http://newamerica.org/cybersecurity-initiative/digichina/blog/translation-cybersecurity-law-peoples-republic-china.
57. "Alliance Canada Hong Kong leader Says a Huawei 5G Network in Canada Would Track Citizens," *Global News*, August 25, 2020, https://globalnews.ca/video/7289169/alliance-canada-hong-kong-leader-says-a-huawei-5g-network-in-canada-would-track-citizens.
58. Ibid.

59. Brittany Jordan, "Chinese Bot Network Used Social Media to Encourage Asian American Protests, Researchers Find," *Federal Inquirer*, September 8, 2021, https://federalinquirer.com/chinese-bot-network-used-social-media-to-encourage-asian-american-protests-researchers-find.

60. Ghalia Kadiri and Joan Tilouine, "In Addis Ababa, the Headquarters of the African Union Spied On by Beijing," *Le Monde*, January 26, 2018, https://www.lemonde.fr/afrique/article/2018/01/26/a-addis-abeba-le-siege-de-l-union-africaine-espionne-par-les-chinois_5247521_3212.html.

61. "China's Strategic Aims in Africa," U.S.-China Economic and Security Review Commission, November 18, 2020, https://www.uscc.gov/sites/default/files/2020-12/Chapter_1_Section_3—Chinas_Strategic_Aims_in_Africa.pdf.

62. Ryan Lovelace, "LinkedIn Looms as China Security Threat, U.S. Officials Warn," *Washington Times*, February 18, 2020, https://www.washingtontimes.com/news/2020/feb/18/linkedin-looms-china-security-threat-us-officials-/.

63. Winnona DeSombre, "Testimony before the U.S.-China Economic and Security Review Commission," U.S.-China Economic and Security Review Commission, February 17, 2022, https://www.uscc.gov/sites/default/files/2022-02/Winnona_DeSombre_Testimony.pdf.

Chapter 14: Proxy Warfare: China's Warfare Outsourcing

1. Gabriel Crossley, David Brunnstrom, and Michael Martina, "U.S. Urges China to Use Influence with Moscow over Ukraine," Reuters, January 27, 2022, https://www.reuters.com/world/europe/uss-blinken-holds-talks-with-chinas-wang-ukraine-situation-2022-01-27.

2. Thomas Chan and Seong Hyeon Choi, "Moon Jae-In: South Korea's Merkel?," *The Diplomat*, May 9, 2022, https://thediplomat.com/2022/05/moon-jae-in-south-koreas-merkel.

3. Tara O, "Unification Minister Hearing: Thae Yong-Ho Asks Lee In-Young about Espousing Juche Ideology, National Security Law, Ji Seong-Ho Asks about South Koreans Detained in North Korea, Park Jin Asks about the Alliance," East Asia Research Center, August 2, 2020, https://eastasiaresearch.org/2020/08/02/unification-minister-hearing-thae-yong-ho-asks-lee-in-young-about-espousing-juche-ideology.

4. "'If You Don't Deal with China, I Will Impeach You.' South Korean People Boycott Chinatown, and Moon Jae-In Is Hard to End," INews, October 28, 2022, https://inf.news/en/world/29904ae8ef5cc9bcbfc43e64f4ee6d43.html.

5. Yonhap, "China Calls on S. Korea to Uphold Former Moon Administration's Policy on THAAD," *Korea Herald*, July 27, 2022, https://www.koreaherald.com/view.php?ud=20220727000814.

6. Kyungji Cho et al., "As Virus Spreads, Koreans Blame Refusal to Stop Chinese Visitors," Bloomberg UK, February 28, 2020, https://www.bloomberg.com/news/articles/2020-02-28/as-virus-spreads-koreans-blame-refusal-to-stop-chinese-visitors.

7. Grant Newsham, "Fraud in South Korea's April 2020 Election: It Probably Happened and Is a Big Deal for the United States," Center For Security Policy, September 24,

2020, https://centerforsecuritypolicy.org/fraud-in-south-koreas-april-2020-election-it-probably-happened-and-is-a-big-deal-for-the-united-states.

8. Sarah Kim, "NEC Chief Apologizes, Vows to Do Better on Election Day," *Korea Joong-Ang Daily*, March 8, 2022, https://koreajoongangdaily.joins.com/2022/03/08/national/politics/National-Election-Commission-Noh-Jeonghee-NEC/20220308165609253.html.

9. Michelle Nichols and Krishna N. Das, "China Foils Bid to Blacklist Kashmir Attacker; U.S., India Vow to Keep Pushing," Reuters, March 13, 2019, https://www.reuters.com/article/us-india-kashmir-un/china-foils-bid-to-blacklist-kashmir-attacker-u-s-india-vow-to-keep-pushing-idUSKCN1QU2S2.

10. Rahul Tripathi, "NIA Chargesheet: NSCN Got Arms from Chinese Firms," *Indian Express*, April 1, 2011, https://indianexpress.com/article/news-archive/web/nia-chargesheet-nscn-got-arms-from-chinese-firms.

11. V. P. Haran, "Challenges in India's Neighborhood Policy," lecture at Central University of Tamil Nadu, July 14, 2017, https://www.mea.gov.in/distinguished-lectures-detail.htm?674.

12. Christopher D. Booth, "Clowns to the Left of Me, Jokers to the Right: The Threat of Increased Insurgency in India's Volatile Northeast," Modern War Institute at West Point, April 25, 2022, https://mwi.usma.edu/clowns-to-the-left-of-me-jokers-to-the-right-the-threat-of-increased-insurgency-in-indias-volatile-northeast.

13. Gurpreet Singh and Rajinder Singh Sandhu, "Naga Separatism in India and Role of External Powers," *Indian Journal of Political Science* 75, no. 2 (April–June 2014): 381–392, https://www.jstor.org/stable/24701145#metadata_info_tab_contents.

14. Joe Kumbun, "Protected by China, Wa Is Now a de Facto Independent State," *The Irrawady*, April 23, 2019, https://www.irrawaddy.com/opinion/guest-column/protected-by-china-wa-is-now-a-de-facto-independent-state.html.

15. "China Supplying Weapons to Insurgent Group 'Arakan Army' to Weaken India, Myanmar: Report," New Indian Express, July 2, 2020, https://www.newindianexpress.com/world/2020/jul/02/china-supplying-weapons-to-insurgent-group-arakan-army-to-weaken-india-myanmar-report-2164324.html.

16. Editors of *Encyclopædia Britannica*, "Maoism," *Encyclopædia Britannica*, May 15, 2018, https://www.britannica.com/topic/Maoism.

17. Robert D. Eldridge, "Memo to Kishida: Komeito's Cozy Relationship with China Risks Japan's Security," Japan Forward, October 19, 2021, https://japan-forward.com/memo-to-kishida-komeitos-cozy-relationship-with-china-risks-japans-security/.

18. "Australia Passes Foreign Interference Laws amid China Tension," BBC Australia, June 28, 2018, https://www.bbc.com/news/world-australia-44624270.

19. Austin F. Cullen, *Commission of Inquiry into Money Laundering in British Columbia* (British Columbia: Cullen Commission, June 3, 2022), https://cullencommission.ca/files/reports/CullenCommission-FinalReport-Full.pdf.

20. John Paul Tasker, "MPs Agree to Probe Allegations of Chinese Interference in Federal Elections," CBC News, November 14, 2022, https://www.cbc.ca/news/politics/mps-probe-chinese-interference-elections-1.6651121.

21. Michael Turton, "Notes from Central Taiwan: Why Taiwan Should Be Concerned about 'Substate Actors,'" *Taipei Times*, April 26, 2021, https://www.taipeitimes.com/News/feat/archives/2021/04/26/2003756353.

22. Alex Vines, "What Is the Extent of China's Influence in Zimbabwe?" BBC News, November 20, 2017, https://www.bbc.com/news/world-africa-42012629.

23. Farai Mutsaka, "Zimbabwe's Imposing New Chinese-Funded Parliament Opens," Associated Press, November 23, 2022, https://apnews.com/article/africa-china-asia-zimbabwe-d7176d0e7ed5997e50c89d226a34d2e9.

24. "President Joao Lourenco of Angola Meets with Special Representative. Liu Yuxi of the Chinese Government on African Affairs," Ministry of Foreign Affairs of the People's Republic of China, September 16, 2022, https://www.fmprc.gov.cn/mfa_eng/wjbxw/202209/t20220919_10767697.html.

25. Georgina Kekea, "We Needed China Deal to Protect 'Domestic Security,' Says Key Solomon Islands Official," *The Guardian,* June 13, 2022, https://www.theguardian.com/world/2022/jun/14/we-needed-china-deal-to-protect-domestic-security-says-key-solomon-islands-official.

26. Grant Newsham, "China's Operations in U.S. Island Territories in the Western Pacific" in *Winning without Fighting: Chinese and Russian Political Warfare Campaigns and How the West Can Prevail,* Vol. 2: *Case Studies* (Washington, D.C.: Center for Strategic and Budgetary Assessments, 2019), 18, https://csbaonline.org/uploads/documents/Winning_Without_Fighting_Annex_Final2.pdf.

27. "FBI Corruption Probe Links Saipan Governor, Casino Operator," Asia Sentinel, November 15, 2019, https://www.asiasentinel.com/p/fbi-corruption-probe-links-saipan-governor-casino-operator.

28. Bethany Allen-Ebrahimian, "When China Stood with African American Activists," Axios, June 16, 2020, https://www.axios.com/2020/06/16/china-racism-black-panthers.

29. Aimee Lamoureux, "The Crazy True Story of America's First Female Terrorists," Grunge, February 12, 2022, https://www.grunge.com/213527/the-crazy-true-story-of-americas-first-female-terrorists.

30. Dan MacGuill, "Did a 'Convicted Terrorist' Sit on the Board of a BLM Funding Body?" Snopes, July 14, 2020, https://www.snopes.com/fact-check/blm-terrorist-rosenberg.

31. Adam Edelman, "Biden's Comments Downplaying China Threat to U.S. Fire Up Pols on Both Sides," NBC News, May 2, 2019, https://www.nbcnews.com/politics/2020-election/biden-s-comments-downplaying-china-threat-u-s-fires-pols-n1001236.

32. Ibid.

33. Bob Bryan, "The Trump Administration Is Reportedly Considering Lifting Some Tariffs on China to Help Get a Trade Deal Done," *Business Insider,* January 17, 2019, https://www.businessinsider.com/trump-china-trade-war-lift-tariffs-deal-2019-1?r=US&IR=T.

34. Julia Horowitz, "Goldman Sachs CEO to Join Trump in China," CNN Money, November 2, 2017, https://money.cnn.com/2017/11/02/news/lloyd-blankfein-trump-china/index.html.

35. Lauren He, "China's 'Revolution' Cost Investors $3 Trillion. So Why Aren't They Running Scared?" CNN Business, September 1, 2021, https://www.cnn.com/2021/09/01/investing/china-investment-tech-crackdown-mic-intl-hnk/index.html.

36. Tunku Varadarajan, "'Principles for Dealing with the Changing World Order' Review: Trouble Ahead, As Usual," *Wall Street Journal*, November 19, 2021, https:// www.wsj.com/articles/principles-for-dealing-with-the-changing-world-order-book -review-ray-dalio-trouble-ahead-as-usual-11637335545.

37. Evelyn Cheng, "Ray Dalio Says None of China's New Leadership Team Appear to Be 'Extremists,'" CNBC, November 18, 2022, https://www-cnbc-com.cdn .ampproject.org/c/s/www.cnbc.com/amp/2022/11/18/ray-dalio-shares-his-outlook -on-covid-real-estate-politics-in-china.html.

38. Andrew Ross Sorkin, "Henry Paulson Sounds Alarm: U.S.-China Relations May Only Get Worse," *New York Times*, November 21, 2019, https://www.nytimes.com /2019/11/21/business/dealbook/henry-paulson-china.html.

39. Personal correspondence.

40. U.S. Department of Defense, "Michael Bloomberg Sworn in as Defense Innovation Board Chair," June 22, 2022, https://www.defense.gov/News/Releases/Release /Article/3070020/michael-bloomberg-sworn-in-as-defense-innovation-board-chair.

41. Personal correspondence.

42. Perry Link, "China: The Anaconda in the Chandelier," China File, April 11, 2002, https://www.chinafile.com/library/nyrb-china-archive/china-anaconda-chandelier.

43. Isaac Stone Fish, "The Other Political Correctness," *New Republic*, September 4, 2018, https://newrepublic.com/article/150476/american-elite-universities -selfcensorship-china.

44. Alex Nester, "George Washington University President Walks Back Criticism of Anti-CCP Posters," Washington Free Beacon, February 8, 2022, https://freebeacon.com /campus/george-washington-president-walks-back-criticism-of-anti-ccp-posters.

45. Josh Horwitz, "A Visit by the Dalai Lama Is Dividing a U.S. Campus Where 14% of Students Are from China," Quartz, June 14, 2017, https://qz.com/1004386/the -uproar-over-the-dalais-lamas-ucsd-visit-has-unveiled-chinas-meddling-influence -over-foreign-campuses.

46. William Lowther, "Owens' Links to PRC Firms Ring Alarm," *Taipei Times*, September 9, 2010, https://www.taipeitimes.com/News/taiwan/archives/2010/09 /09/2003482460.

47. Shirley A. Kan, *U.S.-China Military Contacts: Issues for Congress* (Washington, D.C.: Congressional Research Service, October 27, 2014), https://sgp.fas.org/crs/ natsec/RL32496.pdf.

48. Kerry K. Gershaneck, *Political Warfare: Strategies for Combating China's Plan to "Win without Fighting"* (Quantico, Virginia: Marine Corps University Press, 2020), xvi–xviii, https://www.usmcu.edu/Portals/218/Political%20Warfare_web.pdf/.

49. Shirley A. Kan, *U.S.-China Military Contacts: Issues for Congress* (Washington, D.C.: Congressional Research Service, June 25, 2013), https://apps.dtic.mil/sti/pdfs /ADA585310.pdf.

50. U.S.-China Economic and Security Review Commission, *2011 Report to Congress of the U.S.-China Economic and Security Review Commission* (U.S. Government Printing Office, 2011), 365, https://www.uscc.gov/sites/default/files/annual_reports /annual_report_full_11.pdf.

Chapter 15: The Chinese Military: No One Is Laughing Anymore

1. Office of the Secretary of Defense, *Annual Report to Congress: Military and Security Developments Involving the People's Republic of China 2018* (U.S. Department of Defense, May 16, 2018), https://media.defense.gov/2018/Aug/16/2001955282/-1/-1/1/2018-CHINA-MILITARY-POWER-REPORT.PDF.

2. Office of the Secretary of Defense, *Annual Report to Congress: Military and Security Developments Involving the People's Republic of China* (Washington, D.C.: U.S. Department of Defense, 2022, https://media.defense.gov/2022/Nov/29/2003122279/-1/-1/1/2022-MILITARY-AND-SECURITY-DEVELOPMENTS-INVOLVING-THE-PEOPLES-REPUBLIC-OF-CHINA.PDF.

3. Ellen Nakashima and Cate Cadell, "China Secretly Building Naval Facility in Cambodia, Western Officials Say," *Washington Post*, June 6, 2022, https://www.washingtonpost.com/national-security/2022/06/06/cambodia-china-navy-base-ream/.

4. Kaitlin Schallhorn, "Niger Attack Leaves 4 U.S. Soldiers Dead: What to Know," Fox News, May 10, 2018, https://www.foxnews.com/world/niger-attack-leaves-4-us-soldiers-dead-what-to-know.

5. Henry Chu, "Beijing Orders Army to Give Up Its Businesses," *Los Angeles Times*, July 23, 1998, https://www.latimes.com/archives/la-xpm-1998-jul-23-mn-6350-story.html.

6. Daniel M. Hartnett, "The 'New Historic Missions': Reflections on Hu Jintao's Military Legacy," in *Assessing the People's Liberation Army in the Hu Jinatao Era*, ed. Roy Kamphausen, David Lai, and Travis Tanner (Carlisle, Pennsylvania: U.S. Army War College Press, April 2014), https://apps.dtic.mil/sti/pdfs/ADA599540.pdf.

7. Shannon Tiezzi, "The Real Reason China Is Cutting 300,000 Troops," *The Diplomat*, September 8, 2015, https://thediplomat.com/2015/09/the-real-reason-china-is-cutting-300000-troops.

8. Gregory B. Poling , Tabitha Grace Mallory, and Harrison Prétat, *Pulling Back the Curtain on China's Maritime Militia* (Washington, D.C.: Center for Strategic and International Studies, November 2021), https://csis-website-prod.s3.amazonaws.com/s3fs-public/publication/211118_Poling_Maritime_Militia.pdf.

9. Liu Xuanzun, "China Boosts Defense Budget by 7.1% for 2022 amid Complex Global Situation," *Global Times*, March 5, 2022, https://www.globaltimes.cn/page/202203/1254011.shtml.

10. Ibid.

11. Personal correspondence.

12. Ibid.

13. Maochun Miles Yu, "The Battle of Quemoy: The Amphibious Assault That Held the Postwar Military Balance in the Taiwan Strait," *Naval War College Review* 69, no. 2 (2016)91–107, https://digital-commons.usnwc.edu/cgi/viewcontent.cgi?article=1097&context=nwc-review.

14. "1985–2020: China's Maritime Disputes," Council on Foreign Relations, https://www.cfr.org/timeline/chinas-maritime-disputes.

15. Caitlin Campbell, *China's Military: The People's Liberation Army (PLA)* (Washington, D.C.: Congressional Research Service, June 4, 2021), https://crsreports .congress.gov/product/pdf/R/R46808.

16. "China's Central Military Commission Under Hu Jintao," *Rusi*, March 18, 2005, https://rusi.org/publication/china's-central-military-commission-under-hu-jintao.

Chapter 16: Objective: Tawain

1. Office of the Secretary of Defense, *Annual Report to Congress: Military and Security Developments Involving the People's Republic of China 2019* (Washington, D.C.: U.S. Department of Defense, May 2, 2019), 85, https://media.defense.gov/2019/May /02/2002127082/-1/-1/1/2019_CHINA_MILITARY_POWER_REPORT.pdf.

2. Office of the Secretary of Defense, *Annual Report to Congress: Military and Security Developments Involving the People's Republic of China 2022* (U.S. Department of Defense, 2022), 127–128, https://media.defense.gov/2022/Nov/29/2003122279/-1/ -1/1/2022-MILITARY-AND-SECURITY-DEVELOPMENTS-INVOLVING-THE -PEOPLES-REPUBLIC-OF-CHINA.PDF.

3. Kerry K. Gershaneck, *Political Warfare: Strategies for Combating China's Plan to "Win without Fighting"* (Quantico, Virginia: Marine Corps University Press, 2020), https://www.usmcu.edu/Portals/218/Political%20Warfare_web.pdf.

4. Chris Buckley, "China, Sending a Signal, Launches a Home-Built Aircraft Carrier," *New York Times*, April 25, 2017, https://www.nytimes.com/2017/04/25/world/asia /china-aircraft-carrier.html.

5. Wang Xinjuan, "China Unveils Giant Aircraft Carrier CNS Fujian," Ministry of National Defense of the People's Republic of China, June 18, 2022, http://eng.mod .gov.cn/news/2022-06/18/content_4913347.htm.

6. Chad Peltier, "China's Logistics Capabilities for Expeditionary Operations," U.S.-China Economic and Security Review Commission, April 8, 2020, https://www.uscc .gov/research/chinas-logistics-capabilities-expeditionary-operations.

7. *China Military Power: Modernizing a Force to Fight and Win* (Washington, D.C.: Defense Intelligence Agency, 2019), https://www.dia.mil/Portals/110/Images/News /Military_Powers_Publications/China_Military_Power_FINAL_5MB_20190103 .pdf.

8. Guo Yuandan, "Chinese Military Sends Two Naval Vessels Bearing 2nd Batch of Aid to Tsunami-Hit Tonga, Demonstrates Responsibility, Capacity," *Global Times*, January 31, 2022, https://www.globaltimes.cn/page/202201/1250266.shtml.

9. Alison A. Kaufman, *China's Participation in Anti-Piracy Operations off the Horn of Africa: Drivers and Implications* (Alexandria, Virginia: Center for Naval Analyses, July 2009), https://www.cna.org/reports/2009/D0020834.A1.pdf.

10. Ryan White, "PLA Navy's Type 071 LPD Holds Joint Landing Exercise," *Naval Post*, May 9, 2021, https://navalpost.com/type-071-amphibious-transport-dock -landing-exercise.

11. Kathrin Hille, "China Plans Hybrid Assault Vessel to Strengthen Overseas Power," *Financial Times*, July 24, 2020, https://www.ft.com/content/5f0e15d8-406a-47f1 -9be3-1a9ace242830.

12. Yang Hui and Liu Xuanzun, "China Launches 3rd Type 075 Amphibious Assault Ship," *Global Times*, January 29, 2021, https://www.globaltimes.cn/page/202101/1214361.shtml.

13. Franz-Stefan Gady, "U.S. Navy Takes Delivery of New F-35B-Carrying Amphibious Assault Ship," *The Diplomat*, March 2, 2020, https://thediplomat.com/2020/03/us-navy-takes-delivery-of-new-f-35b-carrying-amphibious-assault-ship/; Megan Rose, "USS Bonhomme Richard Failed on Fire Safety, Documents Show," *Navy Times*, September 25, 2022, https://www.navytimes.com/news/your-navy/2022/09/25/uss-bonhomme-richard-failed-on-fire-safety-documents-show.

14. Armin Rosen, "Chinese State Television Ran Footage of Troops Storming a Mock-up of Taiwan's Presidential Palace," *Business Insider*, July 27, 2015, https://www.businessinsider.com/china-military-drill-taiwan-presidential-palace-2015-7.

15. Anthony Bergin and Jeffrey Wall, "China's Deal with PNG Will Deplete Fishing Stock and Pose Border Risk," Australian Strategic Policy Institute, December 23, 2020, https://www.aspi.org.au/opinion/chinas-deal-png-will-deplete-fishing-stock-and-pose-border-risk.

16. Chris Horton, "COSCO: China's Shipping Giant Expands Its Global Influence," *Financial Times*, May 24, 2022, https://www.ft.com/content/13e606df-9b43-4c9c-9e23-24883d0988f9.

17. Personal correspondence.

18. Erica Downs, Jeffrey Becker, and Patrick deGategno, *China's Military Support Facility in Djibouti: The Economic and Security Dimensions of China's First Overseas Base* (Alexandria, Virginia: Center for Naval Analyses, July 2017), https://www.cna.org/archive/CNA_Files/pdf/dim-2017-u-015308-final2.pdf.

Chapter 17: Will China Launch a Kinetic War?

1. Gordon G. Chang, "China Never Was a Superpower—and It Won't Be One Anytime Soon," Hoover Institution, March 28, 2019, https://www.hoover.org/research/china-never-was-superpower-and-it-wont-be-one-anytime-soon.

2. Evelyn Cheng, "Ray Dalio Says None of China's New Leadership Team Appear to Be 'Extremists,'" CNBC, November 18, 2022, https://www-cnbc-com.cdn.ampproject.org/c/s/www.cnbc.com/amp/2022/11/18/ray-dalio-shares-his-outlook-on-covid-real-estate-politics-in-china.html.

3. Matt Pottinger, Matthew Johnson, and David Feith, "Xi Jinping in His Own Words," *Foreign Affairs*, November 30, 2022, foreignaffairs.com/china/xi-jinping-his-own-words.

4. Norman Angell, *The Great Illusion: A Study of the Relation of Military Power to National Advantage* (New York: G. P. Putnam's Sons, 1913), https://www.gutenberg.org/ebooks/38535.

5. Agnès Andrésy, *Xi Jinping: Red China, the Next Generation* (Lanham, Maryland: University Press of America, 2016), 46.

6. "Xi Jinping Millionaire Relations Reveal Elite Chinese Fortunes," Bloomberg UK, June 29, 2012, https://www.bloomberg.com/news/articles/2012-06-29/xi-jinping-millionaire-relations-reveal-fortunes-of-elite.

7. Mark Moore, "Bloomberg: Xi Isn't a Dictator Because China Doesn't Want Democracy," *New York Post*, February 27, 2020, https://nypost.com/2020/02/27/bloomberg-xi-isnt-a-dictator-because-china-doesnt-want-democracy.

8. Song Geng, "Consuming the Anti-Japanese War on the TV Screen in China: State Ideology, Market and Audience," *Journal of Oriental Studies* 49, no. 2 (March 2017): 1–22, https://www.jstor.org/stable/44645727#metadata_info_tab_contents.

9. "Protests in China Hit Japanese Companies," Al Jazeera, September 17, 2012, https://www.aljazeera.com/news/2012/9/17/protests-in-china-hit-japanese-companies/; Ionut Arghire, "Chinese Hackers Target Japanese Organizations in Large-Scale Campaign," Security Week, November 19, 2020, https://www.securityweek.com/chinese-hackers-target-japanese-organizations-large-scale-campaign.

10. "China's War Blockbuster Sequel Hits 6 Million USD," Xinhua, February 28, 2022, https://english.news.cn/20220228/716a0307749c43bc94df2706782bf473/c.html.

11. Scott Mendelson, "Box Office: 'Wolf Warrior 2' Cracks 100 All-Time Biggest Grossers List," *Forbes*, August 14, 2017, https://www.forbes.com/sites/scottmendelson/2017/08/14/box-office-wolf-warrior-2-cracks-100-all-time-biggest-grossers-list/.

12. "China: May Quake Killed 19,000 School Kids," CBS News, November 21, 2008, https://www.cbsnews.com/news/china-may-quake-killed-19000-school-kids.

13. Michael Dobbs, "With Albright, Clinton Accepts New U.S. Role," *Washington Post*, December 8, 1996, https://www.washingtonpost.com/wp-srv/politics/govt/admin/stories/albright120896.htm.

14. Stephen Burgess, "Confronting China's Maritime Expansion in the South China Sea," *Journal of Indo-Pacific Affairs* (Fall 2020), https://media.defense.gov/2020/Aug/31/2002488087/-1/-1/1/BURGESS.PDF.

15. Iida Masafumi, "New Developments in China's Policy on the South China Sea," *National Institute for Defense Studies*, no. 9 (2008), http://www.nids.mod.go.jp/english/publication/kiyo/pdf/2008/bulletin_e2008_2.pdf.

16. Otto von Stierlitz, "China's Massacre in Spratly Islands [Real Footage 1988]," May 28, 2009, YouTube, https://www.youtube.com/watch?v=Uy2ZrFphSmc.

17. Laney Zhang, "Past Bilateral Border Agreements between China and India and the June 15th Clash," Library Of Congress, July 17, 2020, https://blogs.loc.gov/law/2020/07/past-bilateral-border-agreements-between-china-and-india-and-the-june-15th-clash/.

18. Michael Safi, Hannah Ellis-Petersen, and Helen Davidson, "Soldiers Fell to Their Deaths as India and China's Troops Fought with Rocks," *The Guardian*, June 17, 2020, https://www.theguardian.com/world/2020/jun/17/shock-and-anger-in-india-after-worst-attack-on-china-border-in-decades.

19. Paran Balakrishnan, "Since Galwan Border Flare-up, China Has Installed Massive Military Infrastructure, Says the Warzone," *Telegraph India*, July 12, 2022, https://www.telegraphindia.com/india/since-galwan-border-flare-up-china-has-installed-massive-military-infrastructure-says-the-warzone/cid/1874307.

20. P. C. Katoch, "China in Southern Nepal," SP's Land Forces, December 26, 2022, https://www.spslandforces.com/experts-speak/?id=958&h=China-in-Southern

-Nepal/; Editors of *Encyclopædia Britannica*, "Maoism," *Encyclopædia Britannica*, May 15, 2018, https://www.britannica.com/topic/Maoism.

21. Joe Kumbun, "Protected by China, Wa Is Now a de Facto Independent State," Irrawady, April 23, 2019, https://www.irrawaddy.com/opinion/guest-column/protected-by-china-wa-is-now-a-de-facto-independent-state.html; "Mong Tai Army (MTA) / United Wa State Army (UWSA)," GlobalSecurity.org, https://www.globalsecurity.org/military/world/para/wa.htm; Bertil Linter, "The United Wa State Army and Burma's Peace Process," United States Institutes of Peace, April 29, 2019, https://www.usip.org/publications/2019/04/united-wa-state-army-and-burmas-peace-process.

22. Brahma Chellaney, "China Leverages Tibetan Plateau's Water Wealth," Georgetown University, June 16, 2020, https://gjia.georgetown.edu/2020/06/16/china-leverages-tibetan-plateaus-water-wealth.

23. Meg Sullivan, "UCLA Demographer Produces Best Estimate Yet of Cambodia's Death Toll under Pol Pot," UCLA Newsroom, April 16, 2015, https://newsroom.ucla.edu/releases/ucla-demographer-produces-best-estimate-yet-of-cambodias-death-toll-under-pol-pot.

24. Kerry K. Gershaneck, *Political Warfare: Strategies for Combating China's Plan to "Win without Fighting"* (Quantico, Virginia: Marine Corps University Press, 2020), https://www.usmcu.edu/Portals/218/Political%20Warfare_web.pdf.

25. "Our Ports—World," Hutchinson Ports, 2022, https://hutchisonports.com/ports/world/.

26. Andrew Hosken and Albana Kasapi, "Why Is China Investing Heavily in South-East Europe," BBC News, October 17, 2017, https://www.bbc.co.uk/news/world-europe-41654346.

27. "Chinese-Built Walvis Bay Container Terminal in Namibia Inaugurated," Namport, August 5, 2019, https://www.namport.com.na/news/447/chinese-built-walvis-bay-container-terminal-in-namibia-inaugurated.

28. Jonathan E. Hillman, "Game of Loans: How China Bought Hambantota," Center for Strategic and International Studies, April 2, 2018, https://www.csis.org/analysis/game-loans-how-china-bought-hambantota.

29. H. I. Sutton, "China's New High-Security Compound in Pakistan May Indicate Naval Plans," *Forbes*, June 2, 2020, https://www.forbes.com/sites/hisutton/2020/06/02/chinas-new-high-security-compound-in-pakistan-may-indicate-naval-plans/.

30. "Freely Associated States," U.S. Department of the Interior, July 23, 2019, https://www.doi.gov/ocl/freely-associated-states.

31. Patricia O'Brien, "The 'Framework Agreement' with China Transforms the Solomon Islands into a Pacific Flashpoint," Center For Strategic and International Studies, March 31, 2022, https://www.csis.org/analysis/framework-agreement-china-transforms-solomon-islands-pacific-flashpoint.

32. Jennifer Staats, "Four Takeaways from China's Tour of the Pacific Islands," United States Institute of Peace, June 9, 2022, https://www.usip.org/publications/2022/06/four-takeaways-chinas-tour-pacific-islands.

33. "FACT SHEET: Quad Leaders' Tokyo Summit 2022," The White House, May 23, 2022, https://www.whitehouse.gov/briefing-room/statements-releases/2022/05/23/fact-sheet-quad-leaders-tokyo-summit-2022.

34. "War in Ukraine: Beware of China's Amplification of Russian Propaganda, RSF Says," Reporters Without Borders, April 14, 2022, https://rsf.org/en/war-ukraine-beware-china-s-amplification-russian-propaganda-rsf-says.

35. "Remembering the Hainan Incident," Station Hypo, April 1, 2022, https://stationhypo.com/2022/04/01/remembering-the-hainan-island-incident-2/; Minnie Chan, "How a Mid-Air Collision Near Hainan 18 Years Ago Spurred China's Military Modernization," *South China Morning Post*, April 2, 2019, https://www.scmp.com/news/china/diplomacy/article/3004383/how-mid-air-collision-near-hainan-18-years-ago-spurred-chinas.

36. Raul Pedrozo, "Close Encounters at Sea: The USNS Impeccable Incident," *Naval War College Review* 62, no. 3 (Summer 2009): 1, https://apps.dtic.mil/sti/pdfs/ADA519335.pdf.

37. "USNS Bowditch (T-AGS-62)—December 4, 2017," More Fun, 2017, https://morefun.ph/who-is-on-dock/usns-bowditch-t-ags-62-december-4-2017/.

38. Jim Garamone, "Chinese Trawlers Harass USNS Impeccable," *The Flagship*, March 11, 2009, https://www.militarynews.com/norfolk-navy-flagship/news/top_stories/chinese-trawlers-harass-usns-impeccable/article_217a5b7c-6e43-51df-84f8-7569d1769eee.html.

39. Jon Harper, "Chinese Warship Nearly Collided with USS Cowpens," *Stars and Stripes*, December 13, 2013, https://www.stripes.com/theaters/asia_pacific/chinese-warship-nearly-collided-with-uss-cowpens-1.257478.

40. Sam LaGrone, "Chinese Seize U.S. Navy Unmanned Vehicle," USNI News, December 16, 2016, https://news.usni.org/2016/12/16/breaking-chinese-seize-u-s-navy-unmanned-vehicle.

41. Ronald O'Rourke, *China's Actions in South and East China Seas: Implications for U.S. Interests-Background and Issues for Congress* (Washington, D.C.: Congressional Research Service, August 1, 2018), https://crsreports.congress.gov/product/pdf/R/R42784/86.

42. Brad Lendon, "Chinese Fighter Jet 'Chaffs' Australian Plane near South China Sea, Canberra Alleges," CNN, June 7, 2022, https://www.cnn.com/2022/06/05/australia/australia-china-plane-intercept-intl-hnk-ml/index.html.

43. Brad Lendon, "Canada Says Chinese Warplanes Are Buzzing Its North Korea Reconnaissance Flights," CNN, June 6, 2022, https://www.cnn.com/2022/06/01/asia/canada-china-fighter-jet-harassment-intl-hnk-ml/index.html.

44. Gerry Mullany and David Barboza, "Vietnam Squares Off with China in Disputed Seas," *New York Times*, May 7, 2014, https://www.nytimes.com/2014/05/08/world/asia/philippines-detains-crew-of-chinese-fishing-vessel.html.

45. "Statement of Justice Antonio T. Caprio on the Ramming of F/B Gimver 1," Institute for Maritime and Ocean Affairs, June 14, 2019, https://www.imoa.ph/statement-of-justice-antonio-t-carpio-on-the-ramming-of-f-b-gimver-1.

46. Morgan Ortagus and David Stilwell, "The Risks Americans Face in Traveling to China," CNN, October 26, 2021, https://www.cnn.com/2021/10/26/opinions/china-hostage-diplomacy-ortagus-stilwell-op-ed.

47. Jamie Seidel, "'Sink Two Aircraft Carriers': Chinese Admiral's Chilling Recipe to Dominate the South China Sea," News.com.au, January 2, 2019, https://www.news.com.au/technology/innovation/military/sink-two-aircraft-carriers-chinese-admirals-chilling-recipie-to-dominate-the-south-china-sea/news-story/aaa8c33d57da62e7d5e28e791aa26e0f.

48. Benjamin Jensen, "Shadow Risk: What Crisis Simulations Reveal about the Dangers of Deferring U.S. Responses to China's Gray Zone Campaign against Taiwan," Center for Strategic and International Studies, February 16, 2022, https://www.csis.org/analysis/shadow-risk-what-crisis-simulations-reveal-about-dangers-deferring-us-responses-chinas-gray.

49. Ben Werner, "China's Past Participation in RIMPAC Didn't Yield Intended Benefits of Easing Tensions," USNI News, May 24, 2018, https://news.usni.org/2018/05/24/33834.

50. "The Ebb and Flow of Beijing's South China Sea Militia," Center for Strategic and International Studies, November 09, 2022, https://amti.csis.org/the-ebb-and-flow-of-beijings-south-china-sea-militia.

51. Lonnie D. Henley, *Civilian Shipping and Maritime Militia: The Logistics Backbone of a Taiwan Invasion* (Newport, Rhode Island: China Maritime Studies Institute at the U.S. Naval War College, May 2022), http://www.andrewerickson.com/wp-content/uploads/2022/05/CMSI_China-Maritime-Report_21_Civilian-Shipping-and-Maritime-Militia-Logistics-Backbone-of-Taiwan-Invasion_Henley_202205.pdf.

52. Associated Press, "China Is Using Civilian Ships to Enhance Navy Capability and Reach," CNBC, September 25, 2022, https://www.cnbc.com/2022/09/26/china-is-using-civilian-ships-to-enhance-navy-capability-and-reach.html.

53. Associated Press, "China Has Fully Militarized Three Islands in South China Sea, U.S. Admiral Says," *The Guardian*, March 20, 2022, https://www.theguardian.com/world/2022/mar/21/china-has-fully-militarized-three-islands-in-south-china-sea-us-admiral-says/; Jeremy Page, Carol Lee, and Gordon Lubold, "China's President Pledges No Militarization in Disputed Islands," *Wall Street Journal*, September 25, 2015, https://www.wsj.com/articles/china-completes-runway-on-artificial-island-in-south-china-sea-1443184818.

54. Paul J. Leaf, "Learning from China's Oil Rig Standoff with Vietnam," *The Diplomat*, August 30, 2014, https://thediplomat.com/2014/08/learning-from-chinas-oil-rig-standoff-with-vietnam.

55. Adam Gerval and Mark Henderson, "U.S. Policy in the South China Sea across Three Administrations," E-International Relations, June 27, 2022, https://www.e-ir.info/2022/06/27/us-policy-in-the-south-china-sea-across-three-administrations.

56. Bryan Bender, "Chief of U.S. Pacific Forces Calls Climate Biggest Worry," *Boston Globe*, March 9, 2013, https://www.bostonglobe.com/news/nation/2013/03/09/admiral-samuel-locklear-commander-pacific-forces-warns-that-climate-change-top-threat/BHdPVCLrWEMxRe9IXJZcHL/story.html.

57. Harry B. Harris Jr., Adam Smith, and Mac Thornberry, "Admiral Harry Harris Says U.S. Must Remain a 'Credible Deterrent' to North Korea," Internet Archive, April 26, 2017, https://archive.org/details/CSPAN3_20170426_140100_Admiral_Harry _Harris_Says_U.S._Must_Remain_a_Credible_Deterrent_to_North...

58. Peter Greste, Justin Stevens, and Alex McDonald, "'Misunderstanding' May Lead to Conflict between U.S. and China over South China Sea, Expert Warns," ABC (Australia), October 2, 2016, https://www.abc.net.au/news/2016-10-03/south-china -sea-us-china-misunderstandings-may-cause-conflict/7893012.

59. Personal correspondence.

60. Navdeep Yadav, "Xi Jinping Directs Chinese Troops to Carry 'Special Military Operations' Abroad," MSN, June 15, 2022, https://www.msn.com/en-us/news/world /xi-jinping-directs-chinese-troops-to-carry-special-military-operations-abroad/ar -AAYuCcj.

61. Personal correspondence.

62. Personal correspondence.

63. Yimou Lee and Sarah Wu, "Furious China Fires Missiles near Taiwan in Drills after Pelosi Visit," Reuters, August 5, 2022, https://www.reuters.com/world/asia-pacific/ suspected-drones-over-taiwan-cyber-attacks-after-pelosi-visit-2022-08-04.

64. Personal correspondence.

65. Personal correspondence.

66. "China Pressures Taiwan's President Tsai Ing-wen to Acknowledge One China," CNBC, May 22, 2016, https://www.cnbc.com/2016/05/22/china-pressures-taiwans -president-tsai-ing-wen-to-acknowledge-one-china.html.

67. Tom Phillips, "Chinese and U.S. Officials Scuffled over 'Nuclear Football' during 2017 Trump Visit," *The Guardian*, February 19, 2018, https://www.theguardian .com/world/2018/feb/19/china-and-us-in-skirmish-over-nuclear-football-during -trump-visit-to-beijing-report.

68. Dan De Luce and Abigail Williams, "China Poses 'Biggest Geopolitical Test' for the U.S., Secretary of State Blinken Says," NBC News, March 3, 2021, https://www .nbcnews.com/news/world/china-poses-biggest-geopolitical-test-u-s-says-secretary -state-n1259489.

69. John Garnaut, "How China Interferes in Australia," *Foreign Affairs*, March 9, 2018, https://www.foreignaffairs.com/articles/china/2018-03-09/how-china-interferes -australia; also see Clive Hamilton, *Silent Invasion: China's Influence in Australia* (Richmond, Australia: Hardie Grant Books, 2018).

70. Callum Hoare, "David Cameron's 'Wishful' Thinking Sparked Huawei Threat 10 Years Ago—MoD Insider," *Express UK*, July 16, 2020, https://www.express.co.uk /news/uk/1309924/china-huawei-david-cameron-tobias-ellwood-boris-johnson-5g -network-donald-trump-spt.

71. Michelle Toh and Anna Cooban, "Germany's Leader and Top CEOs Have Arrived in Beijing. They Need China More Than Ever," CNN, November 3, 2022, https://www .cnn.com/2022/11/03/business/germany-china-olaf-scholz-visit-trade/index.html.

72. Richard Louis Edmonds, "Macau and Greater China," *China Quarterly* 136 (December 1993): 878–906, https://www.jstor.org/stable/655595.

73. Allen S. Whiting, "Chinese Nationalism and Foreign Policy after Deng," *China Quarterly* 142 (June 1995): 295–316, https://www.jstor.org/stable/pdf/655418.pdf.

74. Jim Fanell, "Now Hear This—the Clock Is Ticking in China: The Decade of Concern Has Begun," *U.S. Naval Institute Proceedings* 143, no. 10 (October 2017), https://www.usni.org/magazines/proceedings/2017/october/now-hear-clock-ticking-china-decade-concern-has-begun.

Chapter 18: China Attacks: The Political and the Kinetic Combine

1. Personal correspondence.

2. Fumio Ota, "[Speaking Out] Regrettable U.S. Failure to Invite Taiwan to RIMPAC Exercise," Japan Forward, June 28, 2022, https://japan-forward.com/speaking-out-regrettable-us-failure-to-invite-taiwan-to-rimpac-exercise.

3. "Rubio, Colleagues Urge President to Include Taiwan in Proposed Indo-Pacific Economic Framework," Marco Rubio: US Senator for Florida, May 18, 2022, https://www.rubio.senate.gov/public/index.cfm/2022/5/rubio-colleagues-urge-president-to-include-taiwan-in-proposed-indo-pacific-economic-framework.

4. Sarah Zheng, "China Reportedly Paid Taiwan Officer to Surrender If War Started," Bloomberg, November 22, 2022, https://www.bloomberg.com/news/articles/2022-11-22/china-reportedly-paid-taiwan-officer-to-surrender-if-war-started.

5. Jim Garamone, "Austin Meets with Chinese Counterpart in Singapore," U.S. Department of Defense, June 10, 2022, https://www.defense.gov/News/NewsStories/Article/Article/3058994/austin-meets-with-chinese-counterpart-in-singapore.

6. "USNI News Fleet and Marine Tracker: Feb. 24, 2022," USNI News, February 24, 2022, https://news.usni.org/2022/02/24/usni-news-fleet-and-marine-tracker-feb-24-2022.

7. Office of the Secretary of Defense, *Annual Report to Congress: Military and Security Developments Involving the People's Republic of China 2020* (Washington, D.C.: U.S. Department of Defense, 2020), https://media.defense.gov/2020/Sep/01/2002488689/-1/-1/1/2020-DOD-CHINA-MILITARY-POWER-REPORT-FINAL.PDF.

8. U.S. Senate Committee on Foreign Relations, *Left Behind: A Brief Assessment of the Biden Administration's Strategic Failures during the Afghanistan Evacuation* (Washington, D.C.: U.S. Senate Committee on Foreign Relations, February 2022), https://www.foreign.senate.gov/download/02-03-22-risch-report-on-afghanistan.

Chapter 19: How to Defend and Counter

1. Gillian Brockell, "'A Republic, If You Can Keep It: Did Ben Franklin Really Say Impeachment Day's Favorite Quote?," *Washington Post*, December 18, 2019, https://www.washingtonpost.com/history/2019/12/18/republic-if-you-can-keep-it-did-ben-franklin-really-say-impeachment-days-favorite-quote.

2. Patricia McKnight, "Ron DeSantis Establishes 'Victims of Communism Day' Holiday amid CRT Fight," *Newsweek*, May 9, 2022, https://www.newsweek.com/ron-desantis-establishes-victims-communism-day-holiday-amid-crt-fight-1705008.

3. Leo Shane III, "Senator Wants Communist West Point Grad Booted from the Army," *Army Times*, October 4, 2017, https://www.armytimes.com/news/pentagon

-congress/2017/10/04/senator-wants-communist-west-point-grad-booted-from-the-army.

4. "Information about the Department of Justice's China Initiative and a Compilation of China-Related Prosecutions since 2018," U.S. Department of Justice Archives, https://www.justice.gov/archives/nsd/information-about-department-justice-s-china-initiative-and-compilation-china-related.

5. Carl Samson, "Justice Department Ends Trump Administration's 'China Initiative' amid Anti-Asian Claims," Yahoo News, February 24, 2022, https://news.yahoo.com/justice-department-ends-trump-administrations-221259509.html.

6. Rachelle Peterson, "China Is Rebranding Its Confucius Institutes," National Association of Scholars, July 23, 2020, https://www.nas.org/blogs/article/china-is-rebranding-its-confucius-institutes.

7. Niall McCarthy, "The Countries with the Most Stem Graduates," *Industry Week*, February 6, 2017, https://www.industryweek.com/talent/article/21998889/the-countries-with-the-most-stem-graduates/; Prashant Loyalka et al, "Computer Science Skills across China, India, Russia, and the United States," *Proceedings of the National Academy of Sciences* 116, no. 14 (April 2019): 1, https://www.pnas.org/doi/full/10.1073/pnas.1814646116.

8. Personal correspondence.

9. U.S. Senate Permanent Subcommittee on Investigations, *Threats to the U.S. Research Enterprise: China's Talent Recruitment Plans* (Washington, D.C.: U.S. Senate, November 18, 2019), https://china.usc.edu/sites/default/files/article/attachments/us-senate-report-2019-chinese-talent-recruitment-plans.pdf.

10. Greg Myre, "As Scrutiny of China Grows, Some U.S. Schools Drop a Language Program," NPR, July 17, 2019, https://www.npr.org/2019/07/17/741239298/as-scrutiny-of-china-grows-some-u-s-schools-drop-a-language-program.

11. Cristina Laila, "U.S. Citizen, Four Chinese Intelligence Officers Charged with Acting as Secret Police to Harass, Stalk, Spy on U.S. Residents Critical to China," Gateway Pundit, May 18, 2022, https://www.thegatewaypundit.com/2022/05/us-citizen-four-chinese-intelligence-officers-charged-acting-secret-police-harass-stalk-spy-us-residents-critical-china.

12. "FBI Director Christopher Wray's Remarks at Press Conference regarding China's Operation Fox Hunt," Fedearl Bureau of Investigation, October 28, 2020, https://www.fbi.gov/news/press-releases/press-releases/fbi-director-christopher-wrays-remarks-at-press-conference-regarding-chinas-operation-fox-hunt.

13. Ibid.

14. Michael Tamara and Ted Hesson, "FBI Director 'Very Concerned' by Chinese 'Police Stations' in U.S.," Reuters, November 17, 2022, https://www.reuters.com/world/us/fbi-director-very-concerned-by-chinese-police-stations-us-2022-11-17.

15. U.S. Attorney's Office, District of Massachusetts, "People's Republic of China Citizen Arrested for Stalking," U.S. Attorney's Office, District of Massachusetts, December 14, 2022, https://www.justice.gov/usao-ma/pr/peoples-republic-china-citizen-arrested-stalking.

16. Ibid.

17. "Foreign Agents Registration Act," U.S.Department of Justice, https://www.justice.gov/nsd-fara/.

18. "President Xi Jinping Has a Video Call with U.S. President Joe Biden," Ministry of Foreign Affairs of the People's Republic of China, March 19, 2022, https://www .fmprc.gov.cn/mfa_eng/zxxx_662805/202203/t20220319_10653207.html.

19. Ibid.

20. Trump White House Archived, "A Message from Deputy National Security Advisor Matt Pottinger," YouTube, May 6, 2020, https://www.youtube.com/watch?v= dp5h6n6fbUg.

21. Personal correspondence.

22. Personal correspondence.

23. Tim Morrison, "Controlling Chinese Weapons: The Wuhan Virus and Nuclear Weapons," Hudson Institute, April 2, 2020, https://www.hudson.org/national -security-defense/controlling-chinese-weapons-the-wuhan-virus-and-nuclear -weapons.

24. Personal correspondence.

25. Nicholas Wade, "Home Truths on Where COVID Came From," *City Journal*, November 17, 2022, https://www.city-journal.org/gop-controlled-house-should -investigate-covids-origins.

26. Leland Smith et al., "Evidence of Environmental Changes Caused by Chinese Island Building," *Scientific Reports* 9, no. 5295 (March 13, 2019): https://doi.org/10.1038 /s41598-019-41659-3.

27. Kurt Jensen, "Smith Calls Organ Harvesting in China 'a Horror Story' at Hearing on Hill," Catholic News Service, June 10, 2022, https://chrissmith.house.gov/news /documentsingle.aspx?DocumentID=410028.

28. "Motion for a Resolution on Reports of Continued Organ Harvesting in China," European Parliament, May 3, 2022, https://www.europarl.europa.eu/doceo/ document/B-9-2022-0252_EN.html.

29. Ralph Jennings, "China Plans a Single, Chilling Response to the Panama Papers," *Forbes*, April 10, 2016, https://www.forbes.com/sites/ralphjennings/2016/04/10/ china-plans-a-single-chilling-response-to-the-panama-papers/.

30. Barbara Demick, "The Times, Bloomberg News, and the Richest Man in China," *New Yorker*, May 5, 2015, https://www.newyorker.com/news/news-desk/how-not -to-get-kicked-out-of-china.

31. Henry Kissinger, *A World Restored: Metternich, Castlereagh and the Problems of Peace, 1812–1822* (Echo Point Books & Media, 2013).

32. Personal correspondence.

33. Personal correspondence.

34. Kerry K. Gershaneck, *Political Warfare: Strategies for Combating China's Plan to "Win without Fighting"* (Quantico, Virginia: Marine Corps University Press, 2020), https://www.usmcu.edu/Portals/218/Political%20Warfare_web.pdf.

Chapter 20: Saving Taiwan

1. "Factbox: Key Xi Quotes at China's 20th Communist Party Congress," Reuters, October 16, 2022, https://www.reuters.com/world/china/key-xi-quotes-chinas-20th -communist-party-congress-2022-10-16.

2. "China Says U.S. Should Stop Abusing the Concept of National Security," Reuters, December 4, 2020, https://www.reuters.com/article/us-usa-china-military-companies -idUSKBN28E0UX.

3. Diane Bartz and Alexandra Alper, "U.S. Bans New Huawei, ZTE Equipment Sales, Citing National Security Risk," Reuters, November 30, 2022, https://www.reuters .com/business/media-telecom/us-fcc-bans-equipment-sales-imports-zte-huawei-over -national-security-risk-2022-11-25/.

4. Daniel Moritz-Rabson, "China Demands U.S. Remove Tariffs Levied during Trade War for Final Deal," *Newsweek*, October 17, 2019, https://www.newsweek.com/ china-demands-us-remove-tariffs-levied-during-trade-war-final-deal-1465963.

5. Drew Fitzgerald, "U.S. Expands Bans of Chinese Security Cameras, Network Equipment," *Wall Street Journal*, November 25, 2022, https://www.wsj.com/articles /u-s-expands-bans-of-chinese-security-cameras-network-equipment-11669407355.

6. Ibid.

7. Jimmy Quinn, "Former Harry Reid Staffer Lobbies for Blacklisted Chinese Surveillance Firm," *National Review*, June 28, 2022, https://www.nationalreview .com/corner/former-harry-reid-staffer-lobbies-for-blacklisted-chinese-surveillance -firm/.

8. "FACT SHEET: CHIPS and Science Act Will Lower Costs, Create Jobs, Strengthen Supply Chains, and Counter China," The White House, August 9, 2022, https:// www.whitehouse.gov/briefing-room/statements-releases/2022/08/09/fact-sheet-chips -and-science-act-will-lower-costs-create-jobs-strengthen-supply-chains-and-counter -china/.

9. "President Xi Jinping Has a Video Call with U.S. President Joe Biden," Ministry of Foreign Affairs of the People's Republic of China, March 3, 2019, https://www.fmprc .gov.cn/mfa_eng/zxxx_662805/202203/t20220319_10653207.html.

10. Anders Fogh Rasmussen and Ivo Daalder, *Memo on an 'Economic Article 5' to Counter Authoritarian Coercion* (Chicago Council on Global Affairs, 2022), 1, https://globalaffairs.org/sites/default/files/2022-06/CCGA%20Economic%20Article %205%20Brief_vF_0.pdf.

11. National Critical Capabilities Defense Act of 2021, H.R. 6329, 117th Cong. (2021–2022), https://www.congress.gov/bill/117th-congress/house-bill/6329/text.

12. Inu Manek, "Outbound Investment Screening Would Be a Mistake," Council on Foreign Relations, June 30, 2022, https://www.cfr.org/article/outbound-investment -screening-would-be-mistake.

13. David Stilwell, "U.S. Insider on Failed U.S. Policy toward China," *China Unscripted* (podcast), November 8, 2021, https://chinaunscripted.libsyn.com/140-us-insider-on -failed-us-policy-toward-china-david-stilwell.

14. "The Clean Network," U.S. Department of State, https://2017-2021.state.gov/the -clean-network/index.html.

15. "U.S.-EU Trade and Technology Council (TTC)," U.S. Department of State, https:// www.state.gov/u-s-eu-trade-and-technology-council-ttc.

16. "President Xi Jinping Has a Video Call with U.S. President Joe Biden."

17. Brett Marohl, "In 2019, U.S. Energy Production Exceeded Consumption for the First Time in 62 Years," U.S. Energy Information Administration, April 28, 2020, https://

www.eia.gov/todayinenergy/detail.php?id=43515; Javier Blas, "The U.S. Just Became a Net Oil Exporter for the First Time in 75 Years," Bloomberg, December 6, 2018, https://www.bloomberg.com/news/articles/2018-12-06/u-s-becomes-a-net-oil -exporter-for-the-first-time-in-75-years.

18. Adele Peters, "The U.S. Is Still Importing Russian Oil despite the Ban, Report Says," *Fast Company*, June 12, 2022, https://www.fastcompany.com/90760216/the-u-s-is -still-importing-russian-oil-despite-the-ban-report-says; Kevin Liptak et al., "Biden Turns to Countries He Once Sought to Avoid to Find Help Shutting Off Russia's Oil Money," CNN, March 8, 2022, https://www.cnn.com/2022/03/08/politics/joe-biden -saudi-arabia-venezuela-iran-russia-oil/index.html.

19. Vincent Ni, "Xi Jinping Makes No Major Climate Pledges in Written Cop26 Address," *The Guardian*, November 1, 2021, https://www.theguardian.com/environment/2021 /nov/01/cop26-xi-jinping-china-president-sidesteps-videolink-written-statement.

20. Jim Garamone, "Austin Orders Military Stand Down to Address Challenge of Extremism in the Ranks," U.S. Department of Defense, February 3, 2021, https:// www.defense.gov/News/News-Stories/Article/Article/2492530/austin-orders -military-stand-down-to-address-challenge-of-extremism-in-the-ranks.

21. The View, "General Milley Defends Critical Race Theory," YouTube, June 24, 2021, at 9:14, https://www.youtube.com/watch?v=bQ1LuHNJWgw.

22. Paul Szoldra, "Why the U.S. Navy Wants Sailors to Read 'How to Be an Antiracist,'" *Task and Purpose*, June 23, 2021, https://taskandpurpose.com/news/us-navy-reading -list-how-to-be-an-antiracist.

23. Dominic Nicholls, "China Is Launching Equivalent of Royal Navy Every Four Years," *The Telegraph*, October 15, 2021, https://www.telegraph.co.uk/news/2021 /10/15/china-launching-equivalent-royal-navy-every-four-years.

24. Alexandra Stevenson, "Leadership Changes Reveal That in China, Men Still Rule," *New York Times*, October 23, 2022, https://www.nytimes.com/2022/10/23/world /asia/women-china-party-congress.html.

25. "Cobra Gold 2022: Scaled Down and No Cobra Sacrifices," Thai PBS World, February 19, 2022, https://www.thaipbsworld.com/cobra-gold-2022-scaled-down -and-no-cobra-sacrifices.

26. "China Participates in Cobra Gold 2022 HADR Exercise," Ministry of National Defense of the People's Republic of China, February 26, 2022, http://eng.mod.gov .cn/news/2022-02/26/content_4905774.htm; Tita Sanglee, "Thailand-US-China Relations amid the 2022 Cobra Gold Drill," *The Diplomat*, February 3, 2022, https://thediplomat.com/2022/02/thailand-us-china-relations-amid-the-2022-cobra -gold-drill/.

27. Lucy Craft, "Pacifist Japan to Double Defense Spending, Buy Counterstrike Missiles as China and North Korea Fuel Anxiety," CBS News, December 16, 2022, https:// www.cbsnews.com/news/japan-defense-force-spending-budget-doubling-china -taiwan-north-korea/.

28. Reiko Miki, "Japan to Establish Self-Defense Forces 'Joint Command' in 2024," *Nikkei Asia*, https://asia.nikkei.com/Politics/Japan-to-establish-Self-Defense-Forces -joint-command-in-2024.

29. "Quad Leaders Joint Statement," The White House, May 24, 2022, https://www .whitehouse.gov/briefing-room/statements-releases/2022/05/24/quad-joint-leaders -statement.

30. Aamer Madhani and Zeke Miller, "What's the 4-Nation Quad, Where Did It Come From?" Associated Press, May 24, 2022, https://apnews.com/article/nato-shinzo -abe-japan-india-australia-c579b7eb5ea53fb8cc50097de85e6b14

31. Thomas deVries, "U.S. Marines, Australians, Japanese Kick Off Trilateral Exercise Southern Jackaroo," Defense Visual Information Distribution Service, June 15, 2021, https://www.dvidshub.net/news/398916/us-marines-australians-japanese-kick-off -trilateral-exercise-southern-jackaroo.

32. Ibid.

33. Jeff M. Smith, "Democracy's Squad: India's Change of Heart and the Future of the Quad," War on Rocks, August 13, 2020, https://warontherocks.com/2020/08/ democracys-squad-indias-change-of-heart-and-the-future-of-the-quad/.

34. Jim Garamone, "China Military Power Report Examines Changes in Beijing's Strategy," U.S. Department of Defense, November 29, 2022, https://www.defense .gov/News/News-Stories/Article/Article/3230682/china-military-power-report -examines-changes-in-beijings-strategy/.

35. Office of the Secretary of Defense, *Annual Report to Congress: Military and Security Developments Involving the People's Republic of China 2021* (Washington, D.C.: U.S. Department of Defense, 2021), 92, https://media.defense.gov/2021/Nov/03 /2002885874/-1/-1/0/2021-CMPR-FINAL.PDF.

36. Bill Gertz, "U.S. Indo-Pacific Commander Warns about Chinese Nuclear Buildup," *Washington Times*, August 16, 2022, https://www.washingtontimes.com/news/2022 /aug/16/us-indo-pacific-commander-warns-about-chinese-nucl/; Ellie Kaufman and Barbara Starr, "U.S. Military Nuclear Chief Sounds the Alarm about Pace of China's Nuclear Weapons Program," CNN, November 4, 2022, https://www.cnn.com/2022 /11/04/politics/us-china-nuclear-weapons-warning/index.html.

37. Bill Gertz, "Former Los Alamos Nuclear Scientists Aid China's Advanced Weapons, Private Study Says," *Washington Times*, September 22, 2022, https://www .washingtontimes.com/news/2022/sep/22/former-los-alamos-nuclear-scientists-aid -chinas-ad.

38. Ankit Panda and Benjamin Silverstein, "The U.S. Moratorium on Anti-Satellite Missile Tests Is a Welcome Shift in Space Policy," Carnegie Endowment for International Peace, April 20, 2022, https://carnegieendowment.org/2022/04/20/u.s.-moratorium-on-anti -satellite-missile-tests-is-welcome-shift-in-space-policy-pub-86943.

39. Jeremy Page, Carol Lee, and Gordon Lubold, "China's President Pledges No Militarization in Disputed Islands," *Wall Street Journal*, September 25, 2015, https:// www.wsj.com/articles/china-completes-runway-on-artificial-island-in-south-china -sea-1443184818.; Julie Hirschfield Davis and David E. Sanger, "Obama and Xi Jinping of China Agree to Steps on Cybertheft," *New York Times*, September 25, 2015, https://www.nytimes.com/2015/09/26/world/asia/xi-jinping-white-house.html.

40. Office of the Secretary of Defense, *Annual Report to Congress: Military and Security Developments Involving the People's Republic of China 2022* (Washington, D.C.: U.S. Department of Defense, 2022), ix, https://media.defense.gov/2022/Nov/29 /2003122279/-1/-1/1/2022-MILITARY-AND-SECURITY-DEVELOPMENTS -INVOLVING-THE-PEOPLES-REPUBLIC-OF-CHINA.PDF.

41. Dylan Tokay, "U.S. Targets Chinese Fishing Vessels, Russian Detention Camps, with Human-Rights Sanctions," *Wall Street Journal*, December 9, 2022, https://www.wsj.com/articles/u-s-sanctions-china-based-vessels-over-alleged-illegal-fishing-practices-11670598344.

42. Personal correspondence.

Epilogue: It's Our Choice: Pushing Back and Winning

1. "Americans Hold a Nazi Rally in Madison Square Garden," History.com, February 20, 2019, https://www.history.com/this-day-in-history/americans-hold-nazi-rally-in-madison-square-garden.

2. Bret Stephens, "I Was Wrong about Trump Voters," *New York Times*, July 21, 2022, https://www.nytimes.com/2022/07/21/opinion/bret-stephens-trump-voters.html.

3. Joel Kotkin, "Xi Jinping's China Faces Challenges of its Own," American Mind, April 12, 2022, https://americanmind.org/features/beating-china/red-dusk.

4. cPASS @ucsd.edu, "Wallace C. Gregson (Part 1: Talk)—The Indo-Pacific, Big Things, Wicked Problems, No Easy Solutions," YouTube, April 10, 2019, at 7:52 and 24:25, https://www.youtube.com/watch?v=_zwnABZAVns.

Index